Redefining the Role of Language in a Globalized World

Ai-Ling Wang
Tamkang University, Taiwan

A volume in the Advances in
Linguistics and Communication
Studies (ALCS) Book Series

Published in the United States of America by
IGI Global
Information Science Reference (an imprint of IGI Global)
701 E. Chocolate Avenue
Hershey PA, USA 17033
Tel: 717-533-8845
Fax: 717-533-8661
E-mail: cust@igi-global.com
Web site: http://www.igi-global.com

Copyright © 2021 by IGI Global. All rights reserved. No part of this publication may be reproduced, stored or distributed in any form or by any means, electronic or mechanical, including photocopying, without written permission from the publisher.
Product or company names used in this set are for identification purposes only. Inclusion of the names of the products or companies does not indicate a claim of ownership by IGI Global of the trademark or registered trademark.

Library of Congress Cataloging-in-Publication Data

Names: Wang, Ailing (College teacher), editor.
Title: Redefining the role of language in a globalized world / Ai-Ling
   Wang, editor.
Description: Hershey : Information Science Reference, 2020. | Includes
   bibliographical references and index. | Summary: ""This book explores
   the role language will play in a globalized world and how language
   changes over time through its interdependent relationship with
   technology"--Provided by publisher"-- Provided by publisher.
Identifiers: LCCN 2019044156 (print) | LCCN 2019044157 (ebook) | ISBN
   9781799828310 (hardcover) | ISBN 9781799828327 (paperback) | ISBN
   9781799828334 (ebook)
Subjects: LCSH: Language and languages--Globalization. | Languages in
   contact. | Language and culture. | Language and languages--Study and
   teaching--Foreign speakers.
Classification: LCC P130.5 .R43 2020 (print) | LCC P130.5 (ebook) | DDC
   306.44--dc23
LC record available at https://lccn.loc.gov/2019044156
LC ebook record available at https://lccn.loc.gov/2019044157

This book is published in the IGI Global book series Advances in Linguistics and Communication Studies (ALCS) (ISSN: 2372-109X; eISSN: 2372-1111)

British Cataloguing in Publication Data
A Cataloguing in Publication record for this book is available from the British Library.

All work contributed to this book is new, previously-unpublished material.
The views expressed in this book are those of the authors, but not necessarily of the publisher.

For electronic access to this publication, please contact: eresources@igi-global.com.

Advances in Linguistics and Communication Studies (ALCS) Book Series

ISSN:2372-109X
EISSN:2372-1111

Editor-in-Chief: Abigail G. Scheg, Western Governors University, USA

MISSION

The scope of language and communication is constantly changing as society evolves, new modes of communication are developed through technological advancement, and novel words enter our lexicon as the result of cultural change. Understanding how we communicate and use language is crucial in all industries and updated research is necessary in order to promote further knowledge in this field.

The **Advances in Linguistics and Communication Studies (ALCS)** book series presents the latest research in diverse topics relating to language and communication. Interdisciplinary in its coverage, ALCS presents comprehensive research on the use of language and communication in various industries including business, education, government, and healthcare.

COVERAGE

- Non-Verbal Communication
- Media and Public Communications
- Discourse Analysis
- Dialectology
- Language Acquisition
- Interpersonal Communication
- Forensic Linguistics
- Computer-Mediated Communication
- Semantics
- Language in the Media

IGI Global is currently accepting manuscripts for publication within this series. To submit a proposal for a volume in this series, please contact our Acquisition Editors at Acquisitions@igi-global.com or visit: http://www.igi-global.com/publish/.

The Advances in Linguistics and Communication Studies (ALCS) Book Series (ISSN 2372-109X) is published by IGI Global, 701 E. Chocolate Avenue, Hershey, PA 17033-1240, USA, www.igi-global.com. This series is composed of titles available for purchase individually; each title is edited to be contextually exclusive from any other title within the series. For pricing and ordering information please visit http://www.igi-global.com/book-series/advances-linguistics-communication-studies/78950. Postmaster: Send all address changes to above address. Copyright © 2021 IGI Global. All rights, including translation in other languages reserved by the publisher. No part of this series may be reproduced or used in any form or by any means – graphics, electronic, or mechanical, including photocopying, recording, taping, or information and retrieval systems – without written permission from the publisher, except for non commercial, educational use, including classroom teaching purposes. The views expressed in this series are those of the authors, but not necessarily of IGI Global.

Titles in this Series

For a list of additional titles in this series, please visit:
http://www.igi-global.com/book-series/advances-linguistics-communication-studies/78950

Strategies and Tactics for Multidisciplinary Writing
Kemi Elufiede (Carnegie Writers, Inc., USA) and Carissa Barker Stucky (Carnegie Writers, Inc., USA)
Information Science Reference • © 2021 • 315pp • H/C (ISBN: 9781799844778) • US $195.00

Handbook of Research on Discrimination, Gender Disparity, and Safety Risks in Journalism
Sadia Jamil (Khalifa University, UAE) Barış Çoban (Doğuş University, Turkey) Bora Ataman (Doğuş University, Turkey) and Gifty Appiah-Adjei (University of Education, Winneba, Ghana)
Information Science Reference • © 2021 • 459pp • H/C (ISBN: 9781799866862) • US $265.00

Futuristic and Linguistic Perspectives on Teaching Writing to Second Language Students
Eda Başak Hancı-Azizoglu (Indiana University of Pennsylvania, USA) and Nurdan Kavaklı (Izmir Democracy University, Turkey)
Information Science Reference • © 2021 • 353pp • H/C (ISBN: 9781799865087) • US $175.00

Universal Codes of Media in International Political Communications Emerging Research and Opportunities
Mykola Borysovych Yeromin (Vasyl' Stus Donetsk National University, Ukraine)
Information Science Reference • © 2021 • 209pp • H/C (ISBN: 9781799838081) • US $135.00

Handbook of Research on Translating Myth and Reality in Women Imagery Across Disciplines
Roxana Ciolăneanu (University of Lisbon, Portugal) and Roxana-Elisabeta Marinescu (Bucharest University of Economic Studies, Romania)
Information Science Reference • © 2021 • 403pp • H/C (ISBN: 9781799864585) • US $245.00

For an entire list of titles in this series, please visit:
http://www.igi-global.com/book-series/advances-linguistics-communication-studies/78950

701 East Chocolate Avenue, Hershey, PA 17033, USA
Tel: 717-533-8845 x100 • Fax: 717-533-8661
E-Mail: cust@igi-global.com • www.igi-global.com

Editorial Advisory Board

Radwan Ali, *Kennesaw State University, USA*
Yasser Alrefaee, *Al-Baydha University, Yemen*
Manpreet Arora, *Central University of Himachal Pradesh, India*
Neriman Hocaoğlu Bahadır, *Kirklareli University, Turkey*
Eddy Chang, *Taipei Times, Taiwan*
Tzu-Shan Chang, *Tamkang University, Taiwan*
Chien-han Chen, *Tamkang University, Taiwan*
Fu-Yen Chiu, *National Chin-Yi University of Technology, Taiwan*
Iliana Cuellar, *University of California, Riverside, USA*
Maya David, *Central University of Himachal Pradesh, India*
Patricia Deubel, *Nova Southeastern University, USA*
Wanchi Huang, *University of California, Riverside, USA*
Işıl Günseli Kaçar, *Middle East Technical University, Turkey*
Yuh-Chang Lin, *Aletheia University, Taiwan*
Kazuhiko Nakae, *Kansai Gaidai University, Japan*
Aicha Rahal, *Aix-Marseille University, France*
Ylva Sandberg, *Stockholm University, Sweden*
Amanda Sladek, *University of Nebraska at Kearney, USA*
Trini Stickle, *Western Kentucky University, USA*
Patrizia Torricelli, *University of Messina, Italy*
Michael Kai-Yip Tsang, *The University of Hong Kong, Hong Kong*
Rebecca Wheeler, *Christopher Newport University, USA*
Xiaowan Xie, *The University of Edinburgh, UK*
Xiaoli Yu, *Middle East Technical University, Turkey*
Azlin Zaiti Zainal, *University of Malaya, Malaysia*

Table of Contents

Preface xvi

Chapter 1
Are We Living in a Globalized World? Reflections on Language Use and
Global Inequality 1
    Ai-Ling Wang, Tamkang University, Taiwan

Chapter 2
Ideology as Social Imagination: Linguistic Strategies for a Cultural Approach
to Controversial Social Situations 28
    Patrizia Torricelli, University of Messina, Italy

Chapter 3
Post-Truth (Mis)communication as Enigmatic Mystification and Misuse of
Language 43
    Manpreet Arora, School of Commerce & Management Studies, Central
        University of Himachal Pradesh, Dharamshala, India
    Roshan Lal Sharma, Department of English, Central University of
        Himachal Pradesh, Dharamshala, India

Chapter 4
Incompatible Discrepancy Between Low Proficiency of Arabic Language and
Its High Status and Prestige 54
    Kazuhiko Nakae, Kansai Gaidai University, Japan

Chapter 5
Performing Speech Acts: Focussing on Local Cultural Norms in the
Englishes We Use 71
    Maya Khemlani David, University of Malaya, Malaysia
    Aliyyah Nuha Faiqah Azman Firdaus, University of Malaya, Malaysia

Chapter 6
Re-Examining the "Native Speaker Question": Representing Native Speakers on an ELT Website 88
    Lanqing Qin, University of Ottawa, Canada
    Awad Ibrahim, University of Ottawa, Canada

Chapter 7
The EU Language Policy as a Tool 113
    Neriman Hocaoğlu Bahadır, Kırklareli University, Turkey

Chapter 8
Impacts of Globalization on English Language Education Across Inner, Outer, and Expanding Countries 131
    Xiaoli Yu, Middle East Technical University, Turkey
    Veysel Altunel, Hacettepe University, Turkey

Chapter 9
Improving the L2 Interactional and Critical Thinking Skills of University Students Using the CLIL Approach in the 21st Century 159
    Sakae Onoda, Juntendo University, Japan

Chapter 10
The Major Developments of Learner Language From Second Language Acquisition to Learner Corpus Research 184
    Aicha Rahal, Aix-Marseille University, France

Chapter 11
The Role of Technology in Interdisciplinary Language Teaching: Bridging Language and Science Learning 197
    Azlin Zaiti Zainal, University of Malaya, Malaysia

Chapter 12
An Investigation Into In-Service and Pre-Service Teachers' Understanding and Perceptions of Global Englishes in Taiwan 219
    Ethan Fu-Yen Chiu, National Chin-Yi University of Technology, Taiwan

Chapter 13
Internet-Based Text-Matching Software and EFL Preservice Teachers' Awareness of Academic Integrity: A Case Study in the Turkish Context 243
    Işıl Günseli Kaçar, Middle East Technical University, Turkey
    Hale Işık-Güler, Middle East Technical University, Turkey

Compilation of References 306

About the Contributors 347

Index 351

Detailed Table of Contents

Preface xvi

Chapter 1
Are We Living in a Globalized World? Reflections on Language Use and
Global Inequality 1
    Ai-Ling Wang, Tamkang University, Taiwan

The author first points to some prejudiced or inappropriate language use in an era of globalization, for example, distinctions between language and dialect, Global South and Global North, developed countries and developing countries, majority and minority, intercultural education, and multicultural education. Then the author extends the discussion to the inequality in different fields, such as the educational and economic fields. Finally, the author calls for elimination of the biased language use and unequal practice in an era of globalization. This chapter concludes that a real globalization will not be attained without an equal globe and suggests unbiased language use and equal practices in language use in various domains.

Chapter 2
Ideology as Social Imagination: Linguistic Strategies for a Cultural Approach
to Controversial Social Situations 28
    Patrizia Torricelli, University of Messina, Italy

Ideology is a social imagination of world's truth that can be shaped and eventually corrected before it becomes historically dangerous. The methodology of linguistic analysis offers the essential approach to a positive resolution of this problem because it suggests how to prevent risky ideologies, or how to change them once they are established. The suggested linguistic strategies refer, particularly, to the textual analysis of meaning as the key to discover the imaginative value of words in a culture from which the people's mentality derives. Cultural interventions in this field of social life are, obviously, very important to foster mutual understanding, welfare, and world peace.

Chapter 3
Post-Truth (Mis)communication as Enigmatic Mystification and Misuse of
Language 43
*Manpreet Arora, School of Commerce & Management Studies, Central
University of Himachal Pradesh, Dharamshala, India
Roshan Lal Sharma, Department of English, Central University of
Himachal Pradesh, Dharamshala, India*

It would be erroneous to assume that language can only be used in positive sense and that it cannot be misused to cause instability and unrest in our professional as well as personal lives. On the contrary, language can be weaponised to cause irreparable harm/damage to vulnerable communities, ethnicities, marginalized populations, and deprived chunks of humanity. Language has innumerable forms such as genuine and authentic language, truthful and honest language, ingenuine and false language, and fake and deceptive language. Be that negative or positive aspect of language, it can be tilted either way as per one's will and choice; nevertheless, inauthentic and manipulative language can seldom have acceptability among the masses. The term 'post-truth' stems from fabrication of truth and it has a deep connection with politics. Post-truth may be understood as a situation wherein the objective facts are less influential in shaping opinion, and emotions and personal beliefs are important to connect people. In this chapter, the authors have analyzed language in the age of post-truth.

Chapter 4
Incompatible Discrepancy Between Low Proficiency of Arabic Language and
Its High Status and Prestige 54
Kazuhiko Nakae, Kansai Gaidai University, Japan

Muslims are ardent to learn Arabic and study al-Qurʾān, but many of them are not competent in manipulating the Arabic language. The discrepancy of high prestige and status of the language versus low proficiency of the learners is the target of the research in this chapter. The author calls this "incompatible discrepancy." What do they indeed do in the Arabic school and Qurʾānic school? If they are so ardent, they should be highly competent in Arabic. The process of their learning is, exactly to say, rote-learning. In schooling they just memorize phrases from al-Qurʾān and the other religious texts. They start to learn Arabic as a graphic mode. They never learn Arabic as an identity marker without sticking to the way of learning it as a graphic mode. In this globalizing world everything is going to be digitalized. On the other hand, in the Islamic world many of the things remain analog, especially the way of leaning Arabic. The globalizing world is digital while the Islamic world is analog. Digital/analog can be considered as an important perspective for the world.

Chapter 5
Performing Speech Acts: Focussing on Local Cultural Norms in the
Englishes We Use 71
    Maya Khemlani David, University of Malaya, Malaysia
    Aliyyah Nuha Faiqah Azman Firdaus, University of Malaya, Malaysia

When we speak we use speech acts. Examples of speech acts include performing greetings, giving compliments and responding to compliments, making complaints and responding to complaints, making and responding to requests, congratulating, and consoling. In English language textbooks we normally see one response to some of these speech acts. For example, "thank you" as a response to a compliment or "good morning/afternoon/evening" as a greeting. As English has become a world language spoken by non-native speakers of English, many non-nativised cultural norms when performing speech acts are noted in real-time interactions. In this chapter, examples of nativised speech acts expressed in acceptable English are drawn from a number of data sources ranging from both real-time interactions, literary sources, which are a reflection of life, and social media, which encompass Facebook, Messenger, WhatsApp messages. Pedagogical ramifications of such authentic real-time data are discussed. The result will be the teaching of the English emerging from localised cultural norms in the speech acts we perform.

Chapter 6
Re-Examining the "Native Speaker Question": Representing Native Speakers
on an ELT Website..88
    Lanqing Qin, University of Ottawa, Canada
    Awad Ibrahim, University of Ottawa, Canada

This chapter addresses the native speaker question and construct from a representational point of view. Through a critical discourse analysis (CDA) of an ELT website in China's context, the authors discuss what and who is profiled as 'native speaker' and how this category is represented on the website. Existing studies dealing with the 'native speaker' abound, but only in recent years have a few efforts been made on the construction of this discourse, and the online representation of ELT in China is worthy of more examination. Consequently, this chapter aims to problematize the term 'native speaker', deconstruct the process of how a discourse of 'native speaker' takes on shape through online representation, and reveal how it is a racialized category. In conclusion, they offer pedagogical and policy implications.

Chapter 7
The EU Language Policy as a Tool 113
   Neriman Hocaoğlu Bahadır, Kırklareli University, Turkey

The European Union (EU) is a multilingual union, which has 27 official languages. There is no other international or regional organisation that has so many official languages. Since its very beginning, the official languages of the member states are the official languages of the EU. The multilingualism of the EU is not just about the official languages of the EU but also because of the numerous indigenous regional and minority languages. The language policy of the EU can be traced back to the Treaty of Rome and the first regulation. Since then, the language policy of the EU has changed parallel with the developments and changes within the EU and in the world. First, it was evaluated as a tool for personal development and integration, but with the changes in the globalized world, it became a tool to increase the competitiveness of the EU, which can be seen as a soft power at the international level. This chapter aims to show the changing role of the EU's language policy and its current status as a powerful tool in the knowledge-based economies at the international level.

Chapter 8
Impacts of Globalization on English Language Education Across Inner,
Outer, and Expanding Countries 131
   Xiaoli Yu, Middle East Technical University, Turkey
   Veysel Altunel, Hacettepe University, Turkey

This chapter tackles the critical changes that have occurred in English language education in different countries under the progress of globalization. Adhering to comprehensiveness, the changes in representative countries across different categories are discussed. The division of the categories is based upon Kachru's Three Circle Model, namely the Inner Circle, the Outer Circle, and the Expanding Circle. Within each circle, two representative countries are addressed. Major changes related to the field of English language education in these countries include issues such as educational policy, English curriculum designing, English teaching research, methods and techniques, English educators' and learners' perspectives, and so forth. Throughout the synthesizing and comparing process, the common theme that is used to connect the six countries is globalization; discussions are centered on how the changes are influenced by globalization. The chapter concludes by addressing the future issues each country might face and their further directions in advancing English education.

Chapter 9
Improving the L2 Interactional and Critical Thinking Skills of University
Students Using the CLIL Approach in the 21st Century 159
Sakae Onoda, Juntendo University, Japan

This chapter discusses theoretical underpinnings, practical applications, and effects of the CLIL (content and language-integrated learning) approach with a primary focus on the use of group projects on the development of English interactional skills (especially oral fluency), self-efficacy, and critical thinking skills in undergraduate English majors in Japan. The chapter first reviews L2 literature on the use and features of the CLIL approach and then focuses on the use of group projects and their potential effects on three important dimensions of language learning: linguistic, affective, and social. The literature review covers the author's own investigations of the effects of group projects substantiated by students' feedback and statistical data collected as part of his extensive teaching experience in universities. Finally, a number of practical suggestions for implementing group projects are presented along with procedures and worksheets so that interested readers can adopt these in their own teaching context.

Chapter 10
The Major Developments of Learner Language From Second Language
Acquisition to Learner Corpus Research 184
Aicha Rahal, Aix-Marseille University, France

Given the fact that there is a constant debate among monolinguists and pluralists, this chapter aims to explore the main developments in learner language. It focuses on the changes from second language research to learner corpus research. It is an attempt to present second language theories. Then, the chapter draws a particular attention to the limitations of second language acquisition. The discussion turns to learner corpus research to show how language changes from heterogeneinity to diversity. Language is no longer seen as monolithic entity or a standard variety but a multilingual entity.

Chapter 11
The Role of Technology in Interdisciplinary Language Teaching: Bridging
Language and Science Learning 197
Azlin Zaiti Zainal, University of Malaya, Malaysia

In discourses of 21st century learning, there is an increasing emphasis on interdisciplinary learning. In this chapter, the author first looks at previous research on interdisciplinary teaching and learning. Next, the concept of scientific literacy and how this is related to language will be discussed. The intersections between the teaching of science literacy and language teaching and learning will also be explored.

This is followed by research on the use of technology in science education and how technology can enhance science literacy.

Chapter 12
An Investigation Into In-Service and Pre-Service Teachers' Understanding
and Perceptions of Global Englishes in Taiwan...219
    Ethan Fu-Yen Chiu, National Chin-Yi University of Technology, Taiwan

This chapter examined in-service teachers' and pre-service teachers' interpretation, understanding, knowledge, and willingness of promoting Global Englishes. The results of quantitative and qualitative data indicated that the concepts of Global Englishes were more informally delivered than formal instructed channels. Both groups generally had the understanding and knowledge of Global Englishes. The majority of participants of this study preferred Standard English when selecting listening materials, but they were in favor of the idea of introducing Global Englishes into the curricula of the 12-year Compulsory Education. With the goal of achieving appropriate and effective communication, in addition to Global Englishes, ICC should be adequately developed and enforced. The focus of the chapter was to highlight the importance of training teachers with greater awareness and respect of English varieties and to disseminate the concept of Global Englishes at teacher training programs. Findings of the study have some important implications for the English curricula of 12-year Compulsory Education.

Chapter 13
Internet-Based Text-Matching Software and EFL Preservice Teachers'
Awareness of Academic Integrity: A Case Study in the Turkish Context.........243
    Işıl Günseli Kaçar, Middle East Technical University, Turkey
    Hale Işık-Güler, Middle East Technical University, Turkey

Having been investigated from different perspectives across a broad range of disciplines, plagiarism in English as a Second Language (ESL)/English as a Foreign Language (EFL) contexts has not received much attention until very recently. This mixed-methods case study in the Turkish context is a critical analysis of EFL preservice teachers' perceptions, motives, knowledge of, and practices regarding plagiarism, as well as their academic integrity awareness and plagiarism detection ability in a freshman academic writing course at a state university. The quantitative data from the pre- and post-test questionnaires in the study were analyzed through descriptive statistics while the qualitative data from the questionnaires and semi-structured interviews with the preservice teachers were analyzed via thematic analysis. Findings suggested the favorable impact of Turnitin on preservice teachers' self-discovery to overcome and reduce possible plagiarism attempts in the Turkish context.

Compilation of References 306

About the Contributors 347

Index 351

Preface

AN OVERVIEW OF THE BOOK

Redefining the Role of Language in a Globalized World is a collection of thoughts concerning what role or roles language can play in an era of globalization. As we can tell, in an era of a globalized world, there is a strong interdependence between and among countries around the world. For example, the COVID-19 pandemic occurred in 2020 has raised awareness of how people as global citizens are indeed interconnected, irrelevant of their culture, ethnicity, gender, and geographical location. Viewed from this global perspective, language particularly plays a critical role in our daily life and in a world that different types of mobility are common, especially when it comes to communicating with people from different cultures and speaking different languages.

The topic of language actually covers a variety of issues, allowing us to redefine what language is in a globalized world. For example, in this book, the topics cover global perspectives on language, language teacher education, language teaching methodology and learning strategies, language varieties, and language policy. Although there are a lot more relevant issues that need to be discussed and dealt with, our contributors have pointed to some core issues that deserve our attention. These issues may be of interest of different groups of people, including local and international students, college faculties and staffs, school administers, researchers, business owners and managers, agencies of language proficiency tests, policy makers, and practitioners of cross-cultural exchange projects.

ORGANIZATION OF THE BOOK

Thanks to the contributors' enthusiasm in providing thoughtful insights into different issues relevant to language, an essential part of our daily life. Language keeps changing its role as various types of mobility are increasingly growing around the globe. We are happy to see that more and more scholars and experts are getting aware

Preface

of the impacts language can have on our lives. To better present our contributors' chapters, I organize the book into three areas of concern: global perspectives on the role(s) of language, teaching methodologies and learning strategies of language, and language teacher education and training. There are 13 articles contributed by authors from 8 countries collected for this book. We are happy to see that different voices are heard. After all, different languages are used by different groups of people around the world every day.

It has never been easy to edit a book. However, I am definitely not entitled to claim the credit. The credit should go to all the contributors. The book will not come out without their thoughtful input into the wisdom tank that will contribute to the well-being of human lives in term of language. I organize the entire submissions into three sections, namely Global Perspectives on the Role of Language at Local, National, and International Level, Language Teaching Methodologies and Learning Strategies in the Classroom, Teacher Education and Training in an Era of Globalization.

The first section includes Chapter 1 to Chapter 7, all of which deal with how language changes its role in an era of globalization; Section 2 covers Chapter 8 to Chapter 11 in which authors discuss and provide how new ways of teaching and learning languages in an era of great mobility; authors in Section 3, which covers Chapter 12 to Chapter 13, focus their discussions on how teacher education needs to be changed in order for future teachers to be prepared for a culturally diverse classroom. Details of each chapter are listed below respectively.

Section 1: Global Perspectives on the Role of Language at Local, National, and International Level

Chapter 1: Are We Living in a Globalized World? Reflections on Language Use and Global Inequality

The author claims that we cannot claim that we are living in a globalized world unless we can work together to develop an equal global community. The author points to some unequal and biased use of language and treatment commonly found in research report and in the fields of education, politics, and economy. She calls for political politically correct use of language at the global level.

Chapter 2: Ideology as Social Imagination: Linguistic Strategies for a Cultural Approach to Controversial Social Situations

The author first describes that ideology is a sum of true values attributed to the meaning given to things, and every culture is the product of a historical ideology. She states the importance of being able to prevent socially dangerous behavioral deviations. The author finally discusses the linguistic strategies in the cultural field of social life to foster mutual understanding, welfare and world peace.

Chapter 3: Post-Truth (Mis)communication as Enigmatic Mystification and Misuse of Language

The author first describes that the term post-truth refers to the phenomenon in the technology-driven environment in which there are spread of lies, rumors, distorted facts, propagandas and deceit. These untrue facts and false news are spread widely through social media and social websites. The author argues that, in communications, we should not only analyze the way one speaks but also interpersonal relationships. She suggests that the communication ethics, the serious and sustained idea building approach can be taught to educate the public to combat the problems emerged in the era of post-truth.

Chapter 4: Incompatible Discrepancy Between Low Proficiency of Arabic Language and Its High Status and Prestige

The author first describes an interesting phenomenon in Arabic-speaking communities. That is, Muslim people, for example, are enthusiastic in learning Arabic in a globalizing world, even more than learning English, and this has led to the high status of the Arabic language. However, Arabic speaking people are not really proficient in Arabic. The author calls the phenomenon 'incompatible discrepancy'. He investigates into the reality of how Arabic-speaking people learn Arabic and how they perceive Arabic as a language.

Chapter 5: Performing Speech Acts-Focusing on Local Cultural Norms in the Englishes We Use

The author argues that when we are performing a speech act in a globalized world, especially when we are communicating in English, we need to take local cultural norms into consideration. She collects many examples from authentic language in use, including real time interaction, literature, and social media showing how Asians reflect their cultural norms when they use English. The author suggests that teachers of English need to sensitize learners to relationship between speaker and listener and to cultural and religious norms of both parties.

Preface

Chapter 6: Re-Examining the "Native Speaker Question": Representing Native Speakers on an ELT Website

The authors' discussions center on the debate over the dichotomy of native/non-native speakers. They argue that the perceived native speakers are White people who speak "standard English" as they examined a China website organized by the British Council. They found that the perception of nativeness/non-nativeness is actually groundless and discriminatory. The consequence of the perception is that some so-called non-native English speakers are excluded from the ELT field. The authors argue that we need to recognize the many variations of Englishes around the world in a globalized world.

Chapter 7: The EU Language Policy as a Tool

The author explores how the European Union (EU) uses language as a tool to integrate its member states and to gain competitiveness at a global level. She first describes that there are 28 official languages in the EU. The EU language policy changes in accordance with the developments and changes within the EU and in the world. According to the author, as the changes in the globalized world, the EU language policy has become a tool and a soft power to increase the competitiveness of the EU.

Section 2: Language Teaching Methodologies and Learning Strategies in the Classroom

Chapter 8: Impacts of Globalization on English Language Education across Inner, Outer, and Expanding Countries

The authors compare changes in English education in an era of globalization in six countries, the US, the UK, India, Singapore, China and Turkey. The six countries are representatives of the three circles of English speakers initiated by Kachru: the Inner Circle, the Outer Circle, and the Expanding Circle. The authors first examine how globalization have had impact on each of the country in their English language education, and they also compare changes in countries within the same Circle and across different Circles.

Chapter 9: Improving the L2 Interactional and Critical Thinking Skills of University Students Using the CLIL Approach in the 21st Century

To solve the inherent problems of teaching and learning English in Japan, the author proposes the Content and Language Integrated Learning (CLIL) approach that integrates content learning with language learning and the four language skills in the learning activities. This approach features its group projects because group activities can integrate all four language skills and increase interactions and communications.

Chapter 10: The Major Developments of Learner Language: From Second Language Acquisition to Learner Corpus Research

The author describes that traditional research on second language acquisition tends to treat L2 learning as a relationship between the L1 and L2. She argues that L2 learners, in their learning process, use a language that is neither the L1 nor the L2. The researcher proposes Learner Corpus Research, which concentrate on learners' performance, rather than their competence. She explains this approach mainly intends the present major developmental stages of learner language.

Chapter 11: The Role of Technology in Interdisciplinary Language Teaching: Bridging Language and Science Learning

The author argues that language plays a role in the mastery of science concepts and skills, and it is important to enhance the teaching and learning of science and language in an increasingly globalized world. She argues that there is an increasing emphasis on interdisciplinary learning. She argues that non-native speakers of English studying science need to be instructed in both English and Scientific Language Instruction. The author urges that a holistic model of this interdisciplinary learning need to be developed in the context of higher education.

Section 3: Teacher Education and Training in an Era of Globalization

Chapter 12: An Investigation into In-Service and Pre-Service Teachers' Understanding and Perceptions of Global Englishes in Taiwan

The author investigates how in-service and pre-service teachers in Taiwan perceive global Englishes and how they learned the term Global Englishes. He found that most of the in-service and pre-service teachers still favor the so-called standard English and are not quite aware of English varieties. He then suggests that the Ministry of Education (MOE), teacher training programs, and the English Department should provide in-service and pre-service teachers with required information relevant to global Englishes and English varieties.

Preface

Chapter 13: Internet-Based Text-Matching Software and EFL Preservice Teachers' Awareness of Academic Integrity: A Case Study in the Turkish Context

The authors first point out that the issues of plagiarism perceived in ESL/EFL contexts, differences of cultural perceptions of texts and textual growing borrowing may produce different outlooks toward plagiarism. The authors investigated EFL preservice teachers in Turkey into whether the overt use of plagiarism-detection software can help build an awareness of plagiarism and deter plagiarism. Based on the findings, the authors suggest that internet-based plagiarism detection services can build on EFL learners an awareness of plagiarism and academic integrity.

The entire book shows a variety of issues relevant to language. It may draw the attention of language educators, policy makers, and language users to the dynamic nature and the changing role(s) of language. That is, language changes based on how we perceive it, make use of it, integrate it with other domains, and make critical judgement of it. Again, thanks to all the contributors, a variety of issues relevant to language have been shown in this book. It is hoped that readers can get a rough picture of how language works in a globalized world and, more importantly, can get involved in the discussions of the role(s) language plays in our daily life.

Chapter 1
Are We Living in a Globalized World?
Reflections on Language Use and Global Inequality

Ai-Ling Wang
Tamkang University, Taiwan

ABSTRACT

The author first points to some prejudiced or inappropriate language use in an era of globalization, for example, distinctions between language and dialect, Global South and Global North, developed countries and developing countries, majority and minority, intercultural education, and multicultural education. Then the author extends the discussion to the inequality in different fields, such as the educational and economic fields. Finally, the author calls for elimination of the biased language use and unequal practice in an era of globalization. This chapter concludes that a real globalization will not be attained without an equal globe and suggests unbiased language use and equal practices in language use in various domains.

INTRODUCTION

Are we living in a globalized world? Yes and No. The answer is Yes! In a sense that various forms of mobility, either physical or virtual, can be seen around the globe. Physically, people from one country can easily move to another country or state. On campuses, students from different cultures sit in the same classroom and learn together. In a company, people from different cultures may work together for

DOI: 10.4018/978-1-7998-2831-0.ch001

Copyright © 2021, IGI Global. Copying or distributing in print or electronic forms without written permission of IGI Global is prohibited.

the same company. It is also not uncommon that you see merchandise produced in a far-away country displayed in a store near you or a globally well-known store is just several steps away from you. Virtually, you find that establishing friendship with people from different cultures or other countries is just a finger-tip away. You can even take distance courses and get a foreign degree without having to leave your own country. Thanks to modern technologies and transportation, all these seemingly impossible occurrences before have become norms of our daily life. Under this circumstance, "the boundaries between home and away, local and global, here and there are increasingly blurred" (Caruana, 2010, p. 52). Information, people, merchandise and ideas can flow rapidly around the globe.

However, is this the picture faithfully describing the globe? The answer is No! We cannot pretend that we do not see the other side of the globe. We cannot assume that each member of the global community is equally living happily and safely and the globe is peaceful and harmonious. In addition to what the author describes above, the other side of the globe is also apparent and cannot be overlooked. For example, inequality, discrimination, poverty, conflict, war, oppression, illiteracy, drug trafficking, and epidemics prevail in some corners of the world. To solve these global issues is really a big task and it takes the entire global community to work together to eventually reach the goal of globalization.

To address so many global issues is beyond the scope of this chapter. In this chapter, the author focuses only on the language used and hence inequality existing in the seemingly globalized world. In some literature relevant to globalization, there are indeed existing different degrees and different types of discriminations and prejudices. These linguistic expressions are commonly used in literature and people take them for granted without consciously noticing the pitfalls underlying these expressions. In some cases, there might be gaps between the writer and the reader. While the writer may not intentionally write this way, the reader can receive a great impact on how the writer writes. That is, writers may lack in audience awareness and sometimes they use languages or expressions offensive to people from different cultures. In the following sections to come, the author discusses some commonly used linguistic expressions and their inappropriateness in a so-called globalized world.

Background

One of the most important issues that people encounter moving towards globalization is language used in various political, economic, and educational contexts. The inappropriate use of language is actually one of the factors that bar the road towards globalization. The author will point to just some examples showing how language can be inappropriately used in different contexts. The author's intention is to draw people's attention to how unintentional use of language may have great impacts on readers or listeners.

Another important task global citizens have to work together before they can claim it is a globalized world is to combat inequality in the world. There are different types of inequality existing around the world, either in politics, economy or education. In this section, the author will only mention inequality in education and economy respectively. In education, Solga (2016) claims that the principles of meritocracy actually create and promote social inequality. She argues that equal educational outcomes, rather than equal educational opportunity, are solutions to inequality in education. According to Solga, one of the problems with meritocratic principles is that the principles' idea of "survival is the fittest." In this sense, one's accomplishments, and hence rewards, are predetermined by his or her natural, rather than nurtured, intelligence.

Furthermore, education seems to reinforce the potential inequality shaped by stratification by academic outcomes. As a result, better educated people are more secured to access better jobs and to possess higher social status. Viewed from this perspective, it seems that biological birth alone can determine one's accomplishment without having to interact with social environments. Solga (2016) thus urges redistribution of welfare and equally providing people with high levels of quality education.

Another inequality in education is found in the opportunities for first generation college students to study abroad. In their call for creating study abroad opportunities for first generation college students, Martinez, Ranjeet, and Marx (2009) claim that, although study abroad has been actively promoted and practiced in higher education around the world in an era of globalization, higher education institutions did not really provide equal opportunities to each college student. Among those students deprived of their opportunities to study abroad are first generation college students. According to Martinez et al., "[b]arriers that inhibit student participation…include cost, lack of information about study abroad, family constraints, and individual limitations" (p. 529).

Soederberg (2006), on the other hand, focuses her discussion of inequality on economy. She points to the inequality in neoliberal-led globalization. In global economic governance, she demonstrates some important facts that show how inequality, exclusion, and dominance are actually practiced in international settings. For example,

Large segments of civil society—particularly the more 'radical' elements that disagree with neoliberal-led globalization—have been consistently barred at significant international conferences such as the joint annual meetings of the IMF and World Bank and that of the WTO or G7/8 meetings (p. 3)

Soederberg also points to other examples showing unequal human relations "the increasing polices of the United States government" (p. 2), such as the "unwillingness of the majority of the world's population to continue to adhere to global rules governing trade, which have been written largely by a select number of wealthy states" (p. 2).

It is ironic that, on the one hand, we claim to work towards a globalized world and to develop a harmonious, peaceful, and equal global community. On the other hand, we are actually creating a world where inequality, discrimination, and conflict can be found everywhere around the globe in economy, politics, religion, and education. The author argues that a real globalized world cannot be attained without solving some fundamental global issues and without the awareness of members of the global community. As mentioned in the introductory section, this chapter does not intend to present various global issues and suggestions. Instead, the author hopes to start with the basic tool for communication: language. In addition to developing relationships and showing one's good will, language has the potential to cause misunderstandings and conflicts. Politically correct use of language at the global level may contribute in a certain degree to globalization of the world.

From the background information mentioned above, we can see that inequality exists in different domains in an era of globalization. Different types of inequality are actually barriers barring the way towards globalization, Much of the inequality is actually apparent through the use of language or policies or decision-making revealed in language use. It is sometimes the case that language is unconsciously or unintentionally expressed by the author and it leads to great impacts on the reader.

LANGUAGE USE IN AN ERA OF GLOBALIZATION

In this section, the author will list some commonly used terms or expressions in literature in an era of globalization. People may be familiar with these terms and take their appropriateness for granted. However, they need our attention and in-depth discussion to ensure these terms can be properly used.

Language Versus Dialect

As pointed out by Cardinal and Lĕger (2018), "languages and cultures have been more vulnerable by globalization, climate change and global capitalism" (p. 21). First and foremost, the most directly related to the theme of the book, language, is the distinction between language and dialect. In the author's linguistics class, before her lecture to the topic of the distinction between language and dialect, she always asks her students to define language and dialect and wonders how they perceive language and dialect. A majority of students would respond that a language is spoken by a larger number of people and is considered more prestigious; while a dialect is spoken by a smaller number of local people and is considered inferior and less informal and less important. In reality, this view of language and dialect should be discouraged. Fromkin, Rodman, and Hyams (2014) clearly state that each language or dialect is equally complete and expressive and that there is no so-called superior or inferior language or dialect, and a language or a dialect is irrelevant to the number or prestige of its speakers. As a rule of thumb, Fromkin et al. suggest that we may "refer to dialects of one language as mutually intelligible linguistic system, with systematic differences among them" (p. 281). In this sense, English is a language and American English, Scottish English, or Australian English is a dialect respectively. This is in accordance with the concept of language varieties. The same is true, if American English is a language, then African American English, Chicano English, and Hispanic English are dialects. This makes a better sense. Otherwise, it may sound bizarre and illogical if we consider all American English, British English, and Australian English standard English. It is because there exist a lot of phonological, morphological, and syntactic differences among these Englishes. The same is true for other languages, such as Spanish, French, and Chinese. We do not expect that people in Spain and people in Mexico and in South-Eastern American Spanish-speaking countries speak identical Spanish, not to mention the dynamic nature of language.

The development of language is dynamic. That is, new vocabulary words and expressions are invented and created all the time in a certain part of the world because of a particular event, invention or initiation occurred in different parts of the world. It may not temporarily be associated with the other parts of the world. However, because of the great mobility in an era of globalization, these newly-invented vocabulary words and expressions may soon be relevant to other people around the world. Viewed from these perspectives, it may be too narrow-minded to delimitate a language as "standard." Davies and Dubinsky (2018) term language variation "language change." They argue that "language can change…across time and space…[and] language differs across space, inclusive of physical space, social space, ethnic and cultural space, and gender space" (p. 48).

In addition to the dynamic nature of language, the Linguistic Relativity Principle initiated by Sapir and Whorf suggests that "language shapes thought and culture" (Davies & Dubinsky, 2018, p. 85). That is, one cultural element of a group of people may significantly appear in their language or dialect, while it may be missing in another. Viewed from this perspective, language should be able to play a role as an informant in an era of globalization to inform people messages relevant to what happened in a specific corner of the globe. Having a positive attitude towards one's own language or dialect and respect and appreciate others' may be the first step to *globalize* oneself. It is sometimes the case that having a negative attitude towards a language or dialect may lead to a negative attitude towards speakers of it, and vice versa.

Davies and Dubinsky (2018) discuss language rights from the perspective of human rights. They argue that there is "distinction between tolerance-oriented and promotion-oriented rights. Viewed from this perspective, simply tolerating other languages, especially minority languages, is not sufficient to protect language rights as part of human rights. To actively promote and encourage minority languages, for example, teaching minority languages from the very start of school education and using students' mother tongue as an instructional medium, can really preserve minority languages and their cultures. Another issue is that those "who do not speak the state language fluently may be unable to enjoy all the rights and privileges of citizens of the state" (p. 169), and sometimes it is the case that language loss is because of the extinction of some human species.

On the other hand, Davies and Dubinsky (2018) also describe yet another group of scholars who are in opposition to this human rights perspective. Those who oppose the view argue that there is tension between individual and collective rights. If a language is associated with a particular language community, then individuals may jeopardize the integrity of the community if they exercise their individual right, which allows them to speak any language at any time in any place. It is even more complicated when dialects and ethnicities are taken into consideration. As mentioned earlier, languages are dynamic and they change over time. Thus language varieties and dialects are created. One cannot precisely say which language community he or she belongs to. Furthermore, a great deal of population mobility in an era of globalization may force one to relinquish his or her mother tongue. However, his or her "ethnic identity remain intact" (p. 171).

Another issue that "many language right opponents point out [is] that speaking a minority language may be disadvantageous" (p. 171). Some language right advocates suggest that minority students should be taught in their mother tongue and minority languages should be preserved and promoted. However, those who are in opposition of the view argue that it may prevent minority students from social, economic, and educational mobility and global access.

Based on all the arguments above, the author argues that allowing minorities to join social activities and let their voices to be heard is key to eliminate social inequality. Part of the solutions may be promotion of bilingualism or multilingualism. It may be important in an era of globalization. People can feel at ease to speak different languages to different people in different contexts. Simply put it, bilingual education or multilingual education just refer to teaching or using two or more languages in an educational setting. It is irrelevant to threatening the hegemonic power of a particular group of people and the languages they speak. Rather, it aims at providing each ethnic group or country with equal opportunities to express themselves, to participate in the global community, and most importantly, to be respected as global citizens. Henderson's (2019) experience of teaching bilingual classes shows that the

awareness of language variation helps students understand why they use one feature in one context but not another, and why the language of peers is different from the language of an academic text. Therefore, knowing a language is more then knowing grammar terminology; it is about being able to use the different language features to maximize the communicative effect on an audience (p. 107)

Viewing from the perspective of language right, Davies and Dubinsky (2018) argue that "[l]anguage, as a strong symbol of group identity, is sometimes cited as a reason for intergroup conflict" (p. 161). Although language may not really be the reason to cause conflicts between or among different groups of people, "language has been and continues to be a powerful tool (or weapon) in the arsenal of control" (p. 162). Throughout history, there are many cases showing that dominant groups made use of language to control and confine minority groups for fear of losing their power over minority groups. They mandate the use of mainstream languages in public settings, including in the educational context, and prohibit the use of minority groups' mother tongue. For example, Kurdish in Turkey, Māori in New Zealand, Tamil in Sri Lanka, and Ainu in Japan are all cases in history showing how language was used as a means to exert power over minority groups. In addition to language and power, Metz (2019) reminds us of yet another issue called *linguistic prejudge.* He argues that "there is nothing inherently better of worse about a particular language variety; it is the association of the language with powerful or stigmatized social groups that creates a linguistic hierarchy" (p. 73). Metz points out that the stigmatization is not "caused by the language itself but by the association between these groups and their language" (p. 73). In this case, we cannot purposefully ignore the social reality and expect that the language or dialect we speak is equally treated or perceived like all other languages or dialects. Language inequality does exist around the world. In the following paragraphs, the author will present the situations in the United States and in Canada respectively to show how language policies made by decision makers can affect nationals' attitude towards languages.

Language issues are very complicated in the United States. Throughout the early history of the United States, because of the unique history and its great numbers in immigrants, the United Stated has been encountering different languages with different ethnic groups that moved to the United States. Davies and Dubinsky (2018) describe that in the colonial times, the "competition for North America on the part of European power…was primarily an English, French, and Spanish affair" (p. 72), and then Swedish and Dutch speakers and Mexican Americans had different lengths of residence in the United States. Another English versus other-language conflict "was directed at German-speaking inhabitants of Philadelphia" (p. 175). American people were afraid that "German-speaking settlers…and others were polluting the English colonies linguistically and racially" (p. 175). These lingo-phobias were basically related to war and immigration. As accounted by Davies and Dubinsky, even after World War I, it "did not stop the Americans from getting quickly up to speed in targeting German immigrants as a potential enemy" (p. 178), and the government did not certainly discourage the public anti-German hysteria. Actually, "assaults on speakers of other languages for speaking or using those languages has a long and distinguished history in the United States" (p. 180).

In the later history of the United States, Americans have been debating over the issues of official English, English only, and English First. They have been working hard in protecting American hegemony and the dominance of English. Those who advocate official English were "dedicated to preserving the unifying role of the English language" (Davies & Dubinsky, 2018, p. 182). Advocates of English First were actually fighting against bilingual education. They believed that offering bilingual education to immigrants, especially Spanish-speaking Hispanic immigrants, "reduces the need and motivation for immigrants to learn English" (p. 182). The group of people who advocated English Only actually targeted at immigrants, and it has led to the passage of the Immigration and Naturalization Act and the Immigration Reform Act in which "immigration to the United States was managed and constrained through quotas based on national origins…determined by each national group's representation in the US population" (p. 181). According to Davies and Dubinsky, in the context of the Civil Rights Movement, there is "bias in favor of Northern European immigrants over all others" (p. 181). As Wolfram (2019) has pointed out, "it is far beyond linguists to solve problems of language inequality and linguistic discrimination in the U.S." (p. 61).

Unlike the United States, Canada has a very positive attitude towards other languages, especially minority languages or immigrant languages. Cardinal and Lĕger (2018) describe that Canada "has two official languages, English and French, an official multiculturalism policy that encourages the retention and use of non-official languages, and basic measures for the promotion of aboriginal languages" (p. 19). Advocates of multilingualism in Canada argue that if the government's language policy favors English and French, then it "reproduces racial hierarchies of colonialism" (p. 22). Historically and geographically, Canada has a very rich linguistic landscape. Aside from their official languages, English and French, "Canadians reported speaking more than 200 languages at home.…[In Canada, there are] more than 60 Aboriginal languages and a large number of 'immigrant' languages" (p. 29). However, it seems that the Canadian government can manage to plan its language policy to develop a multilingual society.

According to Cardinal and Lěger (2018), throughout the history of Canada, the Canadan government has been actively promoting and preserving minority languages, including aboriginal languages and immigrant languages, as stipulated in official governmental documents. For example the *Canadian Multiculturalism Act*, the *Aborignal Languages Recognition Act*, the *First Peoples Heritage, Language and Cultural Act*, British Columbia's *Language Education policy*, *Inuit Language Protection Act*, and Yokon's *Language Act* were all organized and devoted to protecting minority languages and to developing a multilingual society. As accounted by Cardinal and Lěger, societal multilingualism needs to take linguistic attitudes and language choices of the government and people, and the status and the roles languages play in the society into consideration.

From the above two examples, it is apparent that the government's language policies are greatly affect its nationals' attitude towards languages. With the government's encouragement, people may have more positive attitude towards different languages and their speakers. Most importantly, in an era of globalization, languages should be used for communication and collaboration, rather than for creating conflicts and separation.

Global English Versus World Englishes

In this section, the author would like to narrow the discussion of language down to focus only on English. Many scholars consider the two terms *Global English* and *World Englishes* can be used interchangeably, while others distinguish the two terms based on how cultural elements are perceived in language use. As mentioned by Fromkin et al. (2014), language and culture are the two sides of a coin. It is almost impossible that one learns a language without learning its culture. Some argue that the term 'Global English' implies that English is the most widely used language around the globe and speakers or learners of English have to accept English-speaking people's culture. Unless English is treated as a lingua franca, which is neutral and is used by people who do not know each other's language for communication purposes only. Some consider *Global English* is synonymous with *English as an International Language, English as a Lingua Franca* or *World English* (singular form) (Kachru & Nelson, 2006).

Unlike *Global English* or other terms, *World Englishes* (plural form) imply different Englishes, or English varieties, spoken around the world, including different accents, pronunciations, word or sentence structures, and, of course, cultural elements. Each of the World Englishes contains its specific cultural messages. Scholars categorize speakers or users of English into three Circles: the Inner Circle, the Outer Circle, and the Expanding (Kachru & Nelson, 2006). People in the Inner Circle are those called native speakers of English; people in the Outer Circle are those in countries that have a history of colonization by English-speaking countries and were forced to learn and to speak English; and those in the Expanding Circle are said to learn English as a foreign language. Although it may be helpful to categorize English speakers into the three circles to understand how English is spread around the world and how English has reached its current status, it is not our intention to label and to judge how close non-native speakers' English is to those of native English speakers. As pointed out by Kachru and Nelson (2006), the term *World Englishes* "emphasizes the equality of all the varieties used in the Inner, Outer and Expanding Circles" (p. 2). It is inclusive of all English speakers around the world, and it does not favor any one English speaker with privilege to claim ownership of the English language. Most importantly, it implies that people, as world citizens, are allowed to add their specific cultural elements to the language to convey local messages to the entire world. Language is a social and dynamic product, and it proceeds with social activities, environmental changes, and knowledge advancement. English is no exception. It is inevitable that World Englishes have been developed due to a great deal of population and other types of mobility in an era of globalization. Insisting on the static status of English and on the so-called *standard English* may deny the existence of different ethnic groups in the global community and may, in turn, block the way towards globalization.

Furthermore, language is sometimes viewed as carrying power and ideology. Choosing a particular language or language variety to speak in a specific context with a particular group of people, speaking with a particular accent or a grammatical change, and attitude towards a specific language can be ideological. Those are language rights that each individual possesses and are ways to show one's knowledge, social status, preference, and relationship with the people he or she communicates. Therefore, when one chooses to use a language or a language variety, he or she is claiming the ownership of the language and is entitled to use the language or language variety to perform whatever purposes he or she might have. Viewed from this perspective, the concept of *global English* is not really arguable. Unless it can be used as a lingua franca for communication purposes only and is free of any cultural elements as mentioned earlier. Unlike global English, World Englishes allow language users to choose whatever English variety they think is appropriate to use in a specific context. Although the dominance of English will not fade away in a short period and we do need a language for global communications, it is natural and reasonable to allow World Englishes to flourish in an era of globalization. The cultural and ideological elements in World Englishes may contribute to global understanding and collaboration.

Global South Versus Global North

Definition and Debates over Global South and Global North

In the process moving towards globalization, ironically there are conflict terms existing in literature: *Global South* and *Global North*. Interestingly, *South* and *North* in the terms do not actually have their geographical connotation. Rather, "the Global North represents the economically developed societies of Europe, North America, Australia, Israel, South Africa, amongst others, the Global South represents the economically backward countries of Africa, India, China, Brazil, Mexico amongst others" (Odeh, 2010, p. 338). Odeh further describes that "Global North countries are wealthy, technologically advanced, politically stable and aging as their societies tend towards zero population growth,…[and] Global South countries are agrarian based, dependent economically and politically on the Global North" (p. 338).

Similarly, Royal Geographical Society (n.d.) also states that generally speaking, most richer countries are located in the Northern Hemisphere, while poorer countries are mostly located in the Southern Hemisphere. The dichotomy to distinguish Global South and Global North is really unsounded and illogical. First, economic and technical advancement is not the only factor that accounts for the development of a country as will be elaborated in a later section of this chapter. The culture, religion, natural resources that support economic development, such as agrarian-based economy, geographical environment, and humanity development of a country may contribute to the well-being of its people and may create a society that people can peacefully live together without feeling physically or spiritually threatened. Second, the distinction between South and North not only implies inequality and hierarchy, but also encourages conflicts and separation. Psychologically, people tend to assign themselves to a particular side when two opposite options emerge for them to choose from. Historically, when a country is separated into two, for example, east and west or south and north, people are forced to choose one side and treat the other side as enemy or stranger. The cases happened in history have shown that it always takes a long time for a country to bridge the gap between the two sides once the divide has been created. This is an absurd phenomenon in an era of globalization, which stresses the importance of cooperation, interaction, and peaceful co-existence. Third, the development of a country is actually dynamic, not static. Some countries were considered being poor and were initially assigned to the Global South. However, they shifted to the Global North as they developed to become an economically advanced country, such as Japan, Singapore, and Taiwan (Butler, n.d.). On the other hand, as pointed out by Butler, in a country, there are likely to have both civilized and primitive areas within the country, be it belongs to the South or the North. To dichotomize countries of the whole world based on the economical development appears not arguable.

The Way to Go: An Example of Online Services

Historically and geographically, the South and the North may have their advantages and disadvantages respectively. Arguably, the aim of globalization is to collaborate and interact between or among different countries or ethnic groups and to complement each other towards a better globe. The terms Global South and Global North actually promote segregation and introduce conflicts. In other words, cultural differences should be used as a source of enriching an ethnic group, a country, or the entire globe, rather than as a source of conflict and discrimination. Geographically, historically, and economically, the South and the North may have their specific natural resources, cultures, historical backgrounds, economic developments and intentions to develop their own countries or regions. These differences should be regarded as advantages for cooperation or collaboration. In much literature, the authors tend to underscore the differences and to dichotomize things into two extremes. For example, the North is better developed in its science and technology, while the South is better developed in its humanity and arts. Whether this may sound true or not, one thing we can be sure is that both physical and spiritual lives are important and essential to human life. A well-balanced physical and spiritual life is what globalization is expected to bring to each of the global citizens.

In the discussion of online services, Wentrup, Nakamura, and ström (2017) describe how inequality is manifest between Global North and Global South and suggest practical ways to bridge the gap in demand and supply of online services between the South and the North. They first explore the demand side of the Internet and found that "between 75-80 per cent of households have access in the developed countries, around 30 per cent in the developing country, and 5 percent in less-developed countries" (p. 57). The authors conclude that "the spread of the Internet has not been equal between geographical regions and that the digital divide seems to persist" (p. 58). In the case of contributions to Wikipedia, there is also "a divide pattern between the Global North and the Global South" (p. 59). Countries from the Global North dominate the number of edits, while only some countries from Africa make contributions and the number is far behind that of the Global North.

In the supply side of online service providers, Wentrup, et al. (2017) find that online service providers are dominantly companies from the US and China. However, American providers are much better to reach global markets and Chinese providers can only concentrate on their domestic market. The researchers also find that not "only are the most important online service providers located in the global cities, but they are most often also in central prestigious districts within the cities" (p. 63).

To internationalize online providers in the Global South, Wentrup et al. suggest that they should learn the American experience or the Global North and aggressively making use of strategies such as "acquisitions, mergers or partnerships" (p. 63). They point out that "savvy programmers and knowledgeable highly skilled staff; innovation capabilities; and a mix of investors, academics and entrepreneurs with international networks…are critical for international success" (p. 64).

In sum, there is a gap in online services between Global North and Global South and online services from Global South do not reach the Global North. Wentrup et al. (2017) suggest three reasons that might contribute to the North-South divide. First, "Global South countries are stuck with unfavorable terms of trade in their extant trade patterns with the Global North" (p. 65). Furthermore, the Global South countries do not have efficient ecosystems to connect with international networks and global cities. Finally, countries in Global South tend to lock in their domestic market because of their large domestic population. Wentrp et al. describe that online service industry is seen "a more even playing field between the Global South and the Global North, … [and it makes] the online service geography more even, diverse and dynamic" (p. 66-67). This example of online services points to a very important fact that the gaps or divides can likely to be bridged through global learning or collaboration.

Developed Countries Versus Developing Countries

Being commonly associated with Global South and Global North are the terms *developed countries* and *developing countries*. In an era of globalization, the terms developed countries and developing countries, or the Third World, prevail in the literature of different research reports. Although the authors of these reports may not specifically point out what developed countries and developing countries are, the reader may have his or her predominant ideas as to what countries the authors refer to. However, one question relevant to the issue rises: development in terms of what? Technical development, modernization, education, cultural heritage, economic development, political or militarily power, geographical location, population or even the physical size of the country? We do not have a clear definition of *development*. Many scholars define "development" as "economic development." However, some countries may be stronger in some aspects and weaker in others. A country may be rich in some natural resources and lack of others; a country may have stronger and powerful global status and a shorter length of history compared to other countries. That is, all historical background, geographical location, national resources, cultural heritage, official languages, religion, and birth rates may all contribute to the development of a country. Taking all these factors into consideration, it is really complicated to distinguish between developed countries and developing countries.

Another problem with distinguishing between development countries and developing countries is that the development of a country should be viewed as a dynamic process and should be judged based on how people of a country work together to "develop" the country, rather than a fixed and currently existing facts or situations. A country may change, either for better or for worse, decades later. Especially in an era of globalization, nobody can be sure what will happen to a country in the future. In addition to human factors, natural factors can contribute to the on-going development of a country. For example, natural resources or natural disasters may affect a country's development either positively or negatively.

Viewed from yet another perspective, being well-developed as a country does not necessarily have positive connotations. It sometimes implies "aggressiveness," "invasiveness," "arrogance." "hegemony," and "imperialism." Although distinguishing between developed and developing countries may be the outcomes of competition around the globe as we commonly perceive that survival is the fittest, it may not be the goal of globalization. Interaction and interdependence and cooperation may be. In an era of globalization, we do not want to see that one wins and the other loses; rather, we are looking for a win-win situation and a one-plus-one-is-greater-than-two consequence. In another sense, being a developed or developing country cannot be judged or determined by one's own people. Hartman, Kiely, Boettcher, and Friedrichs (2018) describe a story in which American students and Bolivian students' encounter in a community-based global learning setting. In this encounter, an American student thought himself a pacifist. However, a Bolivian professor claimed that "she had never before met a U.S. citizen who was a pacifist; in fact, she hadn't believed they exist" (p. 84). The encounter occurred during the time of the U.S. and Iraq war. This story reveals an important message that we cannot see our real selves without having reflections from others. People in developed countries may feel less secure and promising in comparison with those in developing countries, and people in developing countries may live at ease and their lives may fill with opportunities to prosper. Viewing from this perspective, it may be more reasonable to judge a country's development based on how people of the country make efforts to *develop* the country and to make improvement, rather than solely on the economic status quo of the country.

Majority Versus Minority

Now let us turn to the discussion of the terms *majority* and *minority,* again another terms popularly used in literature in an era of globalization. The two terms may be easier to be understood and tend to be interpreted in terms of the population of a country or an ethnic group. If an ethnic group appears to have a smaller number of people, compared to those of other groups of people, then it is considered "minority." The problem with this distinction is that it has a strong connotation that the minority has to be submissive to the majority just like the rules of the game played at a meeting. It may be fair at a meeting that the minority follows the majority's decision. However in the case of individual countries, each country has its national identity and is ensured of its political autonomy to practice in its own country. At an international meeting, each country representative has equal rights to speak up for his or her own country and is equally obliged to follow the rules or regulations agreed upon by all the member countries. Viewed from another perspective, the term *minority* does not necessarily imply 'less important' or 'less valuable.' It is sometimes the case that minority groups can reveal the real issues not being widely aware of by the majority of people and can really enrich the lives of human beings, and their voices should be heard if we want to claim that we are living in a globalized world.

Applying the sense of salad bowl to an era of globalization, each ethnic group, whether minority or majority, can contribute to the globe and human beings just like each ingredient of the salad can contribute to the flavor of the entire salad in different ways. In a global setting, it may be more appropriate to refer to the name of an ethnic group or a country. First, as mentioned earlier, each country or ethnic group has its identity. Directly referring to the name of a country or an ethnic group may show respect to the country or the ethnic group as a political entity and may not label it as a more powerful or less powerful group. Like the terms developed and developing countries, the terms majority and minority are actually relative terms. A minority group may become a majority group when compared with another group. It does not really make sense if we term a group as majority simply because it has a larger number of people or is more dominant or powerful in comparison. In this sense, a country or an ethnic group should not be permanently labeled as a majority or minority group.

Historically, we see some cases in some places around the world, and it may be not fair to say that aboriginal residents are minorities when their territories are intruded by more powerful groups of people. Some may argue from Darwinian evolutionary theory *Survival of the fittest*. It may sound ridiculous to go backward to the evolutionary stage when human beings were competing with other animal species for survival. Human societies feature their cooperation, not competition. Even though human beings do compete with each other, the competition is for better societies and for better lives, not to destruct others in order for someone to win and survive. Negative competition is synonymous with *destruction* and may cause conflicts, and, when it comes to negative competition, the destruction ensued is irrelevant to the matter of majority or minority. When conflicts rise, both majorities and minorities are losers. Unlike negative competition, positive competition does not compete for survival. Rather, it competes for construction and contribution to societies. Minorities may be weaker in population, territory, and dominance in comparison with majorities. It does not mean that they contribute less contributive ways to the global community.

Intercultural Education Versus Multicultural Education

To respond to the trends of globalization and great population, information, and knowledge mobility around the globe, many educational institutions around the world practice intercultural education. The situation deserves a great applause if the education can reach its goal of promoting peaceful co-existence of different ethnic groups or different cultures and, most importantly, of encouraging interactions, interconnectedness, and communications between or among people from different ethnicities and cultures towards a better tomorrow and a better globe.

However, as pointed out by Portera (2011), the so-called intercultural education practiced in many countries are actually multicultural education in nature. Practitioners of multicultural education advocate co-existence of different ethnic groups and claim to "tolerate" different cultures. The word "tolerance", according to Portera, "in fact transmits a hierarchical idea: one person is up and has to tolerate the other person's (down)" (p. 26-27). In a sense, multicultural education is actually promote and encourage segregation, rather than interaction and cooperation or collaboration. Underlying the nature of multicultural education, an important message is that, as long as people can live together peacefully, there is no need to communicate and work with people from a different culture for a better global community. In this sense, it implies indifference and inequality. Under this circumstance, people only care about their well beings and consciously or unconsciously treat people from a different culture as strangers and feel no connection with them. As pointed out by Lasonen (2011), schools "can be multicultural, but the practice of pedagogy may be monocultural. Multicultural schools presuppose a change of administration, methods and curricula which come from their students' ethnic cultures and languages" (p. 268).

Multicultural societies do exist in many places around the world in an era of globalization, and multicultural education is also practiced in many countries and institutions. Unfortunately, much of the multicultural education tends to stress only peaceful co-existance of different ethnic groups and, on the other hand, use words that show discrimination, hierarchy, and inequality, such as: minority and majority, colonizer and colonized, and native speaker and non-native speaker should not be reinforced in multicultural education. Multicultural education *per se* deserves encouragement, and, in the treatment of language and culture, discriminatory and biased words should be avoided. "Mere coexistence does not guarantee any mutual interaction and negotiation" (Lasonen, 2011, p. 264).

A very good example of multilingualism practiced in the societies is found in the Nordic countries, namely Denmark, Finland, Iceland, Norway and Sweden). Lasonen (2011) describes how Nordic countries practice multiculturalism in their multicultural societies. According to Lasonen, migration from one Nordic country to another has been very popular since the 1950s. In some cases, Nordic countries allowed free mobility and did not require visas or work permits from the citizens of other Nordic countries. Under this circumstance, Nordic countries have gradually developed their multicultural societies and had to deal with culturally diverse societies. As pointed out by Lasonen, neither

multiculturalism in society nor multicultural education can guarantee the quality of personal encounters and mutual learning with different people....People of the Nordic countries have learned to accept and recognize foreigners as equal citizens in their neighborhood, schools, jobs and communities (p. 624)

Lasonen emphasizes "the dynamic, hybridity and interactive, reciprocal natural of 'inter,' not only its location or existence some where between the cultural" (p. 271), and points out that this type of intercultural competence can be seen in action in Nordic countries.

Unlike multicultural education, intercultural education emphasizes "just, equity and understanding of diversity in democratic multicultural societies" (Lasonen, 2011, p. 268) and stresses the importance of interactions and interdependence. In a globalized world, peaceful co-existence is not enough in terms of developing a better global community. Rather, people from different cultures should work together and, as members of the global community, contribute to the development of a global community in which people feel comfortable and feel at ease to live despite the fact that people may not enjoy the same quality of life and may not have the same opportunities to access education, politics, and business. The key to reach the goal is to abandon ethnocentrism. Ethnocentrism may be developed especially in the era of colonization. It is quite natural that being dominant over other countries may contribute to the development of ethnocentrism for colonizers. However, they should be reminded that colonization does no longer fit into a claimed globalized world. Intercultural education not only stresses respecting each other's languages and cultures, but also encourages collaborating with and learning from each other. Teachers of intercultural education should develop a curriculum demonstrating how different ethnic groups can complement each other and learn from each other. It is also important that students are told to avoid exclusion and domination in a multicultural communication setting.

In research reports or relevant documents, intercultural education and multicultural education should not be considered interchangeable or synonymous. In a culturally diverse educational setting, teachers may purposefully organize activities or group works involving students from different cultures to invite students to personally experience how cross-cultural collaboration may have added benefits to their professional and personal growth. Perhaps the terms intercultural and multicultural *per se* may be not really important. The most important thing is educators' attitude towards a multicultural society-to actively collaborate with people from different cultures for a better living environment or to keep people from different cultures away in a distance and mind only your own interests. That is the question.

Lasonen (2011) also reminds us that internationalization of education and intercultural education are not complementary activities. Internationalization of education focuses on economy at the global level, while intercultural education "aims at mutual learning and intercultural understanding at the local level" (p. 266). That is, recruiting international students and faculty and encouraging student and faculty mobility is one thing; having effective intercultural education to encourage interactions between or among different cultural groups on the campus is another.

GOLBAL INEQUALITY

Inequality in Education and Linguistic In-justice

The above sections present some practical and commonly-found examples showing how language can be inappropriately expressed in a seemingly equal and globalized world. This section deals with more general language use and unequal attitudes towards language use, especially in research reports. It is commonly found that research reports in cross-cultural collaborations or cooperation follow the long-standing Western research format and are reported from the authors' perspectives, not always take partners' perspectives into consideration. For example, researchers may report on how their students gain and are benefited from the collaboration, and they seldom explore how their partner students perceive the collaborations and what they would suggest or comment on the partnership.

In the research domain in education, research reports involving two cultural groups tend to describe the entire project from the dominant group's perspective, and little or no attention has been paid to the less dominant group. Hence, some inappropriate terms are used, such as developed countries vs. developing countries, majority vs. minority, and native English speakers vs. non-native English speakers as mentioned above. As Wang (2014) has pointed out, underlying successful cross-cultural collaborations is being mutually beneficial. Reporting only from one side of the partners may be insufficient in terms of providing the reader with an entire picture of the collaboration and claiming that the collaboration is successful.

In the case of language learning, language learners may learn the target language from native speakers of the language. But how about the native speakers? What do they gain or learn from the partnership? It seems that research reports do not always take the partners' perceptions into account. In service learning or international volunteering, reports mostly focus on how the service providers provide assistance, services, and instruction or materials to the groups in need and how they learn from serving people and gain a sense of accomplishment by helping less advantaged people. Seldom is the case that the reports include the voice of those who receive services. How they perceive the services they receive, what they benefit from the services and how they can learn from the services to improve their future life and to gain basic knowledge required for a better life, and, importantly, whether they feel that they also contribute or try to contribute something to the service providers in return are seldom explored. Like service providers, recipients of service also need a sense of accomplishment and of being respected (Ngo, 2014). Hence languages used in these reports are always based on I-or-we points of view and are somewhat biased. That is, research reports dominantly focus on the reporters' perspectives, and the voice of the less powerful partners is seldom heard.

Another issue relevant to research reports is the language and format used in a research report. Kachru and Nelson (2006) divide English users into three circles: the inner circle, the outer circle, and the expanding circle. People in the three circles constitute the largest English-speaking population. Under this circumstance, research reports have to be written in English, follow the Western writing format, and reviewed by native English speakers. Sometimes research reports are judged by their accuracy and fluency of writers' English, rather than the integrity of the research design and the researchers' contribution to a specific field. Under this circumstance, non-native English speakers may be prevented from presenting their research findings no matter how excellently their research studies are done. It is always the case that drafts submitted by non-native English speakers have to be reviewed or proofread by native English speakers. It may sound reasonable and logical that native English speakers help refine non-native English speakers' wording. However, again, native English speakers may make corrections or provide comments based on the norms and cultures of English speaking countries. Under this circumstance, it is doubtful as to how much of the non-native English speaking author's real voice is left.

Viewed from another perspective, different domains of research may require different formats of presenting their research findings in order for the research findings, be it scientific explorations, literary reviews and reflections, or statistical analyses, to best convey their significant messages to their readers. We may arbitrarily, or bravely, say that the Western world is better developed in its scientific and technical field and the Eastern World is better developed in its humanistic and artistic fields. Both material advancement and spiritual enrichment are equally important to human life, and they are actually the goal of globalization. Limiting the way of presenting research studies may intentionally, or unintentionally, prevent people from getting access to a globalized world.

In addition to linguistic inequality, Gobbo (2018) discusses another issue termed *linguistic justice*, aiming at coping "with the asymmetries quite often found in multilingual context" (p. 145). The debate over linguistic justice actually discovered linguistic in-justice existing in societies. However, there are different opinions and approaches to linguistic justice. The key question is "how to measure the linguistic context under analysis" (p. 146). Gobbo discusses the Calvet language Barometer (CLB) in measuring the altitude of a language's position. Gobbo argues that the weight of a language should not be measured in isolation as does CLB, "linguistic justice refers to languages in contact and mainly to multilingual contexts" (p. 145).

Gobbo (2018) describes various parameters included in CLB to measure the prestige of a language, including the number of speakers, entropy, vehicularity, official status, the role of translation, international literature awards, the number of Wikipedia articles, Human Development Index and total fertility rate. Gobbo carefully comments on CLB and makes some suggestions for improvements based on current situations. Although it may be not our intention to *rank* languages, it may be helpful to manage linguistically diversified societies. As Gobbo has pointed out "it is far easier to depict unjust linguistic situations than to propose improvements-if not solutions-in which all the linguistic actors feel they are being treated on an equal basis" (p. 147). Gobbo describe the two sides of argument over linguistic justice: the liberal-egalitarians and multi-linguists "liberal-egalitarians put the individual citizen and his or her rights first while multi-linguists put group rights first (p. 147). Striking a balance between the two may require the wisdom of decision makers or language planners' in multilingual societies. From the discussions above, it requires attention that combating inequality in language use, presentation, and measurement in the educational field cannot be ignored in an era of globalization.

Inequality in Economy

In global economic governance, Soederberg (2006) describes how inequality has been evident and how global economic governance has been working to eliminate inequality existing in the global market. She states how the Commission on Global Governance (CGG), at the early stage of global governance, had ignored the fact that inequality, exclusion, and dominance were apparent in the global market. In the stage of Bretton Woods System (BWS) (1944-71), global economic governance was seen as a hegemonic period, in which "a dominant state and other social forces…sustain their position through the creation of and adherence to universalized principles that are accepted or acquiesced to by a sufficient proportion of subordinate states and social forces" (p. 6). For example, the US transmitted its so-called universal norms to its subordinate states through "United Nations, the IMF, and the World Bank" (p. 6), and the "organizational structure of the IMF and World Bank also reflected the underlying power of the inter-state system....A member government owns a number of shares that is determined by how much money it has paid into the IMF" (p. 8). Under this circumstance, the fact is that more powerful states in the North controlled over the states in the South.

However, the hegemonic-controlled type of global economic governance were seen weakened in the post-Bretton Woods era, which was considered as the start of globalization by some analysts (soederberg, 2006). Soederberg suggests that three world events might contribute to the breakdown of the US-based world order: the rise in the Euromarkets, hikes in the price of oil by the Organization of Petroleum Exporting Countries, and the end of the fixed exchange arrangements. As stated by Soederberg, "the post-Bretton Woods era is marked by the increased power of markets over states" (p. 11). This era featured its neoliberalism. Although "the US is still the most powerful country, it has lost the consensus it enjoyed during the BWS, and thus exercises its power largely…through coercive force" (p. 12). However, numerous protests aimed at World Bank, IMF, and WTO has shown people's "discontent with an Anglo-American-dominated neoliberal World" (p. 13).

Being distant with US hegemony and dominance, developing countries established the United Nations Conference on Trade and Development (UNCTAD), which "plays a vital role in politicizing and articulating the fact the Third World concerns should also be the broader concern of the international community, [and which challenges] American hegemony in the South" (Soederberg, 2006, p. 14). The trilateral commission emerged under the circumstance of great discontent in the international community, and it argues that "the US no longer wielded a hegemonic position, and thus should adopt a shared form of leadership with Europe and Japan in order to navigate effectively new challenge at the international level" (Soederberg, 2006, p. 15-16). Soederberg argues that "the perceived need for global governance is not only a result of the geo-politics of the New World Order, but also of transformations brought about by globalization" (p. 17). For Soederberg, globalization features its high degrees of interdependence among different cultures and different countries and global economic governance should not follow "hierarchical or hegemonic modes of regulating world order" (p. 19). In other words, the 'new world order' can be seen as "a mixture of private and public partnerships that operate at the local, global, and transnational spaces…on a bottom-up basis as the constituent states find common cause in a deepening interdependence" (p. 21).

As pointed out by Caruana (2010), "in reality the process of globalization is generated in unequal, divergent, and sometimes contradictory ways; in effect there are the 'globalized' and the 'globalizer'" (p. 52). In online services, Wentrup, et al.

(2017) claim that "[Sir Tim Berners, the founder of the World Wide Web] implied that the Internet has not yet come far in connecting people from different geographical regions from different social groups, and from different ethnic origins with each other" (p. 55). It may be true that globalization promotes global competitiveness; it also creates opportunities for global collaboration. The global community "has been re-ordered with old enemies becoming new allies and vice versa" (p. 52). Viewed from this perspective, to distinguish Global South from Global North as mentioned earlier may sound contradictory to the real meaning of globalization. Providing equal opportunities to practice in the economic field for all members of the global community should be the goal of globalization.

SOLUTIONS AND RECOMMENDATIONS

From the discussions above, we may realize that there are still many issues ahead of the road towards globalization. It takes the entire globe to work together to attain the goal of globalization. Politically correct use of language is not new at the societal level. People are aware of the importance of using politically correct language to communicate with people around them. This awareness should be extended to the global level. In an era of globalization, people have significant opportunities to communicate with people from different cultures, to publish articles or books to be read by people in the global community or to let their voice heard via social websites available on the Internet. We need to use language to accomplish our goal. In intercultural education, students should be reminded that language use in an era of globalization should be culturally correct because one linguistic expression right to one culture may be wrong to another.

The role of language in a so-called globalized world should be played as coordinator between conflicts and facilitator of human cooperation, rather than just as a means of communication and expression. The first step to reach the goal may be eliminating biased and discriminatory use of language, and raising awareness of politically correct use of language should start from each person's mind, rather than basic language skills. Viewed from this perspective, language teachers and educators, especially those in intercultural education, should personally demonstrate how language can be expressed appropriately in an era of globalization, rather than just routinely teach the four language skills and professional knowledge. Teachers may need to purposefully collect examples of different expressions of the same idea and invite students to share their ideas and comment on these expressions.

FUTURE RESEARCH DIRECTIONS

Based on the discussions in the entire chapter, the author would like to suggest that further research studies can be conducted to explore how members of the global community can work together to eliminate the barriers ahead of the road towards a really globalized world, including politically correct use of language. However, politically correct use of language is only the basic step in the course moving towards globalization. Ahead of the road, there are still many issues and tasks that may require global citizens to work together for a better global community. Relevant topics may include reducing poverty and inequality, promoting global collaboration, and reporting on successful cases demonstrating how individuals, institutions or organizations, and countries can contribute to globalization in one way or another.

CONCLUSION

The discussions in the entire chapter show that the so-called globalized world actually exists different degrees and types of discrimination, inequality, and imbalanced power relation reflected in language use. The author argues that the goal of globalization cannot be reached without eliminating biased language use and unequal practices in different fields. Politically correct language use and equality should be fundamental to a real globalized world and it is the role language can play in a globalized world.

REFERENCES

Butler, C. D. (n.d.). North And South, The (Global). *International Encyclopedia of the Social Sciences*. Retrieved July 15, 2019 from Encyclopedia.com: https://www.encyclopedia.com/social-sciences/applied-and-social-sciences-magazines/north-and-south-global

Cardinal, L., & Lĕger, R. (2018). The politics of multilingualism in Canada: A neo-institutional approach. In P. A. Kraus & F. Grin (Eds.), *The politics of multilingualism: Europeanisation, globalization and linguistic governance* (pp. 19–37). John Benjamins. doi:10.1075/wlp.6.02car

Caruana, V. (2010). Global citizenship for all: Putting the 'Higher" back into UK higher education? In F. Maringe & N. Foskett (Eds.), *Globalization and internationalization in higher education: Theoretical, strategic and management perspective*. Continuum. doi:10.5040/9781350091122.ch-0004

Davies, W. D., & Dubinsky, S. (2018). *Language conflict and language rights: Ethnolinguistic perspectives on human conflict.* Cambridge UP. doi:10.1017/9781139135382

Fromkin, V., Rodman, R., & Hyams, N. (2014). *An introduction to language* (10th ed.). Cengage Learning.

Gobbo, F. (2018). How to measure linguistic justice? Theoretical considerations and the South Tyrol case study of the Calvet Language Baromer. In P. A. Kraus & F. Grin (Eds.), *The politics of multilingualism: Europeanisation, globalization and linguistic governance* (pp. 145–165). John Benjamins. doi:10.1075/wlp.6.07gob

Hartman, E., Kiely, R., Bottcher, C., & Friedrichs, J. (2018). *Community-based global learning: The theory and practice of ethical engagement at home and abroad.* Sterling, VA: *Stylus.*

Henderson, M. H. (2019). Grammar in the Spanish/English bilingual classroom: Three methods for teaching academic language. In M. D. Devereaux & C. C. Palmer (Eds.), *Teaching language variation in the classroom: Strategies and models from teachers and linguists* (pp. 101–108). Routledge. doi:10.4324/9780429486678-18

Kachru, Y., & Nelson, C. L. (2006). *World Englishes in Asian contexts.* Hong Kong UP.

Lasonen, J. (2011). Multiculturalism in the Nordic countries. In C. A. Grant & A. Portera (Eds.), *Intercultural and multicultural education: Enhancing global interconnectedness* (pp. 261–278). Routledge.

Martınez, M. D., Ranjeet, B., & Marx, II. A. (2009). Creating study abroad opportunities for first-generation college students. In R. Lewin (Ed.), *The handbook of practice and research in study abroad: Higher education and the quest for global citizenship* (pp. 527–542). Routledge.

Metz, M. (2019). Principles to navigate the challenges of teaching English language variation: A guide for nonlinguists. In M. D. Devereaux & C. C. Palmer (Eds.), *Teaching language variety in the classroom: Strategies and models from teachers and linguists* (pp. 69–75). Routledge. doi:10.4324/9780429486678-14

Ngo, M. (2014). Canadian youth volunteering abroad: Rethinking issues of power and privilege. *Current Issues in Comparative Education, 16*(1), 49–61.

Odeh, L. E. (2010). A comparative analysis of Global North and Global South economies. *Journal of Sustainable Development in Africa, 12*(3), 338–348.

Royal Geographical Society. (n.d.). *A 60 second guice to the Global North/South divide*. Retrieved July 15, 2019. https://www.rgs.org/CMSPages/GetFile.aspx?nodeguid=9c1ce781-9117-4741-af0a-a6a8b75f32b4&lang=en-GB

Schutter, H. (2018). Linguistic justice and English as a lingua franca. In P. A. Kraus & F. Grin (Eds.), *The politics of multilingualism: Europeanisation, globalisation, and linguistic governance* (pp. 167–199). John Benjamins. doi:10.1075/wlp.6.08des

Soederberg, S. (2006). *Global governance in question: Empire, class and the new common sense in managing North-South relations*. Pluto Press.

Solga, H. (2016). The social investment state and the myth of meritocracy. In A. Gallas, H. Herr, F. Hoffer, & C. Scherrer (Eds.), *Combating inequality: The Global North and South* (pp. 199–211). Routledge.

Wang, A.-L. (2013). Engaging students in language learning via successful cross-cultural video-conferencing. In M. Hamada (Ed.), *E-learning: New technology, application and future trends* (pp. 241–256). Nova Publishers.

Wentrup, R., Nakamura, H. R., & Ström, P. (2017). Online services: An equalising force between the Global North and the Global South? In N. Beerepoot, B. Lambergts, & J. Kleibert (Eds.), *Globalisation and service-driven economic growth: Perspectives from the Global North and South* (pp. 55–71). Routledge.

Wolfram, W. (2019). Language awareness in education: A linguist's response to teachers. In M. D. Devereaux & C. C. Palmer (Eds.), *Teaching language variation in the classroom: Strategies and models from teachers and linguists* (pp. 61–66). Routledge. doi:10.4324/9780429486678-12

ADDITIONAL READING

Arambewela, R. (2010). Student experience in the globalized higher education market: Challenges and research imperatives. In F. Maringe & N. Foskett (Eds.), *Globalization and internationalization in higher education* (pp. 155–173). Continuum. doi:10.5040/9781350091122.ch-0011

Bücker, J., Bouw, R., & De Beuckelaer, A. (2018). Dealing with cross-cultural issues in culturally diverse classrooms: The case of Dutch business schools. In K. Bista (Ed.), *International student mobility and opportunities for growth in the global marketplace* (pp. 117–133). IGI Global. doi:10.4018/978-1-5225-3451-8.ch008

Dixon, T., & Christison, M. A. (2018). Teaching English grammar in a hybrid academic ESL course. In J. Perren, K. Kelch, J. Byun, S. Cervantes, & S. Safavi (Eds.), *Applications of CALL theory in ESL and EFL environments* (pp. 149–169). IGI Global. doi:10.4018/978-1-5225-2933-0.ch009

Keijser, C. (2017). Changing geographies of service delivery in South Africa: Towards regional value chains? In N. Beerepfft, B. Lambregts, & J. Kleibert (Eds.), *Globalisation and services-driven economic growth: Perspectives from the Global North and South* (pp. 167–184). Routledge.

Meglio, G. D. (2017). Services and Growth in developing countries: A Kaldorian analysis. In N. Beerepoof, B. Lambregts, & J. Kleibert (Eds.), *Globalisation and services-driven economic growth* (pp. 38–54). Routledge.

Moore, R. L. (2016). Interacting at a distance: Creating engagement in online learning environments. In L. Kyei-Blankson, J. Blankson, E. Ntuli, & C. Agyeman (Eds.), *Strategic, management of interaction, presence, and participation in online courses* (pp. 401–425). IGI Global. doi:10.4018/978-1-4666-9582-5.ch016

Tafazoli, D., Parra, M. E. G., & Huertas-Abril, C. A. (Eds.), *Cross-cultural perspective on technology-enhanced language learning*. IGI Global. doi:10.4018/978-1-5225-5463-9

Teräs, H., Teräs, M., Leppisaari, I., & Herrington, J. (2014). Learning cultures and multiculturalism: Authentic e-learning designs. In T. Issa, P. Isaias, & P. Kommers (Eds.), *Multicultural awareness and technology in higher education: Global perspectives* (pp. 197–217). IGI Global. doi:10.4018/978-1-4666-5876-9.ch010

KEY TERMS AND DEFINITIONS

Dialect: Variations derived from a specific language is said to be the dialect of that language.

Ethnocentric: Viewing things from the perspective of one's own culture and ideology.

Global English: The English language featuring its being widely-used by people around the globe.

Global North: Global North refers to those technically and socially well-developed countries, basically located in North America and Europe.

Global South: Global South refers to those technically and socially less-developed countries, basically located in Africa and Asia.

Inequality: Unfairness in treating people found in different fields, such as education and economy.

Intercultural Education: Teaching cross-cultural communications, stressing interaction and interdependence between or among people from different cultures.

Multicultural Education: Teaching cross-cultural communications, stressing peaceful co-existence of different ethnic groups and tolerance of different cultures.

World Englishes: English varieties spoken by speakers of English from different areas of the world with different accents and other grammatical aspects.

Chapter 2
Ideology as Social Imagination:
Linguistic Strategies for a Cultural Approach to Controversial Social Situations

Patrizia Torricelli
University of Messina, Italy

ABSTRACT

Ideology is a social imagination of world's truth that can be shaped and eventually corrected before it becomes historically dangerous. The methodology of linguistic analysis offers the essential approach to a positive resolution of this problem because it suggests how to prevent risky ideologies, or how to change them once they are established. The suggested linguistic strategies refer, particularly, to the textual analysis of meaning as the key to discover the imaginative value of words in a culture from which the people's mentality derives. Cultural interventions in this field of social life are, obviously, very important to foster mutual understanding, welfare, and world peace.

INTRODUCTION

Ideology is a word derived from the ancient Greek ἰδεῖν (idèin) whose meaning is "to see", and λογία (loghìa), whose meaning, broadly, is "science" (Beekes, 2010). Ideology is, therefore, the "science of vision" and belongs to the imaginative process, which is a structural feature of the human mind and its behaviour. Its domain is the individual sphere and the social environment. In the individual sphere, the ideology is called mentality, and depends on the dynamics of human knowledge of the world

DOI: 10.4018/978-1-7998-2831-0.ch002

and on their preservation and transmission. Indeed, the human experience of the world is allowed by the perception of material things and the conceptualization of this perception. Through senses we perceive the experienced reality, and through concepts we know such reality. Therefore, knowledge of reality depends on conceptualization and its quality.

IDEAS AND WORDS

Conceptualization is a metaphorical process (Lakoff & Johnson, 1980). A thing becomes something else without changing its real dimension, but simply transforming the kind of access to itself, which is offered. Particularly, concepts become words, which allow to easily preserve and transmit the known reality, delivering it to the lightness of the phonemes: linguistic sounds easy to be stored in memory and kept always available when needed. A world without words is heavy, like the one that Gulliver meets in his travels in remote nations (Swift, 1726)[1]. Instead, words are the intellectual key that opens the mental file containing the images of the things to which meanings give linguistic resolution, through an equally metaphorical process: phonemes become meanings, which, in turn, become ideas while remaining sounds (Torricelli, 2006).

The process is arbitrary with regard to the results. Nothing, in the existing natural world, links necessarily those sounds with those ideas and vice versa (Saussure, 1921). *Black* is a colour name whose phonemes [b], [l], [ae] and [k] do not have any trace of the chromaticism expressed by the word *black*, so that *white* could equally express the same idea, if the linguistic code was unanimously reversed by speakers. Only the metaphorical value given by the human society to words makes the relation between sounds and meanings essential from a linguistic point of view, warranting its semantic authenticity for the intelligence of the world (Sljusareva, 1980). So, *Black* is equal to the natural black only because English language considers this kind of phonological translation a suitable linguistic metaphor of the known natural reality, and gives it this cognitive value in the imagination of the world culturally shared by its own speakers.

Values, therefore, are imaginative entities, existing only in people's mind (Modell, 2006). But, for this reason, they are the parameters of human reasoning and judging about the world, which every historical culture uses.

Consequently, they govern the social imagination of the world to which each culture gives voice through its words. And words become the essential key to understand this mental process, culturally internalized in what is called intelligence of things, and to be aware of its effects on our life.

IDEOLOGY

The sum of ideal parameters of judgement about world and life shared by a society – that is the inalienable cultural heritage, which accompanies the existence of each individual – represents an intellectual paradigm, whose principles determine individual viewpoints and opinions. It is a code of thought (Boudon, 1995) – an *ideology*[2], indeed, consisting of truth-values (Zalta, 2010) – which functions like a cognitive map from which all human knowledge takes shape, structure and substance (Freeden, 2003; Martin, 2015).

What is, for example, the value of *honour* in the ancient world, where the mythical figure was the warrior hero, supreme symbol of honour and glory, and what is the value of the same word in the contemporary world inspired by other conceptions of social life and human relations that suggest our ideas and feelings about it and, consequently, direct our behaviours in this regard? What is the true value of the concept? Evidently, it resides in the cultural context that enables our way of thinking about the world giving us the intellectual points of view from which to observe it. The framework where the cognitive dynamic – from which the human imaginary of the world arises – is placed and acts.

What is the meaning of *happiness*? Both individual and social happiness, in the western and eastern world? In Africa and America or in China? Its value changes, evidently, following the development of human thought during his historical experience of the surrounding world (Torricelli, 2019). The cultural background of western societies, for example, has long be marked by widespread economic well-being, which has led to exaggerated forms of consumerism. *Happiness* has been delivered to objects rather than to intimate states of mind. In the oriental world, spirituality has for a long time taken more refined aspects. Meditation has become a source of intimate joy. What, then, is the sense of *happiness* that the word holds to communicate it to the speakers? Obviously, what everyone has learned to appreciate because of the education received in his own cultural environment.

And is the meaning of *family* the same? And the feeling that accompanies it? *Family* is a social concept. It is, indeed, the social normalization of affections among people and not an unexceptionable human condition. Without society, love has no rules. Moreover, different historical societies have different family ideas. Polygamy is normal in some States and prohibited in others. There are patriarchal families and new extended families, with multiple couples, or those with same-sex unions. Different societies allow different types of family unions, each one compatible with the parameters established by the system of ideas – the ideology – in whose truth-values they believe.

Ideology as Social Imagination

Finally, does *life* and *death* have the same meaning in every part of the world or does their value change[3] according to the ideal paradigm and its truths in which every society recognizes itself?

The conceptual space - of which the words are the linguistic cypher that help us to remember the rational and sentimental boundaries within which thought can wander – is, evidently, the only responsible for what we feel and do. A cognitive space, that words return to us in the form of a semantic code, in whose mastery our linguistic competence consists (Chomsky, 1965).

The arrangement of ideas and the order of values that govern their disposition in the mind - authorizing consequently the meaning of words - constitutes the intellectual paradigm from which the thought takes shape and content to regulate our behaviours and decisions in life. It is, indeed, the mental synthesis of our world's intelligence.

Values are also the reason of stereotyped social behaviours. Guiding the individual perception of world (Van Dijk, 1998) they exercise a hidden coercion, absolutely unconscious, on actions to be developed and decisions to be taken (Geraeerts, 1997). They are, indeed, the cognitive principle, which justifies both practices and makes them appear reasonable.

The so-called customs, that distinguish people of different nationalities and make their belonging recognizable, are an obvious example.

When, instead, values become intellectual stereotypes, which regulate social and individual life in a self-sufficient way (Boudon, 1986), without any critical reference to reality, *ideology* may take the dimension of a *doctrine*[4], and become a closed, unalterable system, whose consequences are socially and politically dangerous, as ancient - as well as recent - world history shows (Fukuyama, 1992).

To avoid this result, cultural and political institutions must take care of social imagination, considering its formation and development from two points of view:

1. As evidence of a cultural trend of society, to be attentively monitored, in order to foresee its consequences[5];
2. As an intellectual territory of fundamental importance for the future of social and politic life, to which must be given suitable attention, studying its deep dynamics.

To this aim, two reliable ways are:

a. Linguistic inquiry about the imaginary value of the meaning of words;
b. Analysis of dissemination dynamics, to sustain and spread an image of the world as much as possible authentic and conscious.

THE CHANGE OF MEANING VALUE

The semiotic process that gives rise to words is, of course, the best mirror of social imagination of the known world. The metaphorical relationship (Torricelli, 2006) between signifier and signified is an unquestionable example of a kind of imagination that transforms a phonemic series – absolutely unmotivated toward the mentioned reality – into the unexceptionable mental representation of the same reality. Indeed, it is only the imagination of the world – suggested by a culture and entrusted to its core values – that allows the signifier to identify with a signified completely different from it, and allows things to identify with a signifier equally indifferent toward them, as formal differences between languages in the world perfectly show. The *apple* is called *mela* in Italian and *pomme* in French without any reason for it in the form, colour, flavour or in the material it is made of (Saussure, 1921). Its imaginative value depends on the conceptual category (Lakoff, 1987) to which it linguistically belongs, whose cognitive features are different from those of the *rose*, because the prototype – that is, the conceptual pattern around which category is arranged [6] - and its cognitive declension are not the same (Rosch, 1977). The *apple* is a fruit, while the *rose* is a flower and the mind draws them in different imaginative figures, delivered to a range of hierarchically set out words, which form the scalar linguistic category of the conceptual category whose culmination is the prototype[7]. *Fruit*, precisely, in one case and *flower* in the other. With the whole range of the subordinate conceptual and linguistic patterns, which complete their imaginative mental space.

However, conceptualization is a complex operation[8]. Above all, it is an individual skill, depending on specific qualities and life experience of people. Same things do not have the same meaning for everyone[9]. Therefore, a single word is not enough to exactly communicate an idea, but it needs a certain number of words around itself, which add the meanings sufficient to correctly draw the *mental image* conceived by each person, in his real intellectual values, shared by all people (Saussure, 1921). The polysemy of words – which is an important resource for the mnemonic economy of the language - finds a solution only in the linguistic context.

Moreover, the individual is the real cause of the diachronic linguistic change, and it is also responsible for the change of the semantic value of words. Indeed, the change of the conception of the world is an individual action, depending on human intelligence, to which language simply gives expression. Every modern language owes its current form, and the meaning that its words have taken, to the infinite variations introduced by its speakers over time. The word *heart* is the modern version of a previous, now forgotten, old word that sounded approximately **krd-*.

The replacement of the semantic value of the words is an unmistakable signal of the change of mentality in a society. "Political correctness", for example, is the inverse manifestation of the same phenomenon of replacement of values, as it deletes some words because of signifiers no longer allowed in a social culture to be imposed[10].

Semantic replacement, instead, not concerning the signifier – which remains the same – is noticeable only from the different words added as linguistic corollary to make the discourse pertinent to the new intellectual values envisaged by the speaker. Indeed, the value of every meaning – otherwise unmotivated in regard to the things referred – originates only from the semantic game of the discourse: namely, from the compatibility of the mental images evoked by the words, both among themselves and towards the new conceptual image of things conceived by the speaker. Therefore, the conceptual type of individual and social imagination is revealed by the words selected to talk and by the sentences put together to achieve the utterances of a text.

For example, the word *way* has several meanings and boasts a broad phraseology: *the way to the station*; *the way of entertainment*; *the way of doing something*; *to find one's way into*; *I'm on my w*ay; *way of life*; *by way of*, and so on. However, only the words that accompany it in the context allow us to decode correctly the semantic value of every sentence in the use of speakers.

Similarly, *bachelor* is an unmarried man or someone who graduated or a medieval knight during the novitiate period. Only the texts will tell us which of the three it is.

Thus, linguistic inquiry into textual semantics of a discourse can perfectly illustrate the ideal process of imagination of the world, of which language is a witness, and explain its cultural consequences, so that possible unfavourable social effects can be predicted and avoided.

LINGUISTIC STRATEGIES

To this aim, we must plan a program of textual linguistic analysis to extrapolate – from the contexts that linguistically draw and ideally develop the image of the world conceived by a speaker – its cultural value.

The first step is to see which words are attracted by a certain word, in a linguistic context, as a suitable corollary to discuss about what the word refers to. Secondly, we have to analyse, through the linguistic meaning, the imaginary relevance of the other words in their usual linguistic recurrences. Next, we have to discover the imaginative cause that makes the selected words fit together, and the cultural reason of their compatibility. Finally, we have to arrange a list of key-words, with their conceptual values, culturally explained, which bear people's mentality and direct life during the events of political and social history.

The culture feeds the social mentality and is fed by it until a break interposes, cutting the automatic individual connection. Such break makes the relationship between culture and mentality permeable by a new outlook on things previously thought, which can change their appearance.

The semantic change of words in a language is the first evidence of this latent process. When the ancient Greek word *ànemos*, that means "breath, wind" in that specific cultural dimension, is replicated by the Latin *animus*, it means "spirit, courage" in harmony with the Roman military society. But when it becomes the Italian *anima*, after a natural process of linguistic transformation through the centuries, it declines itself in the meaning of "soul", because Christianity has replaced the classical conception of the world with a new cultural paradigm, which entrusts human interiority to God and to the mystery of his dimension. The word, however, has remained the same. Just reading the context in which it occurs, with the help of the other words that surround it in the sentence, allow us to understand that the meaning is different, steeped in religious feelings, and its intellectual and practical implications are, therefore, different. The conceptual category to which it belongs is filled, in scalar order (Rosch, 1978), with new ideas and words to express them. *Sin, confession, punishment, redemption*, have become part of its conceptual, imaginative corollary, next to word like *strict morals, piety, mysticism, immortality*. Today, a lay meaning of the term emerges often from the contexts and makes it synonymous with *conscience*. The ideal category that, in scalar order, surrounds this new intellectual prototype is made of other concepts - expressed by words such as *rights, duties, consistency, honesty, dignity* - which reveal a different ideological approach to the world, and a different interpretation of things and behaviours to be kept towards them. Thus, a new imagination has become, in each of these cases, a new mentality, learning the words to characterize itself in the linguistic competence of the speakers. And the thought has begun to develop into another ideal frame (Fillmore, 1976).

Two are the aims of this program of linguistic analysis, both very important in the world in which we live today. One is to know how different people imagine the things of experience: that is the requirement of any correct process of understanding between people, countries and civilizations in the modern globalized world. The other one is to foresee the ideologies that can arise from this imagination, attempting to correct them if the risk of a transformation in dangerous totalitarian doctrines occurs.

An imagination just begun can easily be corrected, before becoming a strict ideology, averse to every kind of reasoning and novelties. Equally, it can be corrected until it remains a weak ideology. The replacement of ideas, indeed, is a fundamentally communicative operation (Castells, 2009), that follows the same laws of any promotion of an ideal product, made by proper opinion makers. It is sufficient to have:

Ideology as Social Imagination

1. A culturally, linguistically and politically prepared think tank, able to propose new images of the reality that are acceptable by the culture to be modified, and as striking as possible for people with whom the opinion makers interact;
2. A communicative plan, persuasive and efficacious, able to increase the dissemination of new suggested images, with their corollary of complementary ideas;
3. A distributional network, appropriately selected and powerful.

Knowledge of the laws of linguistic communication is, obviously, the natural and essential presupposition of the project; as well as the aforesaid word list, concerning the linguistic meanings of which the imaginative value is to be changed. In this regard, it is important to select prototypical words – that is, the words that named the conceptual centre of the category - to whose cognitive features all the words in use belonging, in different degrees, to the same conceptual category refer their linguistic meaning (Rosch, 1973). In this way, it will be possible to plan a simple but radical intervention, that once started will be able to proceed almost autonomously.

Particularly, from a linguistic point of view, it is important to identify the cognitive prototypes the envisaged values refer to, so as to reach the ideal core of every category of thought analysed. The list, therefore, must focus on the prototypical conceptual features of the meaning of words, and plan the socio-cultural areas of intervention, to prevent or correct the drift of ideas, in accordance with this semantic principle of cognition and thought processing. Insisting on concepts to be enhanced in the mind map, controlled by language, and trying to limit the damage caused by others, less appropriate in the individual and collective imagination.

The main task consists in rearranging the conceptual category, changing the position of the words, as regards the prototype whose imagery is to be corrected, and replacing the offending prototype with another of the same category, which has been marginalized by this, in the scalar internal order, when it established itself as the best conceptual exemplar – the prototype, precisely - of the category. For example, trying to change the degree of proximity to the prototype between *enemy* – to be killed, materially or figuratively – and *adversary*, to fight with dialogue, in the same category of *antagonism* among people. Up to replace – filling, with words of appropriate meaning, the imaginative category that accompanies and completes its conceptualization - the second with the first one in the common sentiment of how to maintain human and social relationships.

Of course, the inquiry must be undertaken in a sectorial manner, circumscribing, in every language, the conceptual and linguistic field to be explored and to begin to choose the most representative words. Then, to select the contexts in which they occur and decode the specific meaning value. Later, to compare the extrapolated meaning with all the scalar meanings of the same category to which they cognitively belong, up to find the most similar, but less intellectually and socially dangerous, that can replace it in the imaginative mental sphere of the speakers – occupying, by degrees, a hierarchically superior position in the scalar order of the category, closer to the prototype (Rosch, 1975) - and become a new habitual resource of its linguistic competence. It is possible to do this removal because the linguistic meaning is just a metaphorical value, conceived by mind and delivered to the individual memory to be used in speaking. Having no reason to be in things[11], but only in our imagination, all metaphors can, therefore, be replaced by others, believed to be more right or convincing or seductive[12], and become the new conceptual prototypes to whose new scalar category the speaker's linguistic competence refers. A prelude, in turn, to a new different mentality, which take the place of the previous one in the universe of human knowledge, and settles in the mental cognitive map acting as an input for a better arrangement of ideas. The behaviours and practices to be adopted will go along the pattern of this new intellectual frame, once acquired by the memory[13].

The gradual replacement favours not only the readjustment of the conceptual order inside the category, but also the alignment of the mental category envisaged with others similar ones, which, adding to it, strengthen its conceptual area in the mnemonic sphere of the mind. Until the world will be imagined in a different perspective, positive and useful for all people living in a society[14]. In this way, the negative conceptual categories can be modified and their consequences eliminated, improving social life and human relations - which are the prerequisites for mutual understanding and peace - in the globalized world in which today we live.

CONCLUSION

Finally, the important points to consider are the following:

1. Ideology is a social imagination of the world, for the discovery of which language is the best access channel. Linguistic meaning, indeed, is the mental image of the reality warranted by a culture, which is in a cause and effect relationship with it.
2. Textual analysis of meaning is the key to discover the imaginative value of words in a culture. Therefore, it supplies the best evidence of people's mentality in a given historical culture.
3. An up-to-date list of key words, with their imaginative value towards experienced reality, is a very important tool: a) for a correct and interactive communication with peoples, which favours reciprocal understanding: prelude, in turn, to cooperation, welfare, and peace; b) to intercept and correct the ideologies most

dangerous for the future of democracy and civil societies in the world, before their diffusion becomes unavoidable.
4. Communication media are the best operative platform for this persuasive strategy.

REFERENCES

Beekes, R. (2010). *Etymological Dictionary of Greek*. Brill.

Boudon, R. (1995). *Le juste et le vrai: études sur l'objectivité des valeurs et de la connaissance*. Fayard.

Castells, M. (2009). *The Rise of the Network Society*. Blackwell. doi:10.1002/9781444319514

Chomsky, N. A. (1965). *Aspects of the Theory of Syntax*. MIT.

Dijk Van, T. (1998). *Ideology: A Multidisciplinary Approach*. Sage.

Fillmore, Ch. (1976). Frame semantics and the nature of language. *Annals of the New York Academy of Sciences*, *280*(1 Origins and E), 20–32. doi:10.1111/j.1749-6632.1976.tb25467.x

Freeden, M. (2003). *Ideology: A Very Short Introduction*. Oxford: UP.

Fukuyama, F. (1992). *The End of History and the Last Man*. Free Press.

Geeraerts, D. (1997). *Diachronic Prototype Semantics*. Clarendon Press.

Lakoff, G. (1987). *Women, Fire and Dangerous Things: What Categories Reveal About the Mind*. University Press. doi:10.7208/chicago/9780226471013.001.0001

Lakoff, G., & Johnson, M. (1980). *Metaphors We Live By*. University Press.

Martin Levi, J. (2015). Ideology. *Sociológia*, *77*, 9–31.

Rosch, E. (1973). Natural categories. *Cognitive Psychology*, *4*(3), 328–350. doi:10.1016/0010-0285(73)90017-0

Rosch, E. (1977). Human categorization. In E. N. Warren (Ed.), *Advances in cross-cultural psychology* (p. 49). Academic Press.

Rosch, E. (1978). Principles of categorization. In E. Rosch & B. B. Lloyd (Eds.), *Cognition and Categorization*. Erlbaum.

Rosch, E., & Mervis, C. B. (1975). Family resemblance: Studies in the internal structure of categories. *Cognitive Psychology, 7*(4), 573–605. doi:10.1016/0010-0285(75)90024-9

Saussure De, F. (1921). *Cours de Linguistique Générale*. Payot.

Sljusareva, N.A. (1980). The heart of F. De Saussure's theory of language. *STUF - Language Typology and Universals, 33*(1-6), 541-545.

Swift, J. (1892). *Gulliver's Travels*. Retrieved from globalgreyebooks.com

Torricelli, P. (2006). Il segno metaforico. Tra motivazione e relatività linguistica. In R. Bombi & G. Cifoletti (Eds.), Studi linguistici in onore di Roberto Gusmani, (vol. 3, pp. 1715-1729). Alessandria: Edizioni dell'Orso.

Torricelli, P. (2019). *Ammetto di non conoscere l'Africa*. Retrieved from http://www.focusonafrica.info/ammetto-di-non-conoscere-lafrica/

Zalta, E. N. (Ed.). (2010). *Stanford Encyclopedia of Philosophy*. Stanford University.

ENDNOTES

[1] "We next went to the school of languages, where three professors sat in consultation upon improving that of their own country... The other project was, a scheme for entirely abolishing all words whatsoever; and this was urged as a great advantage in point of health, as well as brevity. For it is plain, that every word we
speak is, in some degree, a diminution of our lunge by corrosion, and, consequently, contributes to the shortening of our lives. An expedient was therefore offered, that since words are only names for things, it would be more convenient for all men to carry about them such things as were necessary to express a particular business they are to discourse on. And this invention would certainly have taken place, to the great ease as well as health of the subject, if the women, in conjunction with the vulgar and illiterate, had not threatened to raise a rebellion unless they might be allowed the liberty to speak with their tongues, after the manner of their forefathers; such constant irreconcilable enemies to science are the common people. However, many of the most learned and wise adhere to the new scheme of expressing themselves by things; which has only this inconvenience attending it, that if a man's business
be very great, and of various kinds, he must be obliged, in proportion, to carry a greater bundle of things upon his back, unless he can afford one or two strong

servants to attend him. I have often beheld two of those sages almost sinking under the weight of their packs, like pedlars among us, who, when they met in the street, would lay down their loads, open their sacks, and hold conversation for an hour together; then put up their implements, help each other to resume their burdens, and take their leave. But for short conversations, a man may carry implements in his pockets, and under his arms, enough to supply him; and in his house, he cannot be at a loss. Therefore, the room where company meet who practise this art, is full of all things, ready at hand, requisite to furnish matter for this kind of artificial converse. Another great advantage proposed by this invention was, that it would serve as a universal language, to be understood in all civilised nations, whose goods and utensils are generally of the same kind, or nearly resembling, so that their uses might easily be comprehended. And thus, ambassadors would be qualified to treat with foreign princes, or ministers of state, to whose tongues they were utter strangers." (pp. 170-173).

[2] The world has known many ideologies. Europe inherited the Indo-European ideology that is the background of all its different historical cultures. Greek philosophy and Roman law have been the gift of this ideal past. And the rational thought. Christian ideology has added a new spirituality to this heritage. God, faith, hope and charity became the mainstays of thinking and doing. The truth-values that inspired thought. Great became the Europe of Cathedrals, Monasteries, Capitals. Despite some deleterious historical excesses, due to doctrinal rigidity, Christian age made Europe rich in art, literature, philosophy, science and prelude of the modern age. Where other ideologies have arisen. Some, totalitarian, have become doctrines, like Nazism and Communism. With inauspicious consequences, until the ideas that supported them have changed in the collective imagination and new words, with their alternative meaning, have opened other, more convincing windows on the world and on life, putting into the people's mind different truth-values to refer to.

[3] The recent debate on the end-of-life, which has divided the consciences in Italy between the Catholic conception of existence and the secular one, is an exemplar testimony of how the ideological vision of the world changes our relation with it. The decision to end life, when it becomes intolerable, due to serious, insoluble health problems, is up to each of us, according to the secular vision of human existence, and only to God, instead, according to the Catholic vision.

[4] See the previous note. A doctrine does not allow any freedom of thought. Therefore, its effects are often deleterious to those who suffer it.

[5] As we well know, globalization has represented an epochal change. The breaking down of frontiers between Nations has led to a series of consequences that have not been completely resolved. The recent migrations from Africa,

with the arrival of thousands of migrants on the Italian coasts, gave rise to alarmed reactions form the population, unprepared to face this new situation. Words like *invasion, disease, crime* replaced the word *welcome,* which was used when the phenomenon started. A word never declined, however, in an imaginative paradigm that was suited to the socio-cultural Italian context. So that, the population could get a true idea of the proportions and effects of the phenomenon and to know how to act in this regard. This lack of intellectual help from the Institutions - with a trend's operation, that knew how to work on words to intervene on ideas, filling the meaning of words with clear and acceptable imaginative contents, suitable to the Italian mentality, but able to steer the social behaviours towards the best collective solution – left room for socio-political conflicts that did not benefit the Italian society. Although migrants can be a resource for the development of the country, this idea fails to spread in the common mentality, because it has neglected to work on the cultural paradigm that allows us to conceive it. The word *men* - with the natural, inoffensive corollary of universal qualities and defects surrounding its meaning - has not yet replaced the word *migrants* – with all its hostile implications derived from the experience of a welcome so far unresolved - in the minds of people, and an ill-concealed fear remains intact. Therefore, the political instability remains a characteristic of the Nation, with many internal divisions - especially on the issue of migrants - that do not contribute to its easy progress.

6. The prototype is the cognitive core of the category. It is the jagged and flexible conceptual agglomeration that attracts similar items by degree of proximity to one or another aspect of the cognitive area it occupies. *Man,* for example, is the prototype of a category whose gradients, sometime, depend on subjective parameters or cultural reasons. Therefore, all the categories are scalar – that is, the items form gradients of category membership - and, within them, concepts and words gradually fade, until the category to which they belong becomes unrecognizable and merges with others close to itself in the speaker's semantic competence. The degree of closeness to the prototype is, for example, the factor that distinguishes different linguistic registers. Furthermore, the categories are the reason why we understand each other, even if we do not use the same terms. Indeed, everyone knows, uses or prefers certain words of the same category and not others, without preventing, for this reason, communication. What is important, evidently, is the membership of the linguistic items to the same conceptual categories when speaking to someone.

7. Every linguistic category – it is good to repeat it - has a scalar internal structure because it is mentally built around a prototype, which is its intuitive apex. This property of the prototype allows it to be flexible and, therefore, not only

to attract all the words whose meaning approximates to its area, but also to graduate their proximity to one of its aspect considered, for some reason, to be prevalent over others. Thus, an internal hierarchy is established, which is subject to changes over time, if a new aspect of the same prototype becomes more important. In this case, there are two possible outcomes. The category recomposes itself around the same conceptual prototype, graduating differently the precedence scale of the words, or the prototype loses its conceptual value and is replaced by another more effective one.

[8] It is the object of study of cognitive science to which several scientific disciplines, such as psychology, neuroscience, artificial intelligence, anthropology, linguistics and philosophy contribute. The analysis of cognitive science spans many aspects of mind activity, from logic to decision; from planning to learning; from memory to language; from perception to emotion and action, and concerns many mental faculties. The goal of cognitive science is to understand how intelligence operates and what are the mental structures underlying human cognitive ability (Zalta, 2010).

[9] *Working*, for example, can be an aspiration in life or an effort to avoid, and the value of every job, in terms of importance and prestige, changes according to the parameters of social judgement or individual preferences. Therefore, the meaning of the word *work* is absolutely subjective. *Freedom* has a different meaning for a prisoner and a citizen. A *gift* means love but also corruption or deception. *Moon* is different for poets and physicists.

[10] *Coloured* has replaced *nigger* in general linguistic use, when the word was considered depreciative, transferring the same idea into another conceptual category, similar but declined by other linguistic expressions, considered culturally harmless. Globalization has made the linguistic question, that arose in America to compensate for racial segregation, an international phenomenon.

[11] Words are arbitrary linguistic signs and their meaning does not imitate the things to which it refers (Saussure, 1921), how well the languages of the world – that speak all of the same things but giving them different names – demonstrate well. The objectivity of values is a fundamentally cognitive fact. It depends only on our conviction that they are truly such. But *truth* is a relative notion, depending on the cultural dimension in which everyone lives. It takes different forms according to the intellectual parameters applied to the observed situation and made available by the cognitive background culturally acquired by each one.

[12] Publicity and political propaganda are familiar with these unconscious mechanisms that control human cognition and take full advantage of its potentiality. Both insist on a prototypical idea, placed at the centre of their message and surrounded by all its scalar or related ideas that words and their

context decline in the mental images evoked by them. The art of persuasion, exercised by the ancient Rhetoric, followed the same implicit principles when it taught the orators how to arrange words in sentences, and to construct discourse, to get the desired result from the interlocutor, convincing them and bending his will.

13. Language education given at school applies, without knowing it, the same principle. It teaches, indeed, the right words to think according the traditional canons of the current culture and prepares students to see the world and to reason about it in the perspective considered correct. Its social purpose is to transmit knowledge, but also to train the citizens of tomorrow and, therefore, to correct thoughts and behaviours that tend to deviate and to cause personal and social harm. Words are the only means available to achieve both goals, because they are the key for accessing the mind and stimulating rationality and imagination. Which are the two dimensions relevant to human thought.

14. The responsibility of this educational task, obviously, concerns the appropriate social Institutions, perhaps controlled by an ethical code, and involves collaboration of specialists in language, in culture, in cognitive processes, in sociology and communication. Indeed, they own the scientific tools to warrant the correct execution of the operation - respecting people's legal rights - and to ensure its success, for the benefit of the whole society.

Chapter 3
Post-Truth (Mis) communication as Enigmatic Mystification and Misuse of Language

Manpreet Arora
School of Commerce & Management Studies, Central University of Himachal Pradesh, Dharamshala, India

Roshan Lal Sharma
Department of English, Central University of Himachal Pradesh, Dharamshala, India

ABSTRACT

It would be erroneous to assume that language can only be used in positive sense and that it cannot be misused to cause instability and unrest in our professional as well as personal lives. On the contrary, language can be weaponised to cause irreparable harm/damage to vulnerable communities, ethnicities, marginalized populations, and deprived chunks of humanity. Language has innumerable forms such as genuine and authentic language, truthful and honest language, ingenuine and false language, and fake and deceptive language. Be that negative or positive aspect of language, it can be tilted either way as per one's will and choice; nevertheless, inauthentic and manipulative language can seldom have acceptability among the masses. The term 'post-truth' stems from fabrication of truth and it has a deep connection with politics. Post-truth may be understood as a situation wherein the objective facts are less influential in shaping opinion, and emotions and personal beliefs are important to connect people. In this chapter, the authors have analyzed language in the age of post-truth.

DOI: 10.4018/978-1-7998-2831-0.ch003

Copyright © 2021, IGI Global. Copying or distributing in print or electronic forms without written permission of IGI Global is prohibited.

INTRODUCTION

The origin of language, a great extent, could be attributed to the survival needs of Homo sapiens as they had to struggle hard to get food and stay safe from the harsh surroundings. Ever since man could use language, he had an advantage over other species not only from survival perspective but also from the viewpoint of his need to interact with others (Bryant). Not that communication has been impossible without language; we have ample evidence to the contrary as birds and animals communicate nonverbally without language. Nevertheless, humans are different from members of other species majorly because of their ability to use words to articulate and vocalize our thoughts. In common parlance, language is a means of communication in a non-verbal, verbal or written manner. One tends to make use of words while s/he uses language be that in a spoken or written manner. The term 'language' also implies a 'system of communication' practiced by a particular community. Language can also be viewed as "a system of conventional spoken, manual (signed), or written symbols by means of which human beings, as members of a social group and participants in its culture, express themselves" (Robins and Crystal). Besides communication, it is also a means to express our identity, imagination, ideas, emotions and feelings. Since time immemorial, man has been using language in the form of signs, signals and gestures. Prior to the advent of the word, man has been using various nonverbal signs to express his desires and needs. Language as we see it today is an evolved form of self-expression and exchange of ideas.

Language as Communication

As the story of civilization developed, human's narration skills also improved considerably. Language as communication in its highly evolved form has been a serious cause of concern across humanities and social sciences. Language as means to communicate one's inner-self has been core area of concern for linguists and writers. Interestingly, language can be used, misused, abused, over-used and under-used as per volition and choice of the user. In this sense, language can be viewed as a weapon to achieve desired results.

It would be erroneous to assume that language can only be used only in positive sense, and that it cannot be misused to cause instability and unrest in our professional as well as personal lives. On the contrary, language can be weaponised to cause irreparable harm/damage to vulnerable communities, ethnicities, marginalized populations, and deprived chunks of humanity. Language has innumerable forms such as genuine and authentic language, truthful and honest language, ingenuine and false language, and fake and deceptive language. Be that negative or positive aspect of language, it can be tilted either way as per one's will and choice; nevertheless, inauthentic and manipulative language can seldom have acceptability among the masses.

Politics of Language

In recent years we have observed that there is a lot of experimentation being done in the field of language-use. In particular, in political arena, there is much that could be cited as instances of abuse of language. We can observe around us that the political discourse has stooped to a level where it becomes almost impossible to either tolerate or survive it. At this juncture, it would be worthwhile to deal with the politics of language. To use language in the way that one desires to use it with a particular end in view implies that we are employing language politically, or that we are indulging in politics of language. While using politics of language one tends to privilege or marginalize certain aspects of life. For instance, post-truth politics employs a language of deceit to undermine truth / any truthful claim. The politics of language thus implies that language is being used very cautiously, carefully and also manipulatively whenever/ wherever the need be. The question is: what does one tend to achieve when there is the politics of language in operation? The simple answer to such a question could be that it is either to beguile or deceive.

In today's globalised world, if your political ethics are capitalism-driven, there is every probability that you would oppose a market system that is closed and conservative, a system that is local and need-based, and a system that is based on regional as well as native needs and requirements rather than the demands of global market. In such a situation, the idiom/language that counters the demands of globalised world shall naturally be either ignored or sidelined. Nevertheless, if you are an advocate of globalization, you would support the idiom/language which promotes open market and free trade across the world. In this way, the politics of language runs deep in our minds and thus influences our thoughts, actions, behavior, and decisions.

In another case scenario, let us try and analyze the language that people use in socially stratified situations. In a society like India, which is deeply class and caste-based, and which is deeply genderised, the language that one comes across has two types: a) the language used by the empowered and privileged classes, castes and gender categories, and b) the language used by the marginalized classes, castes and gender categories. A critical analysis of language used in a deeply stratified society like India would make us conscious of the politics of power. People coming from underprivileged classes, lower castes and marginalized gender categories would use language with tremendous inhibition, restraint and fear, but people hailing from privileged classes, upper castes and from empowered gender categories would use hegemonic idiom with a view to dominate and marginalize. Politics thus is intrinsic to language.

Language as a Ploy of Manipulation

Ever since language started to be used in various contexts/ situations, it opened up the possibilities to be misused and manipulated multifariously. The term 'manipulation' simply implies operating in a cleverly devious and shrewd manner with a view to benefit oneself. It is also characterized by a malicious intent, dishonest means and false and deceptive behavior. When we view language as a ploy to manipulate, it signifies misinforming or negatively influencing the listener in interpersonal and other situations. What is critical in manipulation is tricking the other person with a view to achieve one's objective of undeserved sense of accomplishment and satisfaction with negative intent. When language is used as a manipulative tool, the speaker behaves in a premeditated intentionality to either actualize one's wish to cause invisible harm to the listener or hide effectively the actual intent of what is being said by using various linguistic strategies.

Another harm that manipulative language causes is blunting the capacity of the gullible listeners to analyze critically the import of what is being said and communicated. At times manipulation of language remains unmotivated but works in the direction of shaping up the opinions of the listeners to an otherwise unforeseeable end. In this case, even the speaker- manipulator is aware of what s/he is doing, and with what end in view. In various socio-cultural and political scenarios, the language and its weaponry of figurative devices tend to defamilarise as well as veil the speaker's intentions. In contemporary political discourse, for instance, manipulative language is used through social media, print and electronic media and various other platforms concerned with social networking in the age of media multiplicity. This politically manipulated language does not subscribe to any sense of ethics and values. Thus, ethical communication and present day political day discourse can never go hand-in-hand. Whereas the ethical communication relies on truth and socio-cultural value registers, the language used in hardcore politics today undermines ethics, morality and principles of genuine and authentic communication. In such a scenario, the phenomenon called post-truth suddenly assumes relevance.

Post-truth as Lies and Deception

The term 'post-truth' stems from fabrication of truth and it has got a deep connection with politics. The political ups and downs which took place in 2016 during US presidential elections made it possible for post-truth to be selected as the word of the year 2016 by Oxford dictionary. Post-truth may be understood as a situation wherein the objective facts are less influential in shaping opinion, emotions, and personal beliefs are more important to connect with and motivate public at large. It also points toward a scenario where the truth remains unimportant and irrelevant as people are not interested in the objective facts and get easily diverted towards their emotions and beliefs. Therefore, we are now living in a world where leaders tend to shape up their careers by appealing more to emotions rather than facts. It is a newer world where we witness that sentiments and emotions are stronger than realities and facts.

It is regarded to be as an era of factual relativism, which means a situation where the traditional sources of information are no longer relevant and important for us. Each one of us believes that s/he is having an independent opinion. For most of us whatever we believe in is the truth. We may have emotional ground for that but that does not matter because whatever we believe is nothing but truth. Once a French philosopher, Emmanuel Levinas (1906-1995) argued that the "essence of discourse is ethical," implying that all our interactions are surrounded by our principal duty to meet each other face-to-face, open and honest, as we are. This attitude was expressed and captured by Levinas in the old Hebrew word *hineni* (signifying 'here I am') (https://www.brusselstimes.com/).

During this current era of post-truth we are surrounded by hoaxes, ruses, fake news, misinformation, and propaganda on internet and electronic media where everything feels to be fabricated. The public debates seem to be surrounded with lies and disinformation. The fact is that the political dealings have always been marked with lies and deception and the language has always been fabricated by many to take advantage out of it. But we never cared about such things in past. With the advent of technology and greater use of social media platforms, the concept of post-truth got highlighted and we started giving more importance to subjective opinions, emotions and sentiments. The technology and greater use of internet has brought so many changes in our lifestyle and being active on social media is one of them. The more we use technology, the more time we devote to remain on-screen, and therefore, the interplay of messages is more. In such a situation, people develop a tendency of spreading rumors via fabricating truth which always has the potential to become viral. The younger generation seems more vulnerable to the ill effects of new media technology. There is a wide variety of content which is shared on these social media platforms, and to a great extent, people manipulate it as well. Fact-checking mechanisms are not always used meaningfully as it takes time to collect such information.

As stated above, post-truth phenomenon means a situation wherein objective facts are negligible compared to successful appeals to emotions and personal belief. The worst aspect of post-truth phenomenon is that facts are totally undermined and what matters the most is winning the perception battle vis-à-vis masses. If you are able to build a discourse with the help of misleading facts that can shape up the perception of the electorate in a society, this guarantees a secure berth for you in the politics of the day. On the contrary, if you are true, honest to the core, and genuinely concerned about weal and welfare of the society/ masses, and therefore use a language that is in complete consonance with the stated purpose, it simply implies that you can be badly drubbed in the political battle and defeated in a humiliating manner. This sets one thinking as to how one conducts one's socio-cultural and political business when manipulation rules the roost, when falsehood reigns supreme, and when truth is completely undermined and chucked to the bin.

Thus, one may understand how post-truth phenomenon has caused serious damage to political discourse. In post-truth politics, what remain important are people's emotions and passions, which are used to undermine the importance of facts by manipulating the sharing of information and authentic data. Viewed thus, the language which is used in post-truth politics is false, selective, manipulative and deceptive. In this way, post-truth communication becomes a process that either tampers with the message, or manipulates it to achieve a narrow, selfish and manipulated end. Each definition of post-truth points towards and addresses people's emotions, passions and beliefs rather than objective, verifiable facts in more ways than one. Post-truth thus comes very close to propaganda as well. It is akin to post-factual politics wherein "factual details about political establishments, policy frameworks and corporate ethics are made to remain beyond the purview of reliable fact checking and ethical code of political, economic and corporate conduct" (Sharma 2018).

Therefore, what matters in post-truth scenario is true of post-factual politics as well. The most serious damage that post-truth causes to language concerns the discourses of justice and ethics. Sharma further observes that post-truth is a "ruse of a sort played on gullible masses who can be easily misled into believing all that has no roots in reality". Another harm that post-truth has caused to language is that it can never become a discourse. As a result everything that stands for truth and justice is dumped shamelessly. Another aggravating force related to communication in post-truth era is the role that media and fake news play. In today's media charged environment, only perspectives seem to matter. Moreover, fake news also causes havoc along with tampered videos that are made viral. Instead of educating the masses about important political and economic problems, media always offer lopsided view of reality. Electronic media may especially be held responsible for spreading fake news and rumors. Most of the prime time channels tend to become mouthpieces of the ruling establishment.

Janna Andrenson and Lee Rainie have also analyzed how there are differing opinions about the future of truth and misinformation online. James Ball in his book, *Post-Truth: How Bullshit Conquered the World* (2017), demonstrates how bullshit actually works and matters. And one of the reasons for bullshit to survive is because of the time that it occupies on prime time TV shows. According to Harry Frankfurt, "Bullshit is greater enemy of truth than lies are". Thus, post-truth causes multifarious damages to language in today's globalised world. Post-truth communication actually is miscommunication and misrepresentation of facts. Likewise post-truth politics has its roots in falsehood, and it lacks of transparency and accountability. Post-truth has variegated modes of voicing people's thoughts and thereby establishing an emotional connection with them. The truth is simply relegated and facts are completely ignored. Now the simple question that remains to be answered is whether there is any anti-dote to post-truth (mis)communication, or not. To deal with it actually, experts from different walks of life such as educationists, journalists, business leaders, politicians, economists, linguists and social scientists have to come together and speak truth to power with a view to obliterate the menace called post-truth. Thus, it can be arguably claimed that truth-based and authentic communication is the need of the hour. We need to nurture and assert values emanating from truth and honesty in our day to day dealings. Likewise, abuse of language as a weapon to assassinate reputations, spread canards, and deflect attention from pressing and crucial socio-cultural, political and economic issues that need to be addressed via refocusing attention on what Vlad Petre Glaveanu suggests, "pressing societal issues such as current uses of social media, inequality and social justice, migration and multiculturalism, terrorism, democracy and democratic values, protest and civic participation, climate change and environmental concerns, political behaviour and the psychology of human rights, among others".

Enigmatic Mystification of Language in the age of Post-truth

The language in the age of post-truth has received a severe jolt because of the latter's total disregard of genuine and meaningful communication. The fact of the matter is that authentic, fact-based, real and genuine communication has been replaced by miscommunication based on falsehood, deception, chicanery and sophistry. The meaning in the process gets either obfuscated or mystified with the result that the real intent behind the message remains through and through elusive. When communication acquires enigmatic proportions, it compromises clarity and lucidity. Rather than illuminating the truth of the matter, enigmatic communication veils/screens the content as well as the purport. Such an enigmatic mystification needs to be countered with factual language that weakens iron-grip of post-truth on genuine and sincere communication.

Thus, the language of post-truth phenomenon is the language that lacks commitment at the level of putting across the right kind of message. Nevertheless, the wrong kind of message gets conveyed very powerfully. So much so that despite outright lies and misinformation, the ignorant masses get influenced and motivated by the speaker. And they can go to any extent in causing unrest and chaos consequent upon getting provoked due to fake news and misinformation. Such a language is steeped in treachery and deception, and is aimed at provoking/ misleading public at large. The language of the post-truth is the language of manipulation. It is the language of jingoism and of narrow nationalism. Besides being the language of fear and intimidation, it is also the language of propaganda and provocation. Instead of aiming at weal and welfare of the masses, this language causes large scale damage and devastation. At times, it is communal and ends up causing feelings of intolerance and enmity, at other, it causes violence. Thus, the language of the post-truth is the language that undermines fundamental ethics of communication at all levels and thus destroys basic fabric of positive values in human life.

Role of Social Media

Social media had its advent in early 2000 with various websites like LinkedIn, Facebook, twitter, etc. These online platforms changed our social as well as personal lives completely. More than ever, it has become very easy to socialize through various social media platforms. Today, on an average, a normal Indian spends 40% of his internet data on browsing social media content. Social media can be helpful in improving our life but it can be harmful as well. It depends on the individual usage as to how purposefully that platform is being used. The language used on social media can even disrupt our life drastically if not used cautiously. Undoubtedly these platforms help us gain knowledge of various aspects of life and society but it really depends on our approach as to how correctly we use it. Some people use social media to improve their skill-sets or to network with people. The far reaching impact of social media has opened up the opportunity to talk, interact and network with people all around the world. It can be a wonderful source of knowing about people and their cultures, their languages and perception about various aspects of life.

These days social media has become a tool for marketing also. Various companies and even political parties have been using various social media platforms to disseminate information about their ventures, products, services, etc. Undoubtedly in such a dynamic environment where we try to reach out to more people with fewer efforts, social media platforms have become an important choice of marketers of various products and services across the globe. With the help of social media platforms, communication has become so easy that people can interact with the outside world and vice versa. However, it is equally true that human nature is easily trapped by falsehood, deception, and lies.

For many of us, Facebook has been the start of our social media journey and many of us tend to use fake profiles, fake photographs and fake identity to show the public at large relatively nicer aspects of our life. From this moment on, everything has changed—the way we communicate, the way we see and perceive others and the way we think about them. This is the starting point where what we perceive starts affecting our daily life. Distorted language, fake news and misinformation, and the way we want others to perceive us are all lies and marked by deception and misplaced sense of the world around us. Many believe that social media also adds stress to our lives as we increase the use of technology by creating muck around us of likes and dislikes of the content which we share. Plenty of face-to-face interactions are replaced by just likes and dislikes on the content which we share on Facebook.

Earlier interaction used to take place when a person used to have his birthday or anniversary or any other important event in his or her life. We would either call or try to meet in person to share our feelings with our friends. Nowadays, just a message on the Facebook wall fulfills that responsibility and we feel that we have communicated our feelings to the other person. We can see all around us people in the race of updating photographs of whatever they have done or whatever they are doing--be it visiting a place, or feeling something. The way we lead our life has totally been changed by the intervention of social media platforms as language is now being replaced by non-verbal cues/icons on Facebook and other social media platforms where posting a photograph is equated with communication of a sort. There is another segment of people who just want to say good things about their lives on these platforms and we can see how a false web of perception/misperception is spun around them in terms of the content they share.

Whatever may be the reason of using any social media platforms, the important aspect is the lack of truth in indulging in online activities. We are probably shifting to a lifestyle towards deception and lies and are trying to control our lives by using more and more social media platforms. Amidst all this, meaningful use of language steeped in truth and honesty is undoubtedly diminishing. People nowadays aspire to showcase only brighter side of their lives through sharing the best moments and pictures duly photoshopped by using some editing tools on social media platforms. We have started counting likes and dislikes like counting the currency and we are in the race of getting as many likes as possible. Many of us have the habit of starting the day by posting a status on say WhatsApp or Facebook, which again is fake or edited, and then waiting for the likes to glorify our false and fake self-image. What we forget is that such metrics of the likes and dislikes indicate that we are getting too far removed from truth.

Summing up

To conclude, we can aver that we are living in the era of post-truth which has dented communication in all walks of life. In particular, political communication has suffered a severe jolt. This is because of the fact that political leaders across the world are so greedy about power that they can stoop down to any level in spreading canards about their opponents besides spreading falsehood to mislead gullible masses through their treacherous and deceptively tantalizing and luring use of language. Modern day politicians seems to have perfected the art of mis(using) language to their maximum advantage. The naïve masses by and large end up becoming victims of their political chicanery. This phenomenon is very recent and has taken root in most of the successful democratic polities of the world. This, in fact, has been further aggravated by the onslaught of post-truth politics. After post-truth politics became the norm across the world, language as communication has been relegated to an inferior position. In today's world, language is used at best to manipulate and at worst to cause irreparable damages. The phenomenon of post-truth and the politics behind it pushes us to a point where we cannot honor communication. It also causes not only ruptures at various levels of language use but also renders the possibility of genuine exchange of ideas/ thoughts meaningless. It is ironical that to justify their erroneous decisions and faulty policy making, the political masters tend to resort to what has been termed as enigmatic mystification of language which at one point in time was employed by the colonizers to intimidate, terrify, mislead or suppress the voices of the oppressed and exploited native population. Such mystification of language breeds falsehood and treachery, deception and dishonesty and trickery as well as manipulation. Post-truth thus nullifies all possibilities of meaningful communication. If at all there is anything that post-truth gives birth to, it is the misuse of language or miscommunication. The responsible citizenry in a society along with the public intellectuals have a serious role to play in such an abysmal scenario where post-truth politics reigns supreme. They can ensure propagation of truth in collaboration with selfless and committed media agencies. We can also rely on meaningful journalistic interventions so that truthful communication and purposeful use of language may become a reality.

REFERENCES

Anderson, J., & Rainie, L. (2017). The Future of Truth and Misinformation Online. Report. *Internet & Technology*. https://www.pewinternet.org/2017/10/19/the-future-of-truth-and-misinformation-online/

Ball, J. (2017). *Post –Truth: How Bullshit Conquered the World*. Biteback Publishing Ltd. Print

Bryant, C. W. (2010). How did language evolve? https://science.howstuffworks.com/life/evolution/language-evolve.htm

Frankfurt, H. G. (2005). *On Bullshit*. Princeton UP.

Glaveanu, V. P. (2017). Psychology in the Post-Truth Era. Editorial. *Europe's Journal of Psychology*, *13*(3), 375–377. doi:10.5964/ejop.v13i3.1509 PMID:28904590

Robins, R. H., & Crystal, D. (2020). Language. In *Encyclopædia Britannica*. Encyclopædia Britannica, Inc. https://www.britannica.com/topic/language

Sharma, R. L. (2018). Communication in the Era of Post-truth. In *Communication, Entrepreneurship and Finance: Renegotiating Diverse Perspectives. Co-edited by Manpreet Arora and Roshan Sharma*. Anamika Publishers & Distributors (P) Ltd.

Chapter 4
Incompatible Discrepancy Between Low Proficiency of Arabic Language and Its High Status and Prestige

Kazuhiko Nakae
Kansai Gaidai University, Japan

ABSTRACT

Muslims are ardent to learn Arabic and study al-Qurʾān, but many of them are not competent in manipulating the Arabic language. The discrepancy of high prestige and status of the language versus low proficiency of the learners is the target of the research in this chapter. The author calls this "incompatible discrepancy." What do they indeed do in the Arabic school and Qurʾānic school? If they are so ardent, they should be highly competent in Arabic. The process of their learning is, exactly to say, rote-learning. In schooling they just memorize phrases from al-Qurʾān and the other religious texts. They start to learn Arabic as a graphic mode. They never learn Arabic as an identity marker without sticking to the way of learning it as a graphic mode. In this globalizing world everything is going to be digitalized. On the other hand, in the Islamic world many of the things remain analog, especially the way of leaning Arabic. The globalizing world is digital while the Islamic world is analog. Digital/analog can be considered as an important perspective for the world.

INTRODUCTION

In this globalized world there are many common phenomena found on all the corners of the globe. Migration is one of them. Political uprisings, economic crises and such urgent reasons as well as searching for working places for their family lives have obliged many people to cross political borders. They have to live and work in places unfamiliar to them. In most of the cases language and culture differ from their own ones. They have to get accustomed to the new living circumstances, including new language acquisition. As migrants are older this language acquisition is more difficult to implement.

As for this new language acquisition there are at least three cases: 1) to acquire the major, mostly official, language used in the host society positively and actively 2) to acquire any, not necessarily major, of the languages spoken around them in the host society unwillingly just for their communication for their lives and stick to their own native language especially in their original native countries 3) to acquire the prestigious and highly valued language in their own culture (including religion), which they much more stick to in their unfamiliar and unstable circumstances even while they might acquire any, not necessarily major, of the languages spoken around them in the host society.

In the area of language acquisition for migrants the waves of globalization can be found: that is to say, as a result of things going on they select English for their purpose of communication with people in the host society. However this globalizing trend contradicts the third case mentioned above. So to speak migrants of the third case tend not to follow the globalizing trend.

The representative one in the third case is Muslim people. They tend to stick to their Islamic culture much more in a new unfamiliar circumstances. The prestigious and highly valued language of their own culture is Arabic. They want to learn and acquire Arabic language ardently much more than they were in their original native countries, keeping in mind that they could communicate with other Muslims in the same language Arabic. Their behavioral tendency signifies that they stick to Arabic language as an **identity marker** of Muslims. That is to say, they emphasize that they themselves are Muslims (**religious identity**) prior to their original ethnic affiliations (**ethnic identity**) such as Arab, Malay, Indonesian, Filipino and the like.

The reason why their prestigious and highly valued language is Arabic is that the sacred text al-Qurʔān is written in Arabic and the **liturgical language** in Islam is Arabic. They are eager to learn and acquire Arabic and study al-Qurʔān even outside the Islamic countries.

It is normal in this globalizing world that people generally want to learn and acquire prestigious and highly valued language such as English so that they can attain the level high enough to communicate with people native of that language.

However many of the Muslims are eager to learn Arabic language. In the case of Arabic language seemingly strange but fascinating phenomenon for research can be found. They are ardent to learn Arabic and study al-Qur'ān but many of them are not competent in manipulating Arabic language. Why does this kind of discrepancy occur ? The discrepancy of high prestige and status of the language versus low proficiency of the learners is the target of my research in this paper. I call this "**incompatible discrepancy**".

PRELIMINARIES

Overview

Here I briefly overview the development of the research framework in the studies on language and religion in general. It is not doubtful that sociolinguistics in general as well as linguistics in general have recognized religion as an important factor for linguistic research. In as early as the 1960s some scholars started to consider religious factors in their researches. Most of them aimed to proceed interdisciplinary approaches to linguistic studies. Fishman et al. (1966), Crystal (1966)[1990], Stewart (1968), Samarin (1976), Ferguson (1982) described the interplay between language and religion from various perspectives. Kaplan and Baldauf (1997) researched the relation of religion with language spread and shift through the study of colonial history with missionary activities. This is a fascinating research focusing on the linguistic ecology, which seems to be the first in the history of this kind of linguistic research.

Contribution of Fishman and Omoniyi

Over the turn of the millennium the interface between language and religion continues to be more systematically focused in the research field of sociolinguistics and the sociology of language. Fishman published Exploration in the Sociology of Language and Religion with Tope Omoniyi in 2006. They well organized this volume to advance the study in this field.

In this volume among all Bernard Spolsky played a leading role to elaborate on the research framework in this field of language and religion. He was an expert of language policy and considered religion function important in the domain of language policy (cf. Spolsky2004).

Afterwards, Tope Omoniyi edited and published The sociology of Language and Religion: Change, Conflict and Accommodation in 2010. This volume showed the advancement of research in this field after the 2006 volume.

The basis of these studies has been Fishman's starting point for linguistic research: He put emphasis on the importance of many concrete case studies as well as the further advancement of each academic sub-discipline which can contribute to the elaboration of a theoretical research framework of the sociology of language and religion. Fishman published "A Decalogue of basic theoretical perspective for a sociology of language and religion" in 2006 as a crystallized theoretical framework which he and his colleague had contributed to.

IDENTITY

The term 'identity' is a very difficult notion to define. Here in my research it has a fluid nature as in Barkhuizen and de Klerk (2006) and Pavlenko & Norton (2007). As for the conceptualization of identity I draw on Norton (1997,410) as follows: "how people understand their relationship to the world, how that relationship is constructed across time and space, and how people understand their possibilities for the future ... Identity relates to desire --- the desire for recognition, the desire for affiliation, and the desire for security and safety".

When I think of the fuild nature of identity for Muslims I think they construct and re-construct their identities through their **imagination process** as Barkhuizen and de Klerk (2006,279) says "We regard this dynamic nature of identity as central to our understanding of participants' articulations of the **imagined processes** involved in their construction". As for the fluidity of identity Schifflin (1996,170) says "our identities as social beings emerge as we construct our own individual experiences as a way to position ourselves in relation to social and cultural expectations...when our sociocultural expectations change, so too do our perceptions of identities". Basically in this analysis I think identity is a fluid and dynamic one and is constructed through the imagination process of religious expectations.

Religious Identity

In the research field of the sociology of language and religion here it is necessary to refer to identity through religion, that is **religious identity**. We have to focus on the important role of language, especially liturgical language, in the construction of religious identity.

What is religious identity ? It can be considered one form of cultural identity. It is not easy to define it briefly by itself. But if we relate it to language it is not so difficult to define it. That is, liturgical language delineates the religious identity which people share with those who have in mind the same system of religious beliefs and religious experiences.

Language for Religious Identity as a Prescribed Code

The way to acquire religious identity is very similar to the one to acquire the native language transmitted by their parents. That is why Jaspal and Coyle (2010) says "religion is an *ascribed identity* and ... the LL (=liturgical language) in which the religious identity is communicated to the individual is also the *prescribed code*" (not italicized in original)

To share transcended liturgical language is an inevitable step to construct and keep **collective religious identity**. Even if they do not yet have acquired liturgical language even the endeavouring process to acquire it as well as to maintain it can contribute to fortify the unifying sense of their religious community and its 'oneness'. This sense is religious identity.

It is natural that the native language transmitted by their parents is a vital role in the construction of their own identity, whereas the liturgical language in which holy scripture is written is an inevitable role in the construction of their religious identity and in the unity of their religious community. The religious community is cohesive and uniform as the liturgical language is cohesive and uniform only with inherent variation if any. This is an important viewpoint in which *language can contribute to the construction and maintenance of religious identity and the unity of its community*.

Thus language can function as being a dominant self-aspect (Simon 2004) in the construction of the religious identity. There are many cases where those whose native language is one of the regional, non-standard, non-prestigious varieties, whether it is not genetically related to the liturgical language or not. People may perceive discrepancy between their religious identity and their affiliation of their speech community. In such a case again people tend to resort to the liturgical language for the construction and maintenance of their religious identity. In the case where their native language is a prestigious variety, especially genetically related to the liturgical language, there can appear an **imagined link** between these two varieties so that their native prestigious variety can co-act and contribute to the construction and, at least, the maintenance of their religious identity.

But in many of the cases except the above exceptional case people attach greatly religious importance to their liturgical language, putting aside their native language. This is because they feel the allegedly pure and homogeneous liturgical language is the best one they attach the religious importance to and associate with their religious identity. As Pargament and Mahoney (2005, 179) say people "go to great lengths to preserve and protect whatever they perceive to be sacred" to maintain their religious identity. That is why Muslims are eager to approach the liturgical language Qurʾānic Arabic through the **pulling-up power** activated by imagination toward their ideal status of religious identity.

IMAGINATION

The term 'imagination' used in this research comes from Barkhuizen and de Klerk (2006). They researched "immigrant-related ideologies of language and identity" and through its analysis focused on identities for pre-immigrants, that is imagined identities before migration. This approach parallels Anderson's (1983,15) analysis, as follows "the members of even the smallest nation will never know most of their fellow-members, meet them, or even the smallest nation will never know most of their fellow-members, meet them, or even hear of them, yet in the minds of each lives the image of their communication". As Pavlenko & Norton (2007,670) says, "we humans are capable, through our imagination, of perceiving a connection with people beyond our immediate social networks". Anderson and Barkhuizen and de Klerk put an emphasis on imagination as one of the social processes. Pavlenko & Norton (2007,670) says "those in power oftentimes do the imagining for the rest of their fellow citizens, offering them certain identity options and leaving other options "unimaginable"". Imagination cannot expand endlessly. The phenomenon produced by imagination could put the concerned separate from the unconcerned.

Here in this paper I explain that through imagination in language, especially liturgical language, Muslims, even outside of the Arabic-speaking area, can expand their Muslim social networks and ascertain their own Muslim identities. And Muslims activate their imagination power to approach the liturgical language Qur'ānic Arabic over their native colloquial vernacular *through the pulling-up power of classical diglossia* in order to ascertain their *ideal status of religious identity*.

DIGLOSSIA FOR IMAGINATION

In this paper I assert that imagined link between vernacular Arabic and Qur'ānic Arabic has been established through **habit and custom**. In the relatedness to this assertion I have to mention the idiosyncratic sociolinguistic feature of Arabic diglossia, which causes the imagination to be activated.

In an idealized and typical diglossic situation one linguistic variety has a higher and prestigious status and the other (or others) has a lower and not-prestigious status, in some cases, stigmatized status. Linguistic functions between these varieties are divided in a complementary way.

Diglossia can be classified into two types. The first one is '**classical diglossia**' and the other one is '**functional diglossia**'. 'classical diglossia' is that "the H and L varieties belong in some sense to the same language, yet are distinguished by clear structural differences" (Owens 2001,423), following Fasold (1984). 'functional diglossia' is "Fishman's functional diglossia (1971: 74), where different languages may fill different functional niches" (Owens 2001,423 n7).

Arabic is a typical language of classical diglossia. "High functions include the use of the language in formal occasions, and literary and religious functions, while low functions include language activity in the home, talk between friends, and the marketplace." (Owens 2001,423). But "in both structural and functional terms differences between H and L varieties are not so sharply delineated as in Arabic" (Owens 2001,423 n7). High variety is Standard Arabic and Low variety is colloquial vernacular. The former Standard Arabic has been established on the basis of classical Arabic, including Qurʾānic Arabic.

Speakers' utopian vision is to be able to use High variety Standard Arabic while they use their colloquial vernacular in a daily life. *They want to approach Standard Arabic as closely as possible.* This '**pulling-up power**' is a symbolic feature in Arabic diglossia, and more in classical diglossia. Owens (2001,423) says "One important element of the high variety is its *link to a valued cultural past*". Arabic-speaking people think that genuine and ideally-attained image of Arabs are in Arabian peninsula before the rise of Islam. This link causes the imagination power to be activated. This encourages speakers to approach Standard Arabic, and ideally and hopefully Qurʾānic Arabic over Standard Arabic, through the pulling-up power.

In a religious domain this imagined link has been intensified so that their utopian target is classical Arabic or Qurʾānic Arabic although the High variety is Standard Arabic in a true scaler of diglossic continuum. As this link gets intensified, what happens in the minds of speakers ? As it get intensified the High variety gets **sanctified**. As a result they want to expel the Lower variety (not prestigious, not urbanized) or any, even little, mixed varieties with the Low variety at least in the religious domain because they feel these varieties stigmatized, even though *they indeed use these varieties in their daily lives*. This is Arabic diglossia.

SANCTIFICATION PROCESSS

As for the definition of sanctification I draw on Pargament and Mahoney (2005,183) as follows: "a process through which aspects of life are perceived as having divine character and significance". Here liturgical language Arabic becomes sanctified through its inherent sacredness owing to the Prophet's use of this language during his lifetime and the God's revelation and its written text al-Qurʾān in this language. Jaspal and Coyle (2010) say: "through this process of sanctification, Arabic is conceptualised as the most desirable linguistic code for Muslims solely because the Prophet used the language himself".

Incompatible Discrepancy Between Low Proficiency of Arabic Language

Jaspal and Coyle (2010) notice an important point which I myself assert here: co-sanctified language. I adduce two explanations from them: "within the context of Islam, the process of sanctification is by no means confined to Arabic" and "**habit and custom** may play a significant role in the sanctification of language; he [= one of the informants in their research] has only heard this religious account in one language and is therefore unable to entertain the idea of receiving it in any other" (bold typed not in original). They refer to the duality of the linguistic situation. Muslims always listen to sermons in their own vernacular, not in the liturgical language so that the latter liturgical language has become a mere name. In their research unfortunately they do not further elaborate on it.

Liturgical language is mostly classical language difficult for ordinary people to comprehend. In the occasions of sermons and congregations ordinary languages attendants use on the daily basis are used to explain what is needed to understand. This way of explanation gets **customary** so that they feel that ordinary language might be specific to the religious activities. *Habit and custom can produce another sanctified language in a religious domain.* In the example of Lithuanian church, as I explain it later, English becomes a special status in a religious context because they habitually listen to and customarily understand what preachers tell only in English.

In Arabic case some imagination proceeds this kind of habit and custom. Arabic-speaking Arabs most of the cases, not all the cases, listen to the sermons and attend congregations using their regional colloquial Arabic. Especially in historically valued cities those colloquial Arabic varieties become co-sanctified and recognized as sanctified from outside those areas. For example in Jerusalem some parts of Friday sermons and some parts of normal congregations are carried out in their colloquial Arabic of Jerusalem. Jerusalemites may not feel such sanctification in this language variety so much but to the people outside this city this language variety is perceived prestigious because it is spoken in the sacred place and used customarily in sermons and congregations. Through this habitual and customary activity this colloquial Arabic variety becomes co-sanctified. It is assumed that this colloquial Arabic through *prestige* from historically valued urbanized city and *sacredness* from holy city like Jerusalem is *imagined to approach the higher level of Arabic, Qur'ānic Arabic.*

Outside Arabic-speaking regions this prestigious colloquial Arabic variety is co-sanctified alongside with Qur'ānic Arabic. If some non-Arabs have any experiences to visit or stay to work in such Arab urbanized cities they feel much more attached to this colloquial Arabic variety and think it is co-sanctified. Muslims imagine that they can attain the Qur'ānic Arabic through this sanctified variety of Arabic. Here *imagination in the religious context proceeds habit and custom in advance.* Linguistically colloquial Arabic is far from Qur'ānic Arabic but they feel imagined link between these two varieties of Arabic language through religious activities and religious social context.

SACREDNESS IN ARABIC

Why is Standard Arabic considered sacred ? Standard Arabic and Qurʾānic Arabic are not the same linguistically. Standard Arabic is just the modernized version of classical Arabic and basically for written purposes. And Standard Arabic, not classical Arabic, is the acrolect as a high pole in the diglossic/multiglossic continuum, which means that Standard Arabic is a prestigious language as a socio-political status. Only in the formative process of Standard Arabic there was not sacredness. Standard Arabic is not the same as Qurʾānic Arabic in a true linguistic sense but it is assumed in the minds of Muslims that these two languages are the same because Standard Arabic is called fuṣḥā (pure) in Arabic. That is why Standard Arabic can be considered sacred through this assumption on the basis of its prestigious and pure characteristics. Here imagined link to the sacredness has been constructed between these two languages through the linguistic features of prestige and purity.

On the other hand colloquial Arabic has another story. Colloquial Arabic is a vernacular spoken in a speaker's region. Why can this vernacular also be considered sacred ? This is an important question to be answered in the studies of the sociology of language and religion and also in the studies of imagined link. At first the liturgical language, here Qurʾānic Arabic, used in the holy scripture and the other religious documents is of course important and of high value to the religion and its believers. Normally this liturgical language is a classical language and needs much effort to understand through special education. It is not so easy to understand the holy scripture and also the religious lecture including words and phrases from the sacred language, whether this lecture may be given in classical Arabic or in Standard Arabic.

The aim of the preaches in a sermon or a congregation is that the attendants understand the preaches. To implement this aim their colloquial vernacular is used to explain their speeches by the preachers. Although there are many discussions on this usage of language in the preaches the communication between preachers and the attendants (believers) has been established by this way of communication in a colloquial vernacular so that the attendants to hear and understand what God wants to convey to them.

This kind of language use has been customary for a long period so that the colloquial language used by the preachers in a religious domain can be considered sacred through co-sanctification process. This co-sanctification can be established on the stable basis of the actual fact of the cognateness of these two languages, although it might be even in the case of non-cognateness. This establishment of co-sanctification means the construction of the imagined link between sacred classical language including Qurʾānic Arabic and colloquial language through this cognateness, and through its customary use in a religious domain as well. It is to be noticed that the paradoxical story can occur because *vernacular Arabic can get a sacred status through the imagination process*.

ARABIC FOR MUSLIM IDENTITY

Here we refer to Arabic language for Muslims in their religious domain. As religion in general has its linguistic demand, Muslims cannot pray without reading al-fātiḥa the first chapter of the sacred text al-Qurʾān only in Arabic. Normally Muslims remember and recite al-fātiḥa the first chapter in Arabic. Without the knowledge of Qurʾānic Arabic they think they cannot participate in the Islamic religious activities. For that reason they, whether Arabs or not, have to expend "considerable investment in terms of time and money" (Rosowsky2006, 313) for the study of Qurʾānic Arabic.

Muslims perceive holiness in Qurʾānic Arabic as a liturgical language, which is also attributed to the religious history of Islam. Jaspal and Coyle (2010) show that if they are not competent in the liturgical language "their access to Islam is somehow 'tainted' due to their having access to the translated meaning of the Koran rather than to the Koran itself." Muslims feel obliged to read al-Qurʾān in Arabic, not through its translation in the other languages.

The Arabic language is the one which Muslims perceive as a language of sacred revelation. On this point Owens (1995b, 181) explains clearly as follows: "For Islam, language and text are an inseparable whole. The relation between language and text, Arabic and the Koran, is thus unique among sacred works: to fully understand Islam one must be able to fully recite and understand the Arabic Koran". That is why all the Muslims all over the world think that this liturgical language is like a lingua franca in the Islamic community worldwide and that through this language they are united. Jaspal and Coyle (2010) say "The utopian vision of Arabic as a language spoken by all Muslims, which would allow individuals to communicate 'anywhere', appeared to signal a nostalgic desire for linguistic unity among Muslims based upon the LL". As they emphasize, it is imaginable that *Arabic language unites Muslims across borders all over the world*.

The way of learning Arabic as a liturgical language is different from the normal way of learning a foreign language, as Rohlfs (1984/1984:213)[from Owens (1995b)]: "Their study consists in nothing more than memorizing the koranic verses necessary for prayer, and mechanically learning to read and write the Arabic script, without being able to understand its contents. (translated from the German)". Through this kind of rote learning Muslims remember so many expressions from al-Qurʾān and other religious texts. From this formulaic expression religious piety is said to be measured as Joseph (2006,167) says: "it can be a matter of depth of religious piety, as measured through repetitions of formulaic invocations of the deity (and avoidance of 'vain' invocations of the divine name), or through general linguistic purism, using whatever language the religious identity is bound to in its most 'proper' form".

PARADOXICAL LINGUISTIC PHENOMENON

Many of the Muslims, especially outside Arabic-speaking regions, tend to have low competence in Qurʾānic Arabic although Arabic has high status and prestige as a liturgical language. This paradoxical relation has symbolically alluded to by Owens (1995a) in the description of vernacular Arabic in Kanuri, Nigeria. This paradoxical linguistic phenomenon is important and of much value to be researched in linguistics but so far has not been dealt with in the field of linguistic research. In the studies of religious language Samarin (1976a,8) suggests that religious language is not different from ones used in the other domains. But in the case of Arabic language as religious language we have to notice the qualitative difference. Arabic language has high status as a religious language whereas they cannot understand it so well. Samarin's suggestion is of much value for studies of Arabic language. Samarin notices this linguistic phenomenon before Owen's suggestion but Owens suggests this using his concrete data.

Why are these two aspects compatible, although it seems reasonable that it has high status with a good comprehension as Samarin's idea that it does not normally have qualitative difference ? I want to call this asymmetrical relation between language competence and language status 'incompatible discrepancy' in religious language between low comprehension and high status. Owens (1995b) refers to this incompatible discrepancy in another paper published in the same year (Note: It is Dr. Selim Ben Said who kindly lead me to pay attention to this paper.) and gave one of the solutions to this incompatible discrepancy using an idea of '**graphic mode**' in the Islamic religion, as follows: "Arabic is learned not as a text but as a graphic, as a form which embodies the holy scripture. This graphic can be broken down into constituent parts for purposes of memorization and its individual parts, its chapters and verses, have different functions, such as employment in the writing of a talisman, but the role of Arabic does not extend outside the role defined by these functions. It is only when the Koran has been mastered that the textual functions of Arabic become important. (196)".

If his description is right, what the Muslim students indeed do when in Qurʾānic school ? Don't they learn Arabic language ? These are questions which appear naturally when we heard this explanation. If they are so ardent they should be highly competent in Arabic. This is the first question to be answered. When learning a language it is normal to take structural approach, that is, to segment words and phrases and to learn grammar and sentence structure at first. But they do not. Owens (1995b,195) gives a very fascinating answer to these questions: "The purpose of koranic schools was not to learn Arabic but rather to learn the Koran". For them the way of learning is reversed in order. This is the way of learning a language as a religious identity and as a liturgical language. *They never learn Arabic as an identity marker without sticking to the way of learning it as a graphic mode.* Owens (1995b,183) also says: "Only after mastery of the Koran did students go on to the active study of the Arabic language and the Islamic sciences". I think this is right.

In this globalizing world everything is going to be digitalized. On the other hand in Islamic world many of the things remain analog, especially way of learning Arabic. Globalizing world is **digital** while Islamic world is **analog**, putting aside which is preferable and of more value. Digital/analog can be considered as an important perspective for the world.

This analysis can be applied to Arabic-speaking world as well as non-Arabic-speaking world. In non-Arabic-speaking world they are using their local languages such as Malay, Indonesian, Filipino and the like. As they have their own native language there is no problem in their communication with local people. In Arabic-speaking world they are using their own local vernacular, which, surprisingly to say, they do not recognize as Arabic although it is also a variety of Arabic language in an academic field. As mentioned above because they have their own native Arabic language there is no problem in their communication with local people. The target of their learning in school is Classical Arabic, including *Qurʾānic* Arabic. In a broad categorization in Arabic language varieties there is a bridge between the vernacular and Classical Arabic, which is Standard Arabic, modernized, sometimes localized, version of Classical Arabic. People have some knowledge of Standard Arabic when they have had higher education. But nobody feels confident in that they have a good command of Standard Arabic. In Arabic-speaking world they tend to learn and acquire Classical Arabic by an analog style.

And this is an integral process of **religious socialization** in an Islamic religion. As Jaspal and Coyle (2010) says this can be called a '**rite of passage**', as follows: "learning the LL is perhaps comparable to a 'rite of passage', a standardized pattern of social behaviour endorsed by the individual's parents, which allows **initiation** into the religious community and thus access to the religion". (bold typed not in original)

Rosowsky (2018,91) calls this 'unfinished nature of language practice' as follows: "in faith contexts, this 'unfinished' nature of language practice is often one of its main linguistic characteristics". In Rosowsky's explanation Muslims have another one or more languages as a language of communication alongside with the religious language. In Arabic-speaking countries they use their regional vernacular Arabic for their daily communication. In non-Arabic speaking countries they use the local secular languages for their daily communications. What is so called, they are in the similar situation of bilingualism. Rosowsky (2018,95) describes this linguistic situation as follows: "Young people interested in their faith must engage with the ancient language forms of their respective faiths and negotiate their linguistic repertoires by combining the latter with contemporary vernaculars and language varieties of the modern world (Rosowsky 2012)". But he (2018,102) feels difficulty in naming this bilingualism as follows: "There will also be varying levels of motivation and interest. To call such complex repertoire 'bilingualism' or even 'multilingualism' seems inadequate".

PRETENDED BILINGUALISM

Muslims endeavor to be able to use liturgical language Qurʾānic Arabic while they are using their own vernacular Arabic. For this dual linguistic situation I want to suggest 'pretended bilingualism' as one of the reasonable naming solutions. This naming originated in Dzialtuvaite (2006). He describes Lithuanian community in Scotland and says (2006,83): "The mass was held in the Lithuanian and English languages and even the parishioners who claimed to be unable to speak or understand Lithuanian, they sang the hymns in the language from specially provided books printed in 1984. In between the hymns, the priest conducted the mass in English mainly with occasional readings in Lithuanian, which *he then found necessary to summarise in English to ensure that all was understood*. The duality of the situation – I will term it 'pretended bilingualism' - may promote curiosity, but it also caused ridicule amongst the third and fourth generation monolinguals" (not italicized in original). His explanation clarifies the asymmetrical situation which I call 'incompatible discrepancy', in his case, between liturgical language Lithuanian and their daily language English, which might be a co-sanctified language in this religious community.

Jaspal and Coyle (2010) also adduce this term 'pretended bilingualism' to explain "the dual linguistic situation of using the LL for symbolic purposes and the community's dominant language to facilitate understanding". They divided clearly two purposes: **symbolic purpose** and **communication purpose**. I agree with them in the division of two purposes in their language use for the explanation of 'incompatible discrepancy' in religious community. But one more explanation is needed for the status of the language of communication purpose in a religious community. As I referred to above I think the latter language for the communication purpose can be co-sanctified in a religious domain.

CONCLUSION

Muslims stick to Arabic language as an identity marker of Muslims. They tend to emphasize that their religious identity prior to their ethnic identity through Arabic language. They are eager to study al-Qur'ān in Arabic even outside the Islamic countries. Arabic language unites Muslims across borders all over the world.

Strange to say, they are ardent to study al-Qur'ān in Arabic but many of them are not competent in manipulating Arabic language. Why does this kind of discrepancy occur ? The discrepancy of high prestige and status of Qur'ānic Arabic versus low proficiency of the learners is the target of my research in this paper. I call this "incompatible discrepancy".

To share transcended liturgical language is an inevitable step to construct and keep collective religious identity. Even if they do not yet have acquired liturgical language even the endeavouring process to acquire it as well as to maintain it can contribute to fortify the unifying sense of their religious community and its 'oneness'. This sense is religious identity. It is important to notice that language can contribute to the construction and maintenance of religious identity and the unity of its community.

In the case where their native language is a prestigious variety, especially genetically related to the liturgical language, there can appear an imagined link between these two varieties so that their native prestigious variety can co-act and contribute to the construction and, at least, the maintenance of their religious identity. In the occasions of sermons and congregations ordinary languages attendants use on the daily basis are used to explain what is needed to understand. This way of explanation gets customary so that they feel that ordinary language might be specific to the religious activities. Habit and custom can produce another sanctified language in a religious domain. It is to be noticed that the paradoxical story can occur because vernacular Arabic can get a sacred status through the imagination process.

Muslims activate their imagination power to approach the liturgical language Qur'ānic Arabic over their native colloquial vernacular through the pulling-up power of classical diglossia in order to ascertain their ideal status of religious identity. Muslims imagine that they can attain the Qur'ānic Arabic through this sanctified variety of Arabic. Here imagination in the religious context proceeds habit and custom in advance. Linguistically colloquial Arabic is far from Qur'ānic Arabic but they feel imagined link between these two varieties of Arabic language through religious activities and religious social context.

What the Muslim students indeed do when in Qur'ānic school? One of the solutions to the incompatible discrepancy was given using an idea of 'graphic mode' by Owens (1995b). Globalizing world is in a digital style while Islamic world is in an analog style.

In Qur'ānic school Muslims study al-Qur'ān, not Arabic language itself. For them the way of learning is reversed in order. This is the way of learning a language as a religious identity and as a liturgical language. This way of study is considered as an integral process of religious socialization in an Islamic religion and initiation into the religious community.

This linguistic situation is considered as pretended bilingualism to explain the dual linguistic situation for symbolic purposes and for communication purpose. Language use can be divided into two purposes: symbolic purpose and communication purpose. Many of the Muslims are ardent to study al-Qur'ān in Arabic for symbolic purpose, that is, for religious identity.

REFERENCES

Anderson, B. (1991). *Imagined communities: Reflections on the origins and spread of nationalism* (Rev.ed.). Verso. (Original work published 1983)

Barkhuizen, G., & de Klerk, V. (2006). Imagined identities: Pre-immigrants' narratives on language and identity. *The International Journal of Bilingualism, 10*(3), 277–299. doi:10.1177/13670069060100030201

Crystal, D. (1990). Liturgical language in a sociolinguistic perspective. In D. Jasper & R. C. D. Jasper (Eds.), *Language and the worship of the church* (pp. 120–146). Macmillan. doi:10.1007/978-1-349-20477-9_7

Dzialtuvaite, J. (2006). The role of religion in language choice and identity among Lithuanian immigrants in Scotland. In *Explorations in the Sociology of Language and Religion* (pp. 79–85). John Benjamins. doi:10.1075/dapsac.20.08dzi

Fasold, R. (1984). *The Sociolinguistics of Society*. Blackwell.

Ferguson, C. (1982). Religious factors in language spread. In R. L. Cooper (Ed.), *Language spread* (pp. 95–106). Indiana University Press.

Fishman, J. A. (1966). *Language loyalty in the United States. The maintenance and perpetuation of non-English mother tongues by American ethnic and religious groups*. Mouton.

Fishman, J. A. (1971). *Sociolinguistics: a Brief Introduction*. Mouton.

Jaspal & Coyle. (2010). Arabic is the language of the Muslims --- that's how it was supposed to be? Exploring language and religious identity through reflective accounts from young British-born South Asians. *Mental Health, Religion and Culture, 13*(1), 17-36.

Joseph, J. E. (2006). The shifting role of languages in Lebanese Christian and Muslim identities. In *Explorations in the Sociology of Language and Religion* (pp. 165–179). John Benjamins. doi:10.1075/dapsac.20.14jos

Kaplan, R. B., & Baldauf, R. B. (1997). *Language planning from practice to theory.* Multilingual Matters.

Norton, B. (1997). Language, identity and ownership of English. *TESOL Quarterly, 31*(3), 409–429. doi:10.2307/3587831

Omoniyi, T. (Ed.). (2010). *The Sociology of Language and Religion: Change, Conflict and Accommodation.* Palgrave Macmillan. doi:10.1057/9780230304710

Omoniyi, T., & Fishman, J. A. (Eds.). (2006). *Explorations in the sociology of language and religion.* John Benjamins. doi:10.1075/dapsac.20

Owens, J. (1995a). Minority languages and urban norms: A case study. *Linguistics, 33*(2), 305–358. doi:10.1515/ling.1995.33.2.305

Owens, J. (1995b). Language in the graphic mode: Arabic among the Kanuri of Nigeria. *Language Sciences, 17*(2), 181–199. doi:10.1016/0388-0001(95)91152-F

Owens, J. (2001). Arabic Sociolinguistics. *Arabica, 48*(4), 419–469. doi:10.1163/157005801323163816

Pargament, K. I., & Mahoney, A. (2005). Sacred Matters: Sanctification as a Vital Topic for the Psychology of Religion. *The International Journal of Religion, 15*(3), 179–198. doi:10.120715327582ijpr1503_1

Pavlenko, A., & Norton, B. (2007). Imagined communities, identity, and English language learning. In J. Cummins & C. Davison (Eds.), *International handbook of English language Teaching* (pp. 669–680). Springer. doi:10.1007/978-0-387-46301-8_43

Rohlfs, G. (1984). Quer durch Afrika. Wissenschaftliche: Buchgesellschaft, Darmstadt. (Original publication 1874)

Rosowsky, A. (2006). The role of liturgical literacy in UK Muslim communities. In *Explorations in the Sociology of Language and Religion* (pp. 309–324). John Benjamins. doi:10.1075/dapsac.20.24ros

Rosowsky, A. (2008). *Heavenly Readings: Liturgical Literacy in a Multilingual Context.* Multilingual Matters.

Rosowsky, A. (2012). Performance and Flow: The Religious Classical in Translocal and Transnational Linguistic Repertoires. *Journal of Sociolinguistics*, *16*(5), 5. doi:10.1111/j.1467-9841.2012.00542.x

Rosowsky, A. (2018). Globalisation, the practice of devotional songs and poems and the linguistic repertoires of young British Muslims. *Culture and Religion*, *19*(1), 90–112. doi:10.1080/14755610.2017.1416645

Samarin, W. J. (1976a). The Language of Religion. In Language in Religious Practice (pp. 3-13). Newbury House.

Samarin, W. J. (1976b). *Language in religious practice*. Newbury House.

Schifflin, D. (1996). Narrative as Self-Portrait: Sociolinguistic Constructions of Identity. *Language in Society*, *25*(2), 167–203. doi:10.1017/S0047404500020601

Simon, B. (2004). *Identity in Modern Society: A Social Psychological Perspective*. Blackwell. doi:10.1002/9780470773437

Spolsky, B. (2004). *Language policy*. Cambridge University Press.

Stewart, W. (1968). A sociolinguistic typology for describing national multilingualism. In J. A. Fishman (Ed.), *Readings in the sociology of language* (pp. 531–545). Mouton. doi:10.1515/9783110805376.531

Chapter 5
Performing Speech Acts:
Focussing on Local Cultural Norms in the Englishes We Use

Maya Khemlani David
University of Malaya, Malaysia

Aliyyah Nuha Faiqah Azman Firdaus
University of Malaya, Malaysia

ABSTRACT

When we speak we use speech acts. Examples of speech acts include performing greetings, giving compliments and responding to compliments, making complaints and responding to complaints, making and responding to requests, congratulating, and consoling. In English language textbooks we normally see one response to some of these speech acts. For example, "thank you" as a response to a compliment or "good morning/afternoon/evening" as a greeting. As English has become a world language spoken by non-native speakers of English, many non-nativised cultural norms when performing speech acts are noted in real-time interactions. In this chapter, examples of nativised speech acts expressed in acceptable English are drawn from a number of data sources ranging from both real-time interactions, literary sources, which are a reflection of life, and social media, which encompass Facebook, Messenger, WhatsApp messages. Pedagogical ramifications of such authentic real-time data are discussed. The result will be the teaching of the English emerging from localised cultural norms in the speech acts we perform.

DOI: 10.4018/978-1-7998-2831-0.ch005

INTRODUCTION

Over the years, identity has excited interest of researchers from a wide range of disciplines; particularly a marked shift has been witnessed from hard-core psycholinguistic models of second language acquisition to greater interest in sociological and anthropological dimensions of language and education. A number of scholars have worked on language and education drawing from socio-cultural, post-structural and critical theory (Norton and Toohey, 2001; Block, 2003). Rather than focus only on the linguistic input or output of second language acquisition, the above scholars have chiefly concentrated on the intersection between the language learner and the larger social world in diverse cultural, social and historical contexts (Norton, 2011).

Background

Identity and classroom pedagogies have inspired much research from scholars in different contexts. Lee's (2008) findings on postsecondary institutions in Canada suggested that there is often a disjuncture between pedagogies conceptualized by the teachers and their actual classroom practices. Various other researchers have worked on the same theme identifying identity related questions in classroom pedagogies and have suggested transformative strategies to expand identities. Clemente and Higgins (2008) drew on their longitudinal study of pre-service English teachers in Mexico to question the dominant role of English in the globalized economy and illustrated the ways in which the non-native English teachers sought to appropriate and perform English without sacrificing local identities. In a more or less similar research, Stein (2008) surveyed the ways in which English language classrooms in under-resourced township schools became transformative sites in South Africa in which textual, cultural, and linguistic forms were re-appropriated and 're-sourced', with a view to validating those practices that had been marginalized and undervalued by the apartheid system. Cummins (2000) presented case studies of three schools in the United States, Belgium, and New Zealand that have made a positive difference in the lives of bilingual-bicultural children by affirming in every facet of the school operation the value of children's languages and cultures. The notion of identity versus language learning is in accord with post-structuralist, socio-cultural and critical theories that conceive of language not only as a linguistic system, but also as a social practice. Being fluent in English does not mean we are abandoning our identity or traditions. Instead, by mastering the English language we are able to compete in the fast-paced global economy while still preserving our culture and values. We can use the English language to communicate about our culture, custom and knowledge with the rest of the world. Proficiency in our own language is also highly important because being bilingual will build our confidence to speak to people from different racial backgrounds.

Hino (2018) promotes the usage of Japanese English who are listed in Kachru's "Expanding Circle" context by providing concrete suggestions for practitioners. He developed an original model of Japanese English, investigating how Japanese values could be demonstrated in Japanese English. An example of this is to create textbooks that teach how *okagesama de* – an expression of modesty to soften a compliment – could be used. For instance, if someone says "It's good you are back from Tokyo", instead of saying "Thank you", it would express the moral aspect of Japanese culture to say "With your kind influence, I am safely back" (p.70).

A number of studies have been conducted on the speech act of congratulations in different languages. Elwood, 2004 compared the speech act of congratulations by American and Japanese Subjects. The results showed there were differences even by those Japanese students writing in English. As for condolences, Allami and Smavarchi (2012) in their study of condolences found that Persian speakers and EFL learners are more direct than native speakers of English (see also Pishghadam and Morady, 2013 on condolence responses in English and Persian).

Al Kayed and Al-Ghoweri, 2019 investigated the strategies of speech act of criticism in Jordanian Arabic. Data was collected from 120 undergraduate Jordanian students living in Jordan using the Discourse Completion Test (DCT). The results of the study showed that the Jordanian students used more indirect strategies compared to direct strategies to perform criticsm. This suggests that the Jordanians knew that perfroming criticsms is a face-threatening act, hence the adoption of more indirect strategies (e.g. request for change, asking/presupposing, say nothing, etc.)

In many studies, a discourse completion test has been used as the methodology to collect the data. In a discourse completion test, respondents are provided with a number of hypothetical situations then asked what they would say in such a situation. The test has been heavily criticised, though much used in the past, as it has been argued that to ask a subject what he would say is not the same as what they actually say.

MAIN FOCUS OF THE CHAPTER

Empowering Learners: Integrating Local Cultural Norms in the Englishes we Speak

What is the purpose of learning a language? This of course depends on the context, area, country we are learning a target language, in this case English. Thirusanku and Melor Md Yunus (2014) state that in Southeast Asia historically, the forces of colonization, international trade and religion have been responsible for the spread of English to the region. Today, the region is characterized by its linguistic diversity, and English plays a dynamic role in both intra- and international communication. The use of English no longer serves as just a means of communication with foreigners from outside Southeast Asia but, increasingly, English serves the role of lingua franca unifying the different ethnic groups that live in the region (Low & Azirah Hashim, 2012, p.1). This chapter argues that if the role of the target language, English is mainly to communicate with fellow countrymen or with other Asians then local cultural norms should be reflected in the target language we teach. In this way we do not alienate learners from their own cultural norms. In fact, we empower them.

Many Asians are less likely to be interested or have the opportunity to use English with native speakers of the language. Being multilingual, the English language has become a common code for communication. This being the case, the communication discourse in this context should reflect the local culture and values, which are valued and appreciated.

Linguists and anthropologists have long recognized that the forms and uses of a given language reflect the cultural values of the society in which the language is spoken. Language learners need to be aware, for example, of the culturally appropriate ways to address people, express gratitude, make requests, and agree or disagree when using English with fellow countrymen or even with others for whom English is not a L1. These are known as speech acts.

Speech Act

A speech act is an utterance that has a function in communication. We perform speech acts when we offer an apology, greeting, request, complaint, invitation, compliment, or refusal. A speech act might contain just one word, as in "Sorry!" to perform an apology, or several words or sentences: "I'm sorry I forgot your birthday. I just let it slip my mind."(carla.umn.edu/speechacts/definition.html). As speech acts include real-life interactions they require not only knowledge of the language but also appropriate use of that language within a given culture. They also require knowledge of the relationship between speaker and listener and the context in which the speech act is realised.

Speech acts are generally difficult to perform in a second language because learners may not know the idiomatic expressions or cultural norms in the second language but more importantly they may transfer their L1 or first language conventions into the second language, as they might assume that such rules are universal. Because the natural tendency for language learners is to fall back on what they know to be appropriate in their first language, it is important that L2 learners understand exactly what they do in that first language in order to be able to recognize what is transferable to other languages.

An example of a speech act is the use of terms of address. For example, in most Asian countries it is considered polite to address interlocutors who are older than the speaker as uncle or auntie, and if they are not older than the speakers the terms sister or brother are sometimes used. The examples below are taken from a conversation in a hospital reception counter:

Eg. 1: *Polite verbal openings: Yes, sister, can I help you?*

Eg. 2: *Polite request: This way, auntie.*

Moreover, in status conscious and hierarchical countries like for example Malaysia, the use of official titles like "Datuk" is very common in dominant English discourse and is considered as a sign of respect.

Titles and honorary terms of address in Malaysian dailies:

Eg. 3: *Selangor police chief Deputy Datuk Khalid Abu Bakar believes that more than two persons were involved in the latest incident. ("Blast heist.' The Star, 25 October 2008.)*

Eg. 4: *Star Publications (M) Bhd group managing director and chief executive officer Datin Linda Ngiam and cast members of Front page attended the event. ("Ways to ensure safety' of kids" The Star, 25 October 2008.)*

Eg. 5: *It is commonplace for post-graduate ESL students to say to their supervisor "What does Prof. think? Rather than "What do you think?" The omission of the pronoun marker you and its replacement with a title reflects respect in a society which puts much premium on displaying respect to people in power.*

Speech acts reflect local cultural norms. One common local greeting in Malaysia is "Have you eaten?" This is a direct transfer from local languages but is in perfectly good English and is understood by fellow Malaysians as a greeting.

Another important speech act is the performance of giving and receiving compliments. In the Asian context, it is polite to negate and reject compliments and praise by contradicting the compliment giver. In this way the compliment receiver emphasizes humility. Example 6 shows how a Malaysian Indian lady negated her interlocutor's compliments by saying that this was her duty. In Example 6, the interlocutors used the words, "work" to denote duty, rather than personal traits.

Eg. 6:

"You're so, what shall I say, sincere?"

"I try to be."

"Try to be, that's good!" he says, laughing. "And does it take great effort?"

"My work always needs effort."

(Maniam, 2003, p. 118)

Indirectness, a common feature of Asian discourse especially among the elderly is noted in the next example when a niece invites them for dinner and enquires what they would like to eat. Even the invitation to a meal is couched indirectly and the choice of food suggested by Amy is never negated openly or directly.

Eg. 7:

My aunt and uncle were about to return to Beijing after a three-month visit to the United States. On their last night, I announced I wanted to take them out to dinner.

Amy: Are you hungry?

Uncle: Not hungry.

Aunt: Not too hungry. Perhaps you're hungry?

Amy: A little.

Uncle/aunt: We can eat, we can eat, then.

Amy: What kind of food?

Uncle: Oh doesn't matter. Anything will do. Nothing fancy, just some simple food is fine.

Amy: Do you like Japanese food? We haven't had that yet.

Uncle: We can eat it.

Aunt: We haven't eaten it before. Raw fish.

Amy: Oh you don't like it? Don't be polite. We can go somewhere else.

Performing Speech Acts

Aunt: We are not being polite. We can eat it.

(Amy drove them to Japantown and they walked past several restaurants.)

Amy: Not this one, not this one either (as if searching for a certain Japanese restaurant). Here it is (in front of a Chinese restaurant).

Aunt: (Relieved) Oh Chinese food!

Uncle: You think like a Chinese.

Amy: It's your last night in America. So don't be polite. Act like an American.

(Adapted from Tan, 2003)

In Chinese society, it is polite to reject offers because it suggests humility as well as letting the listener know that they do not wish to impose or be troublesome in any way. Yet at the same time according to Chinese culture, one must treat guests like royalty-for not doing so implies arrogance. Vincent, a Singaporean Chinese in Example 8 reacted to the rejection by ordering more food. An example follows:-

Eg. 8: *He (Vincent) ordered liberally and soon the table was crowded with plates, bowls, tureens of hot, steaming, delicious smelling food. "Too much, too much," complained his mother, but he continued to summon the stall attendants with more orders.*

(Lim, 2001, p. 54-55)

Vincent's mother was seen as complaining when her son ordered a lot of dishes, but instead of stopping, he kept ordering more.

Social media like the comments to Facebook entries or even responses to an entry in WhatsApp is a minefield of data to demonstrate cultural norms. Table 1 provides data from a group WhatsApp of Indian lecturers who are informed of the death of an Indian linguist. Examples from Table 1 show homage being paid and positive descriptions being made of him as a man and as a linguist. See Examples, 3, 4, 5, 7, 8, 9, 11 and 13. Peace upon his soul (Om shanti) is shown by Example 1 though Hindi words are used in this codemixed utterance. Expressions of peace on his soul are also shown in Examples 10, and 13. Thoughts of the family he has left are expressed in Examples 2 and 12.

Other examples of condolences in English but Religious norms noted in this speech act are shown in Table 2. Reference to God (Allah) is present in Examples 1, 4 and 5. Expressions of peace and paradise (jannah) are shown in Examples 2 and 3.

Table 1. Realisation of speech act of Condolences by Indian Hindus

Examples	Speech act of Condolences
1.	Om shanti, an irrepairable loss.
2.	May god give his family strength to bear the loss.
3.	He was a good friend and a great soul.
4.	My condolences! A pillar of Indian linguistics has fallen. 🙏
5.	It is a sad news. Prof k has been a legendary. His death is a great loss to academics in general and Kashmir to particular.
6.	Today is a tough and sad day for me and many others in linguistic fraternity.
7.	For those who knew Prof he was one of the most honest fair and caring person you would ever meet. He had a smile that would light up the room.
8.	So sad! He was very inspiring personality. Rest in peace. We met in many conferences. Sir was so active and so humble.
9.	An ever-smiling, energetic, eminent linguist.
10.	I pray Almighty to rest his soul is peace.
11.	Oh no! I remember he had come for a session on Endangered languages in my Orientation course. Later I spoke to him about my endangered language. He was very kind and patient and answered all my queries. He will be missed by everyone.
12.	My condolences to his family.
13.	O N K Sir was a beautiful person inside out. May his soul rest in peace.

Multiple reactions to the death of an Indian colleague obtained from a communal WhatsApp group are illustrated in Table 3. Fond memories of the deceased are triggered upon the news of his death as seen in Examples 3, 4, 5, 6, 7, 8, 9 and 10. Wishes of peace are shown in Examples 1, 2, 11 and 12.

Further examples of condolences by members of the Sindhi community to the death of a much loved elder are mentioned in the Table below:

Table 2. Realisation of speech act of Condolences by Muslims

Examples	Speech act of Condolences
1.	Very sad to hear this. May Allah grant her the highest place in jannah.
2.	So sad to hear May the she gets the highest plc in jannah Ameen.
3.	May her soul rest in peace.
4.	May Allah bless her soul.
5.	May God granted her the paradise.

Performing Speech Acts

Table 3. Realisation of speech act of Condolences by Punjabi speakers of English

Examples	Speech act of Condolences
1.	Really sorry for your loss. Condolences to his family members and loved ones. May he always rest in peace. Amen.
2.	May God bless and protect the family. …. May the divine soul rest in peace!
3.	A very sad news. R J was a very dedicated and committed person. I had an opportunity to work with him as co-editor of the felicitation volume on Prof A R, my revered teacher. Despite his age and deteriorating health he saw to it that the volume is brought out. His dedication, involvement and passion for work were quite extraordinary. He had planned to visit Kashmir this summer and had offered to deliver lectures (without any remuneration) in our department. It is a great loss to the linguistic fraternity and a personal loss for me. My heartfelt condolences to his family members.
4.	R was a close associate at the start of my career at Punjabi University Patiala back in 1985. It's a loss to all sincere linguists. Om shanti Om.
5.	It is indeed sad! I met R, and had several interactions with him in Mysuru when, around two decades ago, I was helping in the project of Late Prof JC S J and also after that. He indeed left a strong impression on my young mind. Like the poets he had a cognonym 'R' that indeed is rare for a linguist. I remember him as a person who didn't care for the political correctness of Linguistics, and even academics in general. However there is a price for this, I remember him to be a Research Associate with a white flowing beard!
6.	He very proudly traced his lineage to one of the Sikh Gurus. I remember he was fascinated by the concept of anhad naad, and he talked very passionately about it.
7.	When I met him first, it was the time he was helping his son to set up an eatery, another unconventional thing for an academic of those days! I wish his soul to become one with the anhad naad, and his family members to get the strength to cope up with the great loss. If someone has the phone number of the family members, or his phone number then kindly share it so that the condolence messages can be sent to the family.
8.	Heart deep condolences. Dr. R was a dedicated, focused linguist.
9.	It is extremely sad to know about the passing away of our friend R. I have known him since 1980 when he was a young man with a black beard. He was also an alumini of the Linguistics Dept. of DU. We had met many many times and we always discussed linguistics and his radical views in Punjabi. He was always bubbling with enthusiasm in academic discussions. He was very affectionate and understanding. His passing away is the loss of another good and great human being. May his soul rest in peace.
10.	Words fail to describe my feelings for R who was my contemporary in Delhi University in 1972. Later when I joined CIIL in 2000, he was overjoyed. Many late evening discussions come to my mind.
11.	May his soul Rest In Peace.
12.	RIP.

The following examples of condolences were retrieved from Instant Messages. Religious norms (our Heavenly Father and Offer Divine Mercy prayers) are present in these speech acts on the passing of a loved one.

Table 4. Realisation of speech act of Condolences by the Sindhis

Examples	Speech act of Condolences
1.	Dearest Uncle S words cannot express my heart broken feelings upon hearing that you have left this world. At the same time I know that Krishna has received you with his own hands because you were always such a kind, generous and loving human being. I will never forget my childhood days sitting and joking in Kaka's with you or the times we helped you as you spent your days and nights in the service of the Lord at the Krishna temple. Rest now uncle at His Lotus feet. You will be dearly missed.
2.	Dada we pray ur soul attains mocha. Heartfelt condolences to the families.
3.	It is extremely difficult to believe that our beloved Daddy is no more. Please accept our deepest condolences....may his soul rest in the Lotus feet of Lord Krishna.
4.	Our deepest condolences to the family, may his soul rest in peace and go to the light. Truly an amazing man.
5.	OMSHANTI.
6.	Our heartfelt condolences to the S...ani, B...ani and B...rani families. May the lord guide Dada's soul.
7.	We all love you Daddy. Where ever you are ! (We know ... U R surely, under the lotus feet of Lord Krishna ... your favourite Kurukshetra Hero) plz plz bless all of us. (With loves, R S family).

Examples of congratulations obtained from comments on a Facebook entry show how culture is transmitted via language. If English is our second language, we transmit or express congratulations using our cultural norms and religious beliefs using English and the words we use, albeit in English, disclose our cultural and religious norms. Table 6 shows the responses to a picture of a well-known professor originally from Sri Lanka now an American in a hospital bed. Remarks in the form of relief over the good news are described in Examples 1, 2, 3, 4, 5, 6, 7, 8, 12, 13, 14 and 15. Words of encouragement are depicted in examples 9 and 10 and 11.

SOLUTIONS AND RECOMMENDATIONS

Pedagogical Implications

Real time interactions obtained from literary sources and social media present a wide variety of the realisation of many speech acts. The enactment or realisation or response when we give compliments, condolences or for that matter any speech act like greetings, responses to compliments, refusals etc. depends on our relationship with the interlocutor and on our religious and cultural norms and that of the recipient. Using examples from real time interactions, literary sources or even social media, the teacher can sensitise learners to both relationships between speaker and listener and

Performing Speech Acts

Table 5. Realisation of speech act of Condolences by Christians

Examples	Speech act of Condolences
1.	Oh dear. Stay strong. Offer Divine Mercy prayers in Divine Mercy Church Shah Alam. May her soul rests in peace. Amen.
2.	So sorry to hear this. I share your pain, M. May she go with peace.
3.	Oh no this is really sad M and I connect with Cancer as I lost my son in cancer when he was 18/19. In fact yday was 22 years since he has passed on. May each ones Soul Rest in Eternal Peace. Our heartfelt condolence and sympathy to you and your full family.
4.	Stay calm and accept the will of God. She is free from all pain now.
5.	Sing the HU it will calm you lol
6.	Heart goes out to her son difficult moment for the family. I pray God her soul rests in peace away from all the pain. Please pass on our deepest sympathies to the family.
7.	So sorry to hear that M. Sincere condolences.
8.	Oh dear so sorry to hear this M. May God bless her soul and may she rest in peace.
9.	So very sorry to hear of your niece's passing. My deepest condolences.
10.	Hello M our deepest condolence to you and family tried to call you no answer.
11.	Thats so very sad. My condolences dear M.
12.	That's very sad. I can understand how you feel. When young ones go it seems so unfair.
13.	So sorry to hear. My thoughts and prayers are with you all. Big hug.
14.	So sad to hear. May you get the strength to bear the loss... May her soul rest in peace!
15.	Oh god ..my condolences...
16.	Hi M how are you all doing? We are very sorry to hear the news. Very young to go. I pray that she is with our Heavenly Father at peace now. Our loves to you all. Miss u and love you sweet M.
17.	Oh dear...my condolences to your family. My wife is a cancer survivor. I know how tough this can be for the family.
18.	Sorry to know...
19.	Very sad to know about G! May God give the whole family strength in this time of pain and grief.
20.	Hi mi... so sorry to hear this ... may God rest her soul in peace.... may God grant you all the strength to bear this loss... take care... praying for the family.

religious and cultural norms of both parties. Communicatively competent learners will result from such a approach. Through this approach, it is hoped that language learners will change their conversational styles depending on whether English is used intra-nationally or internationally, with native speakers of English or with Asean speakers using English (David, 2005).

Table 6. Realisation of speech act of Congratulations

Examples	Speech act of Congratulations
1.	Great news and stay blessed.
2.	Great to know that you are fine! Blessings from Brazil.
3.	Glad to learn that you are fine.
4.	Glad to know that good news. May God bless you. Prayer from Sri Lanka.
5.	That's great to know. Stay blessed.
6.	That's really good news S...God has been good & we praise & thank God for His blessings...
7.	Brilliant
8.	That's wonderful news
9.	The Universe spoke and it spoke well!! Keep on cycling Happy Valley and beyond, my friend!! You made my weekend too!!!
10.	You are too smart to surrender!! Keep going!!
11.	Stay well, Dr. C.
12.	Good news! Stay healthy Professor S. C.
13.	Happy to hear that you are doing great sir ...
14.	Hurray
15.	Thank god!!!!

FUTURE RESEARCH DIRECTIONS

Curriculum designers should be made aware of nativised speech acts although in good English and should include this in curricula. Writers should not be afraid to include examples of nativised speech acts in textbooks. Teachers too should not shy away from acknowledging nativised speech acts and use them in the language classrooms.

CONCLUSION

In close reference with theoretical positions the most central issues this study focuses on, are language learner cultural norms and identity (see also Cummins, 1996 & 2000). Smith (1983) claims that as an international language, the English language is not bound to any one culture, and priority is given to communication. There is also no need for non-native users of English to sound like the native speaker, but simply to use language, which is "appropriate, acceptable and intelligible" (Smith, 1983, p. 8). To view the prevalent scenario through spectacles of the above theoretical and conceptual constructs, one could say that many language teachers fail to recognize and establish students' cultural norms and identities. Bourdieu (1977, p. 75) notes, "when a person speaks, the speaker wishes not only to be understood, but to be 'believed, obeyed, respected, distinguished'. Communicative competence should include not only 'the right to speak' but the right to speak in culturally appropriate ways depending on one's interlocutor.

We use language to communicate. Language teachers must bear this in mind and not only focus on syntax. What we say and how we say it depends on the context and our speech partner or interlocutor. This is because real-life acts of speech usually involve interpersonal relations of some kind.

The authors do not deny that the behaviours and intonation patterns that are appropriate in their own speech community may be perceived differently by members of the target language speech community. Learners have to made to understand that, in order for communication to be successful, language use must be associated with culturally appropriate behaviour when using English with fellow countrymen and when using English with native speakers of English. Language learning is not only a linguistic system, but also a social and cultural practice where local and cultural norms and identities are represented.

ACKNOWLEDGMENT

This research received no specific grant from any funding agency in the public, commercial, or not-for-profit sectors.

REFERENCES

Al Kayed, M., & Al-Ghoweri, H. (2019). A socio-pragmatic study of speech act of in Jordanian arabic. *European Journal of Scientific Research*, *153*(1), 105–117.

Allami, H., & Smavarchi, L. (2012). Giving condolence by Persian EFL learners: A contrastive sociopragmatic study. *International Journal of English Linguistics*, 2(1), 71–78.

Block, F. (2003). Karl Polanyi and the writing of the great transformation. *Theory and Society*, *32*, 1–32.

Bourdieu, P. (1977). *Outline of a theory of practice*. Cambridge University Press.

Center for Advanced Research on Language Acquisition. (2019). *What is a speech act?* Retrieved from carla.umn.edu/speechacts/definition.html

Clemente, A., & Higgins, M. J. (2008). *Performing English with a postcolonial accent: Ethnographic narratives from Mexico*. Tufnell Press.

Cummins, J. (1996). *Negotiating identities: Education for empowerment in a diverse society*. California Association for Bilingual Education.

Cummins, J. (2000). *Language, Power and Pedagogy. Bilingual Children in the Crossfire*. Multilingual Matters Ltd.

David, M. K. (2005). Cultural capsules and reading texts: Triggers to cross-cultural language awareness. *TEFLIN Journal, 16*(2), 209–222.

David, M. K. (2011). Extracting discourse norms from novels. *Pratibimba Journals of IMIS, 11*, 24–32.

David, M. K. (2018, January). *Performing Speech Acts- focussing on local cultural norms in the Englishes we use*. Plenary Paper presented at the International Conference on Teaching and Assessing English Language and Literature, Chennai, India.

David, M. K. (2018, July). *Social media- a treasure house for pedagogical resources: Focusing on responses to the speech act of congratulations and condolences*. Plenary Paper presented at the International Conference on English Language Teaching (CONELT), Kuningan, Indonesia.

Elwood, K. (2004). *"Congratulations": A cross cultural analysis of responses to another's happy news*. Retrieved from: http://dspace. Wil. waseda.ac.jp/dspace/handle/2065/6097

Hino, N. (2018). *EIL education for the Expanding Circle: A Japanese model*. Routledge.

Lee, E. (2008). The other(ing) costs of ESL: A Canadian case study. *Journal of Asian Pacific Communication, 18*(1), 91–108.

Lim, L. (2001). Ethnic group varieties of Singapore English: Melody or harmony? In Evolving Identities. The English language in Singapore and Malaysia (pp. 53-68). Singapore: Times Academic Press.

Low, E.-L., & Hashim, A. (Eds.). (2012). *English in Southeast Asia. Features, policy and language in use*. John Benjamins Publishing Company.

Maniam, K. S. (2003). *Between Lives*. Penguin Books Ltd.

Norton, B. (2001). Non-participation, imagined communities, and the language classroom. In M. Breen (Ed.), *Learner contributions to language learning: New directions in research* (pp. 159–171). Pearson Education Limited.

Norton, B., & Toohey, K. (2001). Identity, language learning, and social change. *Language Teaching*, *44*(4), 412–446.

Pishghadam, R., & Morady, M. M. (2013). Investigating condolence responses in English and Persian. *International Journal of Research Studies in Language Learning*, *2*(1), 39–47.

Smith, L. E. (Ed.). (1983). *Readings in English as an International Language*. Pergamon Press.

Speaking English does not mean forgetting our traditions, says Raja Permaisuri Agung. (2019, Oct. 14). *The Star Online*. Retrieved from https://www.malaymail.com/news/malaysia/2019/10/14/speaking-english-does-not-mean-forgetting-our-traditions-says-raja-permaisu/1800182?fbclid=IwAR3hBpBUkPcpYIkZ9Em23MrYGzzms3AXVUZA4O4hRIxT3YOQCL5yO7jvZmc

Stein, P. (2008). *Multimodal Pedagogies in Diverse Classrooms: Representation, rights and resources*. Routledge.

Tan, A. (2003). *The Opposite of Fate: a Book of Musing*. G. P. Putnam's Sons.

The Star. (2008a, Oct. 25). Blast heist. *The Star*.

The Star. (2008b, Oct. 25). Ways to ensure safety of kids. *The Star*.

Thirusanku, J. & Yunus. (2014). Status of English in Malaysia. *Asian Social Science*, *10*(14), 254–260.

ADDITIONAL READING

Ayres, A. (2009). *Speaking like a state: Language and nationalism in Pakistan*. Cambridge University Press. doi:10.1017/CBO9780511596629

David, M. K. (1999). The teaching of communicative strategies and intercultural awareness – core components for effective communication. *English Teaching*, *28*, 1–7.

David, M. K., Dumanig, F. D., Kuang, C. H. & Nomnian, S. (2016). Cross-cultural encounters in giving compliments and making requests through literary texts: pedagogical ramifications. *Malta Review of Educational Research*, *10*(1), 5-22.

David, M. K., & Kuang, C. H. (2012). Politeness strategies in openings and closings of service encounters in two Malaysian agencies. *SEARCH: The Journal of the South East Asia Research Centre for Communications and Humanities*, *4*(2), 61–76.

Gimenez, T., El Kadri, M. S., & Calvo, L. C. S. (Eds.). (2017). *English as a Lingua Franca in Teacher Education: A Brazilian Perspective*. De Gryuter Mouton.

Khorshidi, H. R. (2013). Study abroad and interlanguage pragmatic development in request and apology speech acts among Iranian learners. *English Language Teaching*, *6*(5), 62–70. doi:10.5539/elt.v6n5p62

Nikitina, L., & Furuoka, F. (2019). Language learners' mental images of Korea: Insights for the teaching of culture in the language classroom. *Journal of Multilingual and Multicultural Development*, *40*(9), 774–786. doi:10.1080/01434632.2018.1561704

Placencia, M. E., & Garcia, C. (2012). Speech acts research. In C. A. Chapelle (Ed.), *The Encyclopedia of Applied Linguistics (9)*. Willey-Blackwell. doi:10.1002/9781405198431.wbeal1099

Strubel-Burgdorf, S. (2018). *Compliments and positive assessments: Sequential organization in multi-party conversations*. John Benjamins Publishing Company. doi:10.1075/pbns.289

Tamimi Sa'd, S. H., & Mohammadi, M. (2014). A cross-sectional study of Iranian EFL learners' polite and impolite apologies. *Journal of Language and Linguistic Studies*, *10*(1), 119–136.

Zeff, B. B. (2016). The pragmatics of greetings: Teaching speech acts in the EFL classroom. *English Teaching Forum*. Retrieved from https://americanenglish.state.gov/files/ae/resource_files/etf_54_1_pg02-11.pdf

KEY TERMS AND DEFINITIONS

Condolences: A speech act to express sympathy or sorrow to someone who has experienced some sorrow or a loss.

Congratulations: A speech act used by a speaker to express joy at the good news received by another.

Greetings: Something friendly or polite that you say or do when you meet or welcome someone.

Intercultural Communication: Situated communication between individuals or groups of different linguistic and cultural origins.

Nativised Discourse Norms: Language adopted by the indigenous communities through the process of adaptations and innovations from indigenous cultures. A form

Performing Speech Acts

of language that is an accepted standard or a way of behaving or doing things that most people from their own community understand and agree with.

Social Interaction: An exchange between two or more individuals and is a building block of society. Social interaction can be studies between groups of two (dyads), three (triads) or larger social groups.

Speech Act: An utterance that has a function in communication.

Chapter 6
Re-Examining the "Native Speaker Question":
Representing Native Speakers on an ELT Website

Lanqing Qin
University of Ottawa, Canada

Awad Ibrahim
University of Ottawa, Canada

ABSTRACT

This chapter addresses the native speaker question and construct from a representational point of view. Through a critical discourse analysis (CDA) of an ELT website in China's context, the authors discuss what and who is profiled as 'native speaker' and how this category is represented on the website. Existing studies dealing with the 'native speaker' abound, but only in recent years have a few efforts been made on the construction of this discourse, and the online representation of ELT in China is worthy of more examination. Consequently, this chapter aims to problematize the term 'native speaker', deconstruct the process of how a discourse of 'native speaker' takes on shape through online representation, and reveal how it is a racialized category. In conclusion, they offer pedagogical and policy implications.

DOI: 10.4018/978-1-7998-2831-0.ch006

Re-Examining the "Native Speaker Question"

INTRODUCTION

The 'native speaker question'[1] has been around for a long period in linguistic and language education arenas. As Alan Davis (2003) has shown, the term 'native speaker' has even a longer genealogy and it is certainly not without controversy (see also next section of this chapter). Its definition, especially in the context of English language teaching (ELT), can be hardly pinned down (Ibrahim, 1999) and its legitimacy is questioned by varied scholars (Cook, 1999; Rampton, 1990). "The terms 'native speaker' and 'non-native speaker'," argues Brandt (2006), "suggest a clear-cut distinction that doesn't really exist" (p. 15). In other words, 'native speaker' is not as obvious a term, yet it seems to have been naturalized and persisted in the language use of professionals and scholars (Medgyes, 2001). Moreover, when it comes to ELT, 'native speakers' are often positioned as the ideal teachers, superior to their 'non-native' counterparts (Phillipson, 1992). Specific to the ELT recruitment process, the native status is attributed with superiority and valued more than the professional qualifications (Mahboob & Golden, 2013; Selvi, 2010). According to Amin (2001), a worldwide phenomenon in the field of ELT is the link between native speakers and Whiteness, a link, which we will address in this chapter, that results in discriminatory perceptions and prejudice against 'native speakers' of color. One cannot help but wonder, how has the 'native speaker' without a solid theoretical support been naturalized and become a substance in practices and how come that its attributed superiority is so widely accepted and deeply engrained in this profession? The aim of this chapter therefore is to problematize the term 'native speaker,' deconstruct the process of how the native speaker discourse takes on shape through online representations and reveal how it is a racialized category.

Taking the *British Council in China* website as a site of analysis, we want to revisit the 'native speaker' question by asking: from a representational point of view, who is a native speaker?; and how are they represented? Put otherwise, what are the different 'representational tools' that are used to represent them authoritatively, and in the process, and as a result, who is included in these representations and who is excluded, how and why? Our analysis show, even when you are proven to be grammatically incorrect, if you are mostly male, White and assumed to be of British origin (through your accent), then you are a native speaker. One may argue that it is a British Council website, so it is not surprising that speakers' talk uses British accent. We concur. What is of interest to us is the mechanism, what we are calling 'representational tools,' through which the category is represented, assumed, reproduced, and thus naturalized. Using critical discourse analysis, we show that these representational tools 'create' (Hall, 2013) a racialized White and mostly male category that speaks with authority from an authorized space (Bourdieu, 1991).

In what follows, we will first briefly review the debate around the native speaker model in the ELT context and based on that offer a working definition of native speaker that guides our research. Second, we look at studies that examine the native/non-native dichotomy as embodied in ELT administrative decision making and employment practices and read them from the representational perspective. This helps to understand how 'native speakers' are actually represented and imagined. We then discuss our findings from investigating into the website, which we see as a system of representation (Hall, 1992) where the 'native speaker' is placed at the center. We end this chapter with the conclusions drawn from our study and implications for ELT profession.

Native Speaker: A Terse Genealogy of a Troubled Term

The earliest written record of the term 'native speaker' is offered by Bloomfield who claims, "the first language a human being learns to speak is his native language; he is a native speaker of this language" (as cited in Davies, 1991, p. 43). The recent debate around the 'native speaker,' however, has been vastly aroused by Chomsky (1965) since he defines it as "an ideal speaker-listener, in a completely homogeneous speech-community, who knows the language perfectly" (p. 3). The linguistic intuition of "the idealized native speaker" (p. 24) is held as the standard against which the grammar of a language should be measured. With this idealized model comes critique and discussion from various aspects and fields, especially from applied linguistics.

Applied linguists find the 'native speaker' an unrealistic concept in the first place. Some argue that the 'native speaker' is rather a myth than a real existence (Cook, 1999; Davies, 1991). For example, Paikeday (1985) contends that the term is arbitrarily established and can never happen in reality. Situating his contention within second language acquisition, Cook (1999) argues that "adults could never become native speakers without being reborn" (p. 187). The question of "who is the native speaker" remains unanswerable so far.

Another major critique is around the connoted inferiority associated with its opposite category, 'non-native' speakers, and L2 learners, especially in terms of the English language. To explain, first and foremost, the terminology itself, by using the prefix 'non-,' signifies a deficit and negative impression (Holliday, 2005); meanwhile, it is common to find 'native speakers' attributed with more prestige both by themselves and the L2 learners (Davies, 1991). What's more, the 'native speaker' community itself does not necessarily represent the highest standard of the language. According to Braine (2013), even "native speakers" themselves "do not speak the idealized, standardized version of their language" (p. xv). For Paikeday (1985), the Chomskian construct of native speaker, who possesses the linguistic intuitions of the language, implies no scientific evidence that non-native speakers cannot have them, thus so-called native speakers are not naturally better at the language than their non-native counterparts.

Furthermore, the notion of 'native speaker' connotes a monolingual ideology, presuming that the 'native speaker' speaks only one language, which is not true in the actual world (Jenkins, 2006). In fact, "much of the world's verbal communication takes place by means of languages which are not the users' 'mother tongue,' but their second, third, or nth language, acquired one way or another and used when appropriate" (Ferguson, 1992, p. xiii). Especially in terms of the English language, this monolingualism is even more problematic. The increased mobility of the English language has generated new forms of Englishes around the globe, and speakers of these Englishes can hardly be defined or categorized by the binary terms of 'native' or 'non-native' (Davies, 1991). Moreover, given their local adaptation and cultural embeddedness, these diverse varieties of English have grown into a part of the global cultural flow, and simply using grammar and lexicon as measurements of who is and who is not a 'native speaker' is out of date (Pennycook, 2017).

ELT: Troubling the Dichotomy Between Native and Non-native

Despite the vagueness they embody, "the superordinate terms 'native speaker' and 'non-native speaker' seem to persist in the language use of researchers and teachers alike," and have influenced discussions on language pedagogy and ELT methodology (Medgyes, 2001, p. 429). Although there does exist difference between native and non-native English-language teachers, especially in terms of linguistic competency, Medgyes (2001) argues, this linguistic difference cannot be confused with teaching capacity, where both 'native' and 'non-native' English language teachers have their pros and cons and can produce effective teaching on their own terms. However, in practice, as Medgyes (2001) observes, the dichotomy may cause unequal job opportunities: "Teaching applications from even highly qualified and experienced non-NESTs [non-native English speaker teachers] often get turned down in favor of NESTs with no such credentials," and "non-native teachers of English often feel disadvantaged and discriminated against" (p. 432). Paikeday (1985) quotes one of the responses to his question "Anyone met a native speaker?", that the native speaker construct has moved beyond a linguistic concept onto one that "has even more political and sociological overtones than linguistic ones" (p. 395). Indeed, this issue has taken up another flavor in the ELT profession, one where complex ideologies and power relations are involved (Holliday, 2005).

For Kramsch (1997), 'native speakership' is a social, historical and ideological construct that implies an "acceptance by the group that created the distinction between native and non-native speakers" (p. 363). It confuses language as a tool of communication with language as a symbol of social identification (Rampton, 1990).

Phillipson (1992) describes the attribute of nativeness in ELT practices as the native speaker fallacy. It positions 'native' speaking English teachers as the ideal teachers, superior to their 'non-native' colleagues. As a result, it contributes to maintaining the position of central English-dominant nations such as the US, the UK and Canada in the ELT profession. Along similar lines, Holliday (2005) coins the term "native speakerism" in reference to the "established belief that 'native speaker' teachers represent a 'Western culture' from which spring the ideals both of the English language and of English teaching methodology" (p. 6). It thus suggests an us/them dichotomy, distinguishing 'We' native speakers, the unproblematic and idealized Self, from 'They' non-native speaker, the "imagined, problematic generalized Other," with the latter dismissed as "culturally deficient" (Holliday, 2005, p. 1). Skutnabb-Kangas and Phillipson (1994) further reveal that the use of "languages of different groups as defining criteria and as the basis for hierarchization" (p. 23) is essentially linguicism, a parallel form of racism. According to Phillipson (1992), "Linguicism involves representation of the dominant language, to which desirable characteristics are attributed, for purposes of inclusion, and the opposite for dominated languages, for purpose of exclusion" (p. 55).

Kubota and Lin (2009) also draw upon the intersection of ELT and racism. They point out that the core issue lies in the essentialized equation of 'native speaker' with White and standard English speakers, 'non-native speakers' with non-White and 'non-standard' English speakers. In this process, the linguistic dichotomy is projected onto racial categories. Paradoxically, race is a social construct that has no biological proof (Kubota & Lin, 2009), yet a certain type of phenotypical feature (e.g., skin color) is used for dividing people into White and non-White, and this division is further conflated with English speakers' '(non)native' statuses. We could already see 'nativeness' associated with Whiteness and naturalized as the English language norm whereas 'non-nativeness' rendered the inferior other, thus producing a racial hierarchy (Kubota & Lin, 2009; Shuck, 2006). Furthermore, by essentializing 'non-native' as being non-White, 'native speaker' professionals of colors are left out of the dichotomy, hence even further marginalized in the field (Kubota & Lin, 2009).

Informed by the discussion above, there is a need to offer a working definition of the term 'native speaker' and, for the purpose of this paper, see how it will be applied in our subsequent research. Tautologically stated thus far, 'native speaker' is a problematic concept and its meaning can hardly be pinned down. Firstly, the nativeness of a language cannot be precisely defined (Davies, 1991). The notions vary from one speaker to the next. Whether it is determined by one's mother tongue, or by the first language learned since one was born, or by the dominant language that one has the best command of, there is not a unitary definition. Secondly, the monolingualism ideology implied by the native speaker model does not fit today's context. Concerning the current stage of globalization and the flow of languages and populations (Pennycook, 2007), specifically in the 'English-language world,' it is more difficult to have a unitary category that can be defined as 'the native speaker of English.' Put otherwise, the native status is no longer an effective criterion for categorizing (English) language speakers around the world (Holliday, 2005; Jenkins, 2006).

ELT: Mapping the Troubled Politics of Meaning and Representation in a Field

In this section, we, along with our readers, can learn from the previous empirical works that looked at the category of 'native speaker' with special emphasis on the recruitment practice in ELT, especially within the last two decades. For the benefit of this research, we pay close attention to the question of representation, a notion we will discuss in the next section. Here, we would have to use 'native' and 'non-native' for the categorized English speakers as they are referenced in the studies, and we use quotation marks to show our problematization of the terms.

Mahboob, Uhrig, Newman and Hartford (2004) surveyed 118 administrators of intensive English programs in the US colleges about the importance they placed on different criteria of English teachers. Mahboob et al. found that compared to other criteria, administrators' preference for 'nativeness' can significantly influence the number of 'non-native' English speaker teachers in the whole teaching staff. Later, Clark and Paran (2007) revised Mahboob et al.'s questionnaire and surveyed 90 respondent administrators in the UK context. Their study evidenced a similar correlation between the importance that employers attach upon 'native speaker' criterion and the hiring decisions. If employers highly value the native status, then 'non-native' speaker candidates have little chance to get interviewed, even if they are qualified. Neither of these two studies has given explicit definitions of the 'native English speaker' in the questionnaire. Nor has there been any confusions about the term reported by the respondents. Arguably one can say that the participants involved in these investigations have all assumed there is such an unquestionable identity as the 'native speaker.'

This naturalization of 'native speaker' has also manifested itself in advertised teaching positions. In their study, Govardhan, Nayar and Sheorey (1999) concluded that, although the job titles and their minimum requirements vary greatly, "being native or nativelike – whatever these vague terms mean – was the main and perhaps the only common requirement" (p. 117). In the past decade, as we shall also see, more studies have been conducted to reveal how recruiters filter the imagined (Anderson, 1983) 'native speaker.' In some cases, the vagueness of the term is pinned down through complementary characteristics or requirements.

Here, Wang and Lin's (2013) study is illuminating. It looked at the professional English teaching requirements in four regions in Asia, namely Hong Kong, Taiwan, Japan and Korea. They found that, except for Hong Kong, governments of the other three areas provided a list of traditional English-speaking countries from which their candidates were selected. They also revealed that all governments were subscribed to 'native speaker' norms, which naturally legitimized all the 'native speakers,' with or without teaching qualifications, as superior teachers.

Selvi (2010) pioneered in using content analysis to examine 249 ELT job advertisements from two worldwide repositories. Selvi found that two thirds of the advertisements required a 'native or native-like/near-native proficiency,' and some of them further narrowed the category with residence history in North America, citizenship of specific countries and locations of professional training. Following Selvi (2010), there have been more studies examining other areas than the traditional English-speaking countries like the UK, the US and Canada. Mahboob and Golden (2013) explored what exact criteria were employed to mark a candidate as a 'native speaker' in East Asia and the Middle East. They identified seven key features from the recruitment advertisements, where 'nativeness' was the most cited and required. Apart from direct uses of the term 'native,' some advertisements referred to specific countries or language genres to imply this intention. Also noteworthy is the correlation between race and nativeness in some discourses such as 'white native speakers' and 'Caucasian native speakers.' For the purpose of our paper, a significant conclusion from Mahboob and Golden's study is that this correlation is implied, almost taken for granted but never stated.

Elsewhere, Lengeling and Pablo (2012) used critical discourse analysis (CDA) as a methodology in a study within the Mexican context. The authors examined a variety of public documents that contained ELT employment information, including ads, websites, fliers and signs. Apart from confirming the native speakerism discourse, their image analysis also indicated a tendency of using discourses to convey such information as a) English teachers are young and energetic and can make English learning easy and fun, and b) teaching English in Mexico is an exciting traveling experience.

Also using CDA, Ruecker and Ives (2015) conducted an analysis of online ELT employment advertisements in Southeast Asia. According to our research, this is the closest study to our own (if not the only we could find so far), which takes a similar representational viewpoint. The authors built up a corpus of 59 sites for macro analysis, then specifically focused on two sites for micro analysis. Their results revealed the intertwined relations between language background and race and confirmed the connection between White privilege and native speaker fallacy in ELT. Ruecker and Ives made a significant revelation: they unveiled a rhetorical construction process which produced a 'White native speaker' as the norm of an ideal

English-language teacher. First, the websites they investigated defined the native speakers through profiles of White teachers who come from specified countries, which the authors referred to as 'Inner countries' (Western, English speaking countries: namely, Canada, U.S., U.K., Australia and New Zealand). Second, the destined countries were represented as non-Western exotica; thus, normalizing the discourse and the status of the White 'native speaker' as the naturalized assumed teacher. These conclusions will be directly relevant to our current research.

It is clear, from the reviews above, that few studies have approached the native speaker question from a representational point of view except for Ruecker and Ives (2015). Generally, nonetheless, these studies have all confirmed the native speaker fallacy, and reading from a representational perspective, we can identify some strategies employed by recruiters and policy makers to define the 'native speaker.' While most of existing research examine the recruitment policy or employment advertising, our study is an investigation into an authoritative ELT website, the *British Council in China*. With the background of digital era, websites and other media forms have become popular among educational institutions in self-representation. Our analysis may thus provide insights on how the whole ELT industry is constructing the discourse of 'native speaker' through their online representations.

Methodology vs. Method: Making use of Critical Discourse Analysis (CDA)

Our study makes a distinction between methodology and method. We see the former as the broad theoretical term that underpins a study (CDA in our study), whereas the latter is the technique by which data is collected. Methodologically, "CDA is a type of discourse analytical research that primarily studies the way social power abuse, dominance, and inequality are enacted, reproduced, and resisted by text and talk in the social and political context" (van Dijk, 2015, p. 466). CDA, van Dijk explains, is by virtue a multidisciplinary approach. Since CDA takes discourses as socio-politically situated, they cannot be extricated from their specific contexts. For van Dijk, as contexts flow and change, the strategies for analyzing text and talk also switch accordingly. For Hall (1992), the discourse around a certain event, once built up, can have functions and effects; it leads or limits people to perceive and talk about this event in a certain way. For CDA scholars, discourse is referred to as an aggregation of utterances and signs that are put together to create knowledge about a subject. Here, the study of language use extends to a broader range, considering a myriad of signs but not limited to spoken and written texts in the purely linguistic sense. This may include the non-verbal aspects of communication events, such as gestures, images, tones, face work, body position, and so on (van Dijk, 1993).

Specifically, Hall's (2013) theory of representation is the critical lens through which the 'native speaker' is examined in our study. Representation is the work where signs, languages, text and talk are utilized to signify our ideas and thought. Hall posits that "language, meaning and representation are constitutive" (p. xxii). That is to say, language itself does not reflect events, the reality cannot meaningfully exist outside our systems of representation, and the knowledge about something is created during representation through the work of language. Moreover, Hall (2013) suggests that it is the difference between different signs that signifies and carries meaning, the producing of meaning through representation thus "marks out and maintains identity within and difference between groups" (p. xix). Representation studies, then, are about language use in meaning constructions and representing different social groups or identities.

Therefore, for the interest of our study, we look into what 'representational tools' are employed on the website to imagine and solidify the category of 'native speaker,' and during this process what knowledge is created about it. By representational tools we are referring to the actual and deployed techniques through which the discourse of the 'native speaker' is introduced, repeated and eventually naturalized. These tools include image, verbal and non-verbal utterance where complex messages are communicated. Probing into these tools, our intent is to scrutinize: who the website is assuming and imagining the 'native speaker' to be, what features are they assumed to have, and as a result, who are left out and eliminated by this category?

Methods: Site of Research and Data Collection

The data of our research comes from the British Council's official website in China ("British Council | China," 2019). Specifically, we examine the webpage of its newly launched project, *English is GREAT* ("English is GREAT," 2019). We look into both verbal and non-verbal elements (i.e. representational tools) displayed on it, especially the promotional video of this campaign, the transcript of which is dictated by the authors. The rationale of choosing this website is that British Council is a world-famous English-language learning institution and is often considered an "authoritative" voice in ELT profession (Ruecker & Ives, 2015). Specifically, the *English is GREAT* campaign was launched in early 2018 and thus represents a most relevant example of the present situation and may signal to future trends of the ELT development. For the verbal part, we describe and analyze the texts in titles, subtitles, captions, as well as the transcript. For the non-verbal part, we pay attention to images and the promotional video, where we also take into consideration the subtle features, such as the background, scenes, accents, intonations etc. Next, we offer a general description of the website and the campaign, so as to understand the structure of the website and build up the context of this study.

When it comes to the site of the research, browsing the *British Council in China* website, we first locate the *English is GREAT* campaign at the Learn English project on the homepage. As one of the five major functions of the *British Council in China* website, Learn English is set up to teach English to learners in China (and around the globe). Entering the campaign section, there are seven small units consisting the webpage. Respectively they are: 1) About The Campaign, 2) 2018 Teacher Award – Overall Winner Announced, 3) UK Summer School Photo Competition, 4) English Teacher Development, 5) For Individuals, 6) Love And Change Chosen By You As The Most Popular English Words For 2018, and 7) English Impact. These small units are displayed in the same format, with a picture on top, a title in the middle, and a short textual introduction attached at the bottom. Among all the small units, we zoom in and examine the most eye-catching unit, About The Campaign, since it unfolds most of the information about the campaign and provides access to the promotional video of this program. Each of the other units is further linked with separate projects and websites, which exceed the scale of our research hence will not be fully covered here. We will only analyze their cover pictures, titles and captions as displayed on the current webpage.

About The Campaign unit is obviously given the highest priority. It is singled out at the centre top and takes up the largest space, almost one third of the webpage, while the other six units share the rest of the space equally in two rows and three columns. This unit is the first thing that greets audiences entering this page and is marked by a striking logo with a strong patriotist meaning (the design of the logo is largely inspired by the Union Jack). As its textual introduction suggests, the campaign is a cross-border cooperation between China and the UK, it "was launched in Wuhan on 31 January 2018, in the presence of UK Prime Minister Theresa May, while on her official visit to China" ("British Council | China," 2019).

The promotional video takes the form of interview and is composed of three main parts. The first two are interviews with head figures from prestigious institutions, Roger Walshe, the Head of Learning of the British Library, and Martin Peacock, the director of Global English Product Development of the British Council. The third part reflects students' experiences of studying in the UK. Meanwhile, on the bottom right of the campaign page, there is an external link which leads to a public comment area regarding this video. It is found here that this video was originally used in 2012 as listening exercise material by the Learn English Team and is now serving the campaign promotion with its content unchanged. The comment area is maintained and responded to by the Learn English Team under the British Council.

Tooling Representation, Representing Tools: Findings and Results

Throughout the investigation, four main themes are identified: 'We' as the authority and experts, the global language and genuine English, arbitrator of the English language, racialized profiles of 'native speakers.' In what follows, we elaborate each of them with detailed analyses of the text and talk found on the website.

'We' as the Authority and Experts

The introduction of the Learn English project outlines the context of programs offered by the British Council in China, including the *English is GREAT* campaign. According to the website:

Learn English with the British Council and you'll be learning with the world's English experts.

We've been teaching English for more than 75 years and have helped more than 100 million people in 100 different countries improve their English skills and build their confidence.

Start leaning English with us today. (British Council in China, 2019, n.p.)

Discursively, the first sentence makes an equation of the British Council with "the world's English experts." This equation can be read in multiple ways but for us, it is an indication that, first, the British Council represents the experts of English; second, this expertise is worldwide, at a global level. What is not clear, nevertheless, is whether this expertise is in the English language itself, or in the competence of teaching the English language. What's more, it creates an impression that if "you," the intended audiences of this website as well as the potential learners, learn English with "us," the British Council, then you will have the privilege of learning with these "world's English experts." This immediately diminishes the distance between the general learners and the high-profile experts who usually are out of reach for average people.

The second sentence uses numbers to demonstrate a) its long history, b) its wide range of influence, in both terms of population and geographic regions, hence c) its full of experience and expertise in English teaching. The use of figures makes their declarative statement appear to be strong and more convincing and not simply remain an empty boast.

Re-Examining the "Native Speaker Question"

The third sentence is the slogan, which is printed in a larger font size. Instead of saying "start learning English today," it specifies that it is 'us,' the British Council, the world's English teaching experts, that the potential learners are learning with (if not from). Meanwhile, the using of adverbial "today" indicates that what has been described above is a tangible goal that can be achieved straightaway.

So far, this brief introduction has established a 'We' identity: self-positioning the British Council as an authoritative community of ELT professionals. It is done by three steps, first, claiming itself as the world's English experts; second, using statistics to enhance this statement; third, promising an instant participation and attracting potential learners.

This authoritative 'we' is not left only to the device of the website, but supported by authoritative figures talking authoritatively. On a video promoting the British Council, Roger Walshe reinforces this us/them dichotomy. Even though the video is introduced in a conversational format, both its high production and intent (creating an authoritative 'we') leave little to doubt:

Roger: This is a poem written in the nineteenth century in which somebody has done exactly that; he says 'I wrote to you before' - he uses a number 2, letter 'B,' the number 4.

Host: That's amazing. So what does this tell us about the English language?

Roger: Well, it tells us it's very versatile. It tells us that people play with it and sometimes the changes they make stay. Some of those changes were made 500 years ago, some of them were made 100 years ago. But some of the changes we make now in internet chatrooms and the way we talk to each other and the way people around the world use English will become the future of English as well.

At first glance, there is an innocent sentiment in this conversation, even a warm feeling, but when read discursively, it implies and assumes more than one can imagine. Roger recognizes that the future English language is open to changes – 'changes we make now… and the way we talk to each other and the way people around the world use English.' But who are 'we'? Who actually have the right and power to determine what kind of changes can be accepted and what cannot? One might hazard a guess that 'we' in this example are the same people as mentioned in the introduction text above, 'we' are people alike the speaker himself, who is a 'native speaker' of English and belongs to the authoritative community of teachers, who is recognizable to 'us.' Then who are 'people around the world'? Although not referred to, it is clear that they do not belong to 'us.' In spite of the manifold meanings and diversity among them, they are unitarily categorized into this simplified term, 'people around the world.'

The Global Language and Genuine English

The second theme is promoting the special status of English as *the* global language among all languages, as well as the notion of the genuine English among all type of Englishes. The following excerpt comes from the beginning of the promotional video:

Host: The English language. It's the official language of 54 different countries and is spoken by over a billion and a half people worldwide. Adding together native speakers, people who speak English as a second language or an additional language and people who are learning English, and it's the most commonly spoken language across the globe. So, what makes English so great? And why do people want to learn English?

In this short prologue the host has already done two things, highlighting the role of English and naturalizing the 'native speaker.' The host starts off by impressing the audiences with the significant status of the English language. This is shown by the great number of speakers and its high political status in a wide range of countries. In the second sentence, without giving any definition, the host is already dividing English speakers into different groups among which the 'native speaker' is a solid category. After that, he jumps into the conclusion that English is great; and he does this in an unquestionable fashion, that is, by skipping the argument process and transitioning directly to ask the audience to think of the causes for this phenomenon as if it were a self-evident fact. By doing so, it leaves no space for alternative interpretations of the relevant topic.

The next excerpt of interview with Martin, the Director of the Global English Product Development, suggests a similar proposition:

Host: Martin, tell me about English as a global language.

Martin: OK, well, many people talk about English as being a global language. And the reasons for that are the widespread use of English. It's used in education. It's used in science and technology. And importantly, English is also used in business.

Host: Are there many global languages?

Martin: No, not really. I mean there is the [stressed tone, emphasis added] global language, which is English, in the sense that English is used in these many different contexts. There's only one. There are a lot of languages which are used very widely and spoken by many people in many different places. Cantonese, for example, the variant of Chinese, is spoken in many different places, so it's global in a geographic sense. And it can be global in the numbers, but in terms of the use in different areas, of education, science, research, English is the only [emphasis added] global language.

This conversation starts with general concept of English as a global language but soon moves on to prove the uniqueness of English as 'the' global language. When people attach meanings to things, Hall (1992) argues, they always construct the relations that exist between different things. It is by highlighting the different aspects that one thing can stand out from all other similar items. The same rings true in this excerpt. Among all definitions and features of a global language, Martin pins down that English is the 'the only' global language. Sidestepping coloniality, Martin leaves out any discussion on how the English language became so widely spread and ended up being the official language of many countries. Phillipson (1992) frames this kind of phrasing as part of what he calls the ongoing practice of linguistic imperialism. For Phillipson, the establishment and continuous activities of the British Council have asserted and maintained English dominance through the reproduction of unequal power and resources between the English language and other languages. Thus, one may contend, this 'English as the only global language' claim made by British Council has a strong political meaning and reveals the linguistic imperialist move in a modern age.

In the following conversation, the host and Martin explore varieties of English from an accent perspective:

Host: Are there different types of English?

Martin: Oh yes, there's lots of different types. There's different accents of English. I come from the Northern England and I have a particular accent. So within England itself, within the UK, there're many variations in the English pronunciation. And that extends globally. So you see English in America, or as used in Australia, which is different in accent and also in usages as well.

Here is a misuse of 'there's + lots of + plural nouns,' which will be analyzed later. Apart from that, Martin admits that there are multiple types of English, but he distinguishes the categories largely by accent and pronunciation. Different usages are only briefly mentioned, and the more complex localizations and dynamics of Englishes in other places are left out in the examination of the current status of English in the globalization process (Pennycook, 2007). Moreover, the variety of accents are limited to traditional English-speaking countries, such as the U.S.,

101

Canada and Australia, hence speakers from these regions are also included as 'we.' In so doing, other areas and regions, such as Singapore, India, West and East Africa, where English is localized, are not given acceptance and recognition.

The conversation between the host and Martin continues but this time 'genuine English' is the exclusive factor:

Host: So technology can change the language. But in what way does it help people to learn the language?

Martin: Well, it helps in many ways. In the past, students in locations in other countries didn't have access to much genuine English. They might have a book, or newspaper. But what the internet allows them is to read, and often to read and translate languages, like English, on a massive scale.

Martin brings up the notion of the 'genuine English' as an assumed and already known category. The underlying idea here is that, now the internet allows learners to be exposed to 'genuine English,' this genuine English accessed on the website of the British Council, including the very video that audiences are watching and listening to. Although Martin acknowledges in the previous example the many variants of English, here, he implies an exclusiveness of the genuine English.

One can sense contradictory statements thus far from the previous conversations. Although both speakers (Martin and Roger) acknowledge the versatility and diversity of Englishes worldwide, there is a strong claim for a standard or genuine English that belongs exclusively to the speakers and in turn to the British Council website. Put otherwise, if it is true that the changes and adaptations to English made by 'people around the world' can be recognized as equally as those changes 'we' made, all types of Englishes should be accepted on an equal ground. However, in the speech only traditionally English-dominant countries are recognized for their variants. Furthermore, if all Englishes are legitimately accepted, then what is the point of a special category of the 'genuine English'? And why would it be necessary for learners to access the genuine English from the UK specifically?

Moreover, if authority and authorization work through selection, then it is rather interesting that the two head figures' voice is the only one that is heard. By virtue of their positions as the director of Global English Product Development and the Head of Learning in the British Council, they have access to such an interview and the medium of the internet to persuasively present their interpretations and perceptions of the English language to the world. In Bourdieu's (1991) language, this is a perfect moment where an authorized speaker is speaking with an authorized language and from an authorized position/location. In the case of Martin and Roger, the statements they make is attached with a higher value than that of an average person. They speak as the authority of the English language. Thus, the statement made is actually no longer about language per se, it is a manifestation of social power and political power in the language education and linguistic areas.

Arbitrator of the English Language

Based on the analysis above, the native speakers represented on the website are given an authoritative voice as know-hows of the English language. The examples in this section show that their authority further extends to arbitering the English language usage. As 'native speakers,' they are entitled with rightfulness even when proven to be linguistically wrong.

As mentioned, at the beginning of the video, the host has already divided English speakers around the world into different categories, among which the 'native speaker' is a separate type. Also, in the interviews with the two head figures, they have constructed an 'Us/Them' dichotomy, by dividing English speakers into 'natives' and 'non-natives' and English worldwide into standard and non-standard. This divide implies that 'we natives' speak the standard and genuine English, whilst 'they non-natives' do not. Now, the following examples can shed light on more information about 'we native speakers,' and this is where we come back to the aforementioned false usage of "there's + plural nouns."

This is a grammar error made by both speakers multiple times in the promotional video. For instance, Roger says 'there's lots of reasons,' 'there's no grammars, there's no guides'; and Martin says 'there's lots of different types,' 'There's different accents of English.' In the comment area in the external link, it is found that during the course of six years up to our current analysis, questions about this usage has been raised three times by different users on this website. And the responses by the Learn English Team from the British Council gave different explanations on this:

Kirk replied on 18 December 2018: In informal situations, it's not uncommon for native speakers to use 'there's' with plural nouns. I never recommend that my students speak this way, as they are judged differently as non-native speakers, but it's useful to know that natives speak this way sometimes!

Peter M replied on 6 December 2016: Roger does indeed use these forms and it is common use in some dialects, though it is considered non-standard in most....

AdamJK replied on 27 December 2012: ... it's important to remember that the people in these videos are speaking spontaneously and not writing. Therefore, they may say things that are not perfect English. Strictly speaking, you are right and the correct form is 'There are lots of reasons.' However, it's quite normal to hear people in informal spoken English use there's, probably because it's just easier to say.

As we can see here, none of the three different responses confronts this mistake squarely. Rather, they start with discursively justifying and defending the usage. They either claim that it is common or declare its legitimacy in certain contexts. Meanwhile, their ambiguous attitudes towards this use are expressed through concessions and indirectness. They reluctantly admit that there is inappropriateness to it, then immediately argue: this is understandable. As such, they also avoid directly criticizing that this is plainly wrong, but just is 'not perfect,' 'non-standard,' and it is only considered so 'in most' situations, but not always, hence further mitigating the negative results of this error. Especially, AdamJK's response, 'probably because it's just easier to say,' indicates a sense of reconciliation with the mistake.

Moreover, sometimes this reluctant acknowledgement comes with attached strings, which can be implied by phrases such as 'strictly speaking,' or 'it is important to remember that (this is an informal context).' It delivers an impression that it is only worth concerning when one is being too scrupulous, as if it is the user who asks this question to blame, thanks to a lack of understanding of oral English in informal conversations.

Last but not least, there can be an alternative explanation of this usage as colloquialism or an interpretation that language may change from one context to another, but this is worth a closer examination here. Provided it is true that this is a common usage in English conversations, then it would only be reasonable that everyone, despite their native or non-native statuses, can use it on a same ground. However, it is not the case. According to the latest response made by Kirk, this mistake is forgivable only when the speaker is a 'native speaker,' whereas it is explicitly stated that a 'non-native' will be 'judged differently' for the same error, regardless of the contexts. It is thus apparent that the status of nativeness would result in different perceptions and attitudes to an English speaker. Furthermore, such a comment made by a 'native' English language teacher indicates that 'non-native' students can do nothing about it but be aware of the fact and avoid being judged on a different ground. Underlying the well-intentioned suggestion made by an ELT instructor, this comment is by virtue delivering a message that 'native speakers' are rule makers and arbitrators of the English language. Consequentially, it will only perpetuate the superiority and dominance of 'native speakers' in the ELT field.

Racialized Profile of 'Native Speakers'

In this last section of analysis, we shall unveil the profile of 'us' 'native speakers.' The website has filled up the presumed 'natives' and 'non-natives' through visual languages, mainly pictures and video representations. Because of space, we will focus only on two examples as a way of discussing a pattern we have seen throughout the website. This argument will become more obvious with the table below and in the next few paragraphs.

First, in the Teaching Award unit, which is aimed at celebrating the "excellence in English language teaching by Chinese nationals who are non-native speakers of English" (n.p.), a Chinese female is portrayed on the award poster. This female in a white suit with short black hair and a warm smile is meant to represent the 'Chinese nationals who are non-native speakers of English,' and whose competency are to be arbitrated by the 'native' professionals. Meanwhile, in the Individual Learners unit, several Chinese learners with bright faces are featured. Although this is a preliminary reading, it could be the case that the website is telling the potential learners that this is what they can become as closely as possible should they learn English with the British Council, and that they could also look professional and be confident in conversations.

The second example comes from the English Teaching Development unit, where the introduction reads, "we work in partnership with the Ministry of Education, national associations and educational institutions to support teacher development" (n.p.). The illustration depicts a middle-age White male in a formal wear giving a speech in a conference setting. It is evident that this White male is positioned as the representative of 'us,' the authority community of 'native speakers,' whereas people like the Chinese female mentioned above, are labeled as the 'Chinese nationals who are non-native speakers of English.'

These two groups of contrasting images on the webpage can have direct implications to audience as to who is a 'native speaker' and who is not. Looking systematically and discursively, the following is a table summarizing the main characters and their identities as clearly stated on the *English is GREAT* webpage and in the promotional video.

As we can see, among all figures depicted on the website, and judging from either their accent or the background scene in the images, those who are identified as 'native speakers' are all White people supposedly coming from the UK. Among these 'native speakers,' only two are females, males are predominantly depicted. Although gender complicates the issue, Whiteness remains intact as the common thread.

White actors are the protagonists with authority in their respective contexts. They usually embody a higher social political status, such as the head figure interviewees in the video and the award presenter. In contrast, people of color are largely underrepresented. Take racialized minorities from the UK, although they are 'native speakers' just as their White counterparts, they get no representation on the website. The only few scenes of people of color are where they show up as

Re-Examining the "Native Speaker Question"

Table 1. Characters represented in the British council in China website

Where	Who	Represented as	Assumed (non-)native status	Nationality
2018 Teacher Award	A Chinese female	Allegedly English Teacher	Non-native	Chinese
	Carma Elliot, White, female	Director of the British Council in China	Native	British
	A group of English teachers	Teacher Award winners	Non-native	Chinese
UK Summer School Photo Competition	A Chinese girl	Student	Non-native	Chinese
English Teacher Development	A White male	Representative from authority institutions	Native	British
For Individuals	A group of Chinese learners	Individual learners	Non-native	Chinese
External link	Two female students	Students in Britain	Not specified	Not specified
Promotional video	Host, White, male	Host	Native	British
	Martin Peacock, White, male	Director of Global English Product Development	Native	British
	Roger Walshe, White, male	Head of Learning	Native	British
	Clara, White, female	Student interviewee	Non-native	Italian
	Maximiliano, White, male	Student interviewee	Non-native	Venezuelan
	Alexandra, White, male	Student interviewee	Non-native	Russian
	Anthony, Asian, male	Student interviewee	Non-native	Malaysian
	A White male	ELT instructor	Native	British
	A White female	ELT instructor	Native	British

supporting role in the background, such as the fellow students who attend class and participate in group discussions. These figures are obviously represented as 'non-native speakers' from 'the rest of the world.'

It is also interesting that in the student interview section of the promotional video, although three of the students are racialized White, they also self-identify as non-natives, which may be due to their non-British nationality. As such, in the whole website, there is not just a simple White/non-White dichotomy in parallel with the native/non-native binary, but a sort of hierarchy, where the White, mostly male British speakers are placed at the top, positioned as the native norm and the absolute authority of the English language.

SO, WHAT DOES THIS ALL MEAN?: A DISCUSSION AND A CONCLUSION

Based on the findings above, the way in which 'native speaker' is created crystalized. In light of the theory of CDA, this category takes on shape through a 'system of representation' (Hall, 1992, p. 187) where the 'native speaker' is located at the centre.

From initial, through verbal languages, such as texts and transcripts, the website directly brings up the terms '(non)native speakers' which differentiate English speakers into binary groups and put them in hierarchy. It naturalizes the 'native speaker' as a solid category despite its problematic nature. It also establishes an 'Us/Them' dichotomy where 'we' as the 'natives' have the authoritative voice as well as the ownership of authentic English. In this process, 'native speakers' are positioned as the gatekeepers of the real English. Second, what are these 'native speakers' like? Through images and other visual representations, the website attaches and fixes meaning of 'native speaker' with a group of White speakers from core English-speaking countries, especially the UK in this case. All these images, utterances and the video are 'representational tools' employed by the website. When put together, they build up a discourse of the 'native speaker' of English. According to Stuart Hall (1992), such an idea or concept can have effects and functions, it delimits people's interpretation of and creates knowledge about 'native speaker.' It explicitly tells us that if you are White, mostly male and coming from Britain, then you are a 'native speaker.' Other categories than this, for instance, the Chinese learners portrayed in illustrations and the variously sounded students who do not acquire the British accent, all fall out of this category. What is especially noteworthy is an imposed rightfulness of 'native speakers,' that they cannot be wrong in using the English language. This is best manifested in the case of the grammar fault.

As is shown in the analysis section, the misuse of 'there's + lots of + plural nouns' has been questioned three times by different commentators over the course of six years. From the linguistic aspect, it is plainly a mistake. However, none of the 'native speaker' teachers from the Learn English Team was willing to admit it frankly. They unexceptionally tried to patch up this error and discursively defend this usage. Furthermore, they not only maintain the authoritative image of 'native speakers' at the stake of linguistic standard, but also tend to perpetuate onto their students the differentiated perceptions based on one's '(non-)nativeness.' Everything they say about the English language is made "true" (Hall, 1992, p. 203) because of the power embodied in their native status. This is essentially an imperialist move.

They are establishing themselves as arbitrators of what is authentic English. They make the rule and has the right to judge what is right and what is wrong. At this point, language teaching has turned into an exercise of power. Behind the question of what the right expression is to say versus what is wrong is actually social power and political power. The relevance of these comments also alerts that this imperialist ideology is still prevailing.

Most significantly, this established 'native speaker' contributes to a discourse of exclusion (if not plain racism). First of all, it equates language ability and language teaching capacity with one's nativeness to English, whatever this 'nativeness' refers to. Then, the dominance of Whiteness represented as standing for 'native speakers' and the underrepresentation of people of color in this process suggests an exclusionary racialized category. It projects the native status onto skin color, which is further associated with model English and authoritative English instructor. Following this are exclusions among all English speakers. On the one hand, the equalization of 'nativeness' with Whiteness and standard English works to exclude racialized speakers of color who come from the same regions as their White counterparts, as well as those speakers of different types of Englishes in other areas. On the other, the attribution of 'nativeness' with superior teaching competence contributes to marginalizing speakers of other languages who have acquired high competency in English and English language teaching. It can therefore result in negative impacts on the marginalized groups, one of which is the injustice and discrimination in hiring practices. Employers and administrators ascribed to this ideology will potentially crowd out qualified 'non-native' professionals or treat them distinguishingly compared to the 'native' teachers. As a result, the 'native speaker' discourse, especially in ELT, racializes (nativeness = Whiteness), excludes (nativeness excludes people of color – even though they may speak only English) and it negatively affects racialized minorities. According to Stanley (2014), this triangle (racialization, exclusion and negative effects) creates the perfect storm of what he calls a 'racist system,' which is exactly what we could see in our analysis.

In conclusion, the current study evidenced the native speaker fallacy while unveiling the process of its construction. Through it, we hoped to uncover and understand the mechanism of how 'native speakers' are attributed with the traits they are attributed with and what that tells us about the ELT field. Clearly, there is an urgent need to disturb the naturalization of 'native speaker' and make people realize its problematic nature, both for recruiters and learners. Despite that the TESOL association has issued position statement against discriminatory employment practices based on race and native speakership (TESOL, 2006), the attribution to Whiteness is still prevalent in today's ELT profession. As Rivers (2018) recently shows, the categorization of speakers based on native language status can result in the marginalization of both groups of English professionals depending on the contexts. It is thus not only just to fight for the right of 'non-native speakers' but also to support the qualified 'native' English teachers to develop in this field. On the other hand, as previous investigations suggest (Mahboob et al., 2004; Medgyes, 1992), administrators and recruiters tend to shift the blame of discriminatory employment onto the demand of stakeholders, namely the students and their parents who buy into the 'native speaker' discourse and believe that "the White native speaker is the only valid" English-language teacher (Amin, 2001, p. 98). While the native/non-native division has been abundantly debated within the ELT professionals, more works should be done on how to let these stakeholders outside of the field be aware of their prejudiced perceptions.

REFERENCES

Amin, N. (2001). Nativism, the native speaker construct, and minority immigrant women teachers of English as a second language. *The CATESOL Journal, 13*(1), 89–107.

Anderson, B. (1983). *Imagined communities: Reflections on the origin and spread of nationalism*. Verso.

Bourdieu, P. (1991). *Language and symbolic power*. Harvard University Press.

Braine, G. (2013). *Non-native educators in English language teaching*. Routledge. doi:10.4324/9781315045368

Brandt, C. (2006). *Success on your certificate course in English language teaching*. Sage.

British Council | China. (2019). Retrieved January 19, 2019, from https://www.britishcouncil.cn/en

Chomsky, N. (1965). *Aspects of the theory of syntax*. MIT Press.

Clark, E., & Paran, A. (2007). The employability of non-native-speaker teachers of EFL: A UK survey. *System, 35*(4), 407–430. doi:10.1016/j.system.2007.05.002

Cook, V. (1999). Going beyond the native speaker in language teaching. *TESOL Quarterly, 33*(2), 185–209. doi:10.2307/3587717

Davies, A. (1991). *The native speaker in applied linguistics*. Edinburgh University Press.

Davies, A. (2003). *The native speaker: Myth and reality*. Multilingual Matters. doi:10.21832/9781853596247

English is GREAT. (2019). Retrieved January 19, 2019, from https://www.britishcouncil.cn/en/EnglishGreat

Ferguson, C. (1992). Foreword to the first edition. In B. B. Kachru (Ed.), The other tongue: English across cultures (2nd ed., pp. xiii–xvii). Chicago, IL: University of Illinois Press.

Govardhan, A. K., Nayar, B., & Sheorey, R. (1999). Do U.S. MATESOL programs prepare students to teach abroad? *TESOL Quarterly*, *33*(1), 114–125. doi:10.2307/3588194

Hall, S. (1992). The west and the rest: Discourse and power. In S. Hall & B. Gieben (Eds.), Formation of modernity (pp. 275–320). Cambridge: Polity in Association with Open University.

Hall, S. (2013). The work of representation. In S. H. Stuart, E. Jessica, & Nixon (Eds.), Representation (2nd ed., pp. 1–59). London: Sage.

Holliday, A. (2005). *The struggle to teach English as an international language*. Oxford University Press.

Ibrahim, A. (1999). Becoming Black: Rap and hip-hop, race, gender, identity, and the politics of ESL learning. *TESOL Quarterly*, *33*(3), 349–369. doi:10.2307/3587669

Jenkins, J. (2006). Current perspectives on teaching World Englishes and English as a lingua franca. *TESOL Quarterly*, *40*(1), 157–181. doi:10.2307/40264515

Kramsch, C. (1997). The privilege of the nonnative speaker. *Modern Language Association*, *112*(3), 359–369. doi:10.1632/S0030812900060673

Kubota, R., & Lin, A. (2009). *Race, culture, and identities in second language education: Exploring critically engaged practice* (R. Kubota & A. Lin, Eds.). Routledge. doi:10.4324/9780203876657

Lengeling, M., & Pablo, I. M. (2012). A critical discourse analysis of advertisements: Inconsistencies of our EFL profession. In R. Roux, A. M. Vazquez, & N. P. T. Guzman (Eds.), *Research in English language teaching: Mexican perspectives* (pp. 91–105). Palibrio.

Mahboob, A., & Golden, R. (2013). Looking for native speakers of English: Discrimination in English language teaching job advertisements. *Voices in Asia Journal*, *1*(1), 72–81.

Mahboob, A., Newman, K., Uhrig, K., & Hartford, B. (2004). Children of a lesser English: Status of nonnative English speakers as college-level English as a second language teachers in the United States. In L. D. Kamhi-Stein (Ed.), *Learning and teaching from experience: Perspectives on nonnative English-speaking professionals* (pp. 100–120). University of Michigan Press.

Medgyes, P. (1992). Native or non-native: Who's worth more? *ELT Journal, 46*(4), 340–349. doi:10.1093/elt/46.4.340

Medgyes, P. (2001). When the teacher is a non-native speaker. In M. Celce-Murcia (Ed.), *Teaching English as a second or foreign language* (pp. 429–442). Heinle & Heinle.

Paikeday, T. M. (1985). *The native speaker is dead!* Paikeday Publishing Co.

Pennycook, A. (2007). *Global English and transcultural flows*. Routledge.

Pennycook, A. (2017). *The cultural politics of English as an international language. TESOL Matters*. Routledge. doi:10.4324/9781315225593

Phillipson, R. (1992). *Linguistic imperialism*. Oxford University Press.

Rampton, M. B. H. (1990). Displacing the native speaker: Expertise, affiliation and inheritance. *The Language Ethnicity and Race Reader, 44*(2), 97–101.

Rivers, D. J. (2018). Speakerhood as segregation: The construction and consequence of divisive discourse in TESOL. In B. Yazan & N. Rudolph (Eds.), *Criticality, teacher identity, and (in)equity in English language teaching. Educational linguistics* (pp. 179–197). Springer International Publishing. doi:10.1007/978-3-319-72920-6_10

Ruecker, T., & Ives, L. (2015). White native English speakers needed: The rhetorical construction of privilege in online teacher recruitment spaces. *TESOL Quarterly, 49*(4), 733–756. doi:10.1002/tesq.195

Selvi, A. F. (2010). All teachers are equal, but some teachers are more equal than others: Trend analysis of job advertisements in English language teaching. *WATESOL NNEST Caucus Annual Review, 1*, 156–181.

Shuck, G. (2006). Racializing the nonnative English speaker. *Journal of Language, Identity, and Education, 5*(4), 259–276. doi:10.120715327701jlie0504_1

Skutnabb-kangas, T., & Phillipson, R. (1994). Linguistic human rights: Past and present. In Linguistic human rights: Overcoming linguistic discrimination (pp. 71–110). Berlin: Mouton de Gruyter.

Stanley, T. (2014). Antiracism without guarantees: A Framework for rethinking racisms in schools. *Critical Literacy: Theories and Practices*, 8(1), 4–19.

TESOL. (2006). *Position statement against discrimination of nonnative speakers of English in the field of TESOL*. Retrieved from https://www.tesol.org/docs/pdf/12305.pdf?sfvrsn=2&sfvrsn=2

van Dijk, T. A. (1993). Principles of critical discourse analysis. *Discourse & Society*, 4(2), 249–283. doi:10.1177/0957926593004002006

van Dijk, T. A. (2015). Critical discourse analysis. In D. Tannen, H. Hamilton, & D. Schiffrin (Eds.), Handbook of discourse analysis (2nd ed., pp. 466–485). Chichester: Wiley Blackwell. doi:10.1002/9781118584194.ch22

Wang, L., & Lin, T. (2013). The representation of professionalism in native English-speaking teachers recruitment policies: A comparative study of Hong Kong, Japan, Korea and Taiwan. *English Teaching*, 12(3), 5–22.

ENDNOTE

[1] Before, during and after the World War II, there was a serious epistemological and ontological discussion on what was known as the 'Jewish question': Who is a Jew? Are Jews Europeans (or not)? Should they exist within or outside Europe? Is the Holocaust the right answer to the 'Jewish question'? etc. (Bauman, 1989). Analogously, we are posing the 'native speaker question' as a way to address similar but different questions: Who is a native speaker? Who decides who is a native speaker? How does this decision come about? That is, based on what criteria the category of the native speaker is demarcated, and in turn who is excluded from this category, how and why? etc.

Chapter 7
The EU Language Policy as a Tool

Neriman Hocaoğlu Bahadır
https://orcid.org/0000-0002-3723-5554
Kırklareli University, Turkey

ABSTRACT

The European Union (EU) is a multilingual union, which has 27 official languages. There is no other international or regional organisation that has so many official languages. Since its very beginning, the official languages of the member states are the official languages of the EU. The multilingualism of the EU is not just about the official languages of the EU but also because of the numerous indigenous regional and minority languages. The language policy of the EU can be traced back to the Treaty of Rome and the first regulation. Since then, the language policy of the EU has changed parallel with the developments and changes within the EU and in the world. First, it was evaluated as a tool for personal development and integration, but with the changes in the globalized world, it became a tool to increase the competitiveness of the EU, which can be seen as a soft power at the international level. This chapter aims to show the changing role of the EU's language policy and its current status as a powerful tool in the knowledge-based economies at the international level.

INTRODUCTION

The European Union (EU) is a *sui generis* Union. It has many characteristics, which make the EU unique, and its Language Policy is one of them. The EU is a union with 24 official languages, and it is the only union, which has so many official languages.

DOI: 10.4018/978-1-7998-2831-0.ch007

Copyright © 2021, IGI Global. Copying or distributing in print or electronic forms without written permission of IGI Global is prohibited.

The language policy of the EU has changed and enriched since the Treaty of Rome where the foundations of the language policy were laid. Then, the official languages of the EU were just 4 and today with each enlargement it has become 24. There are also many indigenous regional and minority languages, which are components of European multilingual identity. The founding treaty and the EU's first regulation, Council Regulation No 1/58, which was especially about the official and working languages and their use, show the importance given to this policy area. The language policy of the EU has been supported in many ways within the EU with different objectives. In this chapter, the objectives like sustaining its motto "unity in diversity" and making young people more competitive and may be not just the young people but also the Union itself will be noted clearly (European Commission, (n.d.)a) and tried to be explained how they have been supported and with what aim.

In international affairs, actors use different policies to gain power; some prefers to use soft co-optive power and others prefers hard command power policies. In general, the EU is seen and evaluated as a soft power, which prefers to use soft power resources such as cultural attractions, ideology and international institutions to achieve wanted outcomes (Nye, 1990, 167). In this chapter, it is aimed to see if the language policy of the EU can be used as a soft power tool for the EU to be able to gain more power or to be more competitive as an actor in the globalized world. This is an important question because while language can be seen and evaluated as a power, the EU is not a monolingual actor. It has many official languages, and this is an important point, which makes the subject complicated because of the languages, such as English, French, German and Spanish, which have a more dominant place within the EU. However, the EU has a language policy, and it has been supported seriously and it should have some outcomes both within and outside the EU.

In this chapter, after stating power and soft power, information about the EU is given to clarify it as a *sui generis* union and its language policy is defined as it is one of the features which makes the EU *sui generis*. Here, to be able to make comparison the United Nation (UN) is also mentioned in terms of its official languages. Then the historical development of this policy is given briefly to be able to see the developments and find out how it and its scope have changed since the beginning. As a last point, it is focused on the role of language policy within and outside the EU as a tool in the globalized world. It is aimed to show the changing role of its language policy and the current status of it. Besides, it is also aimed to point out how EU as a soft power uses its language policy to sustain social integration within the Union and gain prominence in the changing world.

The Concept of Power and the EU as a Soft Power

The EU is a *sui generis* union, which consists of 27 member states and 24 official languages. In this part, one additional phrase should be also used to define the EU. In order to determine this phrase, it needs to be asked what kind of power the EU is. The answer can be civilian power, normative power or/and soft power. In this chapter, the EU is generally accepted as a soft power. Before focusing on the concept of soft power, power as a concept is explained to clarify the basis of this research.

The concept of power is defined differently according to different scholars and theories. But here, as power discussion is not within the scope of this research, the definition of oxford dictionary is preferred to form the starting point of this chapter. Even there are 7 different definitions of power in the dictionary. Two of these definitions can be evaluated to be in parallel with the aim of this study. So, according the first definition power is "the ability or capacity to do something or act in a particular way" and the second definition is "the capacity or ability to direct or influence the behaviour of others or the course of events" (oxfordictioneries.com, power). In international relations the actors are states, organisations and people in general. So, the power of a state is about its capability to do something, to act in a way or to direct or influence the behaviour of other states. In similar vein, when the subject is a union as the EU, the power of the EU can be traced in its ability to do something or act in a particular way or to direct/influence other states. Joseph S. Nye (2009, p.160) defines power as; "one's ability to affect the behaviour of others to get what one wants". Proceeding from this point, it is needed to note what kind of power is the EU.

Hedley Bull (1982, p. 149) citing Andrew Shonfield (1974) states that the EU was defined as a "civilian power" by Francois Duchene in the 1970s instead of being noted as traditional military or traditional political power. But in his article Civilian Power Europe: A Contradiction in Terms, he supports the view that the EU should be a military power to be self-sufficient for its defence and he states his reasons as diverging of interest between the Western Europe and the USA, the enduring Soviet Threat to Western Europe and the regeneration of Europe (Bull, 1982, pp.152-156). Here, it should be noted that as the world is changing the threat that Bull noted in 1982 has changed since then. Karen E. Smith (2005, p.70) also opposes to the view that European Union is a civilian power even though it has some activities and policies, which are quite close to civilian ideal-type. According to her, civilian power has four elements; civilian means, civilian ends, persuasion (soft power) and democratic control while at its opposite side military power consists of military means, military ends, coercion (hard power) and no democratic control (Smith, 2005, p.69). Many other scholars discuss and write about defining EU as a civilian power. Ian Manners and Thomas Diez (2007, p.178) also explain the concept of civilian power by citing

Manners they note three characteristics of civilian power; "'diplomatic cooperation to solve international problems' (multilateralism); 'centrality of economic power' (non-military); and 'legally-binding supra-national institutions' (international law)". All these definitions explain the concept of civilian power, but it is not enough to define the EU as a civilian power within the framework of this chapter.

As stated above the EU is accepted as a *sui generis* union and it is evaluated as a new kind of actor in international relations and external relations. In defining this actor, it is also evaluated as a normative power. Manners (2008, p.65) is one of the scholars who evaluated the EU as a normative power and he defines normative power as a power, which changes the norms, standards and prescriptions of world politics away from the bounded expectations of state-centricity. Ian Manners and Thomas Diez (2007) point out that the EU tries to change other states through the spread of norms, and they make another definition, which is in line with the other definitions. According to this definition the EU power is neither military nor pure economic, but it is a power which works through ideas, opinions and conscience (Manners and Diez, 2007, p.175). So, it can be argued that the EU tries to make a change by using ideas and opinions. According to this definition, they are not neglecting economics means as an element of its power, but they first focus on ideas and opinions. They also point out that "normative power is not the opposite of military power" as civilian power is thought to be (Manners and Diez, 2007, p.180). This statement shows the differing natures of these two concepts. But it should be noted that both of these concepts have changed in time because the context itself has changed as Duchene used the term first in 1973 and lots of things have changed both in the world and in the EU. So, it should be noted that the attributions to these concepts have changed, as well.

Another mostly used power concept while defining EU's role or power in international relations or in other words in external relations is soft power Europe. The concept is mostly known with Joseph Nye who also defines smart power and hard power. Smart power is relatively new concept but the other two has discussed more in international relations. According to Nye (2009, p.160), there are three ways of exercising power and they are "coercion, payment and attraction". Starting from this point, he defines hard power as the power, which uses coercion and payment while he defines soft power as the power, which uses attraction to get preferred outcomes and smart power combines both of them (Nye, 2009, p.160). In relation to the EU, the enlargements of the EU can show its attractiveness because the EU then called the European Economic Community had just six member states when it was founded in 1957 and now it has 27 member states, and many others are waiting to be part of it. Especially Turkey, which applied for associate membership in 1959 and for full membership in 1987, has been waiting for a long time. This shows how attractive is the EU for the states, which want to be part of it.

The EU Language Policy as a Tool

After giving the general framework above, it may be better to focus on the soft power concept and the EU. The above given definition is just the general definition of soft power but leaving this definition just in that level may cause to skip some part of the issue. Nye first used this concept in 1990, which was the year when great changes happened in international relation, so it is quite understandable that there were power related changes, as well. Then, Nye (1990, p.166) introduced the concept of co-optive or soft power in world politics. He notes "the ability to affect what other countries want tends to be associated with intangible power resources such as culture, ideology and institutions" (Nye, 1990, pp.166-167). He also emphasizes the importance of soft power by noting, "if a state can make its power seem legitimate in the eyes of others, it will encounter less resistance to its wishes" and added that it is a cheaper way to direct other states than using coercive/hard power (Nye, 1990, p.167). These views of Nye all shaped in relation to the USA's role in the world politics in 1990. And in 2003 he introduced the term smart power as stated above. From then on, both hard power and soft power tools are thought to be beneficial to use according to the situation to be able to get the wanted outcomes. According to another classification of Nye (2004, pp.30-31), there are three kinds of power: military power, economic power and soft power. In his book, the behaviours attributed to soft power are attraction and agenda setting; the primary currencies are values, culture, policies and institutions; and lastly the government policies are noted as public diplomacy, bilateral and multilateral diplomacy (Nye, 2004, p.31). As it can be seen the concept of power is defined clearly by noting the behaviours, means and policies of an actor, which is evaluated as a soft power.

When the concept of soft power thought in relation to EU it can be seen that the EU as an international actor can be accepted as a soft power easily as it uses values, culture, policies and institutions to reach wanted outcomes. For example, its values are part of EU's acquis communautaire and they are noted in the Treaty of Lisbon, which is the last treaty of the EU, as well as the previous treaties. In Lisbon Treaty (2007, p.11), it is stated "The Union is founded on the values of respect for human dignity, freedom, democracy, equality, the rule of law and respect for human rights, including the rights of persons belonging to minorities" (Article 1a). These values are also the values of today's world. So, it is quite easy to import these values while trying to attract people and other states. Nye (2004, p.11) also focuses on this point and states, "When a country's culture includes universal values and its policies promote values and interests that others share, it increases the probability of obtaining its desired outcomes". So, another point is the issue of culture and it also entered into the treaties of EU with the Maastricht Treaty (1992). Title 9 of the Treaty is about culture and there, it is noted, "The Community and the Member States shall foster cooperation with third countries and the competent international organisations in the sphere of culture,.." (Treaty on the European Union, 1992, p.49) and there are other emphases about culture but this one is quite in vain with the actions of a soft power who prefers to use it in order to cause change. Education, which can be used to provide wanted changes, also takes its part with social policy under title 8 in the Treaty (Treaty on the European Union, 1992, pp.46-48). It is also important to note that these both excerpts are from treaties of the EU, so it shows that they are part of EU's existence and they are internalised.

Nye (2004, pp.75-82) notes that Europe is the closest competitor of the USA in soft power resources and he gives some examples. According to the examples, the Europe's art, literature, music, design, fashion, food, its languages, policies related to climate change, freedoms and human rights, the number of troops involved in peacekeeping operations, using multilateral institutions, being economic power and investing more in public diplomacy are some of the issues in which the EU can be evaluated as a forerunner soft power (Nye, 2004, pp.75-82). According to the research of Laurence Vandewalle, (2014, p.4) culture diplomacy, education diplomacy and science diplomacy are instruments of the EU and these contribute to the image of the EU. This is an important focus as positive image is crucial when a power wants to attract the others. There are a lot of culture related developments such as policies and programmes within the EU. Some of the programmes are EU action for the European Capitals of Culture 2020 to 2033, EU's culture work plan (2015-2018), European Capital of Culture, Creative Europe Programme (2014-2020) and European Heritage Label (Eur-lex, (n.d.)a). In the policy documents of the European Commission, it is noted that the European Commission has "a priority to make the EU a stronger global participant, a better international partner and a more important contributor to sustainable growth" to support this priority a strategy for more effective international cultural relations are proposed (Eurelex, (n.d.)b). As it can be understood there are efforts to improve the culture policy of the EU with the aim of strengthening the EU as a global actor. And a communicating tool is needed to present it to the world. At this point, the multilingual structure of the EU is a priceless asset to present it to the world in many different languages.

Language as a soft power tool is the main concern of this chapter and Nye (2004, p.75) explains it clearly by stating that five of 10 most widely spoken languages are European and they are English, Spanish, Portuguese, German and Russian. But this information should be renewed; as according to 2020 estimated data, they are English (16.5%), Spanish (7%), French (3.6%), Russian (3.4%) and Portuguese (3.3%) (Central Intelligence Agency, 2020). German is not one of these languages anymore, but French is. It should be also pointed out that Russian is not one of the EU languages even though it may be evaluated as European. Although French was not in this list before, Nye (2004, p.76) notes that there are nearly 50 Francophone countries and they meet regularly to discuss policies and celebrate their status. So, proceeding from this point it will be better to focus on the EU's language policy.

The EU Language Policy as a Tool

Brief Overview of the EU and its Language Policy

The EU is a union which was first founded as a European Economic Community in 1957 by six member states. Today it has 27 member states and more than five hundred million citizens, many institutions and many different policies some of which are common policies. However, it was not the case when it was first established, the member states came together for economic goals. In the course of time, many things have changed within the EU. Its name changed with Maastricht Treaty and became the European Union in 1992. The number of the member states of the Union changed, as well.

The EU is a *sui generis* union as noted before. It is *sui generis* because it has institutions which functions different than many other organisations' institutions. For example, from the beginning the EU has the Commission, the European Parliament, the Council and the Court of Justice, even though they had different names, but their functioning, responsibilities and duties have changed since then. But what makes these institutions different from other organisations' institutions is that some of these institutions are known as supranational institutions. The Commission, the Parliament and the Court of Justice are some of them. The member states of the EU transfer "some of their sovereign right to the EU" and give power to the EU "to act independently" so, "the EU is able to adopt European legislation which has the same force as national laws in individual states" (European Commission, 2016, The ABC of EU Law). This is what makes it *sui generis*. There is no other institution which acts in this way.

The EU also have some other features which makes it different than the other international organisations such as the concept of "citizenship". The citizens of the member states are the citizens of the EU. Another difference is that there is no other international organisation which has a common currency. Some of the EU member states have been using Euro as their common currency since the beginning of 2000s. The citizens of the EU have right to travel, live and work within the borders of the EU. These are just the most known features of the EU. However, these are not within the scope of this chapter and they will not be explained in detail. Here, it is focused on just one policy area, which also makes the EU *sui generis*, and it is the language policy of the EU.

EU is a multilingual union with 24 official languages which also makes the EU unique when it is compared to other international organisations. Within the international system there is no other international organisation, which has so many official languages. The UN is also an international organisation, but it has just six official languages which are Arabic, Chinese, English, French, Russian and Spanish (United Nations, (n.d.)) while it has 193 member states (Republic of Turkey Ministry of Foreign Affairs, (n.d.)). The UN notes that its official languages and the correct interpretation and translation are important, and they enable "clear and concise communication on issues of global importance" besides, participation, effectiveness, better outcomes within the Organisation (United Nations, (n.d.)). This shows how important is the language policy of a union, but it also shows that while the UN has more member states, it has fewer official languages. In the meetings of the UN, delegates can speak one of the official languages of the UN and they are interpreted into other official languages of the UN. Besides, the delegate may choose to speak in their own official language which is not one of the official languages of the UN. In such a case, the delegate has the responsibility to provide interpretation or the translated text of the speech in one of the UN official languages (United Nations, (n.d.)).

When it is focused on the language policy of the EU it can be noted that it has been developed since its foundation. There are articles related to languages of the Community in the Treaty of the Rome which is the founding treaty of the EEC. The next step of this policy development is the Council Regulation No 1/58 which was about the working and official languages of the EEC and in the first article of the Regulation, these languages were stated as Dutch, French, German and Italian (Eur-lex, 1958). Later, the language policy of the EU developed with each enlargement and today there are 24 official languages but the developments in the language policy is not just about the number of official languages. It is also about the deepening policy of the EU which is shaped with each treaty and the official documents of the EU besides the developments in international relations. Here, all the developments within the EU which can be related with the language policy are not mentioned in order not to deviate from the purpose. So, just the first developments, Lisbon Strategy and the last one are stated to show the development of this policy area.

After the first regulation, next development came with *Resolution of the Council and Ministers of Education on comprising an action programme in the field of education*. In this Resolution, it was aimed to reach as many students as possible to learn at least one of the languages of the Community in a way to contribute to the development of the Community (Eur-lex, 1976, pp.1-4). This aim has a narrow scope as it just aims to sustain learning one other language and it is thought to be a Community language and it can be understood that it is about the development of the Community. Another important development came with the Lisbon Strategy. In the strategy, it was clearly noted that there was a change towards knowledge-based economy because of globalisation and the EU aimed "to become the most competitive and dynamic knowledge-based economy in the world capable of sustainable economic growth with more and better jobs and greater social cohesion" (European Parliament, 2000). And in reaching this strategic goal foreign languages were noted as new basic skills to be provided besides IT skills, technological culture, entrepreneurship and social skills (European Parliament, 2000). So, it can be claimed that foreign languages are evaluated as one of the tools to reach the targets both in the world by becoming most competitive and dynamic economy and within the EU by providing social cohesion. In other words, the target is two dimensional; global and regional and they are both supporting each other.

The last development related to the language policy was the Proposal for a Council Recommendation on a comprehensive approach to the teaching and learning of languages (Eur-lex, 2018). This Proposal was an outcome of European Council Meeting Conclusions and according to this meeting conclusions, European Council calls on member states, the Council and the Commission to take part in "enhancing the learning of languages, so that more young people will speak at least two European languages in addition to their mother tongue" (European Council, 2017, p.3) besides many other actions. So, the proposal was prepared as an answer to the call and it is quite detailed. Here, language competences and learning were related with mutual understanding, mobility, productivity, competitiveness, economic resilience and new opportunities (Eur-lex, 2018, pp.1-2). There, it is also noted that member states are responsible in designing their education system the EU can just support and supplement their action (Eur-lex, 2018, p.5). This means whatever the EU's recommendation is, it is all about the member state to follow it or not. Nevertheless, it shows the intention of the EU to become more competitive and integrated, to teach foreign language to provide better skills for its citizens, to communicate with rest of the world and to gain prominence.

The language policy of the EU consists of multilingualism, official and working languages of the EU; and the way its multilingualism is provided and supported by translation/interpretation services and education/culture related policies and programmes. So, these are the main concepts, which should be mentioned when the EU language policy is explained.

The EU gives importance to its language policy and multilingualism. This can be understood from its official texts but here, it is preferred to show it by referring to recent news:

multilingual communication is a hallmark of the European Union and its cultural diversity. ... It is a powerful vehicle that and underpins the Union's democratic decision-making processes. Multilingual communication is also an enabler for effective development cooperation and multilateralism, at regional and global level. (European Commission, 2019).

This shows the importance attributed to multilingualism as it is evaluated in relation to democratic decision-making, effective development, regional and global cooperation. Starting with the importance of multilingualism, the next step should be defining the concept. According to Charlotte Kemp (2009, p.15), who cited

McArthur, Edwards and Vildomec, multilingual person has "the ability to use three or more languages, either separately or in various degrees of code-mixing." So, in other words, it can be said multilingualism is the state of using several languages. This kind of usage can be seen both within the EU institutions where it is accepted that the EU has 24 official languages, even if it is not the case in practice in terms of working and official languages, and with the individuals who can speak or aimed to make them speak several languages. In terms of individuals' multilingualism, according to a Eurostat article (2019) using data from the adult education survey (2016), 35.2% of the 25-64 year old adults are reported to know one foreign language, 21% of them know two foreign languages and 8.4% of them know three or more foreign languages. So, according to Eurostat article, it can be said that 64.6% of the 25-64 year old adults who took part in this survey and declared their foreign language knowledge are multilingual individuals of the EU. Even though this is quite high rate, it needs to be stated again that it reflects self-reported foreign language skills. Proceeding from these multilingual individuals, it will not be wrong to say that the society consists of these individuals is also a multilingual one.

Working languages and the official languages of the EU is one of the most discussed issues when the subject is the language policy of the EU. As stated before the EU has 24 official languages but all of its official languages are not used with same density within the EU institutions. The issue of official and working languages of the EU has a long history in the EU as it is first mentioned in the first Council Regulation No 1/58 (Eur-lex, 1958). The Regulation is about the working and official languages of the EU (then, it was the European Economic Community- EEC) and in the first article of the Regulation, the official and working languages of the EEC are stated. The next article is about communication between the member states and the institutions of the EEC and between the citizens (then it was not called citizens, the concept of citizenship came with the Maastricht Treaty) and the institutions of the EEC. Here, it is noted that the institutions will reply in the same language in which the communication started as long as it is one of the official languages of the EEC. The last article, which should be mentioned, is Article 7 and according to this article; "The institutions of the Community may stipulate in their rules of procedure which of the languages are to be used in specific cases" (Eur-lex, 1958). So, it can be said that the institutions use all of the official languages while communicating with a party out of the institutions and can decide which languages to be used within the institutions. So, here comes the question of working languages. Today, in the institutions all of the official languages are not used as working languages, the institutions choose with which languages to work. Mostly English, French and German are decided to be the working languages of the institutions. For example, the working languages or, as it is stated in the web page of the Commission, the procedural languages of the Commission are English, French and German (European

Commission, 2013). Another example can be the Court of Justice of the European Union where French is the internal working language of the Court (Court of Justice of the European Union, (n.d.)). Even though, the citizens or other institutions can write to each other in one of the official languages of the EU, the institutions have the opportunity to choose their working languages.

When it is looked how this multilingualism is supported, it should be noted that it is a huge work as translation and interpretation departments of the institutions both have great numbers of officials and a huge workload to provide multilingualism within these institutions because it is believed that "Giving everyone at the table a voice and a document in their own language is a fundamental requirement of the democratic legitimacy of the European Union" (Interpreting and Translating for Europe, (n.d.)). It is also about transparency. Moreover, these departments "guarantee the cultural and linguistic diversity of the EU" (Ginsburgh and Moreno-Ternero, 2020, p.2). Some numbers can be helpful to be able to understand the importance attributed to providing multilingualism in the EU. For example, European Commission has 560 interpreters, 1600 translators and 700 support staff while European Parliament has 294 interpreters, 600 translators and 280 assistants (Interpreting and Translating for Europe, (n.d.)).

Lastly for this part, it should be added that multilingualism is supported with many actions, programmes and policies. Some of the policies are mentioned but examples for actions and programmes can also be given. One of the most known programmes, which can be evaluated as programmes supporting the multilingualism, is Erasmus+ and its first version Erasmus. The budget of Erasmus+ is 14.7 billion Euros and it is aimed the mobility of 4 million people during 2014-2020 (European Commission, (n.d.)b) and the budget for the next period will be more than the previous one as the dedicated budget is more than 26 billion Euros and it has an aim to reach 10 million people during 2021-2027 (European Commission, 2020). Here, it is so clear that budget is nearly doubled, and the number of beneficiaries is aimed to be more than twice the previous programme. Erasmus+ has a huge budget sustaining the mobility of people interacting and sharing their cultures, making lifelong friendship and forming mutual understanding besides adding value to their skills like learning foreign languages. There are also other initiatives, programmes and actions such as European Language Label which is a rewarding initiative to encourage new language teaching and learning methods, European Day of Languages which is celebrated every year on 26th of September (Franke and Heriard, 2018, pp.3-4) and the Digital Language Diversity Programme, which aims sustainability of European regional, and minority languages in the digital world ("The Digital Language.."). Lastly it can be noted that the EU also cooperate with the Council of Europe and its European Centre of Modern Languages, which aims innovative language teaching (European Commission, (n.d.)a).

The Role of EU Language Policy Within and Outside the EU

In the previous parts, it is noted that the EU has both regional and global aims in supporting its language policy, which consists of many languages. First it would be better to note why the EU language policy is important for the EU within its borders and then it will be appropriate to note why its language policy is important within the international system.

In the European Commission's webpage, the importance of linguistic diversity is explained by noting "unity in diversity" which is the motto of the EU and the harmonious co-existence of languages are underlined, and it is asserted "Languages unite people, render other countries and their cultures accessible and strengthen intercultural understanding." (European Commission, (n.d.)a).

To be in line with this view it should also be noted that the languages of the EU are the languages of the sovereign member states. In order to sustain equality among the member states it needs to have an inclusive language policy because languages are important parts of national identities and excluding any national identity may cause integral problems within the EU. So, coexistence of these languages in harmony provides cohesion and integration.

Another point which is highlighted in the Commission webpage is that;

Foreign language skills play a vital role in enhancing employability and mobility. Multilingualism also improves the competitiveness of the EU economy. Poor language skills can cause companies to lose international contracts, as well hindering the mobility of skills and talent. (European Commission, (n.d)a).

Proceeding from this statement, it can be said that supporting multilingualism also increases mobility within the EU and this mobility causes interaction and sustains mutual understanding. This is so important for sustainability of the EU for that reason there are programs like Erasmus + to make people interact, form long lasting relations, understand each other to gain basic skills (as learning foreign language) which will have effect on competitive features of the EU.

The language policy of the EU is also important for its citizens as it enables its citizens to read the basic official documents in their mother tongue and to write the EU institutions in their native language as long as it is one of the EU official languages. This is also crucial for transparency as the citizens have chance to read at least some of the acquis communitaire in their native language.

Communication is important in international relations and the languages can sustain this communication. As Richard Rose (2005, p.4) notes there is a need for common language and sharing understandings to communicate across national boundaries. Here, it can be said that the concept of sharing understanding is the first step to attract other nations. Because people first need to understand and then they may or may not be attracted by the presented culture, values, policies or whatever it is presented. So, here to sustain understanding language is so crucial.

The linguistic diversity of the EU is a tool to communicate across the national/union borders and it is a quite valuable tool as it is noted in the previous parts some of the official languages of the EU such as English, Spanish, Portuguese and French are the languages mostly spoken in the world partly because of the importance of English as a lingua franca and partly because of colonial history of the states using these languages. These languages increase the possibility to reach as many people or states as possible. And these people and states may more possibly share common understanding because of the language they are using. According to statistics, there are around 460 million people speaking Spanish, 379 million people speaking English and there are around 221 people speaking Portuguese (Statista, 2019). These numbers can show the dimension of interaction, which can be sustained among these people most of whom also share other common points such as culture, way of life and a common history. These numbers also attract people's desire to learn these languages because these languages can give the power to communicate with more people, it can increase the chance of employability and mobility. It can also be seen as an important tool to support the EU's aims in being a competitive global actor. Using its language power, the EU can reach many states within the international system. Reaching them and sustaining communication with common understanding will attract these states and the EU may have chance to shape their desire according to its desire.

Here, it should also be noted that in one of the Commission documents it is pointed out that "language skills are must for the modern economy" and it is added that the EU goals are becoming "a smart, sustainable and inclusive economy" beside "increasing growth creating jobs, promoting employability, and increasing competitiveness" (European Commission, 2012, p.4). These goals summarize the importance of languages for the EU, which wants to be a global actor.

RECOMMENDATIONS

In this study, it is found out that the EU uses its language resources as a tool for its role in the globalised world to become more competitive actor. In other researches, it can be compared to other soft powers to see how they use their languages to attract others.

FUTURE RESEARCH DIRECTIONS

Within this study, it is preferred to focus on the language policy of the EU to examine its role as a soft power. Other measures of the EU can also be researched related to its role as a soft power.

CONCLUSION

The EU language policy is a tool for the EU. It has two tasks at different levels. One of its tasks is at the EU level and the other one is at the international level.

Its task at the EU level is related with the integrity of the EU. And this is tried to be supported with a multilingual structure with official languages of its member states. Here, the official languages of the member states are accepted as the official languages of the Union as language is an important component of national identities and none of the member states will be willing to leave aside their national official languages. So, for the existence of the EU and the coexistence of member states in harmony, it was decided to make the official languages of the member states the official languages of the EU. And it takes part in the EU legislation. From then on, the language policy of the EU has developed with each enlargement and related regulations, conclusions, resolutions, projects, programmes, actions and initiatives.

The goals related to languages have changed with the changing world, as well. They were less demanding in the 1970s but now; it is aimed to learn at least two languages in addition to mother tongue. The underlying reason or reasons have also changed at first it was about the union itself; its integrity, cohesion or unity but in time with the globalisation and changing structure of the world languages started to be evaluated as one of the basic skills to increase the competitiveness of the EU. So, at the international level it became a tool for being competitive actor within the knowledge-based economy in the world. And the EU evaluated and acted as a soft power.

As a soft power at the international level, EU uses its languages to attract people and the states to reach what it wants other to do. Today, the EU is an attraction centre with its culture, policies and prosperity. Languages are valuable tools to present its culture and reach people all around the world to make them follow its values, adapt its culture and way of life. Here, common languages provide understanding, interaction, long lasting relations, which is a slow but effective way to motivate people to want what the EU wants. As a last word, EU as a soft power, uses its language policy to get the desired outcomes as well as being competitive actor by reaching most of the markets easily by communicating and making its culture accepted in the globalised world. The values of the EU are the values of the world, so it is not difficult to commercialise it using the different languages it has.

REFERENCES

Bull, H. (1982). Civilian Power Europe: A Contradiction in Terms. *JCMS, 21*(2), 149–170. doi:10.1111/j.1468-5965.1982.tb00866.x

Central Intelligence Agency. (2020). *The World Factbook: People and Society.* Retrieved from https://www.cia.gov/library/publications/resources/the-world-factbook/geos/xx.html

Court of Justice of the European Union. (n.d.). *The Institution: Language arrangements.* Retrieved from https://curia.europa.eu/jcms/jcms/Jo2_10739/en/

Eur-lex. (1958, April 15). *EEC Council: Regulation No 1 determining the languages to be used by the European Economic Community.* Brussels: The Council. Retrieved from https://eur-lex.europa.eu/LexUriServ/LexUriServ.do?uri=CELEX:31958R0001:EN:HTML

Eur-lex. (1976, February 9). *Resolution of The Council and of The Ministers of Education, Meeting Within the Council: comprising an action programme in the field of education.* Retrieved from https://eur-lex.europa.eu/legal-content/EN/TXT/PDF/?uri=CELEX:41976X0219&from=EN

Eur-lex. (2018, May 22). *Proposal for a Council Recommendation on a comprehensive approach to the teaching and learning of languages.* Retrieved from https://eur-lex.europa.eu/resource.html?uri=cellar:1cc186a3-5dc7-11e8-ab9c-01aa75ed71a1.0001.02/DOC_1&format=PDF

Eur-lex. (n.d.a). *Culture Programmes.* Retrieved from https://eur-lex.europa.eu/summary/chapter/culture/1002.html?root=1002&obsolete=true

Eur-lex. (n.d.b). *International cultural relations — an EU strategy.* Retrieved from https://eur-lex.europa.eu/legal-content/EN/TXT/HTML/?uri=LEGISSUM:4298957&from=EN

European Commission. (2012, November 20). *Commission Staff Working Document: Language competences for employability, mobility and growth.* Retrieved from https://eur-lex.europa.eu/legal-content/EN/TXT/PDF/?uri=CELEX:52012SC0372&from=en

European Commission. (2013, September 26). *Frequently asked Questions on Languages in Europe*. Retrieved from https://europa.eu/rapid/press-release_MEMO-13-825_en.htm

European Commission. (2016, December). *The ABC of EU Law*. Retrieved from https://op.europa.eu/webpub/com/abc-of-eu-law/en/

European Commission. (2019, May 29). *Multilingual communication, a vehicle to bring international organisations closer to the citizens*. Retrieved from https://ec.europa.eu/info/news/multilingual-communication-vehicle-bring-international-organisations-closer-citizens-2019-may-29_en

European Commission. (2020, December 11). *Commission welcomes political agreement on Erasmus+ programme*. Retrieved from: https://ec.europa.eu/commission/presscorner/detail/en/IP_20_2317

European Commission. (n.d.a). *About Multilingualism Policy*. Retrieved from https://ec.europa.eu/education/policies/multilingualism/about-multilingualism-policy_en

European Commission. (n.d.b). *Erasmus+; Key figures*. Retrieved from https://ec.europa.eu/programmes/erasmus-plus/about/key-figures_en

European Council. (2017, December 14). *European Council Meeting Conclusions*. Retrieved from https://www.consilium.europa.eu/media/32204/14-final-conclusions-rev1-en.pdf

European Parliament. (2000). *Lisbon European Council 23 and 24 March 2000 Presidency Conclusions*. Retrieved from: https://www.europarl.europa.eu/summits/lis1_en.htm

Eurostat. (2019, April). *Foreign Language Skills Statistics*. Retrieved from https://ec.europa.eu/eurostat/statistics-explained/index.php/Foreign_language_skills_statistics#Number_of_foreign_languages_known

FrankeM.HeriardP. (2018, September). *Language Policy*. Retrieved from https://www.europarl.europa.eu/ftu/pdf/en/FTU_3.6.6.pdf

Ginsburgh, V., & Moreno-Ternero, J. D. (2020, May). *Brexit and Multilingualism in the European Union*. ECARES Working Paper 16.

Interpreting and Translating for Europe. (n.d.). Retrieved from http://cdt.europa.eu/sites/default/files/documentation/pdf/qd0117611en.pdf

Kemp, C. Defining Multilingualism. In L. Aronin & B. Hufeisen (Eds.), *The Exploration of Multilingualism* (pp. 11–26). John Benjamins Publishing Company.

Manners, I. (2008, February 1). *The normative ethics of the European Union.* doi:10.1111/j.1468-2346.2008.00688.x

Manners, I., & Diez, T. (2007). Reflecting on Normative Power Europe. In F. Berenskoetter & M. J. Williams (Eds.), *Power in World Politics* (pp. 173–188). Routledge.

Nye, S. J. (1990, Autumn). Soft Power. *Foreign Policy*, (80), 153–171. https://www.jstor.org/stable/1148580. doi:10.2307/1148580

Nye, S. J. (2004). *Soft Power The Means to Success in World Politics.* Public Affairs.

Nye, S. J. (2008, March). Public Diplomacy and Soft Power. *AAPSS*, 94-109. Retrieved from https://journals.sagepub.com/doi/pdf/10.1177/0002716207311699

Nye, S. J. (2009). Get Smart Combining Hard and Soft Power. *Foreign Affairs*, *88*(4), 160–164. https://www.jstor.org/stable/20699631?seq=4#metadata_info_tab_contents

Power. (2019). In *Oxford Dictionaries*. Retrieved from https://en.oxforddictionaries.com/definition/power

Smith, K. E. (2005). Beyond the Civilian Power debate. *Politique Europeenne*, *1*(17), 63–82. doi:10.3917/poeu.017.0063

Statista. (2019). *The most spoken languages worldwide (native speakers in millions).* Retrieved from https://www.statista.com/statistics/266808/the-most-spoken-languages-worldwide/

The Digital Language Diversity Programme. (n.d.). Retrieved from http://www.dldp.eu/en/content/project

The Republic of Turkey Ministry of Foreign Affairs. (n.d.). *The United Nations Organization and Turkey.* Retrieved from http://www.mfa.gov.tr/the-united-nations-organization-and-turkey.en.mfa

The Treaty of Rome. (1957, March 25). Retrieved from. https://ec.europa.eu/archives/emu_history/documents/treaties/rometreaty2.pdf

Treaty of Lisbon Amending the Treaty on European Union and the Treaty Establishing the European Community. (2007, December 17). Retrieved from http://publications.europa.eu/resource/cellar/688a7a98-3110-4ffe-a6b3-8972d8445325.0007.01/DOC_19

Treaty on European Union. (1992). Retrieved from https://europa.eu/european-union/sites/europaeu/files/docs/body/treaty_on_european_union_en.pdf

United Nations. (n.d.). *Official Languages*. Retrieved from https://www.un.org/en/sections/about-un/official-languages/index.html

Vandewalle, L. (2014). *In-depth Analysis; The increasing role of the EU's culture, education and science diplomacy in Asia*. Retrieved from https://www.europarl.europa.eu/RegData/etudes/IDAN/2015/549050/EXPO_IDA(2015)549050_EN.pdf

KEY TERMS AND DEFINITIONS

European Union: A *sui generis* union with 27 member states which are all located in Europe.

Integration: The state of being together.

Language Policy: A policy area which includes all kinds of regulations and components related to languages.

Multilingualism: The state of using several languages.

Power: An actor who can cause others to do what she/he wants.

Soft Power: A power which uses culture, policies, and institutions to attract others.

Tool: Something which is used to do something easily.

Chapter 8
Impacts of Globalization on English Language Education Across Inner, Outer, and Expanding Countries

Xiaoli Yu
Middle East Technical University, Turkey

Veysel Altunel
Hacettepe University, Turkey

ABSTRACT

This chapter tackles the critical changes that have occurred in English language education in different countries under the progress of globalization. Adhering to comprehensiveness, the changes in representative countries across different categories are discussed. The division of the categories is based upon Kachru's Three Circle Model, namely the Inner Circle, the Outer Circle, and the Expanding Circle. Within each circle, two representative countries are addressed. Major changes related to the field of English language education in these countries include issues such as educational policy, English curriculum designing, English teaching research, methods and techniques, English educators' and learners' perspectives, and so forth. Throughout the synthesizing and comparing process, the common theme that is used to connect the six countries is globalization; discussions are centered on how the changes are influenced by globalization. The chapter concludes by addressing the future issues each country might face and their further directions in advancing English education.

INTRODUCTION

Language and the use of language constantly change. The changes and corresponding language pedagogy are closely related to national as well as international social, economic, and political agendas (Tsui & Tollefson, 2007). With the speedy process of globalization, issues related to changes in language teaching and learning, particularly the English language as the lingua franca, are crucial to discuss. Around the globe, communication and collaboration are taking place through the use of English. From a macro level, a country cooperates with other countries to seek efficient and comprehensive development via English; from a micro level, an individual is able to obtain more opportunities in career development and life quality by speaking English fluently. The development of both levels demands the establishment of a robust English language education (ELE) system. Today, out of 7.5 billion people living on earth, nearly one quarter (1.75 billion) speak English to a certain extent. The population of ELs (English learners) is only expected to keep growing (Beare, 2019). In order to provide effective English education, it is critical to analyze and compare ELE systems across different countries to identify the advantageous practices and avoid unsound moves.

Taking globalization into consideration, this chapter aims to address the impacts that globalization has had on ELE among six different countries that cover the Inner, Outer and Expanding Circles (Kachru, 1992). The six countries include the US, the UK, India, Singapore, China, and Turkey. Different aspects in ELE are analyzed, including educational policy, English curriculum designing, English teaching research, methods and techniques, English educators' and learners' perspectives, and so forth. Comparative investigation approaches are employed to review the impacts and changes more critically.

The discussion starts with the rationale for the selection of the six countries. Major aspects include but not limited to the general impacts of globalization on the country, the country's position in attracting immigrants and international students, the country's status in generating emigrants and sending out international students, and the country's geographic, economic, as well as political importance in the world. In addition to the rationale, the status of English in the six countries and the local contexts of ELE is introduced. Next, in-depth description of each country's ELE system and its changes in different aspects under globalization are presented. For individual countries, the description of the changes is conducted through multi-dimensional approaches which involves general perspectives and mentality towards ELE in each country, policy and curriculum designing in each country, and specific teaching techniques that have been used in each country. During the process of introducing individual countries respectively, synthesizing and comparing of the changes between different countries are emphasized as well. Throughout the descriptions and analyses of the changes in ELE, constant connections are conducted between globalization and the different changes in these countries. Reasons behind the diverse changes are discussed. The last section of the chapter serves as a summative section to conclude and critically reflect on the changes that have taken place in the target countries. From a collective perspective, the crucial role of globalization in the changes of ELE in these countries is examined one more time to unveil the close relationship between globalization and different aspects of ELE. Furthermore, the commonly positive adjustments and innovations in ELE among the six countries are identified. Meanwhile, unsuccessful attempts in the countries are concluded to draw attention from different parties in order to help other countries avoid unsound moves. In the end, future directions in improving ELE in the six target countries are addressed.

BACKGROUND: THE THREE CIRCLE MODEL AND THE SIX TARGET COUNTRIES

Despite some criticisms, Kachru's Three Circle Model (1992) of World Englishes (WE) has been exceedingly influential in highlighting the changing distribution and functions of the English language as it becomes the international language across the globe. The Three Circle Model includes the Inner, Outer, and Expanding Circles of countries. The Inner Circle countries are where monolingual native speakers of English are located, such as the US, the UK, Canada, Australia, and so forth. The Outer Circle countries are those where English has an official status. These countries were usually previously colonized by English-speaking countries and after decolonization, the English language still plays critical institutional functions in those countries. Examples from the Outer Circle are Singapore, India, and Nigeria. Regarding the Expanding Circle, different from the Outer Circle, English does not have a restricted official status nor major domestic functions; instead, English is mainly taught as a subject and used for international communication. China, Japan, Korea, and so forth are representative countries in the Expanding Circle.

Indeed, the English-speaking community around the globe is much more heterogeneous and dynamic than the Three Circle Model suggests (Jenkins, 2003). However, the Three Circle Model does contain relevance for the current realities of WE and provide a descriptive framework which helps general public and scholars of WE better approach the muddled area of the use of English in different countries (Park & Wee, 2009). For the purpose of this chapter, which looks at how globalization has been influencing the ELE in native English-speaking countries, English as a second or official language countries, and English as a foreign language (EFL) countries, the Three Circle Model corresponds to the purpose well.

For the Inner Circle, the US and the UK are selected as the representative countries. The major reason for this selection is that these two countries are where the commonly discussed American English and British English are originally from; in addition, traditionally, the two countries are considered as the representative English-speaking countries by the general public. The US, in particular, is the top country for immigration (Radford, 2019), which has brought the thriving discussions and exploration of teaching English to the immigrants in the country. Moreover, the academic contribution from these two countries to the field of English Language Teaching (ELT) has been widely recognized.

Regarding the Outer Circle, India and Singapore are chosen as the representative country to examine. India, as the country with the largest English-speaking population (more than 129 million) in the Outer Circle, plays a critical role in shaping the field of ELE worldwide (Registrar General & Census Commissioner, 2011). In addition, according to the recent World Migration Report (The UN Migration Agency, 2018), India has been the top country of original for international immigrants. Thus, cultivating the residents to use English as an effective tool for international migration is of critical significance for India. For Singapore, it is a unique example where English has been successfully utilized to drastically boost the development of its economy and the pace of its globalization. Having been consistently ranked as top open and free economy in the world for more than two decades (Min, 2018), Singapore opens its participation in international economy, education, politics and so forth with the help of high quality ELE. Furthermore, within the country, English bridges the communication between the three major ethnic groups (i.e., Chinese, Malays, and ethnic Indians). Hence, it is beneficial to examine the development and changes of ELE in Singapore to gain invaluable experiences for other countries.

Lastly, for the Expanding Circle, China and Turkey are chosen as the examples to illustrate the change of ELE under the impact of globalization. As the second largest economy and the largest population in the world, China has 390 million ELs by estimation, which reveals the large demand in the field of ELE in China (SGO, 2006). In addition, due to China's significant economic and political status in the world, it is worth addressing the impact of globalization on the field of ELE in China. With respect to Turkey, it occupies a crucial political and geographic position that connects two continents. In particularly, with the current political and military conflicts in the Middle East, Turkey has been considered as a major party in shaping the world situation. In the field of ELE in Turkey, despite some key improvement and reforms, Turkish English learners' proficiency level has been consistently low over the years (Özen et al., 2013). Thus, discussing how globalization has influenced and will possibly impact the field of ELE in Turkey is of considerable significance.

In short, the close link between globalization and ELE is the common theme that threads through the six countries selected in the three circles. On one hand, globalization has largely changed the countries' English language teaching and learning; on the other hand, the constant and corresponding changes in ELE in these counties also influence their globalization process in various aspects. Figure 1 provides a visual representation of the six selected countries and the Three Circle Model in this chapter.

THE INNER CIRCLE: THE US AND THE UK

Globalized Social Backgrounds of the US and the UK

The US has always been the hub for international students, immigrants, and refugees. By 2017, there have been more than 40 million people living in the US but were born in other countries, which accounts for one fifth of the world's migrants and almost 14% of the nation's population (Radford, 2019). In the 2014 – 2015 school year, an estimated 4.6 million students were ELs (National Center for Education Statistics, 2018), representing 9.4% of public-school students in the US. Regarding higher education, from 2015 to 2016, 5% of the students enrolled in U.S. higher educational institutions were international students coming from non-English language backgrounds (Witherell & Department of State, 2016). Compared to a decade ago, the percentage of international students studying at US higher educational institutions has increased 85%. In addition, the US has also been the global leader in resettling world refugees since the 1970s. During the fiscal year of 2018, approximately 22,500 refugees were resettled in the country (Blizzard & Batalova, 2019). Moreover, the countries of origin of the immigrants in the country are extremely diverse, which brings virtually all types of languages spoken in the world. Hence, with the English language still being one of the major languages spoken in the US, ELE at different educational levels has been a central topic that integrates different populations and promotes communication in the nation.

Similar as the US, the population demographics has largely changed in the UK as well. For the past two decades, the resident number of non-British nationals and non-UK-born individuals has been growing steadily every year. In 2018, approximately 14% of the UK population were non-UK born (9.3 million) and 10% were non-British nationals (6.1 million) (Vargas-Silva & Rienzo, 2019). Among all immigrants in the UK, international students account for a quarter of the total number (Migration Advisory Committee, 2018). Different from the US, refugees and asylum seekers face a tougher situation in the UK situation. By June 2019, there was an 8% decrease of asylum applications in the UK compared to the previous year. Only 39% of the applications were granted refugee status or humanitarian protection and allowed to remain in the UK ("Asylum in the UK", n.d.).

Figure 1. Three circles of English and the six representative countries

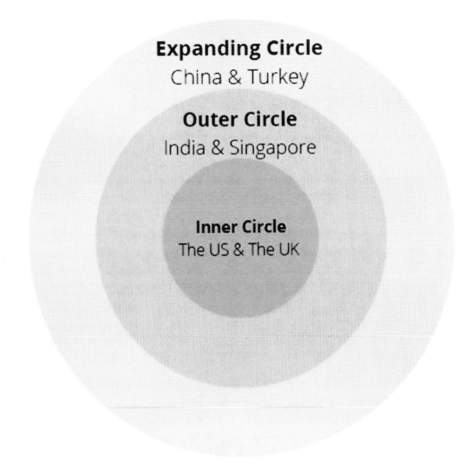

ELE in the US

In the US, from the English-only movement to English-immersion programs to bilingual and multilingual programs, language policies regarding ELE have experienced considerable changes under the influence of globalization. Although the changes are far from smooth, sometimes contradict each other, the major direction of ELE has been toward a more open and inclusive language education, which is in line with the trend of globalization in the country and beyond.

During the colonial period, although European languages other than English were relatively tolerated, other non-English or non-European languages were mostly blocked out from the educational system. In particular, native American languages and cultures were extremely stigmatized (Ricento, 1997). In the beginning of 20th century, teaching or even using foreign languages other than English in classrooms were considered illegal. Unsurprisingly, English-only was the only mainstream approach in ELE across the country.

After the WWII, language policies for language minority students started to relax, bilingual education obtained more attention from the public and the legislations. Starting from 1960s, the US government took some initiatives to promote the use of non-English languages in the education system. For instance, the Bilingual Education Act (BEA) of 1968 authorized the use of non-English languages in educating low-income and language minority students (Lyons, 1992). This change aligned with the social situation at that time when the country accepted a number of war refugees and immigrants. Meanwhile, during this period, methods employed in English as a second language (ESL) education have transformed from merely Grammar Translation Method to more inclusive and diverse ways of teaching. Instead of solely focusing on reading and writing literacy, ESL educators emphasized the significance of listening and speaking skills. The Audiolingual Method was one of the major approaches that were used. In the early stages, specialists in ESL advocated the Audiolingual Method as it deemphasized the traditional rote learning of grammar in foreign language teaching and learning; instead, more opportunities were provided for the learners to practice their listening and speaking skills (Thormann, 1969). However, in the later years, it was recognized that this method was based on the Standard English ideology which neglected the diversity of the English language and reinforced the existing hierarchy of the language in the society. In addition, many scholars have criticized the effectiveness of the Audiolingual Method in enhancing learners' real-life communicative skills as it demands mainly drills and memorization (Richard, 2002).

More and more ESL programs have been initiated by both the federal and state governments from 1980s, such as the National Literacy Act of 1991 and the Immigration Reform and Control Act of 1986 (Burnaby, 1998). Since then, the field of ESL has entered a period of rapid development. The natural approach, communicative language teaching, and recent task-based language teaching approaches are some examples enriching the field of ELE. In particular, the natural approach (Krashen & Terrell, 1983) which emphasizes on comprehensive input in language acquisition has led to profound impact on ELE and other foreign language education programs in the US and beyond. Even today, many language educators continuously use the Natural Approach and its extensions in ESL and EFL classrooms (Shi & Ariza, 2017).

In addition to the changes of language policies and pedagogies in the field of ESL education in the US, participants' and the public's perceptions have also remarkably changed. Language minority population's native languages have gained an increasing acknowledgement in ELE. Numerous research studies suggested that learners' native language does not hinder them from successful second language learning (Byers-Heinlein & Lew-Williams, 2013). Moreover, there has been an increasing number of studies revealing the positive influence from first language literacy on second language learning and academic achievement. Eisenchlas, Schalley, and Guillemin (2013) argue that establishing successful home-language-literacy programs can advocate the enhancement of overall literacy outcomes for ELs. Thus, more educators have recognized the effects of using the learners' native language in fostering the learning of the target language. Furthermore, more immigrant parents in the US tend to support their children to keep speaking the home language besides English in order to have more access to different career opportunities in the future.

Besides the English language policy, pedagogy, and ideology, the English teaching force has also evolved in the US. Recently, nonnative speaker (NNS) English teachers have received increasing recognition from the mainstream practitioners. As the country of origin for the NNS movement, a multitude of scholarly articles and books have been published in the US to raise awareness of the critical role that NNS English teachers play in the field of ELE. From students to administrators to native speaker peers, more opportunities have opened up for NNS English teachers compared to the past (Braine, 2010). In line with the change of the teaching force, the status of so-called Standard English has slowly transformed as well. Instead of establishing one single type of English as the standard, regional English and different types of English have gained more recognition. World Englishes became a formally established and distinct field (Kachru, 2013).

In short, the aforementioned changes correspond to the progress of globalization, which called for the transformation of language policy, teaching methods, general perception of language learning, and practitioners to achieve a more inclusive and diverse magnitude. With the general tendency of a higher level of inclusiveness in ELE, the level of internationalization and globalization in various fields in the US can be potentially promoted as well.

ELE in the UK

As English took up a critical status for international communication in the first half of the 20th century, the British Council, founded in 1934, has played a significant role in the development of ELE in both the UK and beyond (Smith, 2016). Within the UK, the British Council facilitated the establishment of ELT and Applied Linguistics as individual disciplines. Beyond the UK, a number of English teaching institutes had been set up by the British Council since prior to the WWII. In particular, after the WWII, meeting the increasing demand of learning English, the British Council became more involved in curriculum development and teacher training overseas.

Hence, the field of ELT advanced considerably to provide scientific and academic support for the practice in teaching and teacher education. More publications and academic journals in ELT have been issued since 1990s, which have impacted the field worldwide (Smith, 2016). Different from the situation in the US, in the early years, promoting the field of ELE was mainly due to the outward need for the UK rather than accommodating for the inward population. Thus, it is reasonable to argue that instead of being influenced by globalization, the development of ELE in the early years for the UK acted more as a force that pushed globalization forward.

During the 1960s, as in the US, the UK also experienced a tremendous influx of immigrants with varied countries of origin. Particularly in urban areas, the number of students who speak English as an additional language increased tremendously (Harris, Leung, & Rampton, 2001). Both countries have come up with and implemented various policies and programs to support the language minority students. Nevertheless, different from the US where ESL pull-out programs, sheltered English and bilingual education were preferred by many schools and educational institutions, placing ESL learners in mainstream classrooms and providing support from language specialists were more common in the UK (Bourne, 2007). The Swann Report, published in 1985, recognized the ethnical and linguistic diversity in the British society as well as the necessity of supporting ESL learners. Meanwhile, the report noted that there should be no ethnic segregation within the public schooling system. This policy might intend to provide individual students with equal educational opportunities and avoid discrimination; however, the immigrant students from non-English speaking backgrounds were considered as a threat to a school's public performance profile; parents also expressed their complains towards the inclusion of immigrant students (Bourne, 2007). With the relatively high autonomy that the Local Education Authorities (LEAs) had, although the Swann Report called for inclusiveness, many schools did not welcome immigrant and refugee students and other newcomers in practice. Since ESL learners were mainly placed in mainstream classrooms in the UK, the collaboration between ESL teachers and subject teachers was essential (Bourne, 2007; McKay & Freedman, 1990). In many cases, the ESL teacher went into the mainstream classroom to assist the subject teacher. The postgraduate programs in different universities played an important role in training the ESL specialists.

It can be seen from the both cases of the US and the UK that during the progress of globalization, ELE to minority students did not always progress smoothly. Opposite and conservative voices and powers oftentimes came into play, which required solid determination from different key stakeholders to enhance the teaching of English to nonnative speakers.

Recently, with the continuing globalization and increasing mobility, the ethnic and linguistic diversity of ESL learners have been better acknowledged in the UK (Bourne, 2007). The policymakers recognized the significance of providing quality language instruction to ESL learners to improve their learning attainment, thus enhance the quality of education in general. Hence, more training and support have been available for subject teachers to provide accessible instruction to all pupils; additional classes of basic literacy are offered to newly arrived students; accesses to spoken and written forms of students' first languages are also provided. For classroom teachers, with appropriate support and training, they have shown strong awareness of ESL students' needs in language learning and adaption to the new community (Arnot, et al., 2014).

In sum, for both the US and the UK contexts, incoming population from global backgrounds drives the enhancement of ELE and the corresponding teacher training. Accordingly, the acknowledgment of diversity has been strengthened in both countries among key stakeholders. Because of the rapid globalization process and the crucial role of English, as Inner Circle countries, the US and the UK also provide invaluable teaching methods, research findings, as well as practitioners to non-English speaking countries. However, different historical and social contexts have led to various practices in ELE in the US and the UK. One of the major differences between the US and the UK is the placement of ESL students into pull-out programs and mainstream classrooms. For the US, the relatively larger and more diverse population of non-English speaking students may contribute to the set-up of the pull-out programs; whereas for the UK, the more or less similar cultural and linguistic traditions of the ELs may have led to the continuation of placing them in the mainstream classrooms.

THE OUTER CIRCLE: SINGAPORE AND INDIA

Globalized Social Backgrounds of Singapore and India

Different from the US and the UK in the Inner Circle, India and Singapore are categorized in the Outer Circle of the Kachru's Three Circle Model. In this circle, English is not only used as a local language, but more as a global language. In the case of Singapore, since its independence in 1965, English has been determined as the lingua franca and the working language of the government and business sector due to the increasingly important role of English in global economy (Pryke, n.d.). Meanwhile, other three official languages, namely Mandarin Chinese, Tamil, and Malay, also possess an equal status as English in Singapore. As the Education Minister Dr. Tony Tan in 1986 pointed out: English provides a window to the knowledge, technology, and expertise of the modern world; while mother tongues enable children to know what makes them what they are. Thus, ELE in Singapore has always been integrated in a bilingual education system with the mother tongues for the past few decades (Pryke, n.d.).

Different from the case of Singapore, English was given adequate attention from policy makers, administrators, and teachers in India three decades after its independence in the 1980s (Gupta, 2005). Upon its independence in 1947, to establish the national identity and break away from the colonial influence, Hindi was established as the official language of the new country. English was mainly offered in universities and elite schools, which helped English earn an elitist status in India. In addition, compared to the Singaporean society, the cast system is relatively strict in India, which makes it more challenging to spread ELE to the whole population. The socio-economic status and language policies have granted the upper and middle class more privilege in ELE; in contrast, students with low socio-economic status have been mainly educated in vernacular languages and denied more access to English-medium education and opportunities to improve their lives (Ramanathan, 2007).

From different language policies regarding ELE established in Singapore and Indian, one can recognize how the political and economic view of globalization and local or national identities can influence the decisions made on language policies. Considered as a tool for opening up a wider domain in the global economy and development, ELE has been treated as the necessity in Singapore from early on; nevertheless, the strict social system and emphasis on the new national identity after the colonial period hindered the early progress of ELE in India.

ELE in Singapore

In the early years of Singapore's independence from the British colonial rule in 1959 as well as its separation from Malaysia in 1965, English-medium and vernacular-medium education were two major strands in Singapore. In the *1981 English Language Syllabus*, a bilingual language policy was established: English and one of the three vernacular language (i.e., Chinese, Tamil, Malay) have been required to learn in all schools (Zhang, 2006). However, social differences contributed to the various levels of English proficiency for different students. The distinction between Standard Singaporean English (SSE) and Colloquial Singaporean English (CSE) drew attention to numerous scholarly discussions (Tan, 2012). Regarding sociolinguistics, people who speak SSE often took a higher social position than those spoke CSE. Meanwhile, different speakers' educational levels have been regularly taken into consideration regarding the distinction between SSE and CSE (Alsagoff, 2010). On the other hand, Tan (2012) underlined the considerable internal variations within speakers of SSE and CSE.

Throughout the years, ELT has been revised for multiple times with a high centralized approach. Oftentimes, the changes were made in accordance with the country's development and the globalizing process (Zhang, 2006). Starting from the 1950s all the way to 1980s, mastering the accurate grammatical items and using appropriate and formal vocabulary were emphasized since the beginning of ELE in formal education (Mee, 2002). Entering the 1990s, Communicative Language Teaching (CLT) started to gain more attention. Learners were more encouraged to actively participate in the language learning process rather than receiving the instruction prescriptively. The *1991 English Language Syllabus* presented by the Ministry of Education in Singapore noted that the aim of English education was to "help pupils develop their linguistic and communicative competence to meet both their personal, educational, vocational, social and cultural spheres" (Ministry of Education, 1991).

If the early years are considered as the phase to focus on national survival, the more recent decades can be regarded as the period for improving and innovation. To evaluate the successfulness of these different stages, it is not rational to make a clear cut. On one hand, in the early stages, learners' communicative skills were indeed not satisfying; on the other hand, the complete neglect of grammar teaching and greater flexibility also lead to severe problems in ELE. In particular, the effectiveness of English reading and writing was far from ideal (Lim, 1995).

Recognizing the potential problems of eliminating grammar teaching, the *2001 English Language Syllabus* combined the CLT and a systematic teaching of grammar. A text-based approach was employed, moreover, culturally appropriate approaches were highly emphasized to provide effective English language teaching to students from different proficiency and cultural backgrounds. The designing team of this syllabus also intended to cultivate the learners to be confident and capable in meeting the requirement of a globalized knowledge-based economy (Zhang, 2006).

Educated under the quadrilingual policy, Singaporean students have performed constantly well in English reading compared to other English-speaking countries in the international standardized assessments, such as Programme for International Student Assessment (PISA) and the Progress in International Reading and Literacy Study (PIRLS, Zhang, Aryadoust, & Zhang, 2016). Besides focusing on English education, educators in Singapore also increasingly focus on the promotion of bilingualism and multilingualism recently. The program developed to facilitate the communication among teachers of English and other mother tongues to better outcomes in students' biliteracy learning is a representative example (Zhang, Aryadoust, & Zhang, 2016). Undoubtedly, the progressing of globalization stimulated the development of multilingualism.

Most recently, with an increasing population use English as their dominant language at home (36.9%, Lee, 2016), issues related to the ownership of English in Singapore are discussed more frequently. As one of the official languages, English is influenced by its original usages as well as other official languages, including

Mandarin Chinese, Tamil, and Malay. Instead of depending on the structure of English from the Inner Circle countries, Singapore English has earned an increasing recognition globally, attitudes toward Singapore English are also getting more positive, which serves as a critical marker of the Singaporean identity (Siemund, Schulz, & Schweinberger, 2014).

In sum, globalization has been the main force that drives the development of ELE in Singapore; meanwhile, Singaporeans' high English proficiency, varieties of Singapore English, and Singapore's progressive economic development over the years have also boosted its integration in the globalized world and claimed Singapore's unique status in the English-speaking world.

ELE in India

Different from the situation of limited dominant languages in Singapore, the number of languages spoken in India are over 200. The medium of instruction includes 33 different languages; meanwhile, students are required to study a variety of languages, including the mother tongue, the dominant regional language, English, and Hindi (Annamalai, 2003). This is the Three Language Formula in education in India (Vaish, 2008). Although reluctantly adopted English as lingua franca and limited its spread to certain classes in the early years, with the progress of globalization, both the Indian government and the public have recognized the significance of mastering English to gain economic opportunities in the country and internationally. Either as a first, second, or third language, English is the only language instructed in all states across the largest number of schools (Annamalai, 2003). Furthermore, the mastering of English assures one's participation in various social sectors, such as business and industrial sectors, both intra- and internationally.

Regarding English pedagogy in India, before the 1980s, traditional Grammar Translation Method and drills were the major approaches. Entering the 1980s, computer-assisted language learning and communicative approaches have gained more popularity due to the needs from employments from international companies, call centers, and private institutes. Starting from the early 1990s, the Central Board of Secondary Education also have advocated meaningful, relevant, and life-oriented English teaching (Ramanathan, 2016). Consequently, English teaching has changed to more learner-centered in order to meet learner needs (Gupta, 2005). Thus, the major reason for the change of pedagogy can be attributed to the change of the social environment. However, different from Singapore, a systematic and central syllabus and adequate technology has been lacking to guide the practitioners in conducting effective English lessons and tests in India. In addition, teacher education has not been improved in line with the increasing demands of English learning (Ramanathan, 2016).

Furthermore, the quality of English education in different regions as well as social and racial classes differs tremendously in India (Jha, 2014). The most recent Annual Status of Education Reports ("ASER 2018", 2019) shows that the gap regarding reading ability (in mother tongue) between private and government school students has not been decreased; rather, the difference has been gradually enlarged. Thus, the extent of differences between various learners regarding English literacy competence can be easily inferred as well. Besides the considerable gap within the country, internationally, regarding the same PISA test, the reading literacy levels of 80% participants from India were below the baseline of proficiency in 2009 (Rao, 2013). This result differs from Singapore greatly. Scholars have revealed the reasons that contribute to the problematic result, such as the medium of instruction, social gap between the rich and poor, lack of skillful teaching forces and integrated teaching methods, and so forth (Jha, 2014; Ramanathan, 2016; Vaish, 2008).

Turning back to globalization and its impact on ELE, in the case of India, on one hand, the public and the policy makers have both recognized the increasing importance of English proficiency in various social aspects with the development of globalization. It is worth noticing that, as what happened in Singapore, English teaching in India focuses on improving language skills for economic and social purposes. On the other hand, due to the limitation of social conditions, the access to learning English varies critically between different communities. Hence, the English learning results, even the results for general education, differ tremendously within the country. In fact, in the recent years, more and more voices and studies start discussing how to widen the English teaching approaches and methods as well as narrowing the gap between different populations regarding English education (LaDousa, 2014). In additional to educational inequality, English learners' and speakers' identity is another important topic attracting more discussions (Mahapatra & Mishra, 2019). This also mirrors the trend of research in ELE in Singapore.

In short, the appropriate social context, liberalization of the Indian economy, and the increasing globalization encouraged the spread and improvement of ELEn in India; instead of building a uniform national identity through English teaching and learning, successfully using English in communication is considered as a tool for individuals to earn more economic opportunities in the community (Vijayalakshmi & Babu, 2014). However, what is unique and worth tackling is how to provide an equal access to ELE to the general public in India, thus narrowing down the gap in ELE between different learners. Lastly, as a previously colonized country, India faces similar issues as Singapore in ELE, which is related to English learners' cultivation of individual and national identities through English education. Therefore, as a result of globalization, in the Outer Circle countries, English teaching and learning not only helped the participants have more contact and thoughts with a wider outer world, but also their own inner world.

THE EXPANDING CIRCLE: CHINA AND TURKEY

Globalized Social Backgrounds of China and Turkey

Chinese and Turkey are two countries that will be examined in this section as the representative countries in the Expanding Circle. Throughout the history, because of the potential large market, China has always been a major destination for trading; even though in certain time periods, stagnation occurred in economic activities because of political and other reasons. Nevertheless, after experiencing several wars and a closed policy, China has become one of the world's fastest growing economies after applying free market reforms in 1979 (Morrison, 2019). According to the World Bank, China is considered as "the fastest sustained expansion by a major economy in history." Because of the nationwide dedication, China has become the largest producer, trader, foreign exchange reserve holder and the largest economy (Morrison, 2019). In addition, thanks to the rapid economic growth with large scale capital investment and productivity, numerous countries have been trying to make China as their commercial partner and conducting international business with China. Thus, the crucial worldwide economic status of China links it to globalization exceedingly tightly, which largely influences its domestic educational system.

As a country located at the intersection of Europe and Asia, Turkey holds an important position not only strategically but also geographically. After becoming a member of North Atlantic Treaty Organization (NATO) in 1952, Turkey started a series of procedures to be a member of the European Union (EU), and managed to be an associate member of the EU to continue to pursue the desire to be full member of the EU. Considering these facts, Turkey carries an importance role not only for the NATO and EU countries, but also neighboring countries to contribute the peace and tranquility for the conflicts that have been experiencing in the region. Therefore, it is of significant importance to discuss how ELE has been impacted by globalization in both China and Turkey.

ELE in China

Rather than direct control and centralized education system as in Turkey, the Ministry of Education in China only monitors the education system from a macro-level. In each province, the provincial authorities design and administrate the education system; thus, the education system is decentralized in China (National Centre for Education Development Research, 2008). Although different provinces may vary in content designing, there are nine years of compulsory education across China, including primary school and junior secondary school. In terms of ELE, after the establishment of the new country in 1949, it was given little emphasis until the end of the Cultural Revolution, namely the year of 1976. What is more, during the period of 1966 and 1976, ELE was partially banned in China (Bolton & Graddol, 2012). However, after changing political and economic policies after the late 1970s, English started gaining more emphasis with other foreign languages (Adamson, 2002). Joining World Trade Organization (WTO) and hosting the Olympic Games in 2008 gradually promoted the status of English in China as well. Along with the economic growth, international trade opportunities and tourism, learners, parents, teachers, and educational policymakers all recognize the importance of English for the country and individuals. Thus, the age for learning English has been lowered gradually; and English has become an increasingly important subject across all grade levels in China. Students start to learn English at the age of 8 or 9 when they start 3rd grade (Wang, 2007). Also, English is one of the three major subjects in National University Qualifying Exam (i.e., Gaokao), with Math and Chinese. The value of English is also emphasized during college education. Regardless of their major, all college students are required to take College English Test (CET) before graduation (Bolton and Graddol, 2012).

Throughout the past few decades since ELE started to earn more emphasis from various stakeholders in China, great changes have occurred in different aspects in ELE, including curriculum and language policy, assessment, and teaching approaches. Traditionally, foreign language teaching in China, like many other subjects, had solely focused on students' reception and repetition rather than meaningful communication in the target language (Liu, 2016). Methodologically, this also reflects the trend worldwide in the last century, as we discussed previously in the Inner and Outer circle countries. Such a pedagogical approach clearly failed to fulfill the requirement of actively participating and competing in the world economy as a fast-growing country. Correspondingly, in 2011, the standard of the new English curriculum underlines that the aim of language teaching should be developing learners' "language skills, language knowledge, affect and attitude, learning strategies and cultural awareness" (Ministry of Education, 2011, p. 4). Hence, policy-wise, the new curriculum encouraged ELE to embrace the communicative approach, which focuses on meaning and communicative effectiveness rather than rote learning. Despite the policy and curriculum change, standardized exams, in particular Gaokao, are still given the most importance in ELE. Yan's study (2015) of English secondary teachers' perceptions of and the implementation of the new English curriculum noted the lack of alignment between the vision of educational policies on the curriculum reform and the actual practice at school levels. Although the teachers have shown endorsement of the learner-centered communicative approaches, grammar-translation and direct instruction were still widely observed in the classrooms. In addition, it is common that most students study English through examination preparatory books and workbooks only in order to achieve higher grades in the written exams.

Limited time is given to practice English speaking and listening (Shi, 2017) in real English classroom. Thus, due to the high public enthusiasm in learning English and achieving high grades in the exams, it is not uncommon for parents and adult learners to spend a tremendous amount of money in the English training schools and cram classes around the whole country.

Another most recent noteworthy change in ELE in China is the potential removal of English in the national university entrance exam by 2020, brought up in 2013 (Gao & Chen, 2013; Wang & Gao, 2013). Instead, a series of English tests will be conducted to give students better chances of succeeding. Some provinces have taken trials in this reform. Despite the potential benefits of this new policy, which may change the current English teaching and learning practices, it also indicates an unwillingness from the top to let English over penetrate into the social, cultural and linguistic fabric of China (Gil, 2016).

In sum, as in the Inner and Outer Circle countries, globalization has also had enormous impact on ELE in China in the Expanding Circle. What is unique about the context of China is how fast the nationwide changes have taken place economically, politically, and culturally. With the rapid involvement in the global economy and politics, the public and the government have acted fast to recognize the significance of improving the status of ELE and give priority of learning English among all subjects. However, although the teaching methodology has transformed greatly in the field of ELE, the reality of English teaching and learning practice in China has been constrained by the exam-based system. Lastly, with China's increasing power on the international platform in different aspects, its intention to demand more linguistic influence as well rather than merely catering to the needs of the English-speaking world may assumed from the newest education reform.

ELE in Turkey

Designed as a centralized state, the Ministry of National Education (MoNE) determines the national curriculum for every school subject in Turkey. Due to its centralized administration, the K-12 educational system in Turkey is quite directive; teachers and schools have restricted independence in terms of deciding what to cover in lessons (İrican, 2017). Among all subjects, English occupies a significant position since the establishment of the Turkish Republic in 1923. The importance of English for promoting national- and individual-level development has been well recognized; nevertheless, the average proficiency level of students in Turkey has consistently ranked low on various international English proficiency examinations. In the last two decades in Turkey, three major education reforms have been conducted in the year of 1997, 2005, and 2013. Consequently, the curriculum of ELT in Turkey has been drastically changed. The duration of compulsory education has been extended from five to eight to twelve years (4+4+4). Moreover, the grade level of starting teaching English has been changed from the secondary school to the fourth and eventually the second grade of elementary school. Pedagogically, educational technology has been encouraged to be integrated into ELE and the curriculum of ELT has become more communication-focused rather than grammar-based teaching. Kırkgöz (2005) described this change as a milestone in introducing Communicative Language Teaching (CLT) and explained this policy change as "the basic goal of the policy is stated as the development of learners' communicative capacity to prepare them to use the target language (L2) for communication in classroom activities. The curriculum promotes student-centered learning, which replaces the traditional teacher-centered view in ELE. The role of the teacher is specified as a facilitator of the learning process" (Kırkgöz, 2007, p. 221). In response to globalization and the political tendency to integrate in the EU, English Medium Instruction (EMI) has been employed in a number of universities in Turkey. Recently, the increasing process of internationalization for student and academic exchange and mobility is also noteworthy (Kırkgöz, 2017).

The increasing communicative view in ELE also promoted performance-based assessment rather than traditional "paper and pencil" test (Kirkgoz, 2007). However, as in China, the university entrance exam in Turkey still occupies an exceedingly important position in shaping an individual's academic and future development. Scholars have reported that English learners in Turkey tend to "learn to the test" rather than learning the language for communication purposes (Hatipoğlu, 2016), which largely hinders the development of ELE toward a communicative direction and contributes to the gap between the ideal language policy and actual classroom and learning practices.

To sum up, it can be observed that under the impact of globalization, English as a language that provides more opportunities on both individual and national levels has earned sufficient recognition from various key stakeholders in China and Turkey. Teaching methods in ELE have also been enhanced over the years. However, challenges still exist in both countries. Inequality in accessing quality English education among learners from different regions and social class backgrounds is a common issue in both countries. This difficulty was also encountered in India as an Outer Circle country. In China, significant differences in ELE appear between major developed cities and rural areas. The differences contain various aspects, such as available resources for English learning, teacher education, family support, and so forth (Hu, 2003). Similarly, studies have suggested that family income, family's willingness and abilities to spend on extra-curricular tutoring lessons, parents' educational levels significantly correlate to students' academic achievement in English learning in Turkey (Tomul and Savasci, 2012). This difference is obvious in the designated English learning hours in private and state schools. Exam-based

ELE in both countries also contribute to the gap between the classroom practice and the language policy. Although communicative approaches are advocated in both countries, due to the pressure from high-stakes exams, teachers and learners are forced to continue with grammar-based teaching methods in practice, hence listening and speaking are largely neglected. This might be the major reason why many English learners in both China and Turkey struggle in carrying out smooth conversations in English despite years of learning.

CRITICAL REFLECTION ACROSS THE THREE CIRCLES: COMMON TREND, CHALLENGES AND FUTURE DIRECTION

From a collective perspective, the field of ELE in the six countries examined in this chapter has experienced considerable progress and transformation together with the development of globalization. As the lingual franca of international and domestic communication between different groups of people, the teaching and learning of English have moved beyond merely memorizing the grammatical structures in all six countries. Instead, being able to successfully communicate with others from different language or ethnical backgrounds in English becomes key. Furthermore, the authority of native speakers in speaking and teaching the English language has lessened worldwide. More recognition has been given to regional Englishes as well as non-native speaking English teachers. Policy-wise, countries in all three circles have been evolving with the social changes to improve English education policies in order to better embrace the demographic changes domestically and seize the opportunities for economic development. Lastly, with respect to the perspectives of different parties toward ELE, majority of the key stakeholders acknowledge the critical value of learning the English language for individual academic and career development in all six countries.

With respect to positive transformation, involving more varieties of Englishes in teaching has helped promote individuals' self-esteem and their recognition of regional differences in the English language, in particular in the Inner and Outer Circles. Moreover, more emphasis on protecting and preserving mother tongue language education in Inner and Outer Circle countries has been beneficial for improving the language minority's social status as well. For Outer Circle countries, communicative language teaching method and technology have been helping English educators and learners better adjust to the globalized world. Regarding the countries in the Expanding Circle, language policies have been transformed to further promoting the significance of communication in English, learner-centered pedagogical practiced have also been widely advertised. Thus, the aforementioned experiences from the six countries introduced in this chapter shed light on moving the field of ELE forward in other similar countries.

Although the field of ELE has witnessed remarkable progress in different aspects in all six countries, challenges still exist. For the Inner Circle countries, the US and the UK, as more and more immigrants joining the English-speaking communities, it is of significant importance for English language educators to not only teaching the language but also bridging the gap between native and nonnative English speakers in various aspects, such as cultural and ethnic differences. In order to help the newcomers better adjust to the new country, raising awareness of the general public to keep an open mind to different languages and cultures as well as recognize the value that immigrants can bring to the society are crucial. Finally, another challenge for the Inner Circle countries is to preserve and encourage the use of first languages besides English. Globalization does not only encourage English learners to communicate with the world, it also influences native English speakers. Native English speakers may face more challenges to compete with multilingual speakers intra- and internationally. Thus, more efforts are needed to help the immigrant children keep their mother tongue languages and educate multilingual citizens.

Regarding the Outer Circle countries, how to balance the status and usage of English and other official languages is the key challenge under globalization. Because of the essential position of English for communication and official purposes in the Outer Circle countries, the teaching of English has successfully moved beyond the mere emphasis of grammar learning. However, as more and more young people and families use English as their home language, this may lessen the importance of other languages. Furthermore, the unique identity, culture, traditions and so forth that link with the language may lose its importance. In addition, the unequal access to English language education is not uncommon. Taking India as an example, although English is used for official purposes and acts as the lingual franca between different ethnic groups, quality English education is still mainly limited to the wealthy and educated upper caste. The unequal access to English education also exists between urban and rural areas.

Similar as the Outer Circle countries, inequality in ELE also appears in Expanding Circle countries. Unequal access to ELE can be found between urban and rural areas, private and public schools, as well as upper and lower social classes. Such inequality prevents the entire field of ELE from moving forward to reach more individuals and higher teaching quality, thus contributing to more problems on the path to globalization. Besides inequality in education, approaches of English teaching in Outer Circle countries also reveal obstacles. Due to the lack of communication opportunities in the English as a foreign language environment and the exam-based assessment, in many cases, ELE still mainly concentrates on grammar translation and memorization. Learners study English as a subject the same as studying mathematics or physics, rather than a tool for communication. Consequently, it is not difficult to observe that after thousands of hours of study, many English learners in Outer Circle countries still cannot successfully and smoothly communicate with others in English for either academic or work purposes.

In sum, it is critical to acknowledge the impact of globalization on ELE in various countries; meanwhile, the development of ELE also reinforces the countries' participation in globalization and stimulate the evolvement of national and communal identity. With more and more countries participate in international activities by using English and the improvement of English status in many countries, the ownership of English has also transformed. Inner Circle countries are not the sole owner of English; rather, various Englishes that connect unique characteristics of different linguistic origins and ethnical identities in assorted countries become more prevalent than ever. This sheds light on the future of ELE. The teaching of English should not be limited to one type of English; instead, learners should be encouraged to acknowledge and get familiar with other types of Englishes, which is beneficial for effective international communication with different English speakers. Corresponding to the promotion of World Englishes and the importance of all languages, awareness should be raised to preserve English learners' mother tongue languages. This is particularly important for Inner and Outer Circler countries because of the co-existence of multiple languages at learners' homes and the society. Finally, for Expanding Circle countries, in order to cope with the issues related to educational inequality, utilizing technology to reach more disadvantages groups of learners can be an effective approach. The policymakers in the Expanding Circle countries should also consider revising the curriculum and assessment to involve more communicative components to improve the learners' communicative English skills.

REFERENCES

Adamson, B. (2002). Barbarian as a foreign language: English in China's schools. *World Englishes*, *21*(2), 231–243. doi:10.1111/1467-971X.00244

Alsagoff, L. (2010). English in Singapore: Culture, capital and identity in linguistic variation. *World Englishes*, *29*(3), 336–348. doi:10.1111/j.1467-971X.2010.01658.x

Annamalai, E. (2003). Medium of power: The question of English in education in India. In J. W. Tollefson & A. B. M. Tsui (Eds.), *Medium of instruction policies: Whose agenda? Which agenda?* (pp. 177–193). Lawrence Erlbaum.

Arnot, M. (2014). *School approaches to the education of EAL students: Language development, social integration and achievement.* The Bell Foundation. https://www.educ.cam.ac.uk/research/projects/ealead/Fullreport.pdf

ASER 2018. (2019). *Annual status of education report (rural) 2018.* http://img.asercentre.org/docs/ASER%202018/Release%20Material/aserreport2018.pdf

Asylum in the UK. (n.d.). *The UN Refugee Agency.* Retrieved June 28, 2020 from https://www.unhcr.org/asylum-in-the-uk.html

Beare, K. (2019, November 18). How many people learn English? *ThoughtCo.* https://www.thoughtco.com/how-many-people-learn-english-globally-1210367

Blizzard, B., & Batalova, J. (2019). *Refugees and Asylees in the United States.* Migration Policy Institute. https://www.migrationpolicy.org/article/refugees-and-asylees-united-states

Bolton, K., & Graddol, D. (2012). English in China today: The current popularity of English in China is unprecedented, and has been fuelled by the recent political and social development of Chinese society. *English Today, 28*(3), 3–9. doi:10.1017/S0266078412000223

Bourne, J. (2007). Focus on literacy: ELT and educational attainment in England. In J. Cummins & C. Davison (Eds.), *International handbook of English language teaching* (pp. 199–210). Springer Verlag. doi:10.1007/978-0-387-46301-8_15

Braine, G. (2010). *Non-native-speaker English teachers: Research, pedagogy, and professional growth.* Routledge. doi:10.4324/9780203856710

Burnaby, B. (1998). ESL policy in Canada and the United States: Basis for comparison. In T. Ricento (Ed.), *Language and politics in the United States and Canada: Myths and realities* (pp. 243–267). Routledge.

Byers-Heinlein, K., & Lew-Williams, C. (2013). Bilingualism in the early years: What the science says. *LEARNing Landscapes, 7*(1), 95–112. https://www.ncbi.nlm.nih.gov/pmc/articles/PMC6168212/. doi:10.36510/learnland.v7i1.632 PMID:30288204

Eisenchlas, S. A., Schalley, A. C., & Guillemin, D. (2013). The importance of literacy in the home language: The view from Australia. *SAGE Open, 3*(October – December), 1–14. doi:10.1177/2158244013507270

Gao, Y., & Chen, L. (2013, October). China's English fervor under scrutiny. *People's Daily Online.* http://en.people.cn/203691/8426108.html

Gil, J. (2016). English language education policies in the People's Republic of China. In R. Kirkpatrick (Ed.), *English language education policy in Asia* (pp. 49–90). Springer. doi:10.1007/978-3-319-22464-0_3

Gupta, D. (2005). ELT in India: A brief historical and current overview. *Asian EFL Journal, 7*(1), 197–207.

Harris, R., Leung, C., & Rampton, B. (2001). Globalisation, diaspora and language education in England. In D. Block & D. Cameron (Eds.), *Globalization and language teaching* (pp. 29–46). Routeledge.

Hatipoğlu, Ç. (2016). The impact of the university entrance exam on EFL education in Turkey: Pre-service English language teachers' perspective. *Procedia: Social and Behavioral Sciences, 232*, 136–144. doi:10.1016/j.sbspro.2016.10.038

Hu, G. (2005). English language education in China: Policies, progress, and problems. *Language Policy, 4*(1), 5–24. doi:10.100710993-004-6561-7

İrican, E. S. (2017). A comparative study on basic education curricula of Finland and Turkey in foreign language teaching. *International Journal of Curriculum and Instruction, 9*(2), 137–156.

Jenkins, J. (2003). *World Englishes: A resource book for students*. Routledge.

Jha, S. K. (2014). An ethnographic insight into the causal factors of degrading English education in Ethiopia, Libya, and India. *International Journal of Language and Linguistics, 2*(2), 44–55.

Kachru, B. (1992). *The other tongue: English across cultures*. University of Illinois Press.

Kachru, B. B. (2013). History of World Englishes. In C. A. Chapelle (Ed.), *The encyclopedia of Applied Linguistics*. Blackwell Publishing Ltd.

Kırkgöz, Y. (2005). English language teaching in Turkey: Challenges for the 21st century. In G. Braine (Ed.), *Teaching English to the world: History, curriculum, and practice* (pp. 159–175). Lawrence Erlbaum Associates.

Kırkgöz, Y. (2007). English Language Teaching in Turkey: Policy Changes and their implementations. *RELC Journal, 38*(2), 216–228. doi:10.1177/0033688207079696

Kırkgöz, Y. (2017). English education policy in Turkey. In R. Kirkpatrick (Ed.), *English language education policy in the Middle East and North Africa* (pp. 235–256). Springer. doi:10.1007/978-3-319-46778-8_14

Krashen, S. D., & Terrell, T. D. (1983). *The natural approach: Language acquisition in the classroom*. The Alemany Press.

LaDousa, C. (2014). *Hind is our ground, English is our sky: Education, language, and social class in contemporary India*. Berghahn Books.

Lee, P. (2016, March 10). English most common home language in Singapore, bilingualism also up: Government survey. *The Straits Times*. https://www.straitstimes.com/singapore/english-most-common-home-language-in-singapore-bilingualism-also-up-government-survey

Lim, S. (1995). A review of reading and writing research in Singapore: Implications for language education. In M. Tickoo (Ed.), *Reading and writing: Theory into practice* (pp. 492–513). SEAMEO Regional Language Centre.

Liu, W. (2016). The changing pedagogical discourses in China: The case of the foreign language curriculum change and its controversies. *English Teaching, 15*(1), 74–90. doi:10.1108/ETPC-05-2015-0042

Lyons, U. (1992). Secretary Bennett versus equal educational opportunity. In J. Crawford (Ed.), *Language loyalties: A source book on the official English controversy* (pp. 363–366). University of Chicago Press.

Mahapatra, S., & Mishra, S. (2019). Articulating identities – the role of English language education in Indian universities. *Teaching in Higher Education, 24*(3), 346–360. doi:10.1080/13562517.2018.1547277

McKay, S. L., & Freedman, S. W. (1990). Language minority education in Great Britain: A challenge to current U.S. Policy. *TESOL Quarterly, 24*(3), 385–405. doi:10.2307/3587226

Mee, C. Y. (2002). English language teaching in Singapore. *Asia Pacific Journal of Education, 22*(2), 65–80. doi:10.1080/0218879020220207

Migration Advisory Committee. (2018). *Impact of international students in the UK*. https://assets.publishing.service.gov.uk/government/uploads/system/uploads/attachment_data/file/739089/Impact_intl_students_report_published_v1.1.pdf

Min, C. Y. (2018, February 5). Singapore still 2nd freest economy in the world but gap with top-ranked Hong Kong widens. *The Straitstimes*. https://www.straitstimes.com/business/economy/singapore-still-2nd-freest-economy-in-the-world-but-gap-with-top-ranked-hong-kong-0

Ministry of Education. (1991). *English language syllabus*. Curriculum Planning Division, Ministry of Education.

Ministry of Education. (2011). *English curriculum standard*. Beijing Normal University Press.

Morrison, W. M. (2019). *China's economic rise: History, trends, challenges, and implications for the United States*. Congressional Research Service.

National Center for Education Statistics. (2018). *English language learners in public schools*. https://nces.ed.gov/programs/coe/indicator_cgf.asp

National Centre for Education Development Research. (2008), *National report on mid-term assessment of education for all in China*. National Centre for Education Development Research, Chinese National Commission for Unesco. http://planipolis.iiep.unesco.org/upload/China/China_EFA_MDA.pdf

Özen, E. N. (2013). *Turkey National needs assessment of state school English language teaching*. https://www.britishcouncil.org.tr/sites/default/files/turkey_national_needs_assessment_of_state_school_english_language_teaching.pdf

Park, J. S., & Wee, L. (2009). The Three Circles redux: A market–theoretic perspective on World Englishes. *Applied Linguistics*, *30*(3), 389–406. doi:10.1093/applin/amp008

Pryke, W. Y. (n.d.). Singapore's journey: Bilingualism and role of English language in our development. *British Council*. https://www.britishcouncil.cl/sites/default/files/escrito-way-yin-pryke.pdf

Radford, J. (2019). *Key findings about U.S. immigrants*. Pew Research Center. https://www.pewresearch.org/fact-tank/2019/06/17/key-findings-about-u-s-immigrants/

Ramanathan, V. (2007). A critical discussion of the English-Vernacular divide in India. In J. Cummins & C. Davison (Eds.), *International handbook of English language teaching* (pp. 51–61). Springer. doi:10.1007/978-0-387-46301-8_5

Rao, A. G. (2013). The English-only myth: Multilingual education in India. *Language Problems and Language Planning*, *37*(3), 271–279. doi:10.1075/lplp.37.3.04rao

Registrar General & Census Commissioner. (2011). *Census of India 2011: Report on post enumeration survey*. https://www.censusindia.gov.in/2011Census/pes/Pesreport.pdf

Ricento, T. K. (1997). Language policy and education in the United States. In R. Wodak & D. Corson (Eds.), *Encyclopedia of language and education: Language policy and political issues in education* (pp. 137–148). Springer. doi:10.1007/978-94-011-4538-1_13

Richards, J. C. (2002). Theories of teaching in language learning. In J. C. Richards & W. A. Renandya (Eds.), *Methodology in language teaching: An anthology of current practice* (pp. 19–26). Cambridge University Press. doi:10.1017/CBO9780511667190.004

SGO (Steering Group Office for Survey of Language Situation in China). (2006). *Zhongguo Yuyan Wenzi Shiyong Qingkuang Diaocha Ziliao* [Findings and Documents of Survey of Language Situation in China]. Language Press.

Shi, J. L. (2017). English language education in China: Progress, problems, and reflections. *Journal of Literature and Art Studies, 7*(7), 935–938.

Shi, Y., & Ariza, E. (2018). A study on the Natural Approach (NA) and teaching proficiency through reading and storytelling (TPRS). In *Proceedings of the 6th international conference on social science, education and humanities research (SSEHR 2017)*. Atlantis Press. 10.2991sehr-17.2018.92

Siemund, P., Schulz, M. E., & Schweinberger, M. (2014). Studying the linguistic ecology of Singapore: A comparison of college and university students. *World Englishes, 33*(3), 340–362. doi:10.1111/weng.12094

Smith, R. (2016). ELT and the British Council, 1935-2014: Research notes. *Warwick ELT Archive*. https://warwick.ac.uk/fac/soc/al/research/collections/elt_archive/research_projects/britishcouncil/

Tan, P. K. W. (2012). English in Singapore. *International Journal of Language. Translation and Intercultural Communication, 1*(1), 123–138. doi:10.12681/ijltic.14

The UN Migration Agency. (2018). *World migration report 2018.* https://www.iom.int/sites/default/files/country/docs/china/r5_world_migration_report_2018_en.pdf

Thormann, W. E. (1969). The Audio-Lingual Method in the past: "Anti-grammar" in Seventeenth-century France. *Modern Language Journal, 53*(5), 327–329.

Tomul, E., & Savasci, H. (2012). Socioeconomic determinants of academic achievement. *Educational Assessment, Evaluation and Accountability, 24*(3), 175–187. doi:10.100711092-012-9149-3

Tsui, A. B. M., & Tollefson, J. W. (2007). Language policy and the construction of national cultural identity. In A. B. M. Tsui & J. W. Tollefson (Eds.), *Language policy, culture, and identity in Asian contexts* (pp. 1–21). Lawrence Erlbaum Associates.

Vaish, V. (2008). *Biliteracy and globalization: English language education in India.* Multilingual Matters. doi:10.21832/9781847690340

Vargas-Silva, C., & Rienzo, C. (2019). *Migrants in the UK: An overview*. The Migration Observatory. https://migrationobservatory.ox.ac.uk/resources/briefings/migrants-in-the-uk-an-overview/

Vijayalakshmi, M., & Babu, M. S. (2014). A brief history of English language teaching in India. *International Journal of Scientific and Research Publications, 4*(5), 1-4.

Wang, Q. (2007). The national curriculum changes and their effects on English language teaching in the People's Republic of China. In J. Cummins & C. Davison (Eds.), *International handbook of English language teaching* (pp. 87–105). Springer. doi:10.1007/978-0-387-46301-8_8

Wang, X., & Gao, Y. (2013, October). Beijing expected to see exam reforms in 2014. *People's Daily Online*. http://english.people.com.cn/203691/8432022.html#

Witherell, S., & Department of State. (2016). *Open doors 2016 executive summary*. https://www.iie.org/en/Why-IIE/Announcements/2016-11-14-Open-Doors-Executive-Summary

Yan, C. (2015). 'We can't change much unless the exam change': Teachers' dilemmas in the curriculum reform in China. *Improving Schools, 18*(1), 5–19. doi:10.1177/1365480214553744

Zhang, L. J. (2006). The ecology of communicative language teaching: Reflecting on the Singapore experience. In *Proceeding of the annual CELEA international conference: Innovating English teaching: Communicative Language Teaching (CLT) and other approaches*. China English Language Education Association (CELEA) and Guangdong University of Foreign Studies, Guangzhou, China.

Zhang, L. J., Aryadoust, V., & Zhang, D. (2016). Taking stock of the effects of strategies-based instruction on writing in Chinese and English in Singapore primary classrooms. In R. E. Silver & W. D. Bokhorst-Heng (Eds.), *Quadrilingual education in Singapore: Pedagogical innovation in language education* (pp. 103–126). Springer. doi:10.1007/978-981-287-967-7_7

ADDITIONAL READING

Howatt, A. P. R., & Widdowson, H. G. (2004). *A history of ELT*. Oxford University Press.

Jenkins, J. (2007). *English as a Lingual Franca: Attitude and identity*. Oxford University Press.

Kamhi-Stein, L. D. (2000). Adapting US-based TESOL education to meet the needs of nonnative English speakers. *TESOL Journal, 9*(3), 10–14.

Kirkgöz, Y. (2009). Globalization and English language policy in Turkey. *Educational Policy, 23*(5), 663–684. doi:10.1177/0895904808316319

KEY TERMS AND DEFINITIONS

EFL: English as a Foreign Language.
ELF: English as Lingual Franca.
ELT: English Language Teaching.
ESL: English as a Second Language.
Expanding Circle: English does not have a restricted official status nor major domestic functions; instead, English is mainly taught as a subject and used for international communication, e.g. China, Korea, Japan, Turkey, etc.
Inner Circle: Where monolingual native speakers of English are located, such as the US, the UK, Canada, etc.
Outer Circle: Countries that were usually previously colonized by English-speaking countries and after decolonization, the English language still plays critical institutional functions in those countries, e.g. Singapore, India, Nigeria, etc.
WE: World Englishes.

Chapter 9
Improving the L2 Interactional and Critical Thinking Skills of University Students Using the CLIL Approach in the 21st Century

Sakae Onoda
Juntendo University, Japan

ABSTRACT

This chapter discusses theoretical underpinnings, practical applications, and effects of the CLIL (content and language-integrated learning) approach with a primary focus on the use of group projects on the development of English interactional skills (especially oral fluency), self-efficacy, and critical thinking skills in undergraduate English majors in Japan. The chapter first reviews L2 literature on the use and features of the CLIL approach and then focuses on the use of group projects and their potential effects on three important dimensions of language learning: linguistic, affective, and social. The literature review covers the author's own investigations of the effects of group projects substantiated by students' feedback and statistical data collected as part of his extensive teaching experience in universities. Finally, a number of practical suggestions for implementing group projects are presented along with procedures and worksheets so that interested readers can adopt these in their own teaching context.

DOI: 10.4018/978-1-7998-2831-0.ch009

BACKGROUND

Inherent Problems Underlying English Learning in Japan

It is often reported that with advanced English language skills being emphasized in the face of an increasingly globalizing society, teaching EFL learners in secondary schools in Japan is challenging for a number of inherent reasons: 1) students lack strong motivation or need to learn English because they do not clearly perceive any intrinsic learning goals beyond studying English to get good scores in high school or university entrance examinations or for studying abroad) (Onoda, 2014); 2) they have limited exposure to or opportunities for using spoken English outside the classroom (Nation, 2013) unless they take speaking and listening lessons online or in language schools; 3) they do not study English extensively because English is learned generally as a compulsory school subject and the number of classroom learning hours is limited (Vázquez, Molina, & López, 2014); 4) practicing teachers have not developed advanced interactional skills of their own, which makes it difficult to facilitate communication-based teaching; and 5) students usually study in large classes (30-40 on average), which makes it difficult for teachers to implement rich classroom interactions in English (Onoda, 2014; Onoda & Miyashita, 2018; Yamazaki, 2006; Sato, 2012).

As a result, Japanese learners of English have not developed advanced English proficiency, especially in terms of interactional skills, including not only fluent and accurate language use but also the critical thinking skills critical to interaction in authentic language use contexts, both of which might instigate and maintain their further autonomous language learning (Borg, 2013; Onoda, 2019a). Moreover, English language teaching in Japanese universities does not appear to help these students improve their English language skills, mainly for the following reasons:

1. Professional Limitations: English classes are taught by teachers whose majors often vary (for example, from second language acquisition to international relations) and who may lack adequate knowledge of teaching techniques or teaching experience;
2. Curricular Limitations: English language teaching is constrained, in most cases with three or four different English subjects offered each week and a lack of balance between meaning-focused input and output, language-focused learning, and fluency development (Nation, 2013; see below for details). This reflects the reality that in university, majors (e.g., economics in the Faculty of Economics) are placed at the core of the curriculum with English classes relegated to the periphery or designed mainly to help students understand their

majors when taught in English or to get high scores on tests such as TOEFL or TOEIC with a view to securing good jobs involving English;
3. Scope Limitations: While some universities have introduced English-Medium Instruction (EMI) to teach some majors in English in order to foster the types of "Global Citizens" promoted by the Ministry of Education, Culture, Sports, Science, and Technology (MEXT, 2017), as discussed above, typical English language curriculum have not served such a goal and as a result largely failed to improve students' interactional skills to the extent that they could interact effectively with others from diverse backgrounds.

Also worth mentioning is the fact that undergraduate English teacher education programs in Japan are not designed so as to foster effective secondary school English teachers equipped with advanced interactional skills and critical thinking skills (Nishino & Watanabe, 2008; Onoda & Miyashita, 2018; Onoda, Miyashita, & Yoshino, 2017; Yamazaki, 2006). Moreover, there is a lack of research-based inquiries into the underlying causes of this deficiencies, including the lingering effect of the very teaching approaches new teachers themselves have been exposed to. It is no wonder therefore that Japanese secondary school and university learners of English are not expected—let alone guided—to become autonomous, self-regulated learners who can set their own learning goals and are motivated to purse them by using effective learning strategies while regularly reflecting on their learning progress and achievement. This conclusion is especially valid in the area of developing speaking skills, where step-by-step teaching approaches to the acquisition of advanced speaking or interactional skills have not been implemented due to the three major factors listed above. In fact, hardly any systematic English language programs appear to have been designed to progressively improve various aspects of learners' spoken production, including fluency and accuracy (Beglar, 2017). In the following paragraphs, a promising approach to the improvement of L2 motivation and skills of Japanese university learners is thoroughly discussed.

LITERATURE REVIEW

The CLIL Approach

Given the realities of secondary school and university English language learning in Japan, a potentially effective teaching approach that is being increasingly well-documented in contemporary L2 literature, especially in the Netherlands and Finland, appears to be the adoption of CLIL (Content and Language Integrated Learning). This teaching method combines content and language learning, with learners encouraged to actively use all four English language skills while learning subject content and exchanging opinions with their peers. In this approach, English, whether in ESL or EFL contexts, is used as the predominant vehicle for instruction and interaction but also—and crucially—for acquiring information on particular subjects, such as social studies, and for communicating ideas and opinions germane to the subject to and among learners. Importantly, there are not set forms or styles of CLIL teaching because texts and tasks vary from teacher to teacher based on the subject they teach and the proficiency and needs of their students. In some cases, the class is taught by a subject teacher and an English teacher in a tandem fashion after careful preparation and discussion. In principle, there is no reason why this approach should not be transplanted—with adaptations—to Japanese university English teaching contexts.

As can be envisioned from the integration of content and language, the CLIL approach bears a number of similarities to the content-based approach, which has long been employed in English language teaching and is purported to yield comparable pedagogical benefits if adequately implemented. The critical components of the CLIL approach include:

1. Pertinent and meaningful input, with learners engaging in reading or listening;
2. Teaching materials drawn from authentic resources or created by the teacher after careful consideration of the learners' interests and needs;
3. Meaningful input (i.e., reading and listening) is processed deeply through subsequent output activities for communicating information, ideas, and opinions derived from the input materials (i.e., speaking and writing);
4. Speaking and writing activities are incorporated for learners to summarize their understanding by using language (i.e., vocabulary and structures) germane to the subject and giving group presentations or submitting a group report; and
5. Small-group research projects are employed to encourage learners to collect, share, compare, analyze, and evaluate relevant information (Coyle, 2012, 2013).

The benefits of the CLIL approach are equally well-documented in L2 literature (Ellis & Shintani, 2013) and include the following:

1. Making language learning more meaningful and motivating;
2. Offering learners opportunities to acquire knowledge using L2 lexis germane to the subject and theme and to express their knowledge using pertinent language;
3. Research-based learning helps students develop cognitive and critical thinking skills;
4. Group projects, which are often employed under this approach, encourage interactions among learners, thus improving their language skills, especially their speaking skills and social learning skills.

5. Authentic texts and contexts used as part of integrated learning heightens learners' degree of self-efficacy in both language and content learning and facilitates their autonomous learning;
6. Tasks such as grammar learning become more meaningful and help learners acquire language use and grammar rather than simply study them for knowledge;
7. Increased amount of exposure to and use of the L2 and wider opportunities to deeply process and automatize both content knowledge and language use and develop critical thinking skills as well as fluency in language use;
8. Potential solution to a key problem in EFL language learning, where learners possess language skills that are not adequate for the more advanced knowledge and ideas they wish to express, thereby hampering or reducing their motivation for further L2 learning.

Thus, L2 literature abounds in evidence of the positive effects of the CLIL approach on language learning provided the materials and tasks used are well suited to learners' proficiency levels, interests, needs, and expectations. In this sense, the approach has the potential to be adopted in Japanese university English classes, where, as noted above, students with stagnant English skills, especially speaking and writing skills, who cannot effectively deliver their ideas to others are often found.

It should not be assumed, of course, that the CLIL approach is a panacea for L2 teaching. In fact, there are reports that identifying authentic teaching materials and tasks may prove challenging for some teachers, especially those who teach learners with low L2 proficiency (Coyle, 2012).

In the next section, a concrete teaching approach that can be adopted as part of the CLIL framework is discussed.

Tasks That can be Employed as Part of the CLIL Approach

Given the characteristics and pedagogical benefits reviewed above, it is evident that the CLIL approach has major potential for motivating Japanese university learners of English and for improving their interactional and critical thinking skills, which in turn should heighten their self-efficacy and encourage their autonomous English learning.

The Linked-Skills Approach

A promising approach that can be easily adopted in the university English courses is the linked-skills approach advocated in *the four strands of teaching* (Nation, 2013). Nation argues that an L2 should be learned by experiencing four elements: meaning-focused input, meaning-focused output, fluency development, and language-focused learning in a well-balanced way in order to effectively develop communication skills. Although the linked-skills approach does not explicitly include language-focused learning, it effectively integrates the three other critical strands, that is, meaning-focused input, meaning focused output, and fluency development, none of which appears to be actively used in Japanese English teaching contexts (Nation, 2014), mainly, as discussed above, because improvements in students' TOEIC and TOEFL scores have been gaining in importance in university English teaching at universities.

In the linked-skills approach, learners are encouraged to process a single text repeatedly by processing it through a series of carefully designed and sequenced tasks that require them to use all four language skills one after another. This approach can be used in various types of English courses, but most effectively in a content-based setting (Nation, 2014), and therefore as part of CLIL-based teaching (Onoda, 2019a).

A particularly suitable case of task design within the linked-skills framework is the one frequently used in one section of the author's own university Media English course. In this task, learners watch a TV news clip on smartphone addition as a social problem. News clips of this type are often selected because they cover topics that are interesting and familiar to the learners and therefore most of language (lexis) used in them is within the learner's existing knowledge (i.e., at least 98% of the words are already known). This is an important condition for facilitating meaning-focused input. The learners are then are given the script with blanks for key words and are instructed to fill these in while listening again and then check their answers and comprehension of the text in pairs and then with the teacher. These learning behaviors fall into the meaning-focused input and output categories along with a smaller amount of language-focused activity. At the third stage, learners are asked to summarize the story with their comments in 8-10 minutes. Given that at this stage learners have already understood all the language items and expressed their ideas in their own words, this activity can be classified as a fluency development activity, i.e., one designed to improve writing fluency because learners once again make use of what they already know. Although Nation's (2013, 2014) original linked-skills teaching design included three stages, the author normally includes a fourth-stage task, a speaking task, to accommodate learners' willingness to communicate ideas with their classmates, thus improving their speaking fluency and meeting the author's pedagogical objective of developing their interactional and critical thinking skills, which can be most effectively done by engaged them in meaningful authentic contexts. In this task, the learners are encouraged to prepare discussion questions, talk about the news story, and discuss their responses to the discussion questions in 3-5 minutes. The pedagogical design is based on the principle that prescribes how fluency activities should be linked and sequenced.

In sum, the linked-skills procedure enumerated above satisfies the following conditions for improving wiring and speaking fluency (Nation, 2014):

1. The theme is interesting to learners and they are motivated to read, listen to, and speak and write about the text;
2. The language is largely familiar to the learners, with 98% of the lexis already known to them;
3. Learners experience repeated exposure to and use of the same language items in tasks that offer repeated opportunities for comprehensible input and output of the same language items, thereby facilitating automatization of such items; and
4. Learners are pressured to read, listen, speak, and write faster than they normally would.

In addition to considering the four skills (listening, speaking, reading, and writing), Nation (2013) advocates the linked-skills approach from a practical pedagogic perspective as a way to develop fluency and thereby interactional skills and argues that the approach can be effectively incorporated into EFL teaching settings, most favorably in university English classrooms, which generally lack fluency development tasks.

L2 literature amply documents the positive effects of the linked-skills approach on L2 learning. For example, L2 acquisition studies (e.g., DeKeyser; 2007; Onoda, 2012: Segalowitz, 2010) report the following effects:

1. The use of authentic material and authentic interaction opportunities motivates learners to actively engage in the sequenced tasks (intrinsic motivation);
2. Preceding tasks help learners perform well on subsequent tasks, thus facilitating proactive engagement (practice effect and perception of task value);
3. Language items, including collocates and functional multiword-units, are repeatedly encountered and used and thereby processed and acquired while involving three or four different language skills (multiple repetition and automatization);
4. Initial input activities help learners understand the news story and pay attention to and learn key and unknown phrases and words useful for the later summary writing and story-retelling and discussion tasks (noticing and input enhancement);
5. Discussion questions embedded in the summary writing activity encourage deep and emotional processing of the story as well as language items (emotional engagement and personalization);
6. Linked input and output activities are effectively sequenced, thus helping learners repeatedly and deeply process key language items and enhancing automatization, which in turns improves writing and speaking fluency (automatization and fluency development);

7. Writing and speaking activities encourage learners to write, speak, and listen to the same information and key language items a number of times, thus facilitating thoughtful processing of language items (deep processing and automatization);
8. Speaking activities facilitate oral interaction between learners while interactional adjustments (including negotiation of meaning and input adjustment) are frequently observed, thus providing opportunities for receiving comprehensible input and producing comprehensible output and helping learners acquire new language items. (comprehensible input and output, willingness to communicate, and cooperative learning);
9. Sequenced tasks lead to improved writing and speaking fluency and the development of interactional skills and self-efficacy in language use (writing and speaking fluency, interactional skills & self-efficacy enhancement);
10. Discussing the story and the discussion questions helps learners learn new perspectives from their partners, view the issue from multiple perspectives, develop critical thinking skills, and build good relationships among themselves (critical thinking skills improvement and relationship building).

As discussed above, the linked-skills approach is well worth adopting because the sequencing of tasks a range of factors that meet linguistic, affective, and social goals of L2 learning, as summarized below:

1. Linguistic goals: Improving writing and oral fluency as well as receptive and productive knowledge of vocabulary (including functional multi-word units);
2. Affective goals: Nurturing intrinsic motivation, willingness to communicate, and self-efficacy;
3. Social goals: Building good relationships and facilitating cooperative learning.

If these goals are met, the linked-skills approach has the potential to improve English skills, especially interactional skills, but also critical thinking skills among learners in universities in Japan because the approach includes critical elements designed to improve writing and speaking fluency as core constructs of L2 interactional skills. As reviewed above, this approach includes input enhancement, rehearsal, the use of collocates and functional multi-word units, encouragement to speak, repetition, a meaning focus, deep and thoughtful processing, and automatization. Among these, the most critical factor appears to be the automatization of language units because it encourages and subsequently helps speakers perform conceptual, linguistic, and phonetic processes spontaneously (de Bot, 2004; Kormos, 2006), at least to the degree where such operations are conducted unconsciously (de John, 2017; Segalowitz, 2010). L2 literature postulates that multiple exposure to and use of focused items promote automatization and that this is a critical precursor to speaking and writing fluency development as well as that of the other two skills (i.e., reading and listening). Importantly, it is worth stressing here that automatized language operations do not require much working memory capacity or attentional resources, thereby enabling the speaker to deal with more substantial information instantaneously and efficiently (de Bot, 2004; de Jong, 2017; Segalowitz, 2010).

Thus, the linked-skills approach as major potential as part of CLIL-based teaching seems for the improvement of L2 oral fluency and interactional as well as critical thinking skills.

The Linked-Skills Approach as Project Activities

This section introduces an expanded teaching idea that illustrates the linked-skills approach: issue logs (Nation, 2015), a task the author has been using in his content-based university classes in Japan for a number of years and which has been consistently well-received by 3rd- and 4th-year English majors.

This task is in essence a project-type activity and is well-suited to the CLIL teaching framework in the sense that the materials are prepared by learners from authentic materials. The original task, which was developed by Nation (2015), was modified to suit the English proficiency, intellectual curiosity, and motivational levels of English majors. In this expanded project, students individually select a topic in which they are interested, look for a news article on that topic using social media, and prepare a summary, two discussion questions, and their opinion on the issues the news article raises outside of class. In class, they form pairs, take turns in reporting their summary, elicit their partner's opinions regarding the two discussion questions, and write these down in the issue log report. The process is then repeated with three different partners in eight class meetings over one month. At the end of the period, the students submit their report, describing their reflections on their engagement with the task and any benefits they may have derived from it along with their summaries, discussion questions, and their own opinions as well as those of their partners.

L2 literature (Nation, 2013; Onoda, 2014) shows that these expanded projects have similar—though more robust—effects on L2 learning, in addition to those discussed above, as follows:

1. Materials are selected and revised by the learners themselves (intrinsic motivation and willingness to communicate);
2. The language level is adjusted to the speakers' and listeners' capabilities (linguistic adjustment and comprehensible input and output);

3. Genuine interactions are generated in order to exchange information and opinions (authenticity);
4. Sequenced activities provide opportunities to learn cooperatively and give instant feedback to each other in pairs (cooperative learning and peer feedback and self-efficacy enhancement);
5. Repeated pair story-retelling and discussions enable learners to process language items deeply and thoughtfully and reinforce automatization (automatization and fluency development);
6. Exchanging information in pairs stimulates learners' interest and motivation, enriches their knowledge of the world as well as of language, and helps build rapport among them (intrinsic motivation and social learning);
7. Exchanging opinions provides a peer role model for speaking performance (Murphey & Arao, 2000) and the analysis of information as well as impetus for autonomous learning (Zimmerman, 2000) (role model, critical thinking, and autonomous learning or self-regulated learning).

Thus, this teaching approach helps learners engage in actively listening to each other's stories and responding to these with curious and critical minds, thus helping them build rapport and ultimately improve their English interactional skills (intrinsic motivation, critical thinking, and rapport, and interactional skills). Importantly, educational psychology literature lends robust support to the use of issue logs as an approach to promoting effective L2 learning. Finally, the task satisfies the three basic needs self-determination theory postulates (Deci & Ryan, 2000) humans are born with: autonomy, relatedness, and competence.

Taken together, issue log activities have major potential for helping learners engage in critically analyzing information and applying their knowledge to evaluating that information (critical thinking skills improvement) while improving their L2 interactional skills and oral fluency in English classrooms in Japanese universities (interactional skills improvement).

Group projects in CLIL-based teaching

Group projects are good candidates for the implementation of CLIL-based teaching. Various types of project work are reported in the literature on L2 teaching and learning (Gras-Velázquez, 2019) and educational psychology (Alacapinar, 2008) and a number studies have been conducted to investigate the effects of such project work on learning. Group project types vary from video production (Onoda, 2000) to group research (Onoda, 2019b) and problem-solving (Nation, 2013), whether pedagogically designed or as authentic activities. Regardless, project work in L2 learning minimally includes the following objectives:

1. Linguistic skills (e.g., the use of particular expressions to elicit other peoples' ideas, such as *What do you think are some of the negative effects of smartphone use among young people?*).
2. Academic skills (especially critical thinking skills, such as analyzing, comparing, and evaluating information from different perspectives);
3. Discussion and concluding skills (i.e., discussing the issue or problem and deciding on a conclusion based on a consensus);
4. Presentation skills (presenting the completed group project to the whole class effectively and intelligibly and eliciting their feedback) (Gras-Velázquez, 2019). Some examples of group projects are presented and explained in the following paragraphs in terms of the goals discussed above.

L2 literature indicates that project-based learning, whether as part of the content-based or the CLIL framework, yields positive effects on linguistic, affective, and social aspects of L2 learning. For example, studies conducted by Breidbach and Viebrock (2012) and Izumi, Ikeda, and Watanabe (2012) revealed that project-based learning improved social skills, autonomy, critical thinking skills, and self-efficacy as well as language skills, not only for highly proficient learners but also for low-proficiency learners. These studies found that both types of learners continued to see their language improve skills as they engaged in project-based learning, probably because such learning facilitates forced repetition (or "pushed output;" Nation & Newton, 2009), which in turn encourages learners to process language items both receptively and productively in their mental lexicon, thereby enhancing deep processing and facilitating automatization along with interactional skills and their self-efficacy in speaking.

The benefits of project-based learning appear to be substantiated by major principles in teaching materials and task design for L2 teaching, argued in L2 literature (Onoda, 2015; Tomlinson, 2013; Tomlinson & Masuhara, 2017). They include:

1. Facilitation of learners' emotional engagement;
2. Usefulness and value perceived by learners;
3. Generation of meaningful interactions using English;
4. Provision of sufficient guidance and support for the completion of activities;
5. Encouragement of cooperative learning and social learning; and
6. Enhanced learners' self-efficacy;

Most importantly, among the above-mentioned principles, employing project work as part of the CLIL approach facilitates self-regulated or autonomous language learning and appears to be supported by self-regulation literature that draws on social cognitive theory (Bandura, 1997) and self-determination theory (Deci & Ryan; 2000).

It is well-documented that that self-regulated (or autonomous) L2 learning contributes to the improvement of language skills (Onoda, 2012), including interactional skills as well as the use of self-regulation strategies, including metacognition, critical thinking, effort regulation, and peer learning (Pintrich & Zusho, 2002). Moreover, as discussed above, the use of project work within a CLIL approach facilitates self-regulation in a number of processes involved in the completion of the project. These include critical analysis of the project task, planning for completion of the project, selection of effective strategies, evaluation of information and ideas gathered, and reflection on the processes undertaken. Similarly, L2 and educational psychology literature (Onoda, 2012; Pintrich & Zusho, 2002; Zimmerman, 2000) indicates that that intrinsic motivation and self-efficacy influence the use of self-regulated learning strategies, which in turn improves academic achievement and both English speaking (especially, oral fluency and interactional skills) and listening skills (Onoda, 2012). Thus, the above-mentioned principles underlying materials and tasks development are closely connected to those underlying using project work within CLIL because this teaching endeavor stimulates perception of task value and intrinsic motivation and such principles are known to improve critical thinking skills, willingness to communicate, and interactional skills, which in turn enhances self-efficacy (Dörnyei, 2003; Onoda, 2012; Yashima, 2002).Taken together, the CLIL approach has significant potential for improving the English interactional skills as well as the critical thinking skills and self-efficacy in L2 learning and use of university students and pre-service teachers, especially by using English to communicate and to think deeply about how to proceed with and complete the group projects.

Finally, some studies (Izumi et al., 2012; Onoda, 2019a) report the pedagogical benefits of group research-based or problem-solving projects within a CLIL approach, which can be enumerated as follows:

1. Generation of abundant meaningful interaction (i.e., a large amount of rich comprehensible input and output) among learners, which improves interactional skills and facilitates language acquisition;
2. Helping learners learn words and phrases by being exposed to them and being forced to use them repeatedly (i.e., pushed output; Nation & Newton, 2009);
3. Encouraging learners to understand information deeply, critically analyzing it, and expressing their interpretations in English;
4. Enhancing learners' intrinsic motivation and self-efficacy for L2 use, which encourages autonomy in reading, listening, and analyzing information and ideas and communicating their interpretations in English;
5. Stimulating learners to be proactive in authentic communication over information and ideas for solving problems with group members;
6. Enabling learners to feel a sense of ownership of the ideas they discussed;

7. Allowing learners to contribute their particular skills to the completion of group projects and giving them a sense of achievement and evaluation.

In sum, the research-based problem-solving group project is an effective and promising approach to improving learners' critical thinking and interactional skills. However, as with all activities, some disadvantages are reported, including:

1. Not all members are actively and equally involved in every process of the project;
2. Some projects need a great deal of preparation and planning by the teacher;
3. Project work is costly in terms of time and patience and requires a high degree of professionalism from the teacher.

However, according to L2 literature, provided projects are well-designed, well-suited to learners' L2 proficiency and intellectual curiosity levels, and occasional pedagogical support is offered to them, research-based or problem-solving group projects generally yield substantial pedagogical benefits to learners.

Findings From Studies Conducted by Onoda (2013; 2015; 2018; 2019a; 2019b)

Onoda adopted various tasks (including group projects) and used them effectively in his CLIL-based undergraduate Social Issues courses and pre-service English education courses at a university in Japan for a number of years and observed a range of positive linguistic, affective, and social effects on the students' language learning. All of Onoda's studies employed a control and experimental group research design (in most cases with 25 to 30 students in each group) and quantitative data analysis (t-tests) triangulated by the use of qualitative data obtained through interviews, surveys, and the researcher's observation of the learners' engagement. In all of these studies, the participants were English majors (ranging from 2nd-year to 4th-year) in the same university in Japan and demonstrated upper-intermediate English proficiency levels as measured by KEPT (Kanda English Proficiency Test, 2007), with mean scores ranging 3.8 to 4.2 on a 5-point Likert scale measuring speaking skills and by TOEFL ITP, with mean scores ranging from 512.5 to 525.5.

The following paragraph present brief explanations of these studies and their findings along with feedback from participants in the each of the tasks and projects.

1. Onoda (2013) investigated the effects of a teaching approach integrating the four skills within the framework of linked-skills tasks on English speaking fluency development in Japanese university classrooms. Students were instructed to

watch an easy news clip, then read the text, answer comprehension questions, write a summary and reaction, and speak about it to a few partners. This teaching approach is reported to improve speaking fluency as a core element of interactional skills. The rationale derived from the argument by Segalowitz (2010) that speaking fluency and interactional skills development necessitates automatization of language items and that sequenced tasks encourage students to recycle and process vocabulary deeply and thoughtfully (i.e., using the same words a number of times and in multiple contexts), and use formulaic sequences in order to strengthen automatization of the language items they contain. The intervention was conducted in 2nd-year content-based English classes that met twice a week for one entire academic year. Data were gathered from tests administered at the beginning and end of the year. Speaking fluency was measured using an interview test that assessed rate of speech and using the KEPT (2007) speaking section, which uses a group discussion task to elicit speech production. Quantitative findings from both tests showed that speaking fluency significantly, thus lending robust support to the implementation of the linked-skills teaching approach for the improvement of speaking fluency and thereby interactional skills.

2. Onoda (2015) examined the effects of issue logs on L2 oral fluency as a core construct of L2 interactional skills in Japanese university classrooms. In issue logs activities (Nation, 2013), as explained above, students identify a TV news clip or article on their favorite topic, form pairs, and report the story with discussion questions and their opinions to their partners, repeating the process with three different partners. Results show that issue log pair projects enhance learners' intrinsic motivation, promote more active engagement and interaction during the project, and encourage deeper processing of language items and content. As a result, students' critical thinking skills, willingness to communicate, and L2 oral fluency all improved, which concurred with the findings of Onoda (2013).

3. Onoda (2018) study, which was conducted with English majors, indicated that pair project work using linked-skills group projects was effective, as in Onoda (2013), in improving self-efficacy and motivation for using the L2 as well as L2 oral fluency.

4. Studies conducted with 3rd- and 4th-year pre-service English teachers revealed similar results. For example, in his recent study with 3rd- and 4th-year English majors enrolled in undergraduate English teacher education programs at a university in Japan, Onoda (2019a) investigated the effects of group projects on the improvement of the L2 interactional and critical thinking skills that are critical to implementing effective teaching. This study introduced the CLIL approach in English teaching methodology courses, with a primary focus on the

use of authentic problem-solving group projects. The courses were offered to students wishing to obtain secondary school English teaching licenses, and the classes met twice a week, with 30 meetings per term over two academic terms. Participants' English interactional skills were measured using the speaking section of the KEPT (2007) test at the beginning and end of the research period. In addition, interviews were conducted with two focal groups of students and questionnaires administered to measure their perceptions of changes in their critical thinking skills related to the teaching approaches they learned about as well as their perceptions of improvements in their interactional skills.
   a. Close analysis of the quantitative and qualitative data showed that their L2 speaking fluency and interactional skills significantly improved and that their critical thinking skills were also enhanced, lending support to the pedagogical value of authentic problem-solving group projects for students' knowledge and language skills development within a CLIL-based approach in undergraduate English teacher education programs. Onoda concluded that the use of such projects probably satisfied the human need for competence, autonomy, and relatedness postulated by social cognitive theory (Bandura, 1997). In brief, group projects encourage learners to take control of their learning by exercising autonomy and to proceed cooperatively with the project on the basis of consensus among group members over the procedure, thereby facilitating social learning and finally bringing them a sense of achievement and self-efficacy.
5. In another study, Onoda (2019b) employed interactive pair presentations with small-group discussion with undergraduate pre-service EFL teachers (3rd and 4th year university students) in an English teacher education programs in Japan. Their English proficiency (including oral fluency and interactional skills) was measured on KEPT (2007) at the beginning and end of the first term of one academic year in the same fashion as in Onoda (2019a).

In the English teaching methodology classes that met twice a week, participants in an experimental group (25 students) learned about teaching approaches and their theoretical underpinnings, presented the main points of a chapter in the textbook, and engaged their peers in small-group discussions, with participants interacting as they expressed their interpretations, opinions, and learning experiences regarding specific aspects of the presentation. Meanwhile, a control group also presented the main points of a chapter in the textbook but in a teacher-led interactive session aiming to clarify participants' understanding of key concepts by inviting them to participate in small group discussions.

Results show that pair presentations with small-group discussion (the experimental condition) raise participants' intrinsic motivation for authentic interaction and facilitate collaborative learning, which in turn enhances their interactional as well as critical thinking skills, self-efficacy, and a feeling of belonging to a supportive learning community.

Taken together, the group projects reviewed above were shown to be effective in improving students' L2 interactional skills, critical thinking skills, and self-efficacy, as well as intrinsic motivation. However, caution should be exercised since these participants' English proficiency was limited to upper-intermediate levels. Replication studies using participants with different proficiency levels (such as lower intermediate and intermediate levels) should be conducted to verify the findings.

Feedback From Students on Selected Group Project Tasks

Please note that the examples of feedback below are extracted from Onoda (2019a, 2019b) and that comments on linked skills are omitted while those on issue logs are included because, as discussed above, issue logs can be an expanded into linked-skills activities and comments on issue logs may clarify the benefits of these activities better. Please note that the numbers in parentheses indicate the numbers of students out of 20 who made comments similar to those summarized here and judged to fall into the same category.

ISSUE LOG TASKS

1. Linguistic Benefits

By focusing on the same topic, learners repeatedly used the same words and phrases, which helped improve their oral fluency and ease. In addition, the subsequent story-retelling and discussion tasks encouraged effective reading, i.e., reading for main ideas. While they were reading, they thought about key words and how they would write a summary effectively so that they could tell it to their partners. In addition, by discussing the issues, they learned to analyze the information from different perspectives and expanded their views. Finally, the issue log task encouraged them to write and speak intensively with their partners.

2. Affective Benefits

Participants found it pleasurable to retell stories on a topic they liked, saw their partners showing interest in listening to them, sensed that their expertise was appreciated by others, and felt competent because they were treated like experts. In addition, following multiple story-retelling practice on the same topic, their story-retelling became easier and more natural, which made them more motivated and confident.

3. Social Benefits

Participants talked and expanded their horizons on the interpretation of the story they had chosen by getting feedback (comments and questions) from their partners. Equally importantly, they found it beneficial to hear about stories others were interested in because this expanded their views and helped them understand the issues more deeply. Finally, through story-retelling and discussion, they learned about other persons' values and ways of life.

AUTHENTIC GROUP PROBLEM-SOLVING PROJECTS

1. Linguistic Benefits

Problem-solving group projects were effective for integrating SLA theories and teaching skills, which facilitated deeper and critical learning of related theories while improving participants' English speaking and reading ability. In addition, while engaged in problem-solving group projects, they learned new ideas from group members and others, which were useful for understanding SLA theories and teaching methods and their practical application to teaching settings. Learning second language acquisition and teaching methodologies in English was effective for their academic English learning. Furthermore, the projects encouraged them to speak and discuss using a large amount in English because the projects used many key words and phrases encountered in the textbook. Participants first found using technical terms in speech difficult but gradually and with group members' help, they learned to discuss topics using this vocabulary. Finally, critiquing sessions offered opportunities for interactions and were highly effective because listening to other people's opinions helped participants expand their horizons and encouraged them to learn what they did not known. Finally, the critiquing sessions provided opportunities for participants to think about issues deeply from multiple perspectives, including individual learner differences, teaching approaches, and their own various learning experiences.

2. Affective Benefits

Group projects motivated participants to read the textbook deeply and think critically about the issues from many perspectives. Analyzing and solving real-life pedagogical problems stimulated their intellectual curiosity and stimulated their motivation to proactively undertake the necessary cooperative information searching and problem analyzing.

3. Social Benefits

Approaching problems from multiple perspectives facilitated cooperative learning and assisted participants in learning from one another, thus enabling a deeper understanding than they would have reached on their own. Through their longitudinal engagement with the projects from analysis of the problem to presentation of their solution, they got to know one another well and built close relationships among themselves such that they could share a common sense of achievement.

Issue Logs

The following is a transcript of the oral performance demonstrated by a student in an issue log activity:

I … recently… heard an interesting story about … negative effect … of smartphone … people. Do you use … smart phone … often? Can you think of … negative effects? British government recently did research ... with people in … 20s, 30s, and … 40s, and 50s. The result was … many people are … ad … addict… and … their life … communication … changed. Some people can't stop using … them … in … important meeting. Also, when they eat … meals with … family, they put smartphone … on the table and keep looking it … or checking email… So … now family … do not talk to each other … as much as… they talked. Experts say … the increased use of smartphones … have been … caused … by people's working style changes. As you can imagine, nowadays … more people do not go to workplaces … every day … but they work at home … They communicate with their workplaces … using email, for example, for three days a week …, but for two days they go to workplaces and talk to the staff. So communicating by email have been increasing. And … what is worse … children imitate their parents … and use smartphones … until they go to bed. So they use them … more often than before. This has caused another problem. Children do not sleep long enough … and they do not study … much. I think it is a serious situation. Do you agree? Well, in order to improve the situation, the government said … parents and children should limit the smartphone times at home … and parents … should talk to their children at home. These are the main points of the news story…

Suggested Group Projects

English Majors Taking CLIL-Based Courses (English III)

Participants were 3rd- and 4th-year English majors with English proficiency levels ranging from 480 to 635 on TOEFL ITP. The course was named "Exploring Social Issues Reflected in the World of Media" and was one of a number of the five courses students were required to take during their 3rd and 4th years and could select from the online syllabus.

As a final task, they were required to conduct a group research project. Working in groups of two or three, they chose a topic about a social issue, designed a survey, and interviewed 30 people. If time was short, they could conduct an online survey instead. The survey had to have at least 12 questions, including questions about the participants' demographic data, including age, gender, and occupation. Participants then analyzed the data and presented their findings to the class using visual aids such as *PowerPoint*. Each group member had to speak for at least 10 minutes. Students were given the following template for guidance:

Hello, my name is XXX, and this is YYY. We are conducting a survey with people we know as our final project in Prof. Onoda's English III course (a CLIL-based course focusing on learning social issues reflected in media). We would appreciate if you could answer the following questions. We guarantee that we will use your responses for the purpose of this project only and that you will not be identified in any way. (In cases of online surveying, if you have questions, do not hesitate to contact us). Finally, if you do not wish to share your ideas, we understand, and you are free to opt out.

Q1. Please specify your gender: Female / Male (Circle one)
Q2. What is your age? ____
Q3. Are you happy with your life right now? Indicate your degree of happiness on the following scale:

5 (very happy) – 4 (happy) – 3 (neither happy nor unhappy) – 2 (unhappy) – 1 (very unhappy)

Q4. What makes your life very happy or unhappy? List three factors that make you happy or unhappy.
Q5. What has been the happiest experience of your life so far?
Q6. What are some of your hopes regarding your future life? List three hopes.
Q7. What causes stress for you?
Q8. What has been the most stressful experience of your life so far?

Q9. How do you think your future will turn out? Indicate your prediction on the following scale.

5 (a lot easier) – 4 (easier) – 3 (neither easier nor harder) – 2 (harder) – 1 (a lot harder)

Q10. Why do you think so?
Q11. What are some of your worries about your future? List three sources of worry.
Q12. If you were rich and free, what would you like to do? List three wishes.

PRE-SERVICE TEACHERS IN UNDERGRADUATE ENGLISH TEACHER EDUCATION COURSES

English Teacher Education Course Group Project

As a final task in this course, participants engaged in a real-life group problem-solving group project. They were required to consider the objectives of the task, form groups of two or three, choose a pedagogical problem, and follow the steps below as closely as possible. Each group then presented their ideas to the class for 30-40 minutes and then elicited feedback from the audience. After the presentation, students handed in a group report, including their reflections on the ideas they presented.

1. Objectives

a. Improving students' English interactional skills, including the use of functional multiword units and formulaic expressions;
b. Developing higher-order thinking skills (i.e., critical thinking and creative thinking skills);
c. Raising awareness levels over the value of generating solutions to real-life pedagogical problems though collaboration.

   2. Steps

d. Pairs or groups of three students selected a common pedagogical problem they may encounter when they become teachers;
e. Students proposed possible teaching solutions by drawing on second language acquisition theories and teaching ideas described in the textbook: *Teaching ESL/EFL Listening and Speaking* (Nation & Newton, 2009) as well as other

available resources such as websites, news articles, and the views of experts in the field;
f. Students discussed the feasibility and possible effects of these ideas and selected one idea that best suited the problem they selected;
g. Students made a pedagogical plan for implementing the idea and solving (or at least minimizing) the problem;
h. Students presented the teaching idea to the whole class, including the reasons for their choice, and considered critiques and alternatives by eliciting feedback from other students in the class.

3. Real-Life Pedagogical Problems

i. A junior high school student tells you she can't memorize words effectively and often forgets what she studied the very next day. How can you help this student memorize words and retain them for a longer period?
j. A sixth-grade student likes to play baseball. He also wants to be able to speak English and listens to the NHK English Learning Program *Kisoeigo 3* every evening. However, his listening and speaking skills have not improved. How can you help him develop these skills?
k. A first-year university student has very weak L2 reading skills, reading almost word by word, so slowly that she immediately forgets what she read. As a result, she doesn't like reading or learning grammar and vocabulary. How can you help her improve her reading speed and encourage her to read with ease and confidence?

CONCLUSION

As discussed above and as the studies cited indicate, the use of group projects within the framework of the CLIL approach is effective in enhancing the L2 interactional and critical thinking skills of university English majors in Japan. These effects might be due to several factors:

1. Repetition and pushed output encourage learners to process key language items both receptively (reading and listening) and productively (speaking and writing) and thus promotes deep processing and facilitating automatization. Importantly, the resulting enhanced interactional skills improve their self-efficacy in speaking.
2. Learners benefit from being intellectually stimulated to analyze issues from multiple perspectives, apply their knowledge to them, identify possible solutions,

and evaluate their own ideas by eliciting feedback and alternative ideas from peers. As the process involves both cooperative learning and autonomy, it motivates learners to be engaged in critical thinking activities, yielding a sense of achievement and confidence.

REFERENCES

Alacapinar, F. (2008). Effectiveness of project-based learning. *Eurasian Journal of Educational Research, 32*, 17–35.

Bandura, A. (1997). *Self-efficacy: The exercise of control*. Freeman.

Beglar, D. (2017). *Teaching speaking: The key is scaffolding*. Paper presented at the 2017 International JALT Conference, Tsukuba.

Borg, S. (2013). *Teacher research in language teaching: A critical analysis*. Cambridge University Press.

Breidbach, S., & Viebrock, B. (2012). CLIL in Germany: Results from recent research in a contested field of education. *International CLIL Research Journal, 1*(4), 21–35.

Coyle, D. (2012). *CLIL: Content and Language Integrated Learning*. Cambridge University Press.

Coyle, D. (2013). Listening to learners: An investigation into successful learning across CLIL contexts. *International Journal of Bilingual Education and Bilingualism, 16*(3), 244–266. doi:10.1080/13670050.2013.777384

de Bot, K. (2004). *The psycholinguistics of multilingualism*. Benjamins.

de Jong, N. (2017). Fluency in second language assessment. In D. Tsagari & J. Banerjee (Eds.), *Handbook of second language assessment* (pp. 203–218). Mouton de Gruyter.

Deci, E. L., & Ryan, R. M. (2000). The what and why of goal pursuits: Human needs and the self-determination of behavior. *Psychological Inquiry, 11*(4), 227–268. doi:10.1207/S15327965PLI1104_01

DeKeyser, R. (2007). *Practice in a second language: Perspectives from applied linguistics and cognitive psychology*. Cambridge University Press. doi:10.1017/CBO9780511667275

Dörnyei, A. (2003). Attitudes, orientations, and motivations in language learning: Advances in theory, research, and applications. *Language Learning, 53*(S1), 3–32. doi:10.1111/1467-9922.53222

Ellis, R., & Shintani, N. (2013). *Exploring language pedagogy through second language acquisition research*. Routledge. doi:10.4324/9780203796580

Gras-Velázquez, A. (2019). *Project-based learning in second language acquisition: Building communities of practice in higher education*. Routledge. doi:10.4324/9780429457432

Izumi, S., Ikeda, M., & Watanabe, Y. (2012). CLIL: Content and language integrated learning: New challenges in foreign language education at Sophia University: Vol. 2. *Practices and Applications*. Sophia University Press.

Kanda, E. P. T. (2007). *KEPT*. Kanda University of International Studies.

Kormos, J. (2006). *Speech production and second language acquisition*. Lawrence Erlbaum Associates.

Ministry of Education, Culture, Science, Sports, and Technology – MEXT. (2017). *Report on the survey of English language skills of English teachers in Japan*. Retrieved from: http://www.mext.go.jp/component/a_menu/education/detail/__icsFiles/afieldfile/201 7/04/07/1384236_01_1.pdf

Murphey, T., & Arao, H. (2001). Reported belief changes through near-peer role modeling. *TESL-EJ, 5*(3).

Nation, I. S. P. (2013). *What should every EFL teacher know?* Compass.

Nation, I. S. P. (2014). Developing fluency. In T. Muller, J. Adamson, P. S. Brown, & S. Herder (Eds.), *Exploring EFL fluency in Asia* (pp. 11–25). Palgrave Macmillan.

Nation, I. S. P. (2015). *Learning vocabulary in another language* (2nd ed.). Cambridge University Press.

Nation, I. S. P., & Newton, J. (2009). *Teaching ESL/EFL listening and speaking*. Routledge.

Nishino, T., & Watanabe, M. (2008). Communication-oriented policies versus classroom realities in Japan. *TESOL Quarterly, 42*(1), 133–138. doi:10.1002/j.1545-7249.2008.tb00214.x

Onoda, S. (2000). Effectiveness of adopting productive activities in Media English learning with a primary focus on the use of group projects. *Journal of Current English Studies, 39*, 87–102.

Onoda, S. (2012). Effects of repetition of selected news stories on speaking fluency in Media English learning. *Media English and Communication*, *1*, 89–105.

Onoda, S. (2014). An exploration of effective teaching approaches for enhancing the oral fluency of EFL students. In T. Muller, J. Adamson, P. S. Brown, & S. Herder (Eds.), *Exploring EFL fluency in Asia* (pp. 120–142). Palgrave Macmillan.

Onoda, S. (2015). Effects of issue logs on L2 oral fluency development. *Proceedings of the 4th Annual International Conference on Language, Literature, & Linguistics* (pp. 156-163). Singapore: Global Science and Technology Forum. 10.5176/2251-3566_L315.29

Onoda, S. (2019a). Effects of CLIL-based approaches on pre-service teachers' learning in teacher education programs. In R. Raul & A. Lopes (Eds.), *Current issues in language teaching* (pp. 111–122). Editorial Académica Española.

Onoda, S. (2019b). Enhancing L2 interactional skills through interactive pair presentations with small-group discussion. *JALT CUE Journal*, *37*(1), 25–37.

Onoda, S., & Miyashita, O. (2018). Improving learners' interactional skills through innovative undergraduate English teacher education programs. *Juntendo Journal of Global Studies*, *3*, 45–60.

Onoda, S., Miyashita, O., & Yoshino, Y. (2017). Innovating in undergraduate English teacher education programs. *Juntendo Journal of Global Studies*, *2*, 58–65.

Pintrich, P. R., & Zusho, A. (2002). The development of academic self-regulation: The role of cognitive and motivational factors. In A. Wigfield & J. S. Eccles (Eds.), *Development of achievement motivation* (pp. 249–284). Academic Press. doi:10.1016/B978-012750053-9/50012-7

Sato, K. (2012). *Changing a teaching culture: From individual practice to curriculum development*. Paper presented at the 2012 International JALT conference, Nagoya.

Segalowitz, N. (2010). *The cognitive bases of second language fluency*. Routledge. doi:10.4324/9780203851357

Tomlinson, B. (2013). Introduction: Principles and procedure of material development. In B. Tomlinson (Ed.), *Materials development in language teaching* (2nd ed., pp. 25–47). Cambridge University Press.

Tomlinson, B., & Masuhara, H. (2018). *The complete guide to the theory and practice of materials development for language learning*. Wiley Blackwell.

Vázquez, C. P., Molina, M. P., & López, D. J. A. (2014). Perceptions of teachers and students of the promotion of interaction through task-based activities in CLIL. *Porta Linguarum: Revista Internacional de Didáctica de las Lenguas Extranjeras, 23*, 75–91.

Yamazaki, A. (2006). Eigokakyosyokukatei no genjo to kadai [Current situation and problems of university English teacher education programs]. *Musashi University of Technology. Faculty of Environment and Technology Journal, 7*, 103–112.

Yashima, T. (2002). Willingness to communicate in a second language: The Japanese EFL context. *Modern Language Journal, 86*(1), 54–66. doi:10.1111/1540-4781.00136

Zimmerman, B. J. (2000). Attaining self-regulation: A social cognitive perspective. In M. Boekaerts, P. R. Pintrich, & M. Zeidner (Eds.), *Handbook of self-regulation: Theory, research, and applications* (pp. 13–39). Academic Press. doi:10.1016/B978-012109890-2/50031-7

Chapter 10
The Major Developments of Learner Language From Second Language Acquisition to Learner Corpus Research

Aicha Rahal
Aix-Marseille University, France

ABSTRACT

Given the fact that there is a constant debate among monolinguists and pluralists, this chapter aims to explore the main developments in learner language. It focuses on the changes from second language research to learner corpus research. It is an attempt to present second language theories. Then, the chapter draws a particular attention to the limitations of second language acquisition. The discussion turns to learner corpus research to show how language changes from heterogeneinity to diversity. Language is no longer seen as monolithic entity or a standard variety but a multilingual entity.

INTRODUCTION

Second Language researchers (Selinker, 1972; Han, 2005,2004; Ellis, 1994) see learner language as a deviation. According to them, Second language learners' competence depends on a continuum between the first language and the second language. If learners produce output different from Standard English, it is considered as an error. In this context, it has been claimed that L2 learners develop a unique linguistic system, different from both the first language and the target language (TL).

DOI: 10.4018/978-1-7998-2831-0.ch010

The Major Developments of Learner Language From Second Language Acquisition

This linguistic system is called approximative system (Nemser, 1971), idiosyncratic dialects or transitional dialects (Corder, 1971) and interlanguage (Selinker, 1972).

Cook (1993) further argues that "L2 learning only as a relationship between the L1 and the L2. A learner at a particular point in time is in fact using a language system that is neither the L1 nor the L2. Describing it in terms of the L1 and the L2 misses the distinctive features of L2 learning: "a third language system is involved –that of the L2 learner– which also needs to be described" (p. 17). The system of Learner language was investigated by many researchers and they tried to show the effect of these systems on the acquisition of the target language. Based on this perspective, there are different theories, namely the Contrastive Analysis theory, the Error Analysis theory and the Interlanguage theory. "The learner language is viewed as an independent social and psychological phenomenon…It is not a defective version of something else: a chrysalis is simply a chrysalis, not a deformed or defective butterfly" (Phillipson, et al., 1991, p. 61).

Learner Corpus Research studies show that learner language is a creation. They argue for the plural aspect of learner language. Learner Corpus Research has relations with English as a Lingua Franca (ELF). Sridhar and Sridhar (1986) point out, "what is needed is a reevaluation of the applicability of SLA theories to the particular circumstances in which [World Englishes] are acquired" (p.4). They criticized second language acquisition research in particular and applied linguistics in general for relying on "the traditional monolingual conception of bilinguals as being two monolinguals rather than different people from monolinguals in L1" (Cook, 2013, pp. 37-38).

One of the main differences is that Second Language Acquisition studies concentrate on competence. Ellis (1994) states that "the main goal of SLA research is to characterize learners' underlying knowledge of the L2, i.e. to describe and explain their competence" (p.13). Learner Corpus Research studies, on the other hand, focus on performance. Their main aim is to describe the use of language by learners in actual production.

The main objectives of this chapter are to review the major developmental stages of learner language, starting from second language acquisition to learner corpus research. It will also review the major theories in second language acquisition. Methodologically, the proposed study will present the different methodologies that appeared in the developmental stages of learner language. The majority of learner corpus studies are based on raw data. Learner corpora need to be authentic "gathered from the genuine communications of people going about their normal business" (Sinclair, 1996).

Second Language Acquisition

Ellis (1994) defines SLA as "the study of how learners learn an additional language after they have acquired their mother tongue" (p. 5). It refers to the process of mastering a target language after mastering the native language. In defining SLA, Ellis makes the distinction between two processes, namely acquisition and learning. Acquisition refers to "picking up a second language unconsciously through exposure", whereas learning is "the conscious study of an L2" (Ellis, 1994, p. 6).

SECOND LANGUAGE THEORIES

There are a number of second language theories that were developed to investigate learners' acquisition of the target language. These include the contrastive analysis theory, the error analysis theory and the interlanguage theory.

Contrastive Analysis Theory

CA theory developed in 1950s and 1960s. Wilkins claims that "the errors and difficulties that occur in our learning and use of a foreign language are caused by the interference of our mother tongue. Whenever the structure of the second language differs from that of the mother tongue, we can expect both, difficulty in learning and errors in performance" (1972, p.198). This theory is based on 'habit formation'. It conveys the principles of the behaviourist view that "We learn what we do" (Wilkins, 1974, p. 197). It is considered as "an individual tends to transfer the features of his native language to the second language, a comparative study will be useful for the purpose of identifying the likeness and difference between the languages and this enables the linguist to predict areas of difficulty for second language learner" (Stern, 1987, p.159).

Lado (1957, p.vii) argues that contrastive analysis is based on an analysis of the two languages, native language and the target one, for the purpose of overcoming L1 interference: "…the comparison of any two languages and cultures [is] to discover and describe the problems that the speakers of one of the languages will have in learning the other…"

Hassan, Baghdady, and Buslama (1993) argue that:

… it is difficult to fully assess contrastive error analysis because the discipline is very cautious in stating its assumption such as "the most important factor determining ease and difficulty" or "the chief source of the difficulty" (Lado, 1964) … But we

cannot take these reserved expressions into consideration too seriously as long as we have no statistical data to support them. (p.13)

Error Analysis Theory

Error analysis theory believes in the importance of learners' errors which represent a tool to implement the best pedagogy and to choose the suitable methodology. According to Sharma (1980), "Error analysis can thus provide a strong support to remedial teaching". Corder (1974) also states that "The study of errors is part of the investigation of the process of language learning. In this respect it resembles methodologically the study of the acquisition of the mother tongue. It provides us with a picture of the linguistic development of a learner and may give us indications as to the learning process" (p.125). Errors are also a way to know how the system of the language works and this is clearly shown in Corder's (1971) words "A learner's errors, then, provide evidence of the system of the language that he is using (i.e. has learned) at a particular point in the course" (Richard, 1985, p.63).

Error Analysis theory has its limitations. One of the major limitations is that it "fails to provide a complete picture of learner language", and researchers "need to know what learners do correctly as well as what they do wrongly" (Ellis, 1994, p. 67). Additionally, Ellis (2008) mentions another reason for the shortcoming of EA theory, stating that this weakness is due to "weaknesses in methodological procedures, theoretical problems, and limitations in scope"

Interlanguage Theory

According to Stern (1983), "the concept of interlanguage was suggested by Selinker in order to draw attention to the possibility that the learner's language can be regarded a distinct language variety or system with its own particular characteristics or rules" (p.125). As illustrated in the following figure, L2 learning is a non-linear and fragmentary process. It is characterized by fast progression of certain linguistic areas, slow movements of others. Benson (2002) also argues, "Interlanguage (the learner' interim grammar of the L2) is not fixed and rigid like the L1, but 'permeable'" (p. 69).

According to Selinker, IL represents "a metamorphically halfway house between L1 and L2" (Platon, 2013, p.6). McLaughlin (1987) states that 'interlanguage' means "(1) the learner's system at a single point in time and (2) the range of interlocking systems that characterizes the development of learners over time" (p. 60). In Crystal's (2003) words, IL is

The linguistic system created by someone in the course of learning a foreign language, different from either the speaker's first language or the target language

being acquired. It reflects the learner's evolving system of rules, and results from a variety of processes, including the influence of the first language ('transfer'), contrastive interference from the target language, and the overgeneralization of newly encountered rules. (p. 239)

Selinker (1972) provides five processes involved in second language learning, namely language transfer, the transfer of training, strategies of second language learning, strategies of second language communication, and overgeneralization.

Language Transfer

Language Transfer is also called L1 interference. Gass and Selinker (2008) state that "...the learner is transferring prior linguistic knowledge resulting in IL forms which, when compared by the researcher to the target language norms, can be termed positive, negative, or neutral" (p.6).

Transfer of Training

Transfer of Training refers to the effect of some language rules on the learning of others. According to the *Encyclopedic Dictionary of Applied Linguistics* (1999), "...language teaching itself creates language rules that are not part of the L2" (p.175).

Strategies of Second Language Learning

Strategies of learning are methods used by learners to master the TL. They are defined by the *Encyclopedic Dictionary of Applied Linguistics* (1999) as "techniques used by second language learners for remembering and organizing samples of the L2" (p.195).

Strategies of Second Language Communication

Strategies of communication (henceforth CS) are strategies used by learners to overcome communication difficulties. According to the *Encyclopedic Dictionary of Applied Linguistics* (1999), CSs are defined as "techniques for maintaining or repairing a dialogue with an interlocutor when it is in danger of breaking down" (p.195).

Overgeneralization of Target Language Linguistic Materials

Overgeneralization appears when former learning interferes in the learning of new forms and rules. It "…covers instances where the learner creates a deviant structure on the basis of his experience of other structure in the target language" (Richards, 1973, p.99).

These processes can prevent learners from acquiring native like competence. According to Schwartz (1997), most adult second language learners never acquire a second or a foreign language and their ILs can cease to develop at a certain stage. This cessation of learning is what linguists called fossilization. Nemser (1971) refers to fossilization as a "permanent intermediate system and subsystem" (p.14). Similarly, Selinker (1996) defines fossilization as "a process whereby the learner creates a cessation of interlanguage learning, thus stopping the interlanguage from developing…" (cited in Han, 2004, p.15).

According to Selinker (1996), it is defined as:

The process whereby the learner creates a cessation of interlanguage learning, thus stopping the interlanguage from developing, it is hypothesized in a permanent way…The argument is that no adult can hope to ever speak a second language in such a way that s/he is indistinguishable from native speaker of that language. (cited in Han, 2004, p.15)

Han (2004) defines fossilization as the "phenomenon of non-progression of learning despite continuous exposure to input, adequate motivation to learner, and sufficient opportunity for practice" (p.13). She further explains this linguistic phenomenon by station that:

Fossilization – in the eyes of many – is a product as well as a process; it affects the entire IL system as well as its sub-systems; it is literally permanent as well as relatively permanent; it is persistent and resistant; for some researchers it happens to every learner and for others to only some learners. (p. 218)

It seems that there is a common agreement on the definition of fossilization. All the researchers cited above agree that this linguistic phenomenon refers to the permanent cessation of the development of learners' linguistic system overtime.

Studies Conducted on Second Language Acquisition

There are a number of researchers who investigated the role of language interference in the acquisition of a second or a foreign language. Taher (2011) investigated grammatical errors produced by Swedish junior high school students. It was found that the common errors among the participants are verb tense, verb inflection and subject-verb agreement. The researcher explained that the errors are the result of the lack of grammatical knowledge and the incorrect transfer from Swedish into English.

Solano, et al. (2014) conducted a study on Spanish interference in EFL writing skills. The study investigates native language interference toward English Foreign Language writing skills in the written output of Senior High School students in Ecuador. The informants were 351 students from second year senior high school. The students were asked to write a narrative passage. The result showed that most frequent first language interference are misuse of verbs, omission of personal and object pronouns, misuse of prepositions, overuse of articles, and incorrect word order.

Other researchers investigated errors on the written and spoken output of their participants. Hamdi (2005) identified written grammatical errors in the written tasks of 18 third year students from ISEAH Institute of Kef, Tunisia. They were studying Business English. The results presented some difficulties in writing that faced the participants, including prepositions, articles, wrong usage of tenses, verbs and relative pronouns.

Hamdi (2016) also analyzed lexical errors in the English compositions of 20 EFL Tunisian students from ISEAH Institute of Kef, Tunisia. The most frequently reported difficulties in writing involve lexical formal errors, such as suffixation, omissions, over-inclusion and misselection. These can be attributed to several factors, such as fossilization, hypercorrection, faulty teaching and inadequate learning.

Another trend of researchers has focused on IL theory and they investigated learners' IL overtime. Yahya (1980), for example, studied grammatical fossilization made by 59 Tunisian English students from the faculty of Letters and Humanities of Tunis. The informants were in their third year. The researcher collected the written compositions of the informants two times. The results demonstrated that there are many grammatical errors that become persistent. These include prepositions, negation, articles and verbs.

Similarly, Al-Jamal (2017) investigated the fossilized writing errors of EFL Jordanian postgraduate students. The study consists of four phases. The subjects were asked to write four essays at four different times. Based on the results, errors were grouped into structure, article, punctuation, coherence, cohesion, spelling, word form, unnecessary word and others. The results showed that the participants' errors did not drop throughout the four essays.

In a similar research vein, Rahal (2016) has conducted a study on the fossilized pronunciation in the speech of 20 students from the English department of Kairouan. The researcher used an eighteen-month longitudinal study to investigate their IL and to try to show the existence of fossilization. Based on the results, the informants made a number of errors in times 1, 2 and 3. The longitudinal study showed that there are errors that disappeared and there are a number of errors that repeated in times 2 and 3.

Recently, Yakout and Amel (2019) have investigated the persistent pronunciation of the voiceless dental fricative, and the voiced dental fricative sounds in the speech of 20 first-year EFL Students from Tahri Mohamed University, Bechar, Algeria. The results demonstrated that the students tend to pronounce the /t/ and /d/ sounds instead of / θ/ and / ð /. Mother tongue is one of the factors that are attributed to fossilization.

Bias in Second Language Research

The field of SLA was criticized for its support of the view of monolingualism. Some researchers claim that SLA "suffer[s] in its very core... from the ailments that result from taking nativeness and monolingualism as natural organizing principles" (Jenkins, 2006, Sridhar, 1994). Additionally, SLA research has viewed L2 learning from a monolingual standard and they neglected bilinguals and multilinguals. Romaine (1989) insists "it is clear that a reasonable account of bilingualism cannot be based on a theory which assumes monolingual competence as its frame of reference" (p.282). Bilingualism and multilingualism seem to be invisible in SLA research.

Granger (2002) points out that "much current SLA research favours experimental, metalinguistic and introspective data, and tends to be dismissive of natural language use data" (p.5). Based on this argument, it seems clear that SLA researchers still rely on experimental and introspective methods and they are still oriented towards to traditional view of language. Ortega (2010) argues that both nativeness and monolingualism cannot be applied in the study of additional language learning. He calls for abandoning these principles.

Corpus Linguistics: Brief History

The first corpora for the study of language were in the early of the 19th century with the German researcher, Kading, who compiled a huge corpus of 11 million German words. The scholars used his corpus to collect and combine frequency distributions of letters and sequences of letters (McEnery and Wilson, 1996). Corpus-based methodologies were used in different fields. Linguists of the structuralist tradition, for instance, used this methodology to investigate some features in phonetics and grammar (McEnery, Xiao, and Tono, 2005).

The field of language pedagogy also used corpora to create lists of lexical items for second or foreign language learners (McEnery and Wilson, 1996).

Learner Corpus Research

Learner corpus is defined by Granger (2002, p. 7) as "electronic collections of authentic FL/SL textual data assembled according to explicit design criteria for a particular SLA/FLT purpose. They are encoded in a standardized and homogeneous way and documented as to their origin and provenance."

Learner corpus research has special components. These include corpus linguistics expertise, a good background in linguistic theory, knowledge of SLA theory, and a good understanding of foreign language teaching issues (Granger, 2009). Furthermore, Matsumoto (2008) lists the positive potential of learner corpora for language pedagogy: "(i) they can help to decide what features should be particularly emphasized in teaching or even lead to the introduction of so far neglected elements; (ii) results from learner corpus studies can give indications on how to teach certain features; and (iii) results on developmental sequences can help to determine in what order language features should be taught (p.129).

Learner corpus is considered as a pedagogical tool to develop teaching methods. Granger (2003) claims that "learner corpus research opens up exciting pedagogical perspectives in a wide range of areas of English language teaching (ELT) pedagogy: materials design, syllabus design, language testing, and classroom methodology" (p.542). Osborne (2001) further shows the benefits of using corpus data which "not only increases the chances of learners being confronted with relatively infrequent instances of language use, but also of their being able to see in what way such uses are atypical, in what contexts they do appear, and how they fit in with the pattern of more prototypical uses" (p. 486).

The development of learner corpus research shows the limitations of SLA. This field of research can contribute to a better understanding of learner language. One of its main roles is to study how language is used. According to Pérez-Paredes, Sánchez-Tornel and Alcaraz Calero (2011), "has opened new paths for the analysis of language that go beyond the view of the word as the hub of language analysis" (p.3).

Language: From Heterogeneity to Diversity

It seems that language moves from the stability, unity to diversity. Hall (2002) notes that in the psycholinguistic approach language is regarded as abstract systems and individual learners are considered "stable, internally homogeneous, fixed entities in whose heads these systems reside" (p. 31). This is the monolingual view of languages, that is, "the mystic need for separate, perfect, well-balanced mastery of languages" (Moore and Gajo, 2009). Language is regarded as a monolithic entity.

In the global context, language has a multilingual aspect. It becomes plural and plurilingual. Baird, Baker, and Kitazawa (2014) "emphasise the importance of viewing language from multiple dimensions, in which its contextual embodiment is crucial" (p. 190). It is seen as a linguistic repertoire repertoires as plural and multidimensional, shifting in different social contexts (Byrd Clark, 2011).

FUTURE RESEARCH DIRECTION

Future attempts should focus more on the limitations of SLA. More research should be conducted to show how corpus research adds to SLA because some researchers argue that "There is nothing new in the idea of collecting learner data. Both FLT and SLA researchers have been collecting learner output for descriptive and/or theory building purposes since the disciplines emerged" (Granger, 2004, pp.123–4). Moreover, "as tools for linguistic research and not with pedagogical goals in mind" (Braun, 2007). As Cook (1998, p. 57) suggests, "the leap from linguistics to pedagogy is [...] far from straightforward".

CONCLUSION

This study focuses on learner language. It tries to review the development of learner language from second language acquisition to learner corpus research. It draws attention to the major theories of SLA. These include contrastive analysis theory, error analysis theory and interlanguage theory. Then, the study emphasizes the development of learner corpus research which is considered as a crucial resource for SLA. Myles and Mitchell (2004) argue that "It seems self-evident that one of the most precious resources in SLA research, alongside a clear conceptual framework, is a good quality dataset to work on" (p.173). Learner corpus research is seen as a tool for the development of second language research as well as a pedagogical tool for teaching.

REFERENCES

Al-Jamal, D. A. (2017). Students' Fossilized Writing Errors: EFL Postgraduates at Jordanian Universities as a Model. *Journal of Al-Quds Open University for Research and Studies, 19*(6), 1-17.

Baird, R., Baker, W., & Kitazawa, M. (2014). The complexity of ELF. *Journal of English as a Lingua Franca, 3*(1), 171–196. doi:10.1515/jelf-2014-0007

Braun, S. (2007). Integrating corpus work into secondary education: From data-driven learning to needs-driven corpora. *ReCALL, 19*(3), 307–328. doi:10.1017/S0958344007000535

Cook, G. (1998). The uses of reality: A reply to Ronald Cater. *ELT Journal, 52*(1), 57–64. doi:10.1093/elt/52.1.57

Corder, S. P. (1967). The significance of learner's errors. *International Review of Applied Linguistics in Language Teaching, 5*(4), 161–170.

Ellis, R. (1994). *The Study of Second Language Acquisition.* Oxford University Press.

Gass, S., & Selinker, L. (2008). *The role of the native language: An historical overview. In Second Language Acquisition: An Introductory Course.* Routledge.

Granger, S. (2002). A bird's-eye view of learner corpus research. In S. Granger, J. Hung, & S. Petch-Tyson (Eds.), *Computer Learner Corpora, Second Language Acquisition and Foreign Language Teaching* (pp. 3–36). John Benjamins. doi:10.1075/lllt.6.04gra

Granger, S. (2003). The International Corpus of Learner English: A new resource for foreign language learning and teaching acquisition research. *TESOL Quarterly, 37*(3), 538–546. doi:10.2307/3588404

Granger, S. (2009). The contribution of learner corpora to second language acquisition and foreign language teaching: A critical evaluation. In A. Karin (Ed.), *Corpora and Language Teaching* (pp. 13–32). John Benjamins. doi:10.1075cl.33.04gra

Hall, J. K. (2002). *Teaching and researching language and culture.* Pearson Education.

Hamdi, S. (2005). *An analysis of written grammatical errors of Tunisian learners of English in EFL context.* ISEAH Institute of Kef.

Hamdi, S. (2016). An analysis of lexical errors in the English compositions of EFL Tunisian learners. *International Journal of Humanities and Cultural Studies, 2*(4), 643–652.

Han, Z. (2004). Fossilization: Five central issues. *Journal of Applied Linguistics, 14*(2), 212–242. doi:10.1111/j.1473-4192.2004.00060.x

Jenkins, J. (2006). Current perspectives on teaching world Englishes and English as a lingua franca. *TESOL Quarterly, 40*(1), 157–181. doi:10.2307/40264515

Leech, G. (1998). Learner corpora: What they are and what can be done with them. In S. Granger (Ed.), Learner English on computer. London: Addison Wesley Longman.

Matsumoto, N. (2008). Bridges between Cognitive Linguistics and second language pedagogy: The case of corpora and their potential. *SKY Journal of Linguistics, 21,* 125–153.

McEnery, A. M., Xiao, R., & Tono, Y. (2005). *Corpus-based language studies.* Routledge.

McEnery, T., & Wilson, A. (1996). *Corpus linguistics.* Edinburgh University Press.

McLaughlin, B. (1987). *Theories of Second Language Learning.* Arnold Publishers.

Mitchell, R., & Myles, F. (2004). *Second language learning theories.* Edward Arnold.

Moore, D., & Gajo, L. (2009). French Voices on Plurilingualism and Pluriculturalism: Theory, Significance and Perspectives. *International Journal of Multilingualism and Multiculturalism, 6*(2), 137–153. doi:10.1080/14790710902846707

Nemser, W. (1971). Approximative systems of foreign language learner. *International Journal of Applied Linguistics, 9,* 115–124.

Ortega, L. (2010). *The Bilingual Turn in SLA.* Plenary delivered at the Annual Conference of the American Association for Applied Linguistics, Atlanta, GA.

Osborne, J. (2001). Integrating corpora into a language-learning syllabus. In B. Lewandowska-Tomaszczyk (Ed.), *PALC 2001: Practical applications in language corpora* (pp. 479–492). Peter Lang.

Pérez Paredes, P., Sánchez Tornel, M., & Alcaraz Calero, J. M. (2011). *The role of corpus linguistics in developing innovation in data-driven language learning.* Academic Press.

Phillipson, R. (Ed.). (1991). *Foreign/second language pedagogy research.* Multilingual Matters.

Rahal, A. (2016). *Phonetic Fossilization in the Speech of Advanced Tunisian English Students: The English Department of Kairouan as a case study* (Unpublished MA thesis). Faculty of Letters and Humanities of Kairouan.

Romaine, S. (1989). *Bilingualism.* Blackwell.

Selinker, L. (1972). Interlanguage. *International Journal of Applied Linguistics, 10,* 203–230.

Sharma, S. K. (1980). Practical and Theoretical Consideration involved in Error Analysis. *Indian Journal of Applied Linguistics, VI,* 74–83.

Sinclair, J. (1996). The search for units of meaning. *Textus, 9,* 75–106.

Solono, T. (2014). *Spanish Interference in EFL Writing Skills: A Case of Ecuadorian Senior High Schools* (Vol. 7). English Language Teaching Journal.

Sridhar, K., & Sridhar, S. (1986). Bridging the paradigm gap: Second language acquisition theory and indigenized varieties of English. *World Englishes*, 5(1), 3–14. doi:10.1111/j.1467-971X.1986.tb00636.x

Taher, A. (2011). *Error analysis: a study of Swedish junior high school students' texts and grammar knowledge* (Unpublished thesis). Uppsala Universitet.

Yahya, L. (1980). *Fossilized Errors Among Second-cycle Students at the Faculté des Lettres et Sciences Humaines* (MA thesis). University of Tunis.

Yakout, K., & Amel, M. H. (2019). The EFL Learners' Fossilization of the/θ/ and/ð/Sounds. Case Study: First Year EFL Students at Tahri Mohamed University, Bechar, Algeria. *International Journal of Linguistics. Literature and Translation*, 2(4), 219–228.

KEY TERMS AND DEFINITIONS

Contrastive Analysis Theory: Is a theory of second language acquisition; it is based on comparing two or more language to identify the similarities and differences.

Corpus Linguistics: Is the study of language as presented in real samples.

Cross-Sectional Approach: Is a research method that studies learner language at one single point in time.

Error Analysis Theory: Is one of the second language theories; it claims that learners' errors are crucial to study the whole process of learning and to select the appropriate teaching tools.

Interlanguage Theory: Is a linguistic system between the first language and the target language.

Longitudinal Study: Is a research method that studies learner language over time.

Second Language Acquisition: Refers to the process of learning a second language.

Chapter 11
The Role of Technology in Interdisciplinary Language Teaching:
Bridging Language and Science Learning

Azlin Zaiti Zainal
https://orcid.org/0000-0002-0149-9742
University of Malaya, Malaysia

ABSTRACT

In discourses of 21st century learning, there is an increasing emphasis on interdisciplinary learning. In this chapter, the author first looks at previous research on interdisciplinary teaching and learning. Next, the concept of scientific literacy and how this is related to language will be discussed. The intersections between the teaching of science literacy and language teaching and learning will also be explored. This is followed by research on the use of technology in science education and how technology can enhance science literacy.

INTRODUCTION

Language plays a fundamental role in the in the learning of core content. It has been argued that the ability to participate in a global society will depend highly on learners' key literacy skills such as reading, writing and oral communication (Kracjik and Sutherland, 2010). In the context of science learning, literacy skills are needed to understand science. Not only students will need to learn key concepts to be able to understand a scientific phenomenon but also need to be able to describe and explain

DOI: 10.4018/978-1-7998-2831-0.ch011

Copyright © 2021, IGI Global. Copying or distributing in print or electronic forms without written permission of IGI Global is prohibited.

the phenomenon. Accurate language is especially important in communicating an unobservable phenomenon in order to avoid possible misconceptions. In addition, students need to develop argumentative abilities in justifying a claim. Effective argumentation will depend highly on their ability to reason and communicate their understanding of scientific explanations using appropriate scientific terms and provide relevant evidence.

It is critical to examine the intersection between the two educational fields of language and science and the role of technology in facilitating teaching and learning considering the range of literacy practices involved in acquiring science knowledge. This chapter attempts to explore the potential of technology in enhancing the teaching and learning of science and language as an effort to advance the current understanding of interdisciplinary language teaching and learning in an increasingly globalized world. Yore and Treagust (2006) emphasized the critical role of science literacy in science education in order to help learners develop a better understanding of the specific discourse of scientific writing and enhance their critical thinking skills. Others such as Liu, Chiu, Lin and Barrett (2014) argue for the need for non-native speakers of English studying science to be instructed in both English and Scientific Language Instruction (SLI) considering that "scientific writing patterns and critical thinking skills are needed in addition to strong language abilities" (p.828). In countries where English is not the first language but serves as a medium of instruction in universities, the issue of teaching science in English is even more pressing. The challenges of learning a complex subject such as science in a language different from learners' native language, require an examination of how their learning can be supported with the relevant technological tools.

In view of the importance of complementing science education with language, this chapter will look at the role of technology in science teaching and learning and how the achievement of science literacy is contingent on the literacy practices implemented in the science classroom. It is grounded in the recognition that innovation in education is not only about the application of technology in teaching and learning, but also on capitalizing the advantages of interdisciplinary approach to help learners achieve learning outcomes. The current body of research on the use of technology in science teaching and learning appears to focus predominantly on the effectiveness of technology in achieving science content learning outcomes and do not necessarily address the issue of interdisciplinary learning of language and science. Apart from Liu et al., (2014) there has been limited attempt to synthesize research findings on the role of technology in the interdisciplinary teaching of language and science.

Technology has the potential to enhance science curriculum and equip students with the relevant scientific knowledge and skills not only for school level assessment but also to prepare them for the challenges of workplace. Nevertheless, this also prompts some questions about the role of language in science classroom: What are the literacy practices involved when learners engage in discussion and production of science content? What are the communicative purposes of such collaboration? In addition to questions about language role, another crucial question to ask is how does the use of technology in science classroom prepare learners to successfully participate in a global society? The proposed chapter will discuss how content-based teaching can be complemented with language education in the context of technology use. It will begin by introducing the notion of interdisciplinary teaching and learning. It will next look at the concept of scientific literacy and its importance in a globalized world. The chapter will then discuss the role of technology in achieving the outcomes of interdisciplinary language teaching in the context of science education and conclude with pedagogical recommendations and implications for future research.

INTERDISCIPLINARY TEACHING AND LEARNING

In their review of studies of interdisciplinary teaching and learning in higher education, Spelt, Biemans, Tobi, Luning, and Mulder (2009) found that despite the need for more interdisciplinary research in teaching and learning in higher education, research in this area has remained 'limited and explorative'. Since then we have seen a steady increase in research in this area. However, an understanding of how the fields of natural and social sciences can complement each other in higher education is still limited. A recent review by Fischer et al., (2011) on collaboration between natural and social sciences highlights a number of challenges and that more collaboration between university faculties is needed to promote the advancement of interdisciplinary research.

The ability to integrate or synthesise knowledge of disciplines in the context of higher education has often been referred to as 'interdisciplinary thinking', or 'interdisciplinary understanding' (Eisen Hall, Soon Lee, & Zupko, 2009; Spelt et al., 2009). Interdisciplinary understanding has been defined as, "The capacity to integrate knowledge and modes of thinking in two or more disciplines or established areas of expertise to produce a cognitive advancement—such as explaining a phenomenon, solving a problem, or creating a product—in ways that would have been impossible or unlikely through single disciplinary means" (Boix Mansilla, Miller & Gardner, 2000, p.219). Grounded in the performance view of understanding, this definition implies that individuals' understanding of a concept is achieved when they can apply it accurately and flexibly in new contexts (Boix Mansilla et al., 2000). Also, this definition highlights the complex cognitive skills involved in interdisciplinary thinking (Van Merriënboer, 1997), including the ability to view things from different disciplinary perspectives and establish meaningful links across disciplines.

It is suggested that the ability to integrate disciplinary knowledge is a defining feature of interdisciplinary or interdisciplinarity (Klein, 1990). There is a tendency for teaching and learning to remain multidisciplinary, an additive process which does not involve integration, when this complex cognitive skill is not taught (Spelt, Luning, Boekel, & Mulder, 2015). Scholars have emphasized the importance of teaching the skill of integrating interdisciplinary knowledge as an intended learning outcome across interdisciplinary higher education (Eckstein 1976; Gardner 2008; Harrison, Macpherson, & Williams 2007). In view of this, specific intended learning outcomes will need to be constructed and that "for each of the specific learning outcomes of interdisciplinary thinking, the disciplinary perspectives are blended by students to bring about an advance in understanding" (Spelt et al., 2015, p.460). In the context of interdisciplinary teaching of science and language, there is a need to identify the specific intended learning outcomes that can advance students understanding of both scientific concepts and scientific literacy. Airey (2011) suggests that "a suitable basis for collaboration between content lecturers and language lecturers or educational researchers can be found in the content lecturer's disciplinary learning goals" (p. 2). He further suggests that the goals should be both explicit and tacit to achieve disciplinary literacy. Nevertheless, as we shall see in the following section, the interdisciplinary nature of language and science is more formalized in the form of various standards in the context of primary and secondary school education compared to the higher education context.

THE ROLE OF LANGUAGE IN SCIENTIFIC LITERACY

Scientific literacy has been defined in many ways. For example, the National Research Council or NRC (1996) defined scientific literacy as "the knowledge and understanding of scientific concepts and processes required for personal decision making, participation in civic and cultural affairs, and economic productivity" (p.22). Although it is not explicitly stated, this definition implies that language and communication play a role in enabling effective participation in relevant activities and communities. The important role of language in science and science literacy has been emphasized (Osborne, 2002; Yore, 2003). Scientific reasoning (Griere, 1991) is a complex process that requires learners to possess literacy skills. It is argued that "language is a means to doing science and to constructing science understandings" (Yore, Bisanz & Hand, 2003, p.691). This recognition of the critical role of language has implications on the notion of science literacy. Norris and Phillips (2003) distinguish between two forms of science literacy; the fundamental and the derived. A fundamental sense of science literacy views literacy skills such as reading and writing as the core skills needed in accessing and producing scientific content. The derived sense refers to the knowledge and understanding of science.

It is argued that traditional conceptions of literacy have largely been based on the derived sense. As cautioned by Norris and Phillips (2003) "[c]onceiving of scientific literacy only as knowledgeability in science has nurtured a focus upon the substantive content to the neglect both of the texts that carry that content and of the interpretive capacities required to cope with them" (p.233). Others such as Hand et al. (2003) similarly emphasize the integral role of text and the literacy skill of reading to encourage the social practices that promote an understanding of science. Due to their distinctive linguistic characteristics, science texts are not similar to texts of other disciplines (Halliday & Martin, 1993). Complex clause structures, unlike everyday language, is used to organize science knowledge and this can be especially daunting for learners whose first language is not English. Because of this it is important that learners are supported in their reading of such texts. Equally important is to raise learners' awareness of how science texts contribute to the knowledge and understanding of science and the skills involved when readers interact with such texts. It is argued that they are "the artifacts of those past investigations and are used for inductive reasoning about scientific phenomena" (Pearson, Moje & Greenleaf, 2010, p.460). The required interpretive skills in reading science text implies that the development of science literacy will depend also on learners' reading strategies. Hand et al., (2003) have identified the literacy practices involving texts. Such practices include

recording and preserving data; encoding accepted science for anybody's use, reviewing of ideas by scientists anywhere; reexamining ideas at any point in time; connecting ideas to those developed previously (intertextuality); communicating ideas between those who have not met or lived at the same time; encoding variant positions; and focusing attention on a text for the purpose of interpretation, prediction, explanation, or test. (p.612)

In view of the range of social practices involving texts, conceptions of science literacy will clearly need to include the literacy skills of reading and writing. This highlights the importance of teaching scientific texts not only for learners to build their understanding of the scientific content but also for learners to recognize the range of strategies involved in understanding the different purposes of scientific texts which include advancing arguments and presenting the related evidence to support them. Clearly, texts are critical in a science curriculum. It is important that science inquiry is complemented with literacy practices of reading and writing to engage learners' understanding of science and that the texts used in classrooms can support their advancement of knowledge and skills.

A mutual understanding of scientific literacy is needed if educators are to embark on a collaboration of interdisciplinary teaching of science and language. Recent conceptualizations of science literacy have departed from the traditional view. While traditionalist approaches tend to underscore the development of learners' science knowledge skills, in line with Norris and Phillips' (2003) derived sense of science literacy, contemporary thinking regarding science literacy emphasize on experiential science learning. Standards such as A Framework for K-12 Science Education (National Research Council, 2012) and the Next Generation Science Standards (NGSS Lead States, 2013) emphasize on learning science "by doing" which essentially requires substantial language use. These standards also incorporate recent thinking about language learning based on SLA research. This includes looking at language learning from a social theoretical lens as opposed to a structuralist behaviourist approach. These standards also allow freedom for educators to decide the materials to be used and the pedagogical approaches.

Discussions on these standards are useful to clarify the links between literacy practices and the science activities that occur in classroom. A conceptual framework has been proposed by Lee, Llosa, Grapin, Haas, and Goggins (2019) that integrates science and language learning to guide the development of instructional materials based on the standards. Nevertheless, a similar framework is notably lacking in the context of tertiary education. As suggested by Akçayır and Akçayır (2017) a 'holistic model' may need to be developed in the context of higher education involving new technologies. Understanding the link between science and language in such context can guide instructors in incorporating language in the science classroom. As noted by Parkinson (2000) there is a range of literacy practices related to university science. These include

..experimental research and its associated scholarly papers, the student practical session and its associated laboratory manuals and laboratory reports, the tutorial session and its tutorial problems and problem solving techniques, the lecture and its lecture notes, the examination and its examination papers, examination scripts, ``short answers'', problem solving and calculations, and essays. (p.372)

To some extent there will be similarities in terms of the types of social practices engaged by practitioners of science and the social practices commonly expected in a science classroom. What is clearly important is not only to understand what is involved in the real world, but also what is expected of learners when they learn science in classroom. In this way, the approaches and materials can be catered for the development of learners' science literacy. Other than the literacy skills of reading and writing, communication skills are considered essential in the learning of science. Castek and Beach (2013) suggest that a disciplinary literacy of science involves collaboration. This relates to learners' ability to work with others in communicating ideas and knowledge of science. Lemke (1990) proposes that learning to ``talk'' science refers to ``learning to communicate in the language of science and act as a member of the community of people who do so'' (p.1).

Another aspect of science disciplinary literacy as highlighted by Castek and Beach (2013) is the inclusion of multimodality or "the ability to carefully observe and identify specific multimodal, visual features of a phenomenon to explain it" (p.555). With the advancement of technology, the integration of materials of different modalities is made possible within a science curriculum. It is crucial that learners develop the skills that will help them comprehend the function of each multimodal and draw interpretations.

Approaches to Teaching Scientific Literacy

An interdisciplinary approach to the teaching and learning of language and science will necessitate an understanding of the pedagogical practices that can contribute to the development of science literacy. Instruction on the language of science can take place in various domains – either through a content-based language instruction, or through the subject of science itself. To some extent the two fields, science and language, have a close relation as can be seen in studies in the field of English for Specific Purposes (ESP). There has been extensive discussion on the role of the English in content-based learning of science. Research in the area range from research on the metadiscourse of science articles through to preparing learners for science courses. The core focus, however, is language and not mastery of scientific knowledge and processes. Similarly, in science education, the traditional approach involves viewing it as a distinct subject where the focus is on mastery of science content. However, with the shift in thinking of the notion of scientific literacy, which emphasizes on the critical role of language, we see more recommendations of pedagogical approaches that are consistent with such thinking.

Content-Based Approaches

Researchers have highlighted the role of content-based learning in helping learners to acquire literacy skills. From the perspective of language learning, the communicative approach is a way to engage learners in using the language in a contextualized way. This is in line with Airey's (2011) notion of 'communicative practices' in the context of content-based education. Learning language through content helps not only learners to learn the language as they use the language to learn (Mohan, 1986). Through content based-instruction, there is opportunity for contextualized use of language in addition to sentence-level use (Widdowson, 1978). This is a departure from a predominant focus on discrete items such as vocabulary and grammar, as emphasis is given on discoursal aspects of language.

It is therefore important to examine students' participation in a literacy practice within a content-based classroom such as a university science course. Such literacy practices may also be useful to help develop specific intended learning outcomes that integrates the two disciplines of science and language learning. Within an interdisciplinary classroom, pedagogical approaches that can integrate both disciplines would also need to be determined. While content-based approaches are considered important in preparing learners for future studies in the science field, these may not necessarily reflect the actual practices that are found in a science classroom. Also, teachers who are involved in preparing content-based courses in language learning may not necessarily have the expertise in the field of science. It is argued that there are language and literacy challenges that are specific to science (Lee, Quinn & Valdes, 2013) and educators will need to be aware of these in order to implement a pedagogical approach and design instructional materials that are able to address the challenges.

One recommendation by Lee et al., (2013) is to move away from teaching science literacy/ language learning in the form of content-based instruction or what is termed as a "sheltered" mode by focusing on "language-in-use environments". Rather than emphasizing on particular aspects of language, it is suggested that instructors should instead promote language development by contextualising learning and engaging learners in science and engineering practices. This is in accordance with the social oriented approach to learning a language and reflects task-based approaches to language learning. As suggested by Hand et al., (2003), "language practices are embedded in authentic science inquiry to construct meaningful understanding as well as to develop language strategies and understanding of scientific discourse" (p.614).

In developing science literacy, the role of language in achieving learning outcomes will need to be clearly delineated. In this way, decisions regarding the approaches or pedagogical tools to be used can be made based on different aspects of science literacy. In their article, Lee et al., (2013) highlight the language functions that are characteristic of a science classroom. They include: develop and use models, develop explanations for science and design solutions for engineering, engage in argument from evidence and obtain, and evaluate and communicate scientific information. The features of classroom language are also highlighted and are classified according to modality, registers, teachers' and students' language use and tasks. They also outline the science registers that occur in a science classroom such as giving directions, checking for understanding, and facilitating discussions.

Including a component of language of the science classroom is essential in promoting the development of learners' science literacy as it can to help learners to gradually progress from using everyday language to the language of science. This is where it is important to encourage language use among learners. Learners may come from varying backgrounds and with different proficiencies in English. It has been suggested that connections should be made linking students' cultural and linguistic backgrounds and the requirements of a particular academic field (Lee, Buxton, Lewis & LeRoy, 2006). And because of this, instructors will need to be aware of how implementing different science activities in classroom can benefit learners not only in terms of science knowledge but also in their ability to engage in the type of discourse specific to the activity. Such activities essentially should also build on their communicative repertoire. With the rapid development in technology, students leaving university will be exposed to a range of workplace settings, connecting them to communities from different geographical regions and requiring them to communicate with speakers of English from different backgrounds. A goal that educators should consider aiming for in this regard is to develop learners' 'functional nativeness' to enable fluent cross-cultural communication (Nickerson, 2013).

Technology to Promote Interdisciplinary Knowledge

A teaching focus that complements science and language should be accompanied with application of technology that can address interdisciplinary learning goals. Apart from the importance of knowledge of how to use ICT in lessons, teachers need to see how incorporating it would benefit interdisciplinary teaching and learning. It has been suggested that the use of ICT, like the use of English, is predominantly a social practice (Davison, 2005). The development of new social practices will be "transformative to varying degrees, depending on the affordances of the tool, the skills with which human agents learn to use them and their ability to imagine new possible uses" (Somekh, 2007, p.13). With the understanding of the different scientific outcomes that learners are expected to achieve, it is important to examine the role of technology in bridging the two fields within the classroom setting. Technology is fundamental in promoting interdisciplinary teaching and learning. To understand its role, it is important to see how they afford the development of literacy skills and oral communication skills. Through exposure to multiple media forms, learners' engagement in learning can be encouraged. Research findings have indicated that providing learners with a choice of texts in different forms tend to sustain their interest in learning for lengthier durations (e.g. Garner, Zhao & Gillingham, 2002).

Technology as a Resource for the Development of Literacy Skills

Although a communicative approach focusing on the communicative purpose of an activity is suggested to promote science literacy, discussion on how discrete skills such as reading, and writing can be enhanced is necessary. One of the ways is to expose learners to a range of writing resources which include both formal and informal types of writing as they can be used for different aspects of science learning (Hand et al., 2003). The types of texts learners are exposed to are clearly important. In this section we will discuss how exposing learners to different text types can help with the acquisition of discoursal features, scientific concepts and build argumentative skills in writing. In addition, we will look at the role of technology in the enhancement of these areas.

It is important that the instructional materials used in science classroom are intended to highlight the discourse features that are required for students to develop scientific literacy skills. It is common within science classroom to use a textbook as a resource. But considerations should be given to diversify the reading texts learners are exposed to in the classroom. The similarities and differences between textbooks and research articles have been highlighted. Lab reports and research articles have many similarities and yet the latter is not utilized as much in the teaching of undergraduate science courses (Braine, 1989; Jackson, Meyer & Parkinson, 2006; Parkinson & Addendorf, 2004). Jackson et al., (2006) in their study of the reading and writing tasks assigned to students in a foundation science course, found that there is a mismatch between the writing task assigned and what they were expected to read. Although the laboratory report is the genre that is expected for students to produce for their course assignments, the reading materials assigned were mainly textbooks, a genre that is markedly different from laboratory reports. They suggest that research articles should be utilized more in science teaching given that it is a key genre in the discourse community of science. They also call for a more integrated approach to language teaching in the context of science degree. Corpus-based technology may be useful for this purpose as it allows the compilation of large amounts of authentic texts that learners can examine. Using a corpus, Soler (2011) compared the scientific titles in English and Spanish research articles. In another study, Kunioshia, Noguchib, Tojoc and Hayashi (2016) demonstrate how an online corpus can be used to highlight discourse features of science and engineering lectures.

Other than formal scientific genres, we also see emerging studies on the use of other informal genres such as 'popular science' in the teaching and learning of science (Afonso & Gilbert, 2013; Pelger & Nilsson, 2016). Parkinson and Adendorff (2004) argue that although popular science is different in terms of register compared to research reports, they should be utilized in the teaching of scientific writing. Unlike academic texts, they suggest that popular science is 'conceptually simpler' and can help students to understand difficult scientific concepts better. Although popular science may not necessarily be a genre to be used as a model for developing students' scientific writing skills, it is argued that its use can help students to recognize the difference in terms of register between the different genres. The authors recommend that students can be asked to 'translate' the content from popular science to academic texts where this will help them to develop a better understanding of academic texts register. The use of technology such as multimedia and video games with popular science content have the potential to address the learning of conceptual content of science (Li & Tsai, 2013; Lim, Nonis, & Hedberg, 2006). It is essential for students to have mastery of scientific concepts before they could engage in a related problem-solving activity. The visualization capabilities of virtual reality (VR) technology can also be used to relay difficult and abstract concepts (Burdea & Coiffet, 2003).

Conceptual understanding of science phenomenon serves as a building block for learners to construct an argument. Cheuk (2016) argues for the importance of developing learners' argumentative skills in the context of science learning. To make claims and provide evidence in writing are some of the skills that learners will need to acquire as part of scientific literacy (Brickhouse, Dagher, Shipman, & Letts, 2002; Kelly & Takao 2002; Patterson, 2001). Print-based texts may be used to help learners to focus on these specific aspects of writing, but how does technology afford learners to develop skills? Recently we see discussions on how technology use can support learners in promoting their understanding of how arguments can be constructed. As suggested by Castek and Beach (2013) "concept mapping, note-taking/annotation, and screencasting apps allows students to collaboratively share their analyses of observations and data with one another to bolster their claims through evidence" (p.555).

Technology to Promote Communication and Problem-Solving Skills

The role of everyday English should be utilised in the teaching of scientific literacy. Learners should be encouraged to talk about science in ways they know how before gradually using science language. This emphasizes the role of spoken language in achieving interdisciplinary goals. Mercer, Dawes, Wegerif and Sams (2004) found that talk can help develop learners' science reasoning. Because of this, it is recommended that talk-based activities involving teacher led instruction and group-based interaction should be incorporated in science classroom. In implementing such activities, the teacher plays an important role in raising learners' awareness of talk as a tool for thinking. It involves not only the social skills to construct understanding of important ideas in science while collaborating but also to communicate ideas and argue for these ideas (Hand et al., 2003). It is also important for educators to understand the important role of technology in promoting talk in science classroom. In a globalised world where learners' have increasing access to different forms of media, technology has the potential to connect learners from different educational settings. This affordance of technology should be capitalised so that learners could participate in collaborative activities that can enhance their communication skills as they negotiate scientific content. It is therefore important to understand how technology can be utilised to promote active engagement and develop higher order thinking skills through communication.

The type of science content for learning should also be given consideration. Some have argued that it is important to provide learners with opportunities to engage in discussions of socio-scientific issues related to real world situations (Anderson, 2002; Sadler, 2009). In this way learners will use language meaningfully and construct their own understanding of the topic through appropriate discourse. Lawless et al., (2018) adopted a problem-based learning in their study to encourage collaborative exchanges between students. This study demonstrates that interdisciplinary learning can take place when learners participated in problem solving exchanges involving socio-scientific issues. The content of the exchange revolved around problems that link both social studies and science within a simulated environment. They found that the project had a positive impact on students' scientific literacy.

It is recognized, nevertheless, that using technology to enable collaborative exchanges between cohorts of learners from different geographical locations can be met with challenges. Wendt and Rockinson-Szapkiw (2014) found that misconceptions about science were less likely to be resolved when students participated in collaborative discussion online compared to face-to-face discussion. They assert that this may be because of the nature of the online collaboration which is asynchronous. Feedback was not received immediately unlike during face-to-face discussion. The type of technology will also need to paid attention to if online collaboration is to be used in classroom.

Problem-based learning that promotes communication can also be implemented using new technologies such as Augmented Reality (AR) and Virtual Reality (VR). Augmented reality can be referred to as a technology which incorporates the virtual computer-generated object with physical object in the real-world environment (Carmigniani & Furht, 2011). In contrast, VR is described as "a computer-mediated simulation that is three-dimensional, multisensory, and interactive, so that the user's experience is "as if" in-habiting and acting within an external environment" (Burbules, 2006, p. 37). Previous research on AR technology use in educational settings have highlighted many advantages. This includes promoting students engagement in authentic explorations of the real world (Dede, 2009) and facilitating their observation of events which may be difficult to observe with the naked eye when virtual elements are displayed alongside real objects (Wu, Lee, Chang, & Liang, 2013). Cheng and Tsai (2013) summarize the learning process involved in gaming designs of AR for science learning:

Commonly, the role-playing and gaming designs in the context of inquiry-based AR learning generate a learning process that encourages students to (1) observe the phenomena in a surrounding environment, (2) ask questions about the phenomena,

(3) investigate and interpret data, (4) create hypotheses, plausible explanations, or practical plans, and (5) develop conceptual understandings in a collaborative way (p.455)

They further argue that "location-based AR allows students to step outside the classroom and provides an opportunity for inquiring into science issues with the aid of virtual information in a real world or with real phenomena" (p.456). Clearly, AR use afford many opportunities for language use and development as students engage in the processes of learning science.

In a higher education science course, for example, machinery operation may be one of the skills science students need to have when they graduate and join the working world. Through this course, students may be introduced to scientific instruments and machinery. Not only they will need to comprehend how a scientific machinery operates but also need to be able to describe and explain its functions. Furthermore, they may need to apply their knowledge of the machinery through problem solving tasks in order to solve scientific problems based on a given scenario. These knowledge and skills are crucial for science students to have in order to participate in the scientific community when they leave university. Although the best approach for students to understand the operational aspect is to allow students to be able to physically access the machinery, often there are constraints such as accessibility. It is difficult for students to visualize machinery in classrooms without any supporting tools. New technologies such as AR and VR offer the potential for learners to collaborate and have a close interaction with the machine in a virtual environment. However, more research will need to be conducted to understand how students use language in such environment.

Studies on VR use in science education have often focused on the achievement of knowledge-based learning outcomes. For example, in a study on the use VR in undergraduate physics by Martinez et al. (2011), the researchers compared three types of learning environment on the topic of optical aberrations. The environments include: 1) hyper-realistic virtual simulation, 2) traditional schematic simulations and 3) traditional laboratory. In terms of knowledge-based learning achievement, it was found that the group that used hyper-realistic simulation performed significantly better than the other two groups. An implication of their research is that realism is an important aspect of virtual laboratory experiences. If realism in VR technology is a contributing factor to knowledge-based achievement in science learning, further investigation on how realism affects language use in a science learning context could be a possible area of future research.

Nevertheless, we also see studies that have investigated the role of VR on learners' problem -solving skills, which is related to Airey's notion of tacit goal. As pointed out by Huang, Rauch and Liaw (2010) "VR is especially helpful when it comes to address issues that require imagination creativity and high problem-solving ability" (p. 1172). Virtual learning environment does not only allow students to explore new concepts but also helps them to improve their ability to analyze problems (Pan, Cheok, Yang, Zhu, & Shi, 2006). An advantage of virtual learning environment is that it affords a rich and focused environment to visualize and solve problems in groups (Wollensak, 2002). As suggested by Holmes (2007), learners can observe a simulated situation using VR in groups. The environmental parameters can then be altered by a student group to instantly change the simulation. The immersive and interactive environment can motivate learners in learning and developing problem solving skills. Huang et al. (2010) argue that problem-based learning implemented in a virtual learning environment provides a contextualized approach for students to explore the constructs of a problem and compare their thinking. Dryberg et al.,'s (2017) study found that the use of virtual laboratory cases increased students' participation in discussions of a higher level compared to when the programme was not used in the previous year. It was also found that although the use of virtual laboratory did not necessarily increase the students' motivation compared to when they used physical laboratories, it helps them to become more confident and comfortable in handling laboratory equipment. It was concluded that students' participation in virtual laboratories can help students' pre-laboratory preparation. In these studies, the use of VR technology seems to facilitate the development of students' problem-solving skills. More studies, however, is needed to see the aspects of language involved when learners engage in problem solving science activity using technology.

FUTURE RESEARCH DIRECTIONS

The studies above have shown that VR technology can have a positively affect learning. Comparison of the use of high-tech VR and low-tech VR seem to indicate that achievements of learning outcomes are higher when using 3-D tech. However, a finding of a recent study by Makransky, Terkildsen, & Mayer (2017) appear to contradict the findings of such studies. They compared the use of two types of technology, desktop display and the more immersive head-mounted display, on the learning outcome achievement of 52 university students. Despite reporting being more present in the high immersion VR condition, students learned less compared to the low immersion condition. It is argued that learning under the immersive VR condition, although motivating, could distract learners by overloading them cognitively. In view of this, more research is needed to understand how language plays a role in learners' learning of science in the context of both high-tech and low-tech VR.

Additionally, future research on AR and VR application should focus on group-based activities that can be used to promote both mastery of science content and literacy and investigate the effects of its use on students' achievement of science literacy. In their recent review of studies of AR use in education Akçayır and Akçayır (2017) highlighted some of the gaps that can be addressed by future research. They suggest that there is a need for more studies on the development and usability of AR applications and an investigation of learners' perceptions of the usability and preferences of AR based learning environment. In addition, it is recommended that researchers "develop holistic models and design principles (empirically proven) for AR environments" (p.8). They also suggest that more research is needed to examine the effects of AR use. It is pointed out that such research can investigate "the use of AR applications to support ubiquitous learning, collaborative learning, and informal learning, how they should be used, and which methods and techniques should be more effective" (p.8). Similar suggestions could also be applied in the context of VR application.

CONCLUSION

This chapter has attempted to examine how technology can be used to enhance interdisciplinary teaching of language and science. Technology can play an important role in realizing science learning outcomes which embed current understanding of science literacy. The importance of providing learners with opportunities to examine texts in multiple forms and an understanding of how technology can afford learners with such opportunities is one of the takeaways of this chapter. Technology in this sense acts as a resource for storing language with science content and as a visualization tool which can be used by teachers to teach specific discourse features and science concepts deductively or for learners to discover them themselves inductively. Furthermore, technology functions as a tool for communication and potentially can connect learners from various language and cultural backgrounds. The role of technology in promoting language use and development during collaboration and problem-solving activity within science learning is also discussed in this chapter. We also see that new technologies such as AR and VR offer affordances for a more immersive learning environment. Their use encourages learners to experience science inquiry within a virtual space, modelling real world practices of science inquiry.

Although research on the use of technology in science education has mainly focused on the explicit learning outcomes of knowledge-based achievement and not on the tacit aspects such as the development of literacy skills for problem solving, we see an emerging body of literature that investigated the use of technology for interdisciplinary learning, highlighting the tacit aspects of science learning. Future research agenda should entail further investigations of technology use in science education that balances both the achievement of science knowledge and development of literacy skills to reflect current thinking of scientific literacy. To ensure learners are well prepared to participate in a global scientific community, research on technology use will also need to address how technology can support learner diversity in their development of scientific literacy. Furthermore, more research on technology use for interdisciplinary language in the higher education context should be conducted to extend our current understanding of the role of technology in bridging language and science.

REFERENCES

Afonso, A. S., & Gilbert, J. K. (2013). The role of 'popular' books in informal chemical education. *International Journal of Science Education. Part B*, *3*(1), 77–99.

Airey, J. (2011). The disciplinary literacy discussion matrix: A heuristic tool for initiating collaboration in higher education. *Across the Disciplines, 8*(3).

Akçayır, M., & Akçayır, G. (2017). Advantages and challenges associated with augmented reality for education: A systematic review of the literature. *Educational Research Review*, *20*, 1–11. doi:10.1016/j.edurev.2016.11.002

Anderson, R. D. (2002). Reforming science teaching: What research says about inquiry. *Journal of Science Teacher Education*, *13*(1), 1–12. doi:10.1023/A:1015171124982

Boix Mansilla, V., Miller, W. C., & Gardner, H. (2000). On disciplinary lenses and interdisciplinary work. In S. Wineburg & P. Grossman (Eds.), *Interdisciplinary curriculum: Challenges of implementation* (pp. 17–38). Teachers College Press.

Braine, G. (1989). Writing in science and technology: An analysis of assignments from ten undergraduate courses. *English for Specific Purposes*, *8*(1), 3–15. doi:10.1016/0889-4906(89)90003-3

Brickhouse, N. W., Dagher, Z. R., Shipman, H. L., & Letts, W. J. (2002). Evidence and warrants for belief in a college astronomy course. *Science and Education*, *11*(6), 573–588. doi:10.1023/A:1019693819079

Burbules, N. C. (2006). Rethinking the virtual. In J. Weiss, J. Nolan, J. Hunsinger, & P. Trifonas (Eds.), *The international handbook of virtual learning environments* (pp. 37–58). Springer. doi:10.1007/978-1-4020-3803-7_1

Burdea, G. C., & Coiffet, P. (2003). *Virtual reality technology*. John Wiley & Sons. doi:10.1162/105474603322955950

Carmigniani, J., & Furht, B. (2011). Augmented reality: an overview. In B. Furht (Ed.), *Handbook of augmented reality* (pp. 3–46). Springer. doi:10.1007/978-1-4614-0064-6_1

Castek, J., & Beach, R. (2013). Using apps to support disciplinary literacy and science learning. *Journal of Adolescent & Adult Literacy*, *56*(7), 554–564. doi:10.1002/JAAL.180

Cheng, K.-H., & Tsai, C.-C. (2013). Affordances of augmented reality in science learning: Suggestions for future research. *Journal of Science Education and Technology*, *22*(4), 449–462. doi:10.100710956-012-9405-9

Cheuk, T. (2016). Discourse practices in the new standards: The role of argumentation in common core-era next Generation Science Standards Classrooms for English Language Learners. *The Electronic Journal of Science Education*, *20*(3), 92–111.

Davison, C. (2005). *Information technology and innovation in language education* (Vol. 1). Hong Kong University Press.

Dede, C. (2009). Immersive interfaces for engagement and learning. *Science*, *323*(5910), 66–69. doi:10.1126cience.1167311 PMID:19119219

Dyrberg, N. R., Treusch, A. H., & Wiegand, C. (2017). Virtual laboratories in science education: Students' motivation and experiences in two tertiary biology courses. *Journal of Biological Education*, *51*(4), 358–374. doi:10.1080/00219266.2016.1257498

Eckstein, B. (1976). Overcoming non-cognitive problems in interdisciplinary engineering work. *European Journal of Engineering Education*, *1*(3), 217–221. doi:10.1080/03043797608903428

Eisen, A., Hall, A., Soon Lee, T., & Zupko, J. (2009). Teaching water: Connecting across disciplines and into daily life to address complex societal issues. *College Teaching*, *57*(2), 99–104. doi:10.3200/CTCH.57.2.99-104

Fischer, A. R., Tobi, H., & Ronteltap, A. (2011). When natural met social: A review of collaboration between the natural and social sciences. *Interdisciplinary Science Reviews*, *36*(4), 341–358. doi:10.1179/030801811X13160755918688

Gardner, H. (2008). *Five Minds for the Future*. Harvard Business School Publishing. doi:10.1086/591814

Garner, R., Zhao, Y., & Gillingham, M. (Eds.). (2002). *Hanging out: Community-based after school programs for children*. Greenwood.

Giere, R. (1991). *Understanding Scientific Reasoning* (3rd ed.). Holt, Rinehart & Winston.

Halliday, M. A. K., & Martin, J. R. (1993). *Writing science: Literacy and discursive power*. The Falmer Press.

Hand, B. M., Alvermann, D. E., Gee, J. P., Guzzetti, B. J., Norris, S. P., Phillips, L. M., Prain, V., & Yore, L. D. (2003). Message from the "Island Group": What is literacy in science literacy? *Journal of Research in Science Teaching, 40*(7), 607–615. doi:10.1002/tea.10101

Hand, B. M., Wallace, C., & Yang, E. M. (2006). Using a Science Writing Heuristic to enhance learning outcomes from laboratory activities in seventh-grade science: Quantitative and qualitative aspects. *International Journal of Science Education, 26*(2), 131–149. doi:10.1080/0950069032000070252

Harrison, G. P., Macpherson, D. E., & Williams, D. A. (2007). Promoting Interdisciplinarity in Engineering Teaching. *European Journal of Engineering Education, 32*(3), 285–293. doi:10.1080/03043790701276775

Holmes, J. (2007). Designing agents to support learning by explaining. *Computers & Education, 48*(4), 523–547. doi:10.1016/j.compedu.2005.02.007

Huang, H. M., Rauch, U., & Liaw, S. S. (2010). Investigating learners' attitudes toward virtual reality learning environments: Based on a constructivist approach. *Computers & Education, 55*(3), 1171–1182. doi:10.1016/j.compedu.2010.05.014

Jackson, L., Meyer, W., & Parkinson, J. (2006). A study of the writing tasks and reading assigned to undergraduate science students at a South African University. *English for Specific Purposes, 25*(3), 260–281. doi:10.1016/j.esp.2005.04.003

Kelly, G. J., & Takao, A. (2002). Epistemic levels in argument: An analysis of university oceanography students' use of evidence in writing. *Science Education, 86*(3), 314–342. doi:10.1002ce.10024

Klein, J. T. (1990). *Interdisciplinarity: History, Theory, and Practice*. Wayne State University Press.

Krajcik, J. S., & Sutherland, L. M. (2010). Supporting students in developing literacy in science. *Science, 328*(5977), 456–459. doi:10.1126cience.1182593 PMID:20413490

Lawless, K. A., Brown, S. W., Rhoads, C., Lynn, L., Newton, S. D., Brodowiksa, K., Oren, J., Riel, J., Song, S., & Wang, M. (2018). Promoting students' science literacy skills through a simulation of international negotiations: The GlobalEd 2 Project. *Computers in Human Behavior, 78*, 389–396. doi:10.1016/j.chb.2017.08.027

Lee, O., Buxton, C. A., Lewis, S., & LeRoy, K. (2006). Science inquiry and student diversity: Enhanced abilities and continuing difficulties after an instructional intervention. *Journal of Research in Science Teaching, 43*(7), 607–636. doi:10.1002/tea.20141

Lee, O., Llosa, L., Grapin, S., Haas, A., & Goggins, M. (2019). Science and language integration with English learners: A conceptual framework guiding instructional materials development. *Science Education, 103*(2), 317–337. doi:10.1002ce.21498

Lee, O., Quinn, H., & Valdés, G. (2013). Science and language for English language learners in relation to Next Generation Science Standards and with implications for Common Core State Standards for English language arts and mathematics. *Educational Researcher, 42*(4), 223–233. doi:10.3102/0013189X13480524

Lemke, J. L. (1990). *Talking science: Language, Learning and Values*. Ablex.

Li, M. C., & Tsai, C. C. (2013). Game-based learning in science education: A review of relevant research. *Journal of Science Education and Technology, 22*(6), 877–898. doi:10.100710956-013-9436-x

Lim, C. P., Nonis, D., & Hedberg, J. (2006). Gaming in a 3D multiuser virtual environment: Engaging students in science lessons. *British Journal of Educational Technology, 37*(2), 211–231. doi:10.1111/j.1467-8535.2006.00531.x

Lin, S. Y., Wu, M. T., Cho, Y. I., & Chen, H. H. (2015). The effectiveness of a popular science promotion program on nanotechnology for elementary school students in I-Lan City. *Research in Science & Technological Education, 33*(1), 22–37. doi:10.1080/02635143.2014.971733

Liu, G. Z., Chiu, W. Y., Lin, C. C., & Barrett, N. E. (2014). English for Scientific Purposes (EScP): Technology, trends, and future challenges for science education. *Journal of Science Education and Technology, 23*(6), 827–839. doi:10.100710956-014-9515-7

Makransky, G., Terkildsen, T. S., & Mayer, R. E. (2017). Adding immersive virtual reality to a science lab simulation causes more presence but less learning. *Learning and Instruction*, 1–12.

Martinez, G., Naranjo, F. L., Pérez, A. L., Suero, M. I., & Pardo, P. J. (2011). Comparative study of the effectiveness of some learning environments: Hyper-realistic virtual simulations, traditionalschematic simulations and traditional laboratory. *Physical Review Special Topics. Physics Education Research, 7*(2), 020111-1, 020111–020112. doi:10.1103/PhysRevSTPER.7.020111

McNeill, K. L. (2008). Teachers' use of curriculum to support students' in writing scientific arguments to explain phenomena. *Science Education*, *93*(2), 233–268. doi:10.1002ce.20294

Mercer, N., Dawes, L., Wegerif, R., & Sams, C. (2004). Reasoning as a scientist: Ways of helping children to use language to learn science. *British Educational Research Journal*, *30*(3), 359–377. doi:10.1080/01411920410001689689

Mohan, B. A. (1986). *Language and content*. Addison-Wesley.

National Research Council. (2012). *A framework for K-12 science education: Practices, crosscutting concepts, and core ideas*. National Academies Press.

National Research Council (NRC). (1996). *National science education standards*. National Academic Press.

Next Generation Science Standards Lead States. (2013). *Next Generation Science Standards: For states, by states*. The National Academies Press.

Nickerson, C. (2013). English for specific purposes and English as a lingua franca. In B. Paltridge & S. Starfield (Eds.), *The handbook of English for specific purposes* (pp. 446–460). Wiley-Blackwell.

Norriss, S. P., & Phillips, L. M. (2003). How literacy in its fundamental sense is central to scientific literacy. *Science Education*, *87*(2), 224–240. doi:10.1002ce.10066

Osborne, J. (2002). Science without literacy: A ship without a sail? *Cambridge Journal of Education*, *32*(2), 203–218. doi:10.1080/03057640220147559

Pan, Z., Cheok, A. D., Yang, H., Zhu, J., & Shi, J. (2006). Virtual reality and mixed reality for virtual learning environments. *Computers & Graphics*, *30*(1), 20–28. doi:10.1016/j.cag.2005.10.004

Parkinson, J. (2000). Acquiring scientific literacy through content and genre: A theme-based language course for science students. *English for Specific Purposes*, *19*(4), 369–387. doi:10.1016/S0889-4906(99)00012-5

Patterson, E. W. (2001). Structuring the composition process in scientific writing. *International Journal of Science Education*, *23*(1), 1–16. doi:10.1080/09500690117425

Pearson, D., Moje, E. B., & Greenleaf, C. (2010). Literacy and science: Each in the service of the other. *Science*, *328*(5977), 459–463. doi:10.1126cience.1182595 PMID:20413491

Pelger, S., & Nilsson, P. (2016). Popular science writing to support students' learning of science and scientific literacy. *Research in Science Education*, *46*(3), 439–456. doi:10.100711165-015-9465-y

Sadler, T. D. (2009). Situated learning in science education: Socio-scientific issues as contexts for practice. *Studies in Science Education*, *45*(1), 1–42. doi:10.1080/03057260802681839

Soler, V. (2011). Comparative and contrastive observations on scientific titles written in English and Spanish. *English for Specific Purposes*, *30*(2), 124–137. doi:10.1016/j.esp.2010.09.002

Somekh, B. (2007). *Pedagogy and learning with ICT: Researching the art of innovation*. Routledge. doi:10.4324/9780203947005

Spelt, E. J. H., Biemans, H. J. A., Tobi, H., Luning, P. A., & Mulder, M. (2009). Teaching and learning in interdisciplinary higher education: A systematic review. *Educational Psychology Review*, *21*(4), 365–378. doi:10.100710648-009-9113-z

Spelt, E. J. H., Luning, P. A., Van Boekel, M. A. J. S., & Mulder, M. (2015). Constructively aligned teaching and learning in higher education in engineering: What do students perceive as contributing to the learning of interdisciplinary thinking? *European Journal of Engineering Education*, *40*(5), 459–475. doi:10.1080/03043797.2014.987647

Van Merriënboer, J. J. G. (1997). *Training complex cognitive skills: A four-component instructional design model for technical training*. Educational Technology.

Wendt, J. L., & Rockinson-Szapkiw, A. (2014). The effect of online collaboration on middle school student science misconceptions as an aspect of science literacy. *Journal of Research in Science Teaching*, *51*(9), 1103–1118. doi:10.1002/tea.21169

Widdowson, H. G. (1978). *Teaching language as communication*. Oxford University Press.

Wollensak, A. (2002). Curricular modules: 3D and immersive visualization tools for learning. *Computers & Graphics*, *26*(4), 599–602. doi:10.1016/S0097-8493(02)00110-3

Wu, W.-H., Wu, Y.-C. J., Chen, C.-Y., Kao, H.-Y., Lin, C.-H., & Huang, S.-H. (2012). Review of trends from mobile learning studies: A meta-analysis. *Computers & Education*, *59*(2), 817–827. doi:10.1016/j.compedu.2012.03.016

Yore, L., Bisanz, G. L., & Hand, B. M. (2003). Examining the literacy component of science literacy: 25 years of language arts and science research. *International Journal of Science Education, 25*(6), 689–725. doi:10.1080/09500690305018

Yore, L. D., & Treagust, D. F. (2006). Current realities and future possibilities: Language and science literacy—empowering research and informing instruction. *International Journal of Science Education, 28*(2-3), 291–3142. doi:10.1080/09500690500336973

Chapter 12
An Investigation Into In-Service and Pre-Service Teachers' Understanding and Perceptions of Global Englishes in Taiwan

Ethan Fu-Yen Chiu
National Chin-Yi University of Technology, Taiwan

ABSTRACT

This chapter examined in-service teachers' and pre-service teachers' interpretation, understanding, knowledge, and willingness of promoting Global Englishes. The results of quantitative and qualitative data indicated that the concepts of Global Englishes were more informally delivered than formal instructed channels. Both groups generally had the understanding and knowledge of Global Englishes. The majority of participants of this study preferred Standard English when selecting listening materials, but they were in favor of the idea of introducing Global Englishes into the curricula of the 12-year Compulsory Education. With the goal of achieving appropriate and effective communication, in addition to Global Englishes, ICC should be adequately developed and enforced. The focus of the chapter was to highlight the importance of training teachers with greater awareness and respect of English varieties and to disseminate the concept of Global Englishes at teacher training programs. Findings of the study have some important implications for the English curricula of 12-year Compulsory Education.

DOI: 10.4018/978-1-7998-2831-0.ch012

INTRODUCTION

In a fast-moving globalized world, English has increasingly become the common language that people use for global communication. During the past decades, people use English in almost all fields such as science, entertainment and commerce for communication purpose (Crystal, 2003). The spread and use of different varieties of English as a global or international language in the modern era have become a well-known phenomenon (Yang, 2013). The population of English users reside worldwide with native speakers and non-native speakers. Bilingual speakers of English outnumber native English speakers (Vettorel & Corrrizzato, 2016). People from native speaking nations are no longer the lone representatives of English. English users in a global community have the right to be associated with English (Crystal, 2003; Galloway, 2013). These phenomena necessitate the study of Global Englishes, which includes not only nation-bound varieties but also non-nation-bound development. Thus, English is the language increasingly used as a global lingua franca and it has drastically changed sociolinguistic landscape.

In Asia alone, the Ministries of Education in different countries or regions have enacted policies to increase learning hours as well as to elevate English education from the elementary level because of the growing importance of English learning worldwide (Nunan, 2003). In 2001 English became a compulsory and essential course for primary school and secondary school students in Taiwan. English was integrated into a language curriculum category with Mandarin Chinese, Taiwanese and other local language varieties called "Language Arts," which was one of seven major areas of study for the Nine-year Joint Curriculum Plan (Chen, 2013). English language teaching (ELT) has always focused on native norms, aiming to achieve native like proficiency and cultural understanding. Nonetheless, the concept of Global Englishes has not been addressed until the recent 12-year Compulsory Education. In this ever-connected world, English users come from different regional, linguistic and cultural backgrounds. English learners therefore need to adapt themselves to mastering it as a global language for their communication needs. As the number of non-native English speakers is expanding, it is foreseeable that every individual who speaks the global language may encounter more speakers with indigenized variety of English than Standard English (Graddol, 2006; Wajnryb, 2008; Yang & Wong 2009). According to Kachru and Smith (2008) and Kirkpatrick (2007), following native speaker model and behaving like a native English speaker are neither sufficient nor effective. In other words, ELT should emphasize a multilingual paradigm prioritizing competence in a repertoire of multilingual resources. In response to the trend of Global Englishes, the MOE in Taiwan started to promote Global Englishes in its new English curriculum guidelines with the hope that students can accustom themselves to different kinds of English accents. Students are expected to understand English varieties spoken by diverse interlocutors worldwide when they are at the upper secondary level of English studies (National Academy for Educational Research, 2017). In its place, Global Englishes Language Teaching (GELT) is a current trend putting emphasis on the diversity and the functionality of English as an international lingua franca. Global Englishes becomes necessary in both the teaching and processing of English learning (Galloway & Rose, 2015). It is the teachers' obligation to keep pace with the changing expectation of English users so that students will be prepared for the realities they encounter in today's globalized world.

Previous studies try to examine college teachers' opinions about English as a Lingua Franca (ELF), English as an International Language (EIL), or World Englishes (WE). Students' and/or teachers' attitudes towards English as well as necessities to incorporate WE, EIL and ELF into teacher education programs can evidently be found. Nevertheless, those researchers neglect to figure out how these concepts have been put into practice to both in-service teachers' and pre-service teachers at the secondary school level.

This chapter intended to compare the awareness and practice of pre-service and in-service teachers in an attempt to shed light on whether the concept of Global Englishes had been introduced to teacher education. Pre-service teachers referred to those who choose to be secondary school teachers as their career path. In-service teachers were those who currently teaching at secondary schools. Their willingness of promoting Global Englishes was investigated as well. In addition, teachers' preferences for choosing English varieties in their listening materials were discussed. Suggestions on how English education could be reformulated in Taiwan were summarized.

LITERATURE REVIEW

Global Englishes and Intercultural Communicative Competence

The term "Global Englishes" was applied to this chapter as it was referred to the MOE for the new English curricula guideline of the 12-year Compulsory Education. According to the new curricula, English has been a global lingua franca because of the increasing political and economic impacts from English speaking countries. Since the beginning of the 21st century, the population of English users has gradually spread all over the world in addition to native English-speaking countries. It seems countries or individuals using the language can claim the ownership of English. As there are different English varieties, some discrepancies in English are allowed.

Consequently, Global Englishes is the term invented to explain the phenomenon (National Academy for Educational Research, 2015).

People with different mother tongues or without common shared cultures often use English for communication (Seidlhofer, 2005). Since English is not merely spoken by native speakers, cultures from native norms could not represent the whole English-speaking world. It is necessary to redefine the cultural concept and the relationships between cultures and languages (Baker, 2009). As a result, it is insufficient for efficient communication if non-native speakers can only follow native English speakers' culture as a standard. Byram (1997) advocates that developing the intercultural communication and a non-native speaker model for language teaching. These two characteristics are feasible pedagogies for ELT. One of the objectives listed on the curricula for English guidelines is to develop language teaching diversity in order to understand and respect different cultures. The cultivation of international views and global sustainability are equally important. Since English is used as a tool to convey one's own culture and understand that of others, mutual understanding and cross-cultural communications can be achieved and enhanced via the common language (National Academy for Educational Research, 2015). The idea conforms to Vurdien and Puranen's view (2018) in the context that "ICC means that learners should be capable of understanding the language and behavior of the target group and describe it to their own community and vice versa."

Sharifian (2013) points out that 'intercultural competence' is recognized and viewed as a core element of 'proficiency' in English when it is used for international communication. Because of frequent intercultural contact and interchange, Chao (2016) suggests that English language teachers should be cultural facilitators or cultural mediators. They could develop and recognize the competence in intercultural teaching so that their students could be promoted to intercultural speakers. Consequently, the development of ICC is essential for foreign or second language education in the era of globalization and internationalization.

Previous Research on Related Areas

Some research efforts have been conducted to investigate college students' and/ or teachers' attitudes towards Global Englishes, EIL, WE and ELF (Galloway, 2013; Galloway and Rose, 2014; Liu & Cheng, 2017).

Galloway (2013) examined 52 Japanese university students' perceptions of Global Englishes by questionnaires and interviews. Pre-course questionnaires and post-course questionnaires were carried out to mark how students' attitudes changed. In the pre-course questionnaires, more students revealed that their views of learning English were to communicate with native English speakers instead of non-native English speakers. In addition, they preferred native norms, American English in particular. They showed more interests in imitating American English in interviews as it was perceived as a real and standard norm. However, after taking the Global Englishes course, students expressed less preferences for varieties from the Inner Circle. Frequencies of English varieties from the Outer circle and the Expanding circle were chosen from 7 times to 19 times in the pre- and post-course questionnaire data respectively. Students' preferences for American English teachers especially declined by almost 20% in the post-course questionnaires.

Galloway and Rose (2014) analyzed the listening journals of 108 Japanese university students. The journals consisted of 1,092 reflections on Global Englishes exposures. The listening journal provided students with amble opportunities to contact a wide range of speakers from different parts of the world with 367 from the Inner Circle varieties, 186 from the Outer Circle varieties and 459 from the Expanding Circle varieties. Apart from the listening journals, ten interviews were conducted to investigate the attitudes toward the Global Englishes course. The results indicated that native English varieties were not the priority when students chose materials to listen. Students were willing to listen to and communicate with speakers from diverse lingua-cultural backgrounds. However, American English was believed to be the standard and the preferred yardstick to measure English proficiency. The study concluded that listening journals served as a useful tool to highlight students' awareness of the use of ELF worldwide. In addition, the researchers recommended applying careful guidance so that mutual intelligibility could be improved besides native-like proficiency.

Liu and Cheng (2017) explored 17 college teachers' and 300 students' attitudes toward EIL by questionnaires in Taiwan. From the participants' view, English was regarded as a tool to communicate with people from different cultures and linguistic backgrounds. As the goal of learning English was to communicate fluently with others, they agreed that speaking fluently was more vital than having correct pronunciation and grammar. However, in terms of the ownership of English and the awareness of English varieties, students and teachers showed different opinions in the study. More students than teachers agreed that English did not belong to any particular countries or people. Teachers seemed to be more aware of other English varieties in addition to British or American English than students did. Students tended to hold a monolithic view of English and regard British or American English as Standard English. They believed that British or American English were the standard to be learned. Meanwhile, more teachers than students agreed that it was useful to know the different accents and ways of speaking English. Although both groups had positive attitudes toward EIL, they still had an ambivalent feeling about some of the EIL concepts. They agreed that communication skills were more important than native-like competence. Nevertheless, students were more willing to learn to sound like native speakers so that they would not feel inferior to native speakers and in attempts to boost confidence. Most of the teachers and students accepted English varieties but considered Taiwanese English accent as an undesirable one.

The studies related to teacher education include Chang (2014), Zacharias (2014) and Deniz, Özkan & Bayyurt (2016). These researchers suggest fostering WE/ELF/EIL awareness in teacher education for pedagogical implications with regard to ELT.

Chang (2014) carried out a project with a WE framework to explore Taiwanese university students' preferences toward native speaker and non-native teachers. 22 university students enrolled in a WE course taught by Chang who used students' final reflection papers to illustrate WE-related topics. The participants agreed that WE should be incorporated into English instructions. For example, the course helped them acquire a deeper understanding of language beyond rote learning of American and British standards. Students were more aware of different English varieties and became more critical in perceiving, learning and using English. Students were also more open-minded about the legitimacy of Englishes, more confident in using and learning English as non-native speakers. In addition, those who planned to become English teachers in their future career path were willing to embed WE in existing curriculums.

Zacharias (2014) used focus group discussions and interviews to investigate ten bilingual English student-teachers' experience on practicing EIL pedagogy. The participants expressed their willingness to localize English in the classroom. Participants still brought other Englishes in their self-created teaching materials. For example, one of the student-teacher devised a lesson plan, which integrated American and Thai Englishes. It is devised to raise students' awareness of the differences in these English varieties. The finding indicated that all student-teachers showed enthusiasm in teaching English through EIL pedagogy. EIL pedagogy should be integrated into existing pre-service teacher education curriculum.

Deniz, Özkan and Bayyurt (2016) explored 42 pre-service teachers' perceptions and pre-occupied assumptions on ELF related issues by interviews and questionnaires with open-ended questions in Turkey. The participants took part in an English language teacher education program. The findings demonstrated that a great majority of the respondents refused to adopt ELF approach in their language teaching context despite their acceptance of the realities of ELF. More than half of the participants were in favor of keeping rules of Standard English. Consequently, in order to raise awareness of ELF, the study urged that language teachers should have to be well educated and the concept of integrating ELF into language teacher education programs should be disseminated.

Participants from previous studies originally believed varieties from the Inner Circle were learning models, especially American English and British English. However, after receiving trainings, student-teachers changed their attitudes. Their views toward English varieties became more open-minded. Generally speaking, they were more confident in using and learning English as non-native English speakers. They were more willing to bring other English varieties together with varieties from the Inner Circle in their classes.

Studies Related to International Communication Competence

Speaking of ELT, culture is an indispensable element. Rather than teaching Anglo-American cultures or other specific national cultures, one of teachers' responsibilities is to raise students' cultural awareness and foster their ICC development (Ke, 2012). As the range of globalization becomes wider and the pace becomes and faster, it becomes more frequent than before that people with different linguistic and cultural backgrounds interact with one another. Therefore, intercultural understanding and ICC are vital for genuine communication and mutual understanding. Different cultural identities can result in miscommunication and misunderstanding so it is essential to acquire intercultural understanding and ICC to prevent potential miscommunication and misunderstanding (Yang, 2018).

Chao (2016) explored the non-native English teachers' (NNETs) intercultural capabilities and teaching practices in an Asian context. The researcher discovered that a few of her participants had employed intercultural strategies in their classrooms. The participants still preferred to introduce the cultures of English-speaking countries when promoting the acquisition of intercultural knowledge and skills. Furthermore, some NNETs seemed insensitive to the ELF or EIL related issues in ELT. They ignored the issues when selecting textbooks and cultural contents. In addition, NNETs lacked explicit guidance in terms of intercultural education. The lack of ELF-related materials for intercultural teaching and intercultural training in teacher education made them incapable of instructing various Englishes. They overlooked the importance of developing students' awareness and acquiring knowledge of one's own culture along with other cultures. Evidently, English education programs must elucidate the notion of culture and interculturality as well as ICC related training and assessment. Intercultural perspectives with English curriculum and instruction should also be integrated. It is recommended that intercultural education and teachers' awareness of English varieties in teacher education should be established.

Studies related to incorporation of online activities to imbue ICC with teacher educational programs can be found. Prapinwong (2018) applied a blended learning course, face-to-face and web-enhanced activities to raise pre-service teachers' intercultural awareness. Based on the perspective of Global Englishes and the interconnection of language and culture, the course integrated the diversity of languages and cultures to help pre-service teachers develop a deeper understanding of language and culture pedagogy. "Pre-service teachers can develop a deeper understanding of the global social contexts where language and culture pedagogy draw on the complex relationships among language, culture, society and the individual" (p.135). Accessing to the online materials enabled and increased the learners' willingness to participate and engage in the activities. Thus, learners' intercultural experiences could be expanded. Additionally, through the blended course of effective class management, traditional instructions could be transformed into multimodal modes, which enhanced the intercultural awareness and linguistic abilities.

Lawrence and Cohen (2018) examined the impact of telecollaboration between teacher-learners in two Applied Linguistics Master's programs in Canada and Israel. Language teachers were given the opportunities to work with ICT tools within an international community of practice. Both sides explored teachers' collaboration, technology-mediated intercultural language teaching and learning as well as their potential impacts on curriculum development and teaching practice. The researchers indicated that 21st century teaching skills, intercultural learning, technological pedagogical content knowledge, and critical reflective self-awareness among teachers could be potentially developed by cross-cultural telecollaborative approaches. As telecollaborations could keep up with the trend of globalized and technologically-mediated classrooms better than the traditional language teacher education modalities, they could also help develop language teaching strategies such as recognizing identities, enhancing digital literacy, and incorporating reflective activities. By applying telecollaborations to discuss intercultural aspect both sides could avoid misunderstandings and conflicts. In that light, telecollaborations were potentially helpful for developing critical, reflective teaching practices and international communities. Telecollaborations could furthermore foster ongoing teachers' development for language educators in the 21st century, as long as they were actively and carefully implemented.

With English being de facto communicative tool globally, the relationship between the English language and culture is no longer restricted to a particular culture and nation. Instead, the correlation of English and culture is shared in a wide range of different cultural contexts (Baker, 2012). Thus, pedagogy related to Global Englishes, WE, ELF or EIL is supposed to be one part of teacher education programs. In addition, teachers should be equipped with the awareness of multilingual and multicultural understanding with respect to the settings of English use in order to trigger a better communication in global environments.

MAIN FOCUS OF THE CHAPTER

Methodology

Based on the research purposes, the author aimed to explore pre-service teachers' and in-service teachers' knowledge of Global Englishes. Their awareness as well as perceptions of Global Englishes was also explored. In order to shed light on the degrees of understanding and the methods of implementation, mixed methods, a questionnaire first and semi-structured interview afterwards, were utilized to investigate the participants' attitudes and perceptions toward Global Englishes. The specific purposes of conducting this research were as follows:

1. To examine how pre-service teachers and in-service teachers know Global Englishes.
2. To examine pre-service teachers' and in-service teachers' understanding and perceptions of Global Englishes.
3. To examine what variety/ varieties pre-service teachers' and in-service teachers are inclined to select listening materials in terms of similarities or differences between the two groups.

Participants

Participants of the present study were divided into two groups, the pre-service group and the in-service group. Pre-service teachers, recruited by convenience sampling, were still under training on English teaching at Educational Programs in five universities in Taipei City and New Taipei City. The five universities are either public or private comprehensive universities in northern Taiwan. Additionally, according to Cheers Magazine, the five universities are ranked among top 20 universities in Taiwan favored by Taiwanese enterprises. Therefore, all of the five universities are considered to be prestigious higher education institutes in Taiwan. 79 pre-service teachers took part in the quantitative survey. The author delivered the questionnaires to student-teachers who were taking the course called "Methods and Materials for English Teaching" in the second year of their Educational Programs. Meanwhile, student-teachers who were doing their practicums at junior high schools or senior high schools were also invited. The participants were 15 (19%) male and 64 (81%) female student-teachers; 31 (39.2%) of them studying at public universities and 48 (60.8%) of them studying at private universities. The pre-service teachers' group consisted of 55 (69.6%) undergraduate students and 24 (30.4%) graduate students. The average teaching experience for the pre-service teachers was 2.27 years. They had some teaching experiences at private English schools and/or tutoring experiences.

On the other hand, in-service teachers, invited by snowball sampling, were teaching English at secondary schools in the northern part of Taiwan, namely Taipei City, New Taipei City and Keelung. These three areas are so called "The Taipei–Keelung metropolitan area." As the secondary school teacher certificates can be applied to both lower secondary and upper secondary levels, in-service teachers recruited for the study included both junior high school and senior high school teachers in either public or private schools. 146 in-service teachers, 26 (17.8%) male and 120 (82.2%) female, filled out the given questionnaires. 114 (78.1%) teachers were teaching at public schools while 32 (21.9%) teachers were teaching at private schools. The average teaching experience of the in-service teachers was 13.14 years. 63 (43.2%) in-service teachers obtained their teachers' certificates from comprehensive universities, followed by 58 people (39%) from normal universities, 18 teachers (12.3%) from post-bachelor program, 3 teachers (2.1%) from other institutes, 2 teachers (1.4%) from University of Science and Technology. 2 teachers (1.4%) did not reveal the source of their teachers' certificates. In addition, 43 (29.4%) teachers had bachelor's degrees. 99 (67.8%) of them obtained master's degrees. Moreover, 4 teachers held doctoral degrees (2.7%).

The reasons why there is a gap in numbers of both groups are because student-teachers need to apply for the Educational Program and go through a selective process. Furthermore, questionnaire respondents of the study were student-teachers in their second-year study at their Educational Programs or interns who had taken professional courses related to English instructions. On the other hand, since English is one of the major subjects in secondary schools, the availability of in-service teachers is higher than pre-service teachers.

Data Collection

A total of 241 questionnaires were sent to five Educational Programs at five universities and 13 public or private secondary schools in "The Taipei–Keelung metropolitan area". 225 out of 241 questionnaires were returned. This was an overall response rate of 93.4%. The responses from the 225 participants were analyzed to answer the research questions in the study. The questionnaire results had a Cronbach's alpha coefficient value of 0.71, which is an acceptable and reliable value for Social Sciences.

After 225 questionnaires were collected, 16 semi-structured interviews were conducted to yield further information. The interviews involved four males and 12 females. Nine in-service teachers took part in semi-structured interviews while seven pre-service teachers also contributed to qualitative study.

All of the interviews were carried out voluntarily as teachers had already left their names and contact details on questionnaires before they were completed. Pseudonyms were employed to protect the identity of the respondents. Each interview lasted for approximately 30-40 minutes and was recorded. Qualitative data collection compared and broadened the information from the questionnaire surveys. The main purpose of using a semi-structured interview is to add to, revise or expand on previous questions depending on the participants' responses so that a more in-depth analysis of participants' understanding and attitudes toward Global Englishes can be made.

FINDINGS AND DISCUSSIONS

Findings of this chapter were divided into three major sections. The first section presented how both groups know Global Englishes. The second section provided information about their understanding and perceptions of Global Englishes. The third section explored participants' choices and suggestions on the listening material selections.

In What Ways do Teachers get to Know Global Englishes?

On the first section of the questionnaire for both pre-service teachers and in-service teachers, the author listed four possible channels that Global Englishes might have been known to pre-service teachers and five possible ways for in-service teachers. For in-service teachers, there is one more choice "workshop or trainings carried out by the Department of Education of the city governments." It is because those teachers are required to participate in continuing education. These options are:

1. Educational Programs for Secondary School Teachers,
2. English Departments,
3. the MOE,
4. workshop or trainings carried out by Department of Education city governments in "The Taipei–Keelung metropolitan area," and
5. never heard of it.

According to descriptive statistics, English departments or related majors were the most frequently stated reason. 39.2% pre-service teachers stated they had learned Global Englishes via courses offered by English Departments. 33.6% in-service teachers expressed that they had been taught Global Englishes by the same way. Related majors were further elucidated through semi-structured interviews. One interviewee stated that her major, Translation and Interpretation Studies, made her realize different English varieties spoken in the world as well as accent and pronunciation discrepancies in each variety.

Figure 1. Channels Teachers know about Global Englishes

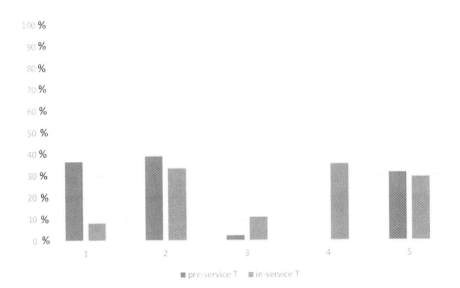

Seven interviewees indicated that they learned the notion of Global Englishes through subjects such as "Introduction to English Linguistics (4)," "Introduction to English Language Teaching (1)," "Introduction to Sociolinguistics (1)," and "Phonetics (1)." These courses were offered by English Departments in different universities. Interestingly, one of the participants indicated that there was a non-native English professor from Japan teaching English Literature courses at her department.

Although the Japanese professor speaks English with a Japanese accent, his English is proficient. He is very professional and knowledgeable in English Literature. (Kimmy)

The situation was in line with what Matsuda's view (2003). Matsuda encourages universities to recruit fluent speakers of English from the Outer Circle and the Expanding Circle for students to interact with EIL users and comprehend World Englishes.

Based on the descriptive statistical result, only 36.7% of pre-service teachers and 8.2% of the in-service teachers knew Global Englishes from previous Educational Programs. A $\chi 2$ analysis ($\chi 2 = 27.921$, P value=.00<.001) revealed a significant difference between the two groups who learned the concept of Global Englishes. More pre-service teachers than in-service teachers were being introduced to Global Englishes when they were under training at the Educational Programs for Secondary

School Teachers at their universities. Global Englishes is a relatively new field that reflects the current global use of English. According to The Republic of China Education Yearbook (2016), senior high school teachers' age between 30 and 50 makes up 73.7% of all teachers nationwide. As the in-service teachers' average teaching experience was 13.14 years, the pedagogic implications of Global Englishes might not have been promoted during their training. This might explain why in-service teachers were not familiar with the concept of Global Englishes.

Workshops and trainings seemed to be inadequate in promoting Global Englishes. From questionnaires, only 35.6% of the in-service teachers claimed they had been informed of Global Englishes via the continuing education. Five in-service teachers at semi-structured interviews further revealed that they were merely trained to be familiar with the changes and policies related to the 12-year Curriculum Education. Global Englishes was the issue subordinated to the curriculum.

I have attended workshops for teachers but as far as I know, these workshops seldom deal with Global Englishes. These workshops mainly propagate the idea of interdisciplinary. (in-service teacher, Anna)

Global Englishes was known to only 2.5% of pre-service teachers and 11% of in-service teachers via the promotion of the MOE. According to χ^2 analysis (χ^2 =4.946, P <.026), there was a significant difference between the two groups when the concept of Global Englishes was promoted through the MOE. One of the in-service teachers mentioned in the interview that he was involved in the development of the new curriculum. The teacher worked at a public high school in Taipei City. Additionally, he attended meetings at National Academy for Educational Research, helping the organization plan the curriculum. It is possible that pre-service teachers do not have as many opportunities as in-service teachers who need to attend workshops and trainings and to receive official documents from the MOE. This may also explain the fact that pre-service teachers are less likely to be in contact with the MOE.

Surprisingly, formal educational and teacher training programs were not yet promoting Global Englishes. 31.6% of pre-service teachers and 29.5% of in-service teachers were never being introduced to that concept. Two interviewees from the in-service group expressed that they did not know Global Englishes until they attended graduate schools. 69.6% of pre-service teachers were undergraduate school students and 30.4% of them were graduate school students. Since the majority of the pre-service teacher group were undergraduate students, English Departments and formal Educational Programs are recommended to offer professional courses to equip future teachers with Global Englishes.

On the other hand, informal channels such as life/overseas experiences, English proficiency tests, and mass media stood in contrast with disseminating Global

Englishes. Life experiences were the most frequently mentioned factor. Experiences such as working abroad, traveling and studying overseas were frequently ticked as the initiators. Eight out of 16 interviewees indicated they paid attention to different varieties of English and the function of "English as a lingua franca." They noticed that English contained different regional accents and pronunciations. Despite these discrepancies, people still used the language to communicate. Moreover, five interviewees stated they had interactions with global citizens at many international exchange activities and they knew how English was used in the world.

When I studied at the graduate school in the U.K., my professors told us English was a tool for communication. I lived in Birmingham where there were immigrants from India and Arabian countries. Therefore, I got a feeling that English was a "diverse" language on pronunciation, lexicon and usages. I also studied in Vienna majoring in linguistics as my second master's degree. My classmates came from European countries. English played a role as a common language because we could not speak each other's language. (in-service teacher, Alice)

English proficiency tests such as TOEIC, TOFEL and IELTS were also influential in promoting Global Englishes. Teachers admitted that they noticed different accents and pronunciations spoken in the listening comprehension section when they prepared for and took these tests. Mass media was another channel that brought the notion of Global Englishes to teachers. This included print media such as textbooks and magazines, broadcast media, and digital materials.

The result of the study was similar to that of Özmen, Çakır and Cephe (2018). They discovered that 851 Turkish English teachers had little contact with English as an International Language during their participants' education. However, personal experiences, the Internet, and high-stake tests gave them the opportunities to use English to communicate. Since non-native English speakers outnumber that of the native speakers, and countries that use English as a foreign language also develop their own varieties and speech communities, they suggest that intercultural communication and a non-native speaker model are more reasonable for language teaching. Teachers should be imbued with the perspective and insight of EIL. Also, non-native English teachers' image is a cultural representation and identification of the linguistic content. As a result, they are responsible for instilling learners with the tendency for intercultural communication.

Teachers' Understanding and Views of Global Englishes

In order to investigate teachers' understandings of Global Englishes, questions below were compiled. The questions dealt with varieties of accents and the ownership of

English. Semi-structured interviews were utilized to explore teachers' views and opinions toward the following statements.

1. I think Global Englishes refers to English with different varieties in accent.
2. I think the ownership of Global Englishes belongs to those who use English as a global language.
3. I believe those who are fluent enough to speak English without major problems have rights to use English.
4. I believe anyone who attempts to learn English has a right to use English.
5. I believe the ownership of English belongs to everyone no matter what one's nationality is.

74.6% of the pre-service teachers and in-service teachers had realized that there was a diversity of English accents including native English origins and non-native ones. The majority of questionnaire respondents agreed and understood that various English accents were the characteristics of Global Englishes; therefore, questionnaire respondents agreed on the statement "Global Englishes refers to English with different varieties in accent." Eight interviewees also pointed out that they understood a variety of English accents spoken throughout the world from their overseas experiences, university majors, and examination preparations. From participants' viewpoints, single English variety did not exist anymore.

In terms of the ownership of English, 78.4% of the questionnaire respondents believed that people who used English for global communication were eligible to claim the ownership of English. These English users not only use "standard English" but also create words from their indigenous languages. Four interviews realized that English was a common language used in the world. Because of the British Empire colonization and development and of technology, new words were developed in different regions and periods of time.

Some English words are created by one's L1 together with English roots. "Kiasuism" is developed by Singaporean who combines Holo with English to make the word. Some new words such as phubbing and selfie are developed because of the invention of smartphones. (Pre-service teacher, Kimmy &Sheng)

Furthermore, 81.7% of the participants agreed the ownership of Global Englishes fell to those who could speak English fluently without major problems. Students' learning motivation was especially worthy noticing. 92% of questionnaire respondents believed that students who were willing to learn English were also eligible English users.

It is meaningful to teach students the issue of the ownership of English. They would realize English owners were not limited to native speakers. They will be more confident in speaking English. I believe this will motivate students to learn English. (in-service teacher, Joey)

Additionally, 80.3% of questionnaire respondents did not view one's nationality as a crucial factor in the ownership of English. Five interviewees pointed out that the ownership of English was "cross-boundary," not restricted to Americans and Britons.

It is evident enough from the quantitative and qualitative data that participants seemed to have open-minded attitudes. They accepted the fact that English accents and pronunciations was diverse and the language was used for communication worldwide. The ownership of English was no longer limited to the Inner Circle. Instead, it transcended national and cultural boundaries. To use English as a global communication tool was more important than emphasize its native-speaker authority.

The results from quantitative and qualitative data are compatible with Matsuda's (2003) view. Matsuda points out that English has been changed in forms and functions. The demographics of English users also reshape the language. Nonetheless, a quarter of questionnaire respondents did not realize that English varieties were pluralistic. As a result, similar to Murphy's (2014) recommendation, it is essential to raise teachers' cognizance of the reality that English comprises many native and non-native varieties.

Judging from the quantitative data, most of questionnaire respondents agreed that the ownership of English had nothing to do with any particular countries or people. The findings of the present study deviated from previous ones (Sifakis & Sougari, 2005; Monfared & Safarzadeh, 2014). For these two studies, participants chose native speakers as the rightful owner of English and showed strong norm-bound perspectives. First, more than half of the respondents in these studies said that English native speakers or to people with native speaker competence were rightful owners. Furthermore, less than one third of the respondents said that fluent English users without major problems were eligible to claim the ownership of English. Finally, less than a quarter of participants took an EIL perspective: speakers of the language without major issues were rightful owners. In contrast, the participants' orientation towards nativism was not as strong as the previous ones in this study, which was consistent with Liu and Cheng's results (2017). They discovered that student and teacher participants in their university believed that English did not belong to any particular countries or people. Both groups were aware of other varieties of English in addition to American or British English. Pre-service teachers and in-service teachers in the present study had a more open-minded view. They believed that people who could speak English fluently had the rights to use English. Nonetheless, from Liu and Cheng (2017), only student participants showed positive attitude toward the statement-- English belongs to those who can speak English fluently. Results from these two studies may indicate that Taiwanese teachers and students had more flexible perspectives. The ownership of English did not need to be norm-bound. This attitude built up English instructors' confidence so they did not need to feel inferior to native speakers when communicating and teaching English.

Data collected from interviews revealed teachers might be confused about terminologies. Some interviewees experienced using English in an ELF context. But one of them was not aware of the term "lingua franca." One in-service teacher shared her experience in Australia. She joined church activities where there were Australians and immigrants from other parts of the world. They used English to communicate because of their various mother tongues. Another pre-service teacher seemed to understand indigenized varieties, one of the characteristics of WE, but she failed to use the term. For example, "Kiasu" is an English word developed uniquely in Singapore. Since teachers might have difficulty in differentiating these nuances among ELF, WE, and Global Englishes, it is necessary to involve scholars specializing in the field to teachers' continuing education and Educational Programs. This way, in-service teachers may have a better understanding to weave these concepts in their classes. An in-service teacher particularly replaced the terminology "Global Englishes" with "World Englishes" during the interview. A possible explanation for the confusion over the terminology was that its corresponding translation in Chinese was printed and used for documentation. Therefore, the MOE was recommended to use a better Chinese translation for the terminology to avoid misconception.

Material Selection

Both quantitative and qualitative data were applied to collect pre-service teachers and in-service teachers' preference for selecting English varieties in a listening textbook. 76.8% of the questionnaire respondents expressed that they preferred using conversations between or among native speakers in a listening textbook. 12 out of 16 interviewees expressed they would put native English speakers' varieties especially American English and British English into consideration when selecting listening materials. From their opinions, these varieties provided learners with the "correct" input. They were afraid that their students would have confusions over learning English. They would also take into account of the students' English proficiency and age before exposing them to other English varieties. Besides American English, which was seen as the main stream in teaching English in Taiwan, teachers also noticed that British English should also be introduced. It is because England is the origin of English and British English is one of the major English varieties. The availability of purchasing listening materials is the other reason. Interviewees stated that textbooks published by Oxford University Press and Cambridge University Press could be bought in Taiwan. Lastly, one third of in-service teacher interviewees obtain their masters' degrees from British universities so that they were aware of the necessity to include British English into English classes. In addition to American English and British English, other Inner Circle English varieties such as Australian and New Zealand English were preferred as they could be heard in English proficiency tests and College Entrance Examination and these varieties were easier for class preparation. They were easier to be understood than other Englishes from the Outer Circle and the Expanding Circle. On the other hand, a quarter of the interviewees expressed they would introduce varieties from the Outer Circle as they wanted to let their learners know the varieties and the pluralistic characters of English. Three interviewees stated that they would choose varieties from Kachru's three circles depending on their teaching topics or contents.

When I teach Great Barrier Reef, I play documentaries filmed and spoken by Australians. When we are debating on the issue whether to kill and eat whales, I let my students watch documentaries spoken by Norwegian and Japanese. Besides the Inner Circle varieties, I also choose other English varieties.(In-service teacher, Laura)

The present study indicates a changing phenomenon. Dissimilar to previous studies (Tsou & Chen, 2014; Tse, 1987), in which American English enjoyed a prestigious status for ELT in Taiwan, the participants of the present study chose other English varieties from the Inner Circle when selecting English listening materials. Nevertheless, the results of the present study were still far from Galloway and Rose's (2015) GELT approach. GELT approach focuses on diversity and the function of English as an international lingua franca when it comes to teaching listening skills. As a result, if the MOE wants to integrate GELT into English curriculum for the 12-year Compulsory Education, English teachers should take Tsou's advice (2015). "English teachers from K-12 and higher education all need to understand how the English language has undergone changes in the past decade so they can in turn help students adjust their mindsets and embrace the exciting changes which are taking place in the English language (p.59-60)." Ke (2012) urges English teachers in Taiwan not to ignore the trend of ELF. Teachers are supposed to modify their teaching to help students adjust to the need for future ELF use. In doing so, students will benefit from the teaching in the long run.

SOLUTIONS AND RECOMMENDATIONS

According to the qualitative and quantitative data, formal settings inadequately provided teachers with the concept of Global Englishes. The author suggested that the insight of Global Englishes should be promoted via English teacher education programs for pre-service teachers, as well as the continuing education for in-service teachers' training programs to reinforce teachers' concepts of Global Englishes. This in turn should help the in-service teachers to integrate the concept into their teaching (Snow, Kamhi-Stein & Briton, 2006; Sifakis, 2007; Coskun, 2011). It is also recommended that the MOE distribute official documents and/or teachers' manuals to secondary schools and Educational Programs for Secondary School Teachers at universities to promote Global Englishes. In Taiwan, to become a qualified teacher at secondary schools, teachers must take teachers' recruitment tests after they obtain their teachers' certificates. Questions related to the concepts of Global Englishes should be included in the tests. If teachers can be aware of the diversities of English during the examination preparations, they will be more aware of introducing a variety of Englishes into their classrooms and adopting materials that include a variety of Englishes.

Data obtained in the present study indicated that teachers seemed to understand Global Englishes via life experience, interactions with native speakers and/or non-native speakers, taking English proficiency tests, and from the mass media. These personal experiences were beneficial in forming the notion of Global Englishes. High school teachers and students can make good use of both face-to-face and virtual communication opportunities. Global Englishes scholars acknowledge that English is diverse in the forms of linguistics, culture and functions. Matsuda (2003) suggests that teachers and students should take advantage of these opportunities to participate in international exchanges to enhance their interactions with EIL users. Baker (2012) indicates language and culture are intertwined. Therefore, it is inextricable to teach language and the culture in the context used. Bayyurt (2006) promotes that teaching ELF pedagogy in the Expanding Circle as ELF pedagogy can lead to better intercultural communication. Currently, some high schools have overseas institutions as partners. Therefore, teachers and students have the mutual benefits to develop their ICC on both sides. In addition to face-to-face interactions, virtual communications are a part of norm in education settings. Dimitriadou, Palaiologou and Nari (2014) encourage multicultural schools to design and implement e-learning training educational systems to provide additional teaching methods for teachers and students. Vurdien and Puranen (2018) suggest videoconferencing can give university students opportunities to share experiences and build friendship. It can heighten students' knowledge of both cultures. Videoconferencing is also an effective tool to foster intercultural learning. In a similar study, Saquing (2018) suggests the need of integrating intercultural communication in English curriculum for English major students to develop their ICC for internationalization.

CONCLUSION

While the notion of Global Englishes was not well-informed through formal channels, life experience, English proficiency test preparations, and mass media made up for teachers to acquire the concept. Quantitative and qualitative data from the participants showed positive attitudes toward Global Englishes. They believed that native English speakers from the Inner Circle were not the solely eligible owners of English. Generally speaking, they also approved of exposing students to a variety of Englishes. However, prior to this, participants were inclined to choose English varieties printed and recorded from the Inner Circle. They believed that the first priority is to make students adapt to the so-called Standard English. It is essential to take advantage of international exchange events, extracurricular activities and Internet resources to fulfill the learning objective addressed in the English curricula for 12-year Compulsory Education.

REFERENCES

Baker, W. (2009). The Cultures of English as a Lingua Franca. *TESOL Quarterly*, *43*(4), 567–592. doi:10.1002/j.1545-7249.2009.tb00187.x

Baker, W. (2012). From Cultural Awareness to Intercultural Awareness: Culture in ELT. *ELT Journal*, *66*(1), 62–70. doi:10.1093/elt/ccr017

Bayyurt, Y. (2006). Non-native English Language Teachers' Perspective on Culture in English as a Foreign Language Classrooms. *Teacher Development*, *10*(2), 233–247. doi:10.1080/13664530600773366

Byram, M. (1997). *Teaching and assessing intercultural communicative competence*. Multilingual Matters.

Chang, Y. J. (2014). Learning English Today: What can World Englishes Teach College Students in Taiwan? *English Today, 30*(1), 21-27.

Chao, T. C. (2016). A preliminary study of Taiwanese NNETS' self-assessment of intercultural communicative competence in English language teaching. *Taiwan Journal of TESOL., 13*(1), 71–103.

Cheers 快樂工作人雜誌 (2017). 2017最佳大學指南 [Best Universities 2017]. Retrieved January 31, 2018 https://topic.cheers.com.tw/issue/2017/college/article/2-2.aspx

Chen, A. H. (2013). An Evaluation on Primary English Education in Taiwan: From the Perspective of Language Policy. *English Language Teaching, 6*(10), 158–165. doi:10.5539/elt.v6n10p158

Coskun, A. (2011). Future English Teachers' Attitudes towards EIL Pronunciation. *Journal of English as an International Language, 6*(2), 46–67.

Crystal, D. (2003). *English as a global language* (2nd ed.). Cambridge University Press. doi:10.1017/CBO9780511486999

Deniz, E. B., Özkan, Y., & Bayyirt, Y. (2016). English as a Lingua Franca: Reflections on ELF-Related Issues by Pre-Service Language Teachers in Turkey. *The Reading Matrix: An International Online Journal, 16*(2), 144–161.

Dimitriadou, C., Palaiologou, N., & Nari, E. (2014). E-Learning Training Courses on Multricultural Education: An Example from Greece. In V. Zuzeviciute, E. Butrime, D. Adžgauskiene, V. Fomin, & K. Papadakis (Eds.), *E-Learning as a Socio-Cultural System: A Multidimensional Analysis* (pp. 322–345). IGI Global. doi:10.4018/978-1-4666-6154-7.ch006

Galloway, N. (2013). Global Englishes and English Language Teaching (ELT)- Bridging the Gap between Theory and Practice in a Japanese Context. *System, 41*(3), 786–803. doi:10.1016/j.system.2013.07.019

Galloway, N., & Rose, H. (2014). Using Listening Journals to Raise Awareness of Global Englishes in ELT. *ELT Journal, 68*(4), 386–396. doi:10.1093/elt/ccu021

Galloway, N., & Rose, H. (2015). *Introducing Global Englishes*. Routledge. doi:10.4324/9781315734347

Graddol, D. (2006). *English next*. The British Council.

Kachru, Y., & Smith, L. E. (2008). *Cultures, contexts and world Englishes*. Routledge. doi:10.4324/9780203891346

Ke, I. C. (2012). English as a lingua franca (ELF) in intercultural communication: Findings from ELF online projects and implication for ELTC in Taiwan. *Taiwan Journal of TESOL, 9*(2), 63–93.

Kirkpatrick, A. (2007). *World English Implications for International Communication and English Language Teaching*. Cambridge University Press.

Lawrance, G., & Cohen, E. (2018). Examing International Telecollaboration in Language Teacher Education. In D. Tafazoli, M. Gómez Parra, & A. Cristina (Eds.), *Cross-Cultural Perspectives on Technology-Enhanced Language Learning* (pp. 264–282). IGI Global. doi:10.4018/978-1-5225-5463-9.ch018

Liu, P. H., & Cheng, Y. C. (2017). Attitudes toward English as an International Language: A Comparative Study of College Teachers and Students in Taiwan. *English as an International Language Journal, 12*(1), 66–85.

Matsuda, A. (2003). Incorporating World Englishes in Teaching English as an International Language. *TESOL Quarterly, 37*(4), 719–729. doi:10.2307/3588220

Monfared, A., & Safarzadeh, M. M. (2014). Pronunciation issues and varieties of English from an EIL perspective: A survey of outer and expanding circle learners' beliefs. *International Journal of Applied Linguistics and English Literature, 3*(6), 212–223.

Murphy, J. (2014). Intelligible, Comprehensible, non-native models in ESL/EFL Pronunciation Teaching. *System, 42*, 258–269. doi:10.1016/j.system.2013.12.007

National Academy for Educational Research. (2015). 十二年國民基本教育語文領域(英語、第二外語)課程綱要研修說明公聽會版本(國民中小學及普通型高中) [The Curricula for English Guidelines of 12 year Education: The Language Arts Learning Area]. Taipei: National Academy for Educational Research. Retrieved June 11, 2017 from http://www.naer.edu.tw/files/15-1000-10472,c639-1.php?Lang=zh-tw

National Academy for Educational Research. (2016). 中華民國教育年報105年版 [The Republic of China Education Yearbook 2016]. Taipei: National Academy for Educational Research. Retrieved November 1, 2017 from https://www.naer.edu.tw/files/15-1000-13943,c1310-1.php?Lang=zh-tw

National Academy for Educational Research. (2017). 十二年國民基本教育課程綱要國民中小學暨普通型高級中等學校語文領域-英語文課程手冊初稿更新第五版[The Curricula for English Guidelines of 12 year Curriculum: The Language Arts Learning Area (The fifth version)]. Taipei: National Academy for Educational Research. Retrieved November 1, 2017 from https://www.naer.edu.tw/files/11-1000-1590-1.php?Lang=zh-tw

Nunan, D. (2003). The Importance of English as a Global Language on Educational Policies and Practices in the Asia-Pacific Region. *TESOL Quarterly, 37*(4), 589–613. doi:10.2307/3588214

Özmen, K., Çakır, A., & Cephe, P. (2018). Conceptuation of English Culture and Accent: Idealized English among Teachers in the Expanding Circle. *Asian EFL Journal*, *20*(3), 8–30.

Prapinwong, M. (2018). Blended learning course design and implementation to foster the intercultural awareness of preservice teachers in an EFL context. *Asian EFL Journal, 20*(12.2), 131-152.

Saquing, J. (2018). Intercultural communicative competence of Bachelor of Science in Secondary Education (BSED) major in English students: A basic for a proposed integration of internationalization in the BSED major in English curriculum. *Asian EFL Journal, 20*(2), 8–29.

Seidlhofer, B. (2005). English as a lingua franca. *ELT Journal*, *59*(4), 339–341. doi:10.1093/elt/cci064

Sharifian. (2013). Globalization and Developing Metacultural Competence in Learning English at an International Language. *Multilingual Education, 3*(7), 1-11.

Sifakis, N. C. (2007). 'The education of the teachers of English as a lingua franca: A transformative perspective. *International Journal of Applied Linguistics*, *17*(3), 355–375. doi:10.1111/j.1473-4192.2007.00174.x

Sifakis, N. C., & Sougari, A. M. (2005). Pronunciation Issues and EIL Pedagogy in the Periphery: A Survey of Greek State School Teachers' Beliefs. *TESOL Quarterly*, *39*(3), 467–485. doi:10.2307/3588490

Snow, M. A., Kamhi-Stein, L. D., & Brinton, D. M. (2006). Teacher Training for English as a Lingua Franca. *Annual Review of Applied Linguistics*, *26*, 261–281. doi:10.1017/S0267190506000134

Tse, K. P. (1987). *Language Planning and English as a Foreign Language in Middle School Education in the Republic of China*. Crane Publishing Co.

Tsou, W. (2015). From Globalization to Glocalization: Rethinking English Language Teaching in Response to the ELF Phenomenon. *English as a Global Language Education (EaGLE). Journal*, *1*(1), 47–63.

Tsou, W., & Chen, F. (2014). EFL and ELF College Students' Perceptions toward Englishes. *Journal of English as a Lingua Franca*, *3*(2), 363–386. doi:10.1515/jelf-2014-0021

Vettorel, P., & Corrizzato, S. (2016). Fostering Awareness of the Pedagogical Implications of World Englishes and ELF in Teacher Education in Italy. *Studies in Second Language Learning and Teaching*, *6*(3), 487–511. doi:10.14746sllt.2016.6.3.6

Vurdien, R., & Puranen, P. (2018). Intercultural Learning Via Videoconferencing: Students' Attitudes and Experiences. In D. Tafazoli, M. Gómez Parra, & A. Cristina (Eds.), *Cross-Cultural Perspectives on Technology-Enhanced Language Learning* (pp. 264–282). IGI Global., doi:10.4018/978-1-5225-5463-9.ch015

Wajnryb, R. (2008). *You know what I mean?: Words, contexts and communication.* Cambridge University Press. doi:10.1017/CBO9780511487064

Yang, J. H. (2013). Taiwanese Perceptions of Indian English: A Perceptual Change in the Learning of English Variation. *English Teaching & Learning, 37*(4), 91–146. doi:10.6330/ETL.2013.37.4.03

Yang, J. H., & Wong, W. (2009, November). *Linguistic standards and realities of English use for international business interaction.* Paper presented at the 2009 Applied Linguistics and Sociolinguistics: The Form and the Content, Taipei, Taiwan.

Yang, P. (2018). Developing TESOL Teacher Intercultural Identity: An Intercultural Communication Competence Approach. *TESOL Journal, 9*(3), 525–541. doi:10.1002/tesj.356

Zacharias, N.T. (2014). Integrating EIL Pedagogy in a Pre-service Teacher Education Program. *TEFLIN Journal: A Publication on the Teaching and Learning of English, 25*(2), 217–232.

Chapter 13
Internet-Based Text-Matching Software and EFL Preservice Teachers' Awareness of Academic Integrity:
A Case Study in the Turkish Context

Işıl Günseli Kaçar
Middle East Technical University, Turkey

Hale Işık-Güler
Middle East Technical University, Turkey

ABSTRACT

Having been investigated from different perspectives across a broad range of disciplines, plagiarism in English as a Second Language (ESL)/English as a Foreign Language (EFL) contexts has not received much attention until very recently. This mixed-methods case study in the Turkish context is a critical analysis of EFL preservice teachers' perceptions, motives, knowledge of, and practices regarding plagiarism, as well as their academic integrity awareness and plagiarism detection ability in a freshman academic writing course at a state university. The quantitative data from the pre- and post-test questionnaires in the study were analyzed through descriptive statistics while the qualitative data from the questionnaires and semi-structured interviews with the preservice teachers were analyzed via thematic analysis. Findings suggested the favorable impact of Turnitin on preservice teachers' self-discovery to overcome and reduce possible plagiarism attempts in the Turkish context.

DOI: 10.4018/978-1-7998-2831-0.ch013

Copyright © 2021, IGI Global. Copying or distributing in print or electronic forms without written permission of IGI Global is prohibited.

INTRODUCTION

Plagiarism in English as a Second Language (ESL) and English as a Foreign Language (EFL) contexts is a topic that has engaged researchers in a heated discussion in recent years (Amin & Mohammadkarimi, 2019; Balbay & Kilis, 2018; Bailey, 2015; Gokmenoğlu, 2017; Jereb et al., 2018; Rets & Ilya, 2018). As pointed out in a recent study by Rets and Ilya (2018), there is still no consensus on a comprehensive definition of the notion of plagiarism that has a "longstanding history" (p.195), despite an escalating rate in plagiarism in higher education suggested by Jackson (2006). The ambiguity that resides in plagiarism demonstrates itself in diverse types of plagiarism depicted in the research literature, revealing its global prevalence (Decoo, 2008, Lei & Hu, 2015). In fact, over the last two decades, in the related literature, plagiarism incidents have become an issue of immediate relevance (Rets & Ilya, 2018). Although in the first /native language (L1) context the focus has been on whether it should be judged as 'stealing' (Kolich, 1983, p. 143) and 'cheating' (Murphy, 1990, p. 889), in ESL/EFL literature, with a different outlook due to the "language factor", research has centered around differences of cultural perceptions of texts and textual borrowing (Yamada, 2003). Several studies have been concerned with contrasting the viewpoints of ESL/EFL writers and those of American and North European teachers as regards to the practice of copying source texts without acknowledgement (Buranen, 1999; Dryden, 1999; Sherman, 1992). Others have investigated the attitudes of Asian ESL/EFL writers toward Western literary conventions (Curie, 1998; Deckert, 1993; LoCastro & Masuko, 1997). Another line of research has adopted a more ideological approach and questioned the authorship of texts as well as the relevance of plagiarism (Pennycook, 1996; Scollon, 1994, 1995) in connection to the writing habits of ESL/EFL writers whose backgrounds do not value textual ownership. Thus, it is evident that more studies are still needed to bridge the global and local concerns and practices.

This debate on plagiarism with a distinct focus on differences in cultural perceptions in textual borrowing has provided interesting descriptions for researchers and teachers, enabling them to develop valuable insights into the developmental discourse practices and cultural notions of ESL/EFL writers (Gibson & Chester-Fangman, 2011; McCabe & Trevino, 1993; Scollon, 1995). There is still a growing need to look into the reasons why plagiarism is still regarded as a growing concern and how classroom practices and technology can help.

These concerns provided an impetus to the present study in this book chapter which investigated the plagiarism-related *perceptions, knowledge and practices* of 80 EFL pre-service teachers and how the use of a text-matching software (i.e., Turnitin) altered them.

The research questions that guided the current study are as follows:

1. What are EFL pre-service teachers' *perceptions* regarding plagiarism?
    i) How do EFL pre-service teachers in the undergraduate program define plagiarism?
    ii) How do their previous educational background and expectations impact their definition of plagiarism?
2. What are EFL pre-service teachers' *knowledge* and *practices* regarding plagiarism?
    a. To what extent do they know how to document sources appropriately?
    b. What are the major difficulties they face in source documentation practices?
    c. What are the culture-based contextual motives that underlie their misconduct in plagiarism-related practices?
3. Does plagiarism *training* and the *use* of Turnitin affect EFL pre-service teachers' *perceptions, knowledge and practices* in plagiarism?
    a. Does plagiarism training affect their ability to notice plagiarized materials/texts?
    b. How do they view the integration of Turnitin into coursework, the advantages and shortcomings of using Turnitin?

Especially in the EFL context, such case studies delving into plagiarism practices of learners are crucial as such environments limit exposure and language production opportunities for many learners. As learners may be discouraged from experimenting with language, they can fail to develop language awareness and decrease their chances of developing and using their voices effectively in written communication as second/foreign language (L2) authors. As they deter from getting creative with language, their chances of engaging in critical thinking is also affected along with their interlanguage development. At this point, this book chapter is also an attempt to disclose how technology might help administrators and teachers in rectifying these practices.

BACKGROUND

Academic honesty is associated with scientific integrity underlying any kind of research or educational endeavor (Dolzhenko et al., 2016). Plagiarism can be described as "an unauthorized appropriation of another's work, ideas, methods, results or words without acknowledging the source and original author" (Mavrinac et al., 2010, p. 196). It is regarded as a threat to academic integrity that strongly undermines the key considerations such as being honest, being trustworthy, being fair, being respectful and being responsible in academic circles (Hughes & McCabe, 2006). The research literature into plagiarism manifested that there has been a surge in plagiarism cases over the past decades (See Heron, 2001; Park, 2003), which is mainly attributed to the speedy and relatively uncomplicated access to information via technology.

Research indicates a substantial rise in the number of plagiarism cases among undergraduate students (Selwyn, 2008; Sentleng & King, 2012), ranging from 19% in the USA (Scanlon & Neuman, 2002) to 81% in Australia (Marsden et al., 2005). However, it is said to be hard to correctly estimate the number of actual plagiarism incidents due to the self-reporting research methodology adopted in the majority of the studies (Bretag, 2013). The most common form of collecting data on plagiarism incidents are questionnaires based on the self-reporting of student plagiarism or the students' perceptions of their peers' plagiarism practices as indicated by Rakovski and Levy (2007) and Scanlon and Neumann (2002).

Unlike in the past, plagiarism is regarded as quite a serious concern and students' academic work and scientific/research activities are subject to screening for plagiarism in most higher education institutes to ensure the production of novel and authentic student/author contributions through free online resources and commercially available softwares. However, it is also acknowledged that students' perceptions on plagiarism, their knowledge and understanding of the issue and their interpretation of academic integrity show variations in line with their previous experiences and their cultural perceptions and may interfere with their academic writing practices (Dolzhenko, et al., 2016). Today many institutions of higher education use text-matching software to assess the originality of the texts and to discover the degree of similarity between a text with other information sources. Furthermore, quite a few universities have prepared detailed guidelines for students or disseminated information about academic research ethics and research quality to them by holding some short courses, in-class sessions or workshops to facilitate their understanding of different ways of plagiarism, raise their awareness of the concept and to point out ways to refrain from it. According to Dolzhenko, et al. (2016), a lot of recommendations have been made to instructors as to how to address this issue properly in their teaching contexts. Nevertheless, to date there has been no agreement on what should be done to effectively handle plagiarism incidents and to radically eliminate the problem or to deter students from committing plagiarism completely.

This chapter, hence, aims to reveal how and to what extent students' attitudes and their educational background regarding writing experiences and the use of a text-matching software, Turnitin, have an impact on their motivation or engagement in plagiarism in their academic writing practices. Another purpose is to highlight recommendations for the students, instructors, policy makers and administrators to prevent plagiarism.

STUDENTS' NOTION OF PLAGIARISM

The previous research into plagiarism put forward that the main factor underlying the growing number of plagiarism incidents students are engaged in is the students' vague understanding of the concept of plagiarism (See Ryan, et al., 2009). It was also indicated that the background factors, different aspects of plagiarism of graduate as well as undergraduate students such as epistemological, cultural and ethical perspectives are said to play a part in students' opaque interpretation of the term (Dolzhenko, et al., 2016).

It was pointed out that even though students develop some kind of general awareness towards plagiarism, they do not have a detailed understanding of the issue (See also Breen & Maassen, 2005; Gullifer & Tyson, 2010; Ledwith & Risquez, 2008; Löfström & Kupila, 2013). Some other studies such as Ashworth, Freewood, and Macdonald (2003), on the other hand, showed that students' understanding of plagiarism is shaped by their personal background to a great extent, which is also in line with the findings of Sohrabi, Gholipour and Mohammadesmaeli (2011), who investigated the issue in a culturally different context. In the same vein, the findings of Lake's (2004) study, which explored the cultural differences in the academic writing practices of Chinese students, and the impact of these students' previous academic writing experience on these practices, indicated that the majority of the Chinese students in the study lacked familiarity with the acknowledgement of an author in a piece of academic writing. Similarly, Powell (2012) stated that students' different previous learning experiences that they bring along with them to higher education contexts might account for their plagiaristic behavior. This is consistent with Kayaoğlu et al. (2015), displaying that EFL students in the Turkish higher education context lack of awareness towards plagiarism due to a heavy emphasis on the exam-oriented education system and '"textbook based" teaching approach' (Hayes & Introna, 2015, p. 225) in their K-12 educational backgrounds. The Turkish EFL learners at university mostly tend to come from language learning environments that do not focus on productive English language skills, i.e., speaking and writing, and hence do not feel confident enough to use English, as pointed out by Hayes and Introna (2015). They are likely to have the inclination to be engaged in unintentional plagiarism due to their lack of awareness towards source documentation and academic integrity issues. Also, Unal et al. (2012) maintained that plagiarism awareness-raising activities are not common in vocational schools, universities and graduate programmes in Turkey. In addition, there are mainly two types of penalty for plagiarism: namely, a warning or expulsion from the institution. Due to the severity of the latter, the former tends to be administered; however, it does not seem to have a deterring impact on those who committed this academic malpractice (Kayaoğlu et al., 2015). Furthermore, the ethics boards at various Turkish universities may have different penalties for similar plagiaristic behaviour (Kayaoğlu et al., 2015).

In relation to the investigation of the attitudes of Asian ESL/EFL writers toward Western literary conventions research by Currie (1998), Deckert (1993), Leki & Carson (1997), LoCastro & Masuko (1997) and most recently Löfström (2011) indicated that students from the West regard plagiarism as "unethical behaviour contradicting academic integrity" (Dolzhenko, et al., 2016, p. 846). In her study on the role of ethical issues in academic writing, Löfström (2011) found that students regarded flawed citation practices as only one aspect of ethical concerns in research. Another study by Scanlon and Neumann (2002) pointed out that the overwhelming majority of the 698 undergraduate students (89.3%) from different American universities, in different degrees, considered patchwriting (copy a text and paste it into one's own without accrediting the author) from an internet source to be an illicit academic writing practice while 3.1% disagreed. Interestingly, however, starting with Howard (1999) and continuing with the work of Abasi and Akbari (2008) and later Davis (2013) and Li (2013), currently 'patchwriting' is considered as a useful developmental transitory stage that helps learners develop rhetorical awareness on their way to becoming expert writers in an L2 (see Pecorari & Petric, 2014 for a further discussion). In a similar vein, Mustafa (2019), in a recent study investigating EFL students' understanding of plagiarism in academic writing classes, found that in the higher education context in Indonesia, patchwriting was regarded as an ethical practice in academic writing as opposed to a form of plagiarism.

At this point, the role of intention and the relationship of deceitful and undeceitful plagiarism are worth mentioning. For some researchers working in the field, "if the writer did not intend to copy or intend to cheat by doing so, the act cannot legitimately be called plagiarism" (Pecorari & Petrić, 2014, p. 271). In a recent study in the Turkish context, Köse and Arıkan (2011) revealed that for nearly one-third of the participants (27.5%) in their sample, plagiarism is not regarded as a serious breach of academic integrity, which is reflected in the high rate of plagiarism incidents among a student cohort. In a study by Handa and Power (2005), which was conducted among 80 Indian undergraduate students and 15 postgraduate students in Australia who received their undergraduate degrees in India, showed that the students did not have a clear understanding of plagiarism and proper source documentation and citation practices. Another study by Gitanjali (2004) also confirmed the findings of the previous studies into the Indian students' perceptions of cheating behavior, which indicates that Indian students do not regard plagiarism as unethical behavior. Similarly, in the Indian context, the feedback from university lecturers was in line with the undergraduate students' responses in that the former thought the latter were not expected to have mastered proper documentation and citation skills, as reported by Handa and Power (2005). According to Dolzhenko, et al. (2016, p.846), however, it must be kept in mind that in relation to the discussion on plagiarism, the emphasis should not be placed on the local "national" and cultural perspective rather on the global "poor academic culture and low education".

THE ORIGINS OF STUDENT PLAGIARISM

As brought up earlier, student plagiarism phenomenon can be investigated in terms of its origin - whether it is an unintentional practice (one where the student is engaged in due to a lack of awareness) or an intentional one (one where the student is aware of his/her breach of academic integrity). Intentional plagiarism, which is regarded as a violation of academic integrity, is reported to be quite a widespread phenomenon (Ryan, et al., 2009), among students and students are reported as having a positive attitude towards this type of academic misconduct (Ryan, et al., 2009).

The motives underlying such cases of intentional/unintentional plagiarism fall into three categories: personal, contextual, and institutional, which for the most part are shaped by the faculty's attitude and behavior (Hughes & McCabe, 2006). Personal factors are related to "culture, language issues, and attitude" while institutional and contextual aspects are concerned with the "academic policies, honor code, the penalties for academic misconduct, peers' attitude toward cheating and cheating individuals" (Dolzhenko, et al., 2016, p. 850). Regarding the personal factors, recent studies corroborate the previous research findings in that students' plagiaristic behavior could be attributed to poor academic writing skills and their relatively low level of proficiency in English (Hui-Fang, 2019; Guraya & Guraya, 2017; Patak et al., 2020;) as well as students' poor understanding of appropriate citing, paraphrasing and summarizing practices (Hui-Fang, 2019) as well as their avoidance to practice the citation and references practices due to a lack of confidence (Hui-Fang, 2019) and their inexperience in source-based writing (Hayes & Introna, 2015). Apart from these aforementioned personal factors affecting plagiarism, convenient access to online academic sources was also stated as one factor leading to plagiaristic behavior (Graham-Matheson & Starr, 2013; Patak et al., 2020). As a result of the recent breakthroughs in the field of technology, the open-access materials have become more and more common, rendering student plagiarism relatively easy and tempting. Such easy and effortless accessibility of the online materials has promoted the global relevance of plagiarism research for the last two decades (Hui-Fang, 2019; Nova & Utami, 2018; Rets & Ilya, 2018). Also, in a comprehensive plagiarism-related project in the Turkish context by Gökmenoğlu (2017) revealed that despite a rise in awareness towards legal and ethical concerns, plagiarism is still considered an issue that deserves a great deal of attention. With respect to the contextual factors affecting the student engagement in plagiarism, the previous research pointed out the inconsistent stance, knowledge and approach towards student plagiarism (Espinoza & Nájera 2015). The recent research confirmed the previous findings, indicating that some instructors' attitudes, which were not aligned with the academic integrity policies adopted by the university, tended to exacerbate the perpetuated plagiaristic student behavior (Hui-Fang, 2019). The instructors' certain assessment practices such as the traditional assessment (i.e., paper and pencil tests) as opposed to the real time assessment (via online platforms) were found to fuel student plagiarism, by creating a conflict between policy and practice (Arslan & Üçok-Atasoy, 2020).

Some other personal factors are also involved in the process of students' decision-making regarding plagiaristic behavior such as poor time management skills, the heavy workload or the high task challenge (Devlin & Gray, 2007). Extensive pressure and expectations of high marks or being in a competitive learning atmosphere may lead students to commit plagiarism (Galus, 2002). It is also of utmost importance that learning should be emphasized at all costs and awareness should be raised against devaluing some particular topics as opposed to others, which is likely to trigger academic misconduct by lowering the students' ethical standards (Heron, 2001).

Peer behavior, one of the personal factors, is also likely to make an impact on students' approach to plagiarism (Carrell, Malmstrom, & West, 2008; McCabe, Trevino, & Butterfield, 2011) and act as a support mechanism for cheating. In fact, those who do not cheat feel isolated from the cheaters (McCabe & Trevino, 1993). It was indicated that the strongest deterrent factor against plagiarism is the risk of being caught (Dolzhenko et al., 2016). As revealed by Gibson and Chester-Fangman (2011), McCabe and Trevino (1993), and Scanlan (2006), students perceive quite accurately how the faculty members respond to academic dishonesty. Scanlan (2006) indicated that 90% of college students believed cheaters do not get caught or are not punished appropriately.

As to the global and local impact on culture as a variable shaping students' perceptions of plagiarism, several studies highlighted the differences in understanding plagiarism in the Western and Eastern cultures (Gu & Brooks, 2008; Maxwell et al., 2008). Maxwell et al. (2008) indicated that learners in the Asian EFL context did not regard illicit paraphrasing and verbatim copying as paraphrasing as much as the ESL learners in the Australian context. This difference in the ESL/EFL learners' perceptions of plagiarism might be attributed to the notion that learning in Asian countries is mainly focused on covering the textbook content as opposed to the view of learning in western countries that emphasizes critical and creative thinking (Hayes et al., 2005). Some other previous research studies on the plagiarism practices of ESL learners, Hyland (2001), Pecorari (2001), Sowden (2005), also confirmed that the cultural values and practices of multilingual students are sometimes at variance with Western academic practice in relation to plagiarism. In fact, Gu and Brooks (2008), in a qualitative study in the Chinese ESL context explored the changes in the plagiarism perceptions of international students in the British academic community. They concluded that plagiaristic behavior can be considered sociocultural as the students in the study needed to cope with the emotional issues arising from the shift in their plagiarism-related cognition, sense of identity, and sociocultural values.

Contextual variables also come into play in relation to the student engagement in plagiarism. The limited direct contact between students and educators, restricted opportunities to receive feedback from instructors, the lack of constructive feedback from academics for students were also indicated to be contributing to the high rates of plagiarism among students. International students were reported to be suffering from the linguistic and cultural obstacles that interfere with the proper contact with the academic staff (Dolzhenko, et al., 2016). Some differences were also observed between the students in the ESL and the EFL context in terms of their familiarity with the concept of plagiarism. Deckert (1993) claimed that the ESL university students in Hong Kong were not only unfamiliar with plagiarism, but found it difficult to identify. Unlike EFL students, ESL students were more aware of the implications of plagiarism than it was thought to be (Deckert, 1993). Leki and Carson (1997, p. 59) found that the non-native students in their study at a university in the US were actually very aware of teacher expectations with regard to plagiarism. Their research based on in-depth interviews concluded that transforming source texts to avoid plagiarism was something that ESL students found very difficult, and that it was also a major concern, especially for postgraduate students.

As regards the impact of the interaction between instructors and students on the students' attitude towards plagiarism, it was indicated that the growing staff-student ratio contributes to the increase in the number of plagiarism cases (Angelova & Riazantseva, 1999; O'Donoghue, 1996). As the instructor feedback time allocated to the discussion of the plagiarism issues decreases, the staff tends to have limited opportunities to raise students' practices concerning academic writing practices. Hyland (2001) reported that writing instructors' oversensitivity to "student feelings" and "understanding potential cultural differences" (2001, p. 381) prevents them from efficiently pointing out to students' infelicities in their essay that may be judged as plagiarism. Carroll (2002) asserted that the continual pressure to achieve high marks led students to be involved in plagiarism. Other studies such as Errey (2002) suggested that poor time management skills on the part of students or the pressure to meet the deadlines of many course work submissions at the same time are likely to lead students to plagiarism.

Research pointed out that the following motives lead students to abstain from plagiarism: being fair to the original author as well as avoiding guilt and fear. However, those who do not have a well-developed sense of academic integrity tend to be engaged in academic dishonesty more readily (Compton & Pfau, 2008; Guraya & Guraya, 2017). Previous research literature demonstrated that the students' perceptions of the source documentation rules (the things that need to be documented and those that do not need to be documented) determine their boundaries of the academic misconduct as well as their attitudes towards plagiarism (Scanlan, 2006). What is interesting is that some studies found the prevalence of positive attitudes towards plagiarism among learners, which is believed to have led the issue to perpetuate in higher education contexts (Ghajarzadeh, Norouzi-Javidan, Hassanpour, Aramesh, & Emami-Razavi, 2012).

Unintentional plagiarism, also associated with the students' perception of plagiarism, is related to the extent to which students are knowledgeable about plagiarism (Park, 2003). In relation to motives underlying student plagiarism, Carroll (2002) suggested that most students are unsure what plagiarism is. She argued that this lack of understanding of what is and what is not plagiarism leads to a rise in unintentional student plagiarism. It is also maintained that some students are not quite clear about the type of knowledge that is included in the common knowledge domain (Park, 2003), which may be the reason for their (unintentional) plagiarism from the internet. It must be underlined that education plays an important role in the establishment and maintenance of ethical standards.

AUTHORSHIP/OWNERSHIP OF TEXTS

Another line of research has adopted a more ideological approach and questioned the authorship of texts as well as the relevance of plagiarism (Pennycook, 1996; Scollon, 1994, 1995) in connection with the writing habits of ESL/EFL writers whose backgrounds do not value textual ownership. In fact, Scollon (1995) indicated that the concept of plagiarism is intertwined with the social, political and cultural issues and that it is not possible to consider it on its own. As claimed by Bloch (2001), it should be acknowledged that there is no universal consensus on the concepts of authorship, intellectual property, and the institutional policy on plagiarism. In regard to the complexity of plagiarism in cross-cultural education, Scollon (1995), Pennycook (1996), and Currie (1998) asserted that ESL students tend to have various perspectives concerning plagiarism. In relation to the complexity of the plagiarism issue, Scollon (1994) suggested that separating the ownership of the texts, their wording, and the facts , may be problematic for non-native writers, who may not conceptualize plagiarism in the same way as their teachers. These views are supported many others. Sherman (1992) found that her Italian students saw copying wholesale from original texts as both legitimate and as showing respect for the original author. In fact, with respect to the different interpretations of plagiarism, Pennycook (1996) argued that all language learning is to some extent a process of borrowing other people's words, and that the distinction between intertextuality and plagiarism is a very fine line. As Buranen (1992) revealed, owing to the strong resistance among some researchers to admitting the presence of authorship in texts and their reluctance to make plagiarism an issue in ESL/EFL setting, debates on plagiarism have failed to yield substantial and realistic support for novice writers. However, as far as the academic reality inexperienced writers faces is concerned, plagiarism turns to have a distinct meaning in most academic institutions.

In relation to the ESL students' difficulties with the authorship, Ercegovac and Richardson (2004) and Paxton (2007) argued that controlling authorial voices, i.e., their own voices and the voices of the sources they use, poses problems for novice writers, which results in their failure to incorporate their individual voices in their works. Student writers were observed to borrow a lot from their textbooks that they found quite authoritative while writing essays.

Furthermore, in a case study of how novice L1 and L2 academic writers of English deal with textual appropriation in an Anglophone university, Angelil-Carter (2000) discussed the difficulties faced by novice academic writers in identifying voices within the sources (i.e., identifying interpretations offered in the sources) as well as developing their own voices using such sources (i.e., the novice writers themselves developing their own interpretations of the sources). The insights she offered are different from those in previous research in that rather than denying the presence of "authorial voice" (Angelil-Carter, 2003, p. 3), she acknowledged it and stated that while "no writers have their own words, they have particular ways of working with those words which are their own" (2002, p. 29).

The studies by Hyland (2001) and Angelil-Carter (2003) suggested that it is time researchers and teachers took a fresh look at plagiarism and saw it as a developmental problem that could be responded to. As Hyland (2001) revealed, some instructors are likely to regard giving students feedback on plagiarism practices as a challenge and feel uncomfortable in this respect, which might be attributed to their awareness that the students' culture determines their approaches to the issues of authorship and acknowledgement. Hyland (2001, p. 380) stated the following in this respect:

For many ESL students' plagiarism is an act of desperation. After they mentally compare their texts with target 'expert texts', they may feel so overwhelmed by the distance between what they are expected to achieve and what they feel capable of doing, that plagiarism seems the most realistic strategy.

THE GAME-CHANGER: BEST TIMING TO FOCUS ON ACADEMIC INTEGRITY ISSUES

Plagiarism incidents are not only limited to students at the undergraduate level but also apply to those at the graduate level. In fact, as Bretag (2013) indicated, it was demonstrated that 43% of research proposals by graduate students and 27% of master theses are engaged in some form of plagiarism. Wadja-Johnson, Handal, Brawer, and Fabricatore (2001) found that the most common (55%) type of dishonest behaviours self-reported in a survey, among graduate students in USA was "not copying word for word but changing the wording slightly" (p.293).

Although EFL university students seemed to have some basic understanding of plagiarism, an analysis of their work shows that they cannot apply this knowledge to their academic writing practices (Hui-Fang, 2019; Rets & Illya, 2018). No obvious relationship seemed to be found between students' plagiarism awareness and their plagiaristic behaviour (Hui-Fang, 2019). The causes of this failure in the practical component is attributable to "poor writing skills and wrong perception about plagiarism" (Dolzhenko, et al., 2016, p. 845) which has been carried over from previous schooling.

In order to alleviate or eliminate the plagiarism problem students are facing in higher education, it is essential to introduce the concept of citation, referencing, source documentation, academic integrity and academic honesty at the pre-tertiary level (i.e., the high school level). Integrating a research component into writing classes of the high school curriculum would be a suitable place for this purpose. A report writing task could be inserted into the curriculum and students can be asked to prepare it making use of different sources and applying proper source documentation and referencing skills.

Williamson and McGregor (2011) suggested that two pedagogical approaches could be combined to successfully prevent plagiarism cases, which can be managed by the integration of well-designed research projects into the high school curricula. The first approach focuses on the improvement of students' academic writing skills, students' ability to notice plagiarism, appropriate quoting, paraphrasing, referencing and source documentation skills, academic integrity, academic misconduct, and authorship practices, which high school students are not likely to be familiar with. The second approach focuses on the development of higher-order thinking skills through the idea generation (Williamson & McGregor, 2011). The combination of both approaches are likely to enhance students' respect and adherence to the principles of academic misconduct (Scanlan, 2006) although a restricted number of high schools appear to have integrated such research projects to integrate both approaches. The study by Holt, Fagarheim, and Durham (2014) confirmed the effectiveness of such training programs for students. The findings evidently indicated that in the long run both online and face-to-face training groups were more successful than the group with no education on academic dishonesty.

ACADEMIC INTEGRITY SOFTWARE RESEARCH AND TURNITIN

Issues of academic plagiarism in educational institutions are often played out in the public arena. Although a variety of motives can be listed for the growth and spread of plagiarism, the problem is mostly attributed to the internet (Maddox (2008, p.125). It was argued that the internet aggravates the plagiarism problem for "educational institutions" (Maddox, 2008). Such cases are currently referred to as 'digital plagiarism' Even though internet technology can be blamed for the rise in plagiarism rates, it also offers a solution to this problem as well, which also involves the utilization of a leading anti-plagiarism program 'Turnitin' (Köse & Arıkan, 2011), which is commonly used at universities "as a means through which to detect and deter plagiarism" (Sutherland-Smith & Carr, 2005).

Text-matching software is widely used to screen plagiarism incidents at educational instructions around the globe. The most popular software that is used worldwide is reported to be Turnitin for universities (Batane, 2010). This internet-based originality checking service was launched in 1997 to safeguard academic integrity (Turnitin.com, 2018). It indicates the similarities between the submitted papers and the documents from its database (Davis & Carroll, 2009). However, Turnitin has been reported to have a major limitation in that it can only detect word-for-word or direct plagiarism in electronic sources (Hui-Fang, 2019). In other words, if the submitted work is from paper-based sources, it is hard to detect plagiarism (Goh, 2013). Although the total elimination of plagiarism is not likely by using such plagiarism-detection software, Turnitin can assist in detecting intentional plagiarism (Walker, 2010). Besides, it is likely to drop the rates of unintentional plagiarism in the revised assignment (Ledwith & Risquez 2008; McKeever 2006).

The Turnitin anti-plagiarism software package is used for the detection and deterrence of plagiarism by means of a matching overview and similarity index acknowledged in a wide range of countries on a global scale (Bruton & Childers, 2016; Handerson, 2008; Scaife 2007; Sutherland-Smith & Carr, 2005).

Although Turnitin has been foreshown as an effective measure to prevent plagiarism for over a decade, more empirical research needs to be undertaken to examine user perceptions of its effectiveness (Sutherland-Smith & Carr, 2005; Nova & Utami, 2018). At the university where the study was conducted, Turnitin has long been utilized for detecting plagiarism in Academic Writing and Research Skills and Academic Reading and Writing courses for EFL preservice teachers as well as giving feedback on assignments and student presentations in Academic English courses for non-EFL majors (Balbay & Kilis, 2019). Despite being a well-developed program, though quite effective in some respects, Turnitin, for some instances/samples, "was not observed to be as effective in student presentations as it was in student essays since it was unable to detect the similarities in slides due to its identification of the text on the pictures as pictures, and could not detect the similarities of slides" (Balbay & Kilis, 2019, p. 26; also see Halgamuge, 2017).

Of such previous studies, while some focused on the text matching power of software and its consequences, some others focused on learner and instructor perceptions regarding their effectiveness and use, yet on the concept of digital plagiarism and the inappropriate reliance on Turnitin, Royce (2003) revealed that overreliance on Turnitin could produce false plagiarism claims as the system can sometimes match texts over abundantly, leaving on the other hand, many real instances undetected. As compared to these measures to deter plagiarism, some authors do not approve of extensive emphasis on explicit teaching related to referencing, documentation skills and academic writing conventions and suggest that students should refer to academic manuals on their own (Standler, 2012). On the other hand, as the students' knowledge and awareness concerning plagiarism display great variation, the introduction of the concepts of academic integrity and academic misconduct should be made early on at the university level, as indicated by Taylor, Usick and Peterson, (2004).

At the institutional level, some questioned whether Turnitin's traditional use as a policing tool neglects the learning process (John Hopkins University, 2006). Others pointed to the potential for inappropriate reliance on Turnitin, which is augmented by the natural limitations of Turnitin's methodology. Still some others argued that Turnitin still has a negative effect on academia because it cultivates a culture of distrust between professors and students (Read, 2006). However, with the recently added PeerMark function, Turnitin enabled peer review activities with multiple Turnitin features such as commenting tools, composition marks and PeerMark questions. In a recent study by Li and Li (2017), it was found that PeerMark fostered students' online peer review and promoted their critical thinking skills. Yet, although Turnitin-based peer review provided constructive feedback for students, it was underscored that prior well-structured training is necessary for the effective implementation of Turnitin peer review activities.

From an instructional value perspective, Ryan and Eckersley (2004) at the University of Newcastle, Auckland, found that lecturers were using the Turnitin software as a learning tool allowing students to review plagiarism reports on their assignments. The staff reported the implementation of the Turnitin to have generally been successful at the University with an overwhelming majority of staff, 89.9%, supporting the use of Turnitin overall and expressing the belief that the software deters students from plagiarism. The software was useful specifically to identify assignments where plagiarism was a problem. Teachers considered the color-coding system of identifying the text match by quantity, and presenting it as a total percentage of the whole work, assisted them in deciding whether to check the assignment further.

There is research evidence indicating the positive impact of Turnitin on the reduction of student plagiarism rates in the tertiary context, not only in the undergraduate level (See Batane, 2010) but also in the graduate level (See Baker, Thornton, & Adams, 2008). Also Turnitin was found to be more effective in reducing plagiarism compared to manual methods (Jocoy & DiBiase, 2006) as well as other online plagiarism detection services (Scaife, 2007). Regarding student perceptions of the effectiveness of Turnitin, studies highlighted both positive and negative views. To illustrate, Nova and Utami (2018) revealed that EFL students in the Indonesian higher education context raised their awareness towards academic integrity and plagiarism as well as writing similarity and originality in addition to developing their academic writing, critical and creative thinking skills. However, the study showed that the inability of Turnitin to differentiate direct quotations, common phrases, and citations led students to hold negative views regarding the effectiveness of Turnitin's. In fact, in the study, the Turnitin system was found to identify everything as similarity not only in the content of the paper but also in things such as the author's name, references, and common terms on the web page (Nova & Utami, 2018), which corroborated Bakhtiyari et al. (2014), indicating factors affecting unconsciously plagiarism such as accidental similarity, fixed definitions, text recycling, and self-plagiarism. This unintentional plagiarism issue was also in line with Jones' conclusion (2008), suggesting Turnitin's overemphasis on checking the match or similarity of the paper with any sources on the internet, which rendered it hard to provide an exact judgement of a plagiaristic attempt. Unlike the study results by Nova and Utami (2018), in a very recent mixed methods study by Hui-Fang (2019) aiming to explore how the use of the plagiarism detection software Turnitin and plagiarism awareness training could affect instances of plagiaristic behavior in students' EFL writing, revealed quite positive student perceptions in terms of Turnitin use. The researchers found that the use of Turnitin promoted a significant reduction in student plagiarism rates, and that it served as an effective tool for educating students on plagiarism-related issues. The findings of Hui-Fang (2019), are reinforced by Heckler, Rice, and Bryan (2013), reporting the use of Turnitin as an effective tool in educating students on plagiarism. They are also in line with the previous studies (Chien, 2016; Martin, 2005), which recommended the use of a detection system in a university writing class to alleviate plagiaristic behavior.

While some studies, such as the one above, have a distinct learner focus, others have had an instructor focus involving teachers' perspectives on Turnitin in raising issues of educational integrity. The study by Sutherland-Smith and Carr (2005) was conducted to explore teachers' perceptions of the usefulness and applicability of

Turnitin in tertiary classrooms. The staff were asked to comment as to how Turnitin might be used as an educative tool. It was found that the software could not accomplish the task of indicating plagiarized material on its own without the manual screening the teachers needed to perform once text matching statistics had been calculated by the software. In addition, "students still require explicit teaching of the concept of textual attribution, often with subject-specific examples to understand acknowledgement conventions within academia" (2005, p. 94). Similarly, Cheah and Bretag (2009) reinforced the findings of previous research, indicating the effectiveness of Turnitin services in improving the understanding of and attention to academic integrity. It was also demonstrated that Turnitin could be used as a formative assessment tool for students to help them avoid plagiarism, decrease the student tendency to over-rely on sources, improve citation practices and improve paraphrasing skills (Davis & Carroll, 2009; Goddard & Rudzki, 2005, Gannon-Leary, Trayhun & Home, 2009). It was, in addition, found to be a popular feedback tool among the staff (Rolfe, 2011) and students (See Dahl, 2007; Sheridan, Alany & Brake, 2005).

Despite the favorable views on Turnitin in terms of being a formative assessment tool and enhancing student academic integrity (Rolfe, 2011), several studies issued a word of caution regarding the overreliance on Turnitin (See Badge & Scott, 2009; Wright, Owens, & Nigel, 2008), indicating that for it to be an effective student deterrent, students should be educated about plagiarism penalties and consequences. The sole use of an electronic detection service fails to deter students from plagiarism effectively. As pointed out by Wright, Owens and Nigel (2008), Turnitin should be considered only as a support tool for the detection of plagiarism; rather as a tool to be used along with the traditional tools for the academic integrity assessment (e.g., to identify abrupt changes in the written structure and style).

PLAGIARISM IN THE TURKISH CONTEXT

The issue of plagiarism in the Turkish context is relatively underexplored. Regarding the Turkish university students' perceptions on plagiarism and their evaluation of the effectiveness of an online plagiarism deterrence tool, the findings of a recent study by Köse and Arıkan (2011) revealed the existence of intentional plagiarism and the positive impact of the online plagiarism detection device Turnitin on the reduction of the rate of plagiarism in an academic writing class. With respect to the university students' problems in undergraduate student writing, Razı (2015a) found a relatively strong impact of Turnitin similarity reports on students' overall scores in academic writing and the gender differences on plagiarism (male students plagiarising more than female ones). In another study, Razı (2015b) found that freshman students mainly had difficulty in "deciding whether citation is needed or not' and the 'use of in-text citation rules" (p. 156). Students found paraphrasing exceptionally difficult which resulted in unnecessary over-quoting. The study also revealed the most commonly employed self-reported strategies to overcome academic writing problems as follows: "checking match of references, checking in-text citation rules, checking reference entries, checking grammar, checking vocabulary choice, checking vocabulary choice, checking punctuation, checking the flow of ideas, checking spelling, and asking for proofreading" (Razı, 2015a, p. 156).

Also, the study by Yazıcı, Yazıcı and Erdem (2011) into the faculty and student perceptions of in-class and out-of-class cheating behaviours suggested that faculty and students showed slight variations in their attitudes towards "collegiate cheating" and the underlying motives. The findings also pointed out that there is a significant correlation between the perceptions of out-of-class cheating, but not with out-of-class cheating behaviors. It was found that the duration of experience in out-of-class assessment marks the ethical attitude towards out-of-class cheating. A more recent study by Rets and Ilya (2018) investigating EFL preservice teachers' perceptions of plagiarism in the Turkish higher education context displayed that they held negative attitudes towards plagiarism with some differences concerning the degree of seriousness and acceptability of plagiarism. The findings showed that EFL preservice teachers had difficulty identifying and accounting for the plagiarism cases, which underscored the need for further training and awareness-raising activities.

METHODOLOGY

The case study reported in this book chapter adopted a mixed methods exploratory research design. The study aimed to investigate Turkish EFL preservice teachers' plagiarism *perceptions, knowledge and practices* and whether or not 15 assignments/samples submitted to a text-matching program to fulfil course requirements for the duration of one semester had any impact on awareness for plagiarism practices. The study also aimed to look into the impact of a variety of issues that affected the self-reported engagement preferences of Turkish EFL preservice teachers with plagiarism practices: the learners' previous schooling experience concerning writing, context-based motives and perceptions regarding plagiarism, and their ability to notice plagiarism in actual texts, as well as whether or not assignments/samples to the text-matching program for the duration of one semester had any impact on their perceptions of plagiarism and their ability to detect plagiarism in a given text.

The study adopted both a qualitative and a quantitative perspective into plagiarism. In addition to a pre-test and a post-test questionnaire to see possible changes in perceptions, knowledge and practice, students' perceptions related to the plagiarism were also probed by semi-structured interviews with a group of volunteer students at the end of the semester.

PARTICIPANTS

The participants were 80 English Language Teaching (ELT) majors, enrolled in a 4-year undergraduate program, who were training to become EFL teachers. They were enrolled in two sections of a freshman academic writing course in Spring 2014-2015 at a large English-medium university in central Anatolia, Turkey. The age range of the participants was between 17 and 20. Convenience sampling was adopted in the formation of the participant group. The participants were all Turkish and had an upper-intermediate/advanced level proficiency in English. They passed the in-house English language proficiency exam administered by their institution with a minimum score of 60 (out of 100), a score that is equivalent to 86 on TOEFL IBT (Internet Based Test), and above. Due to the natural make-up of the department/bachelor's program, the female participants outnumbered those of males (70% females and 30% males). They were considered to have adequate computer literacy skills as prior to their involvement in the study, they all successfully completed a basic computer literacy course and a computer education and instructional technology course as part of their curriculum.

It needs to be noted at this point that although the study initially started off with 80 participants, after the participants who did not participate in both the pre and the post test, and those with incomplete questionnaires for either were removed from the data set. Thus, data from a total of 66 participants was eventually subjected to the final analysis.

THE WRITING COURSE

The freshman academic writing course during which the data were collected aimed to develop students' linguistic competence in English through expanding their knowledge of English grammar and writing. It was organized with the intention of increasing student awareness of how meaning is created through structure and how structure and meaning are related. Emphasis was placed on critical thinking, university level essay development, reading comprehension, vocabulary improvement, certain grammatical structures, usage and mechanics, the ability to identify credible sources and integrate these sources into a text with the aim of training students to become more accurate and less inhibited about expressing themselves in written

English. More specifically, the course explored formal rhetorical patterns including classification, comparison, causation, and argumentation.

DATA COLLECTION TOOLS

The data were obtained through a (i) pre-test questionnaire (containing open-ended, multiple choice and Likert-scale items) administered to the students prior to the course and the very same tool as a (ii) post-test questionnaire after the course, and (iii) semi-structured interviews following the post-test. (see Appendix A and B for the full questionnaires.)

The tools were designed by the researchers themselves to reflect concerns/issues as found in past literature on plagiarism in similar contexts. Expert opinion was also sought at the time. All three data collection tools (i.e., pre/post-test questionnaires and the semi-structured interview questions) were piloted with a separate group of students who were not participants in the final study to test usability and problematic items.

The questionnaire, which was prepared in English, was composed of the following general parts: (1) previous schooling experience, (2) individual participant motives for engaging in plagiarism-related practices, (3) ability to notice plagiarism and knowledge of appropriate source documentation (4) overall perceptions on plagiarism, issues related to ethics and integrity. Some of the questions on the questionnaire and the extracts used to assess pre-service teachers' ability to notice acts of plagiarism were adapted from Deckert (1993).

The pre-test[1] questionnaire was administered in class (in both course sections) by the researchers simultaneously. The participants were given 50 minutes (1 class hour) to complete it, which was found to be sufficient by the participants. In order to avoid misunderstandings and to obtain reliable data the students were allowed to switch to Turkish whenever they needed while answering the items[2].

Part 1 contained questions related to previous exposure to academic integrity related issues in high school and beyond (i.e., whether or not academic writing was expected at high school and whether or not training was received about plagiarism priorly). In Part 2, pre-service teachers were asked to list motives underlying plagiarism behavior. In Part 3, they read one writing sample and 6 extracts where the original sample had been quoted/paraphrased/used in some way. They were then asked to judge whether and to what degree there was 'wrong/unacceptable/unethical use' of the original source. In Part 4 of the pre-test, keeping in mind the extract they indicated as carrying the worst case of plagiarism in the previous section, pre-service teachers were asked how they perceived the act in terms of who it is unfair to (i.e., themselves, classmates, their university, the original author, etc.) and why it is unfair for the parties involved. Their views related to digital plagiarism, the role of the internet and possible prevention strategies were also requested at the end of the questionnaire.

The post-test questionnaire, except for the first part (demographic information about participant background), contained the same sections as the pre-test questionnaire. Additionally, it contained a separate section on their views on the source documentation practice in relation to their use and experience of the software Turnitin during the course. This section also had specific questions on participants' perceived benefits, difficulty, effectiveness/ineffectiveness of Turnitin in avoiding plagiarism.

The post-test which was also designed by the researchers was administered in class in the same fashion as the pre-test. The time allotted to the completion of the questionnaire was 50 minutes (1 class hour) which was found to be sufficient by the participants. Like the pre-test questionnaire, the students were allowed to switch to Turkish whenever they felt like while answering the items.

In addition, the following 15 assignments/writing samples were submitted to Turnitin by the preservice EFL preservice teachers during the EFL freshman writing course: 4 essays (one classification, one cause-effect, one comparison-contrast, and one argumentative essay), 5 reflection journals and 3 peer review reflection assignments. Except for the final argumentative essay, the participants submitted two drafts for each essay type.

At the end of the course, semi-structured interviews were conducted with 12 of the participants (preservice teachers enrolled in the freshman writing course) by one of the researchers in her office. The students were randomly chosen amongst the volunteers for the interview who had ticked a box in the post-test questionnaire. The interviews took between 40 to 55 minutes. They were mainly designed to tap into participants' in-depth personal insights into plagiarism awareness and practices, building mainly on the questionnaire sections/questions. During the interview, the researcher used questions to trigger individual stories in relation to the motives underlying plagiarism and how Turnitin helped/hindered preservice teachers' progress in the course.

DATA ANALYSIS

The quantitative data in the study (the items on the questionnaire except for the open-ended items) were analyzed with SPSS 21.0. Descriptive statistics were computed. The qualitative data (from the open-ended portions of the pre- and post-test questionnaire and the semi-structured interviews) were analyzed via content analysis to gain deeper insights into participant opinions and practices related to plagiarism and the impact of the use of an online text-matching detection software on these perceptions.

RESULTS

Participant Definitions of "Plagiarism'

The EFL preservice teachers in the study all defined 'plagiarism' in a similar way with slightly different wording. Their definitions contained references such as the following: the usage of ideas of other people without crediting them, a kind of theft, a kind of stealing another person's work, opinions and sayings, copying one's work without permission or giving any source, stealing someone's ideas and pretending that you invented them, presenting someone else's works, words as one's own without giving any source, using the information that belongs to someone else and without including your own thoughts, copying or indicating the writer's opinions while you are writing on a subject, copy and paste, downloading our homework from the internet or copy some parts of it, making use of other people's words, works or research without documenting it in our writings, taking one's words without permission and using them as if your own words. In Turkish, they gave the following equivalents to the term 'plagiarism': "bilgi hırsızlığı" (knowledge theft), "ahlaksızca bir davranış" (an immoral deed), "esinlenme" (inspiration), "korsancılık" (piracy). Except for "esinlenme" (inspiration), all the words associated with the act produced in Turkish had negative valence.

From High School to University: Changing Expectations

With respect to the familiarity with plagiarism in their past schooling experience, over one half of the participants (64.19%) indicated that they were not informed of the concepts of plagiarism, academic dishonesty and academic integrity, which is in line with Deckert (1993). This could be attributed to the nature of the assignments that they were asked to do during their K-12 education. The types of writing assignments they were engaged in were mostly reflection and reader-response type papers in which they could not find opportunities to use higher–order critical skills such as evaluation, analysis and synthesis. Although they wrote longer essays, they were not required to use any outside sources. The following quote by one participant from the interview data on her high school years is quite revealing in this respect:

Especially, we were not given information to us about the plagiarism. It is possible that our assignments were generally based on grammar rules or exercises not the comments in a special writing or composition. Also, when the teacher wanted a comment or critique, we didn't need any help or sources. We wrote only our thoughts due to the nature of the assignments (Interview, P14)

In the same line, the majority of the EFL majors in the study (59.71%) indicated that there was no requirement to document sources at high school. The overwhelming majority (86.57%) pointed out that plagiarism was not considered a serious crime at all in high school. They reported that the teacher usually just lectured to them without giving them any penalty or gave them an unofficial warning by informing them of the improperness of plagiarism and advised them not to do it again. On rare occasions, if the teacher wanted to, he/she could have the students write the text again using their own words or could decrease the students' grades.

The great majority of the participants (85%) reported that their teachers did not warn them about any plagiarism related to their academic work while only a small minority (3%) reported being warned about plagiarism once or twice at school, which is in accordance with the findings of Hyland (2001). However, none of the participants reported being punished for copying others' words due to not indicating the source.

As to the source documentation styles at high school, the participants reported adopting the following documentation styles: not having and list but only in text mention of sources, writing website links at the end of their work, encyclopedias from which they found the information, writing the sources (only the name of the source book or site without any author information) that they made use of while writing, listing the sources that they have used on a separate paper, writing sources as a reference without having the original text at hand (only having access to secondary citations of it). Only a fraction stated that they "provided the part, even if it is just one sentence, that is cited in the reference section at the end of the assignment".

With respect to plagiarism-related information transfer at the university level, the great majority of the participants (87.8%) remarked that they were informed of plagiarism-related issues such as academic integrity and ethics and that for over two-thirds of the participants (71.2%) proper source documentation was a requirement in all the courses that they were taking.

Motives Underlying Misconduct

With regard to the motives underlying EFL preservice teachers' plagiarism attempts/practices at the tertiary level, the participants listed the following 25 reasons/motives. They have been listed below according to the order of frequency in the data. Earlier studies that have compatible findings have also been provided.

1. the lack of overall language proficiency (when producing the text in the L2),
2. the difficulty in certain structural and lexical aspects of English when compared to the L1,
3. the difficulty in the written mode of communication (See Scollon, 1994, 1995; Dolzhenko, et al., 2016),
4. the inability to create a point of view/own voice (See Ergovac & Richardson, 2004; Paxton, 2007),
5. the lack of extensive reading habits (both in L1 and L2),
6. low self-esteem,
7. not considering own point of view reliable enough to report,
8. negative self-perceptions on the writing ability,
9. students' poor time management skills (See Devlin & Gray, 2007) and concentration problems,
10. the lack of knowledge on the topic or the topic being beyond their level,
11. a lack of interest in the assigned topic (See Heron, 2001),
12. the inability to see the immediate relevance of the assignment,
13. a concern/desire to get higher grades and the instructors' excessive emphasis on perfection and time pressure (See Galus, 2002),
14. finding shortcuts,
15. laziness,
16. carelessness,
17. the reluctance to do homework and difficulties conducting research and synthesizing findings,
18. procrastination,
19. the unwillingness to write a reference list,
20. previous schooling experiences (a lack of emphasis on creative thinking and a lack of awareness on plagiarism),
21. regarding plagiarism as a springboard for idea development (See Angelil-Carter, 2000; Pecorari, 2001),
22. the unconscious internalization and the ownership of sources (See Pennycook, 1996),
23. facing problems in determining topics to write about (when learners are free to choose their own topics),
24. learner perceptions on instructors' lack of sensitivity towards the learners' work (Gibson & Chester-Fangman, 2011; McCabe & Trevino, 1993; Scanlan, 2006),
25. heavy workload and task challenge (Devlin & Gray, 2007).

Challenge: What Needs to be Documented?

When the results of the pre-test and the post-test questionnaires are compared (See Table 1 and Table 2 below), it is evident that prior to their involvement in the study, the participants did not have a detailed understanding of plagiarism. They were not quite sure of what kind of things needed to be documented, which reinforces the findings of Ashworth, Bannister, and Thorne (1997), Breen and Maasen (2005), Gitanjali (2004), Handa and Power (2005), Ledwith and Risquez (2008), and Park (2003). The pre-service teachers' perceptions seemed to be confused as to what is/ isn't regarded as plagiarism. The participants reported having difficulty deciding on what counts as common knowledge in academia. To illustrate, they indicated that some unimportant sentences, unnecessary information or other people's work or ideas which aren't special/unique on a subject or small details should not be considered plagiarism. They also pointed out it was not necessary to document words that one is inspired by, which is a very vague and troublesome notion regarding plagiarism.

Difficulties Faced in Source Documentation Practices

Table 1. A comparison between the pre-test and the post-test results in terms of the things participants believe to be documented

THINGS REPORTED AS "NEED TO BE DOCUMENTED"	
PRE-TEST	**POST-TEST**
– Encyclopaedia articles – Original texts when discussing supporting ideas – Paragraphs which were taken from outside sources	– Everything/ everything we mentioned directly in our writing/ – Paraphrases – Particulars of a Reference list – Personal communications with someone, friends, etc – Personal ideas of a person other than the writer – Quotes / Citations / Quoted parts of the text – Resources: articles, essays, books, newspapers, internet sources, statistics, etc. – The definitions of some technical words

As far as the reported difficulties the participants faced in source documentation are concerned, they could be divided into two main groups: (a) the difficulties concerning the proper application of the APA style manuals and (b) the lack of information for proper documentation. The following quotations are concerned with the participants' views related to the first difficulty from the post-test data:

As I cannot apply the APA style documentation rules properly, I cannot document the sources clearly. I do not know which order to follow in source documentation (P1)

Table 2. A comparison between the pre-test and the post-test results in terms of the things participants believe need not be documented

THINGS REPORTED AS "DOES NOT NEED TO BE DOCUMENTED"	
PRE-TEST	**POST-TEST**
– Personal details about the writer – The things except reflections – The words that are used – Things that are related to culture – Some sentences which are not important – Other people's writings or ideas who aren't special on a subject – No need for small details – Websites – Unnecessary information – Works/ideas one has been inspired by	– *Everything we take from other sources should be documented* – *Feelings/experiences* – *General information that can be found everywhere/Common beliefs* – *Our own ideas/comments* – *Our own research (perhaps)*

I hadn't documented sources in high school so I had difficulty in it. (P3)

The rules are very complex. While writing sources to references, I got confused. Particularly the sequencing of references is so hard. (P5)

I worked on it a lot to correct APA documentation. I could not learn how to document sources for a long time. Even now I have some doubts. (P8)

I am having problems with in-text citation. References in text citations are very difficult for me to implement. (P10)

I sometimes forget the order of references order such as, whether the date comes earlier than the name of the journal or not. (P16)

Some participants also referred to the lack of availability of the documentary information as one of the challenges they faced in proper source documentation especially for online sources. The following extracts from participants from the post-test questionnaire and interview data could be regarded as representative in this regard:

Sometimes I couldn't reach information about the author's name and the publication date. (P 28)

I only have difficulty mentioning the dates and author names on the web because most of the websites do not give any exact information about them. In some essays the writers are unknown or there are no documentation dates. (Interview, P35)

There was little information on sources. Some sites didn't have the info for the reference. (P30)

Some EFL majors emphasized that having access to credible sources posed a big problem for them. The following quote from the interview data expresses this challenge quite clearly:

Some internet sources are insufficient and unreliable. It is hard to find internet-based sources for some topics. (Interview, P40)

Plagiarism Noticing Ability

Participants' noticing ability was assessed based on two parallel sections on the pre/post-test questionnaires. In these sections the participants were presented with one original short writing sample by author A and accompanying 6 extracts by other authors where the original sample by author A had been quoted/paraphrased/used in some way. In some texts there was proper use of source documentation while for others there were differing degrees of acceptability which participants were asked to judge.

The section on noticing plagiarism in the post-test questionnaire at the end of the course revealed an increase in understanding of proper source documentation, with participants' plagiarism noticing ability increasing from 43.4% to 60.3% over course of 12 weeks. This difference was found as statistically significant ($p<0.05$). According to the participants, the use of Turnitin and the text-matching statistics received from it by the participants proved to be a major factor in the development of this ability.

The Effect of Instructor Preferences

With respect to the EFL preservice teachers' views on their university instructors' preferences concerning credible sources, they reported that the overwhelming majority of their instructors (73.5%) favored library sources, as opposed to one-fourth (26.4%), who also favored internet source use. The following quotes from the pre-test data are indicators of this stance:

… Because library sources are more reliable than internet sources. (P49)

They prefer library sources to internet. I think that's because internet has a much more wide content and it's easier to plagiarize. (P50)

Probably, they are trying to avoid plagiarism and they want us to study on more reliable sources. (P66)

In line with a rise in the participants' awareness as to the credible source use via the training program and the instructor's efforts as well as Turnitin use, the participants reported that their rate of library/hardcopy source use raised noticeably. The majority of the participants indicated that they used such sources either *always* (24%) or *often* (35.7%) after the course use of Turnitin while the rate of those who used these sources ranged from *sometimes* (36.9%) to *never* (22.3%) before the course. A comparison between the pre-test and the post-test results also indicated that the participants experienced less difficulty with source documentation at the end of the study from both hardcopy and credible online sources.

The Role of the Internet

As for the participants' beliefs about role of the internet on plagiarism, they expressed contradictory opinions. While one group emphasized that the internet plays an important role in plagiarism practices, which is in line with Maddox (2008), the other group did not think highly of the role of the internet in such practices (See Köse & Arıkan, 2011). To illustrate, the following quotes from the post-test and the interviews by various participants revealed that the internet contributed to the rise in plagiarism cases:

I think internet seems easy to find and copy information. Due to that students use internet sources much more than any other source (P15)

It is easy to reach the internet sources. There are many sources on the net, so it's very easy to copy one's job. It makes easy to plagiarize. It is an easy way to plagiarism as in the internet there are a lot of pages about the subject and dozens of writings that can be copied directly (Interview, P29).

Students find them easily and think that their teachers can't find them (P40).

The following interview extract, on the other hand, is representative of the participants who thought that internet sources do not directly play a role in plagiarism practices; the kind of source does not lead people to plagiarize but it is the person who is engaged in such practices:

I think they (internet sources) don't have a role, the one who use them in a bad way is guilty, not the source (Interview, P45).

Participant Opinions on the Integration of Turnitin

With respect to the EFL preservice teachers' opinions about Turnitin, the majority of the participants regarded Turnitin as quite beneficial. In fact, nearly two-thirds of them described their general Turnitin experience as very beneficial (63,2%), which is in line with Ryan and Eckersley (2004) and Sutherland-Smith (2005).

The participants divided the benefits for the EFL situation into five major categories: (1) Increase in plagiarism awareness and the development of documentation skills; (2) Help in acquiring study skills (since Turnitin use helped participants to take matters seriously and pushed them to meet deadlines), (3) Bringing with it the sense of fairness and control; (4) Opening up opportunities for peer learning (since it involved peer correction/review), and (5) Development of their computer skills via online text-matching software use.

In relation to plagiarism awareness, the participants were of the opinion that it discouraged plagiarism and raised their awareness towards how to detect plagiarism, which reinforces the findings of Ledwith and Risquez (2008). The following quotes from the post-test and interview data are quite revealing in terms of the participants' perspectives concerning the benefits of Turnitin as a tool to raise plagiarism awareness:

Turnitin taught me how I can avoid plagiarism - and help me develop my creative thinking (P35)

I learnt how to document sources (P48)

I learned to see the rate of plagiarism and I saw what plagiarism may include. (P47)

Sometimes I thought that I cited sources correctly, however, when I see plagiarism, I understood my mistake (P43)

I find Turnitin very useful as it warns me when there is plagiarism. Even when we are not aware of it, it informs us when we commit plagiarism. (P50)

It (Turnitin) showed my mistakes in documenting sources and I tried to correct them. (P61)

Plagiarism training was really useful but the use of Turnitin as a plagiarism device was complimentary to training. It helped me raise my awareness towards the plagiarism issue. The online device was really useful for us to learn how to document our sources properly using the APA style. (Interview, P18)

For the Likert scale item on the post-questionnaire probing the extent of Turnitin usefulness for students in avoiding plagiarism, 78.1% reported that they found it (very) beneficial. In reference to the actual reported impact of Turnitin, Table 3 below reports frequencies of self-reported plagiarism engagement by the participants in the pre- and post-questionnaires. The quantitative findings suggest that the use of Turnitin (with around a 30% increase in the rarely/never category) acted as a deterrent which has also been expressed in the open-ended data.

Table 3. Pre and post-test/course questionnaire results for self-reported engagement frequency with plagiarism

	Pre-test	Post-test
Always	13%	3%
Sometimes	26%	11%
Rarely	36%	33%
Never	25%	53%

With respect to the benefits of the Turnitin in terms of study skills and meeting deadlines, the participants pointed out the main benefit lies in the opportunity to have access to the list of assignments and see the deadlines. They stated that online submissions enabled them to organize their time much more efficiently as they had to follow the deadlines and online alerts. Many expressed the importance of being able to see all their work in an online portfolio fashion which Turnitin provided for them. Furthermore, they considered Turnitin a safe repository for assignments and an indicator to monitor their academic progress in writing. The following quotes from the post-test data are illustrative in this respect:

The submission of the assignments to the Turnitin helped me to keep my work in order as an e-portfolio and develop my study skills. I can access to all my previous work whenever I like. (P27)

The Turnitin triggered me to make my assignments properly, without delay (P63)

The Turnitin also allows me to retrieve our lost work. Sometimes we lose our essays and we can take them from turnitin or I downloaded again the documents I lost. (P5)

Submitting my assignments to the Turnitin was safer than giving by hand. (P7)

I have been able to see my progress in academic writing since I started the course as I revisited my assignments regularly (P42).

I was able to see all the works I' ve done throughout a semester. (P23)

Apart from these aforementioned major benefits, a group of participants believed that the use of Turnitin conveyed a sense of fairness as it brought the feeling of control. They believed that Turnitin led them to be fair and respect other people's work as it helped not only the participants but also the instructor control plagiarism. It also encourages the teacher to take control of the students' writing process. The following post-test comments are revealing in terms of this aspect:

I can be sure that there is no unfairness because everybody does their assignments themselves. (P37)

It is useful for plagiarism so I can be sure that there is no unfairness because everybody does their assignments themselves. (P56)

It increases the teacher's control in that it warns people so it is very important and necessary. (P63)

The participants also listed the peer review opportunities used during the course as a further benefit of Turnitin since it opened up opportunities for peer learning. The following are some related comments:

We can peer review our friends and get feedback. (P32)

We can give our feedbacks to our friends without any difficulty. (P45)

It gave the chance to look at other's work in getting accustomed to regular writing. (P 31)

Turnitin gives us an opportunity to give feedback to our classmates. (P39)

The amelioration of computer skills with the experience of regular submission, is another benefit of Turnitin the participants reported. The following interview comments indicate these sentiments quite succinctly:

I learned much about using computers and my usage of the internet and skills increased a lot. (Interview, P41)

It was easy to submit assignments online also for other courses after I started using Turnitin. (Interview, P22)

On Turnitin: Still Room for Development

Along with the benefits of Turnitin, the participants also indicated some ineffective features of Turnitin. They reported that it fails to be effective for correcting errors and indicating the progress in student writing. It was pointed out that Turnitin does not allow the participants to make any corrections on the essays after the submissions nor does it allow late submissions although this is a matter of the initial set up configuration preferred by the instructors, which participants were probably not aware of.

Furthermore, the participants also indicated that Turnitin did not detect all the plagiarized material but only some parts, which is in line with problems expressed in Chaudri (2008). In fact, as one participant (P12) reported, "sometimes it can detect plagiarism in some certain phrases or words" but not all. On the other hand, one participant (P15) stated that Turnitin may also sometimes "*detect your own work as plagiarism. For example; in one of my works, 2% plagiarism was detected. However, I wrote it on my own. It sometimes detected plagiarism in my work although I avoided plagiarism*". A small number of other participants also expressed such disappointments (i.e., on getting a high rate of text-match on their Turnitin originality reports), stating that sometimes the matches that Turnitin gave them were completely inaccurate and misleading.

The participants also reported that Turnitin sometimes reported the web addresses that they listed according to the APA style as plagiarism. The following are some revealing post-test comments in relation to the above-mentioned ineffective features of Turnitin:

It sees references as plagiarism (P15)

It (Turnitin) sees common expressions as plagiarism (P28)

Even if I used only one word from one book or anything else, it shows that as plagiarism (P37)

It detects wrong plagiarism. It shows as if I did plagiarism (P16)

It (Turnitin) shows plagiarism the things that actually aren't considered plagiarism. Sometimes it comes up with sources which I have not used in my essay. It shows plagiarism even if I didn't do (Interview, P39)

Participants' Recommendations on Plagiarism and Turnitin use for Educational Stakeholders

As end-users, the participants were asked to make some recommendations to different groups (i.e., the university/school administration, students, the community/educational policy makers to) and to instructors to prevent plagiarism. Instructors were recommended to inform students of the seriousness of plagiarism and specifically train them in how to avoid it by teaching them how to document sources properly and how to apply the APA style in a more systematic fashion. Instructors were also advised to lower their expectations from students in that they should assign fewer assignments, which means using fewer sources to consult, and less demanding topics and more attainable objectives. They were expected to act as role models for their students by using sources other than the internet for their own teaching. Apart from that, the instructors were also invited to exercise learner autonomy by encouraging students to write their own opinions, respect and value diverse student points of view and by allowing students to choose their own writing topics. They were also recommended to check student assignments more closely and more attentively.

In addition to the instructors, the participants made some suggestions to the university administration to prevent or discourage plagiarism practices. In their opinion, the students should be made aware that plagiarism is a serious malpractice. In order to raise student awareness in this respect, conferences, teacher-student sessions should be held to inspire students to use the library; library orientations should be organized for students and the university should encourage instructors to integrate computer programs into academic writing classes. The students were of the opinion that the university administration should encourage (and if necessary, obligate) the implementation of plagiarism detection tools throughout the university. In addition, they believed that some websites (where students can download/purchase essays online or retrieve summaries of novels, etc.) can be blocked on campus so that students cannot access them using an university IP address.

The participants also made some suggestions to their counterparts (other students) so as to prevent plagiarism. They recommended them to display a stance of academic integrity, with utmost respect towards others' opinions and act as responsible agents who check the reliability of the source they use, and give credit to others' intellectual work. They also advised others to act as deterrent/monitoring mechanisms against plagiarism in that they should warn their friends/classmates to produce their own ideas instead of copying others' work effortlessly.

With respect to the participants' recommendations to the policy makers/community for the prevention of plagiarism, they pointed out that community and educational policy makers should take immediate action to raise all stakeholders' (including the students and teachers'/instructors' awareness) levels towards the nature of plagiarism and to take precautions against it by regulating the educational system to penalize the doers, and by educating people at the beginning of schooling (perhaps even as early as primary school). They pointed out the importance of emphasizing exploratory teaching and discovery learning (as opposed to rote learning), directing students to investigate on their own in the process.

CONCLUSION

The study highlighted EFL pre-service teachers' perceptions, knowledge, and practices regarding plagiarism and the impact of plagiarism training and Turnitin on these. Regarding the EFL pre-service teachers' perceptions concerning plagiarism, the study found that there is a lack of consensus among EFL preservice teachers concerning the definition of plagiarism, which is consistent with previous research (Balbay & Kilis, 2019; Ivanic, 2004; Rets & Ilya, 2018). The study revealed that the EFL preservice teachers' background and expectations had an impact on the way they interpreted the notion of plagiarism (Yazıcı et al., 2011). The prospective teachers reported their lack of awareness regarding the notions of plagiarism, academic integrity, the types of assignments they were asked to do. The believed that lack of knowledge about academic source documentation and referencing styles during their K-12 education largely shaped their plagiarism practices (Yazıcı, et al., 2011). In fact, the study indicated the importance of previous schooling experiences in preservice teachers' plagiarism practices (e.g., a lack of emphasis on creative and critical thinking activities in K-12 education). The findings indicated a variety of motives underlying their academic misconduct ranging from language proficiency-related factors (Dolzhenko, 2016) to task-related factors such as task challenge (Devlin & Gray, 2007; Yazıcı et al., 2011), and personal factors. The cultural motives (i.e., viewing plagiarism as a preliminary step for idea generation) were also found to play an important role in students' plagiarism practices (Angelil-Carter, 2000; Pecorari, 2001). Regarding the impact of Turnitin on their plagiarism awareness and practices, EFL preservice teachers thought their use of Turnitin raised their awareness towards plagiarism-related issues and academic integrity. They were found to hold a favorable attitude towards the online plagiarism detection device Turnitin.

Overall, the findings of the study suggest that Turnitin is thought to be useful as a deterrent rather than as a solution to internet-assisted plagiarism and that it would be wise to currently pursue other methods in combination with text matching software to reduce the problem of plagiarism in higher education. This study contributed to the related literature by investigating variations in perceptions of plagiarism as well as plagiarism practices of participants in a relatively under-researched disciplinary context (i.e., the EFL preservice teachers at the department of English Language Teaching at a state university in Turkey) and the impact of Turnitin use on their perceptions and practices related to academic integrity. The results shed light into the higher education institution where it was conducted and shaped later teaching practices of the course instructors. They also are promising in terms of revealing to EFL instructors at university the positive impact of Turnitin on raising the EFL preservice teachers' awareness towards plagiarism and deterring them from academic dishonesty at university.

In spite of the limited sample size and the duration of the study, which constituted the limitations in the study, the findings of the study are likely to shed light into the EFL pre-service teachers' plagiarism knowledge, their awareness, practices and attitudes towards the adoption of online plagiarism devices in other similar undergraduate programs both locally and globally.

SOLUTIONS AND RECOMMENDATIONS

Based on the findings obtained in the study, several recommendations can be made to multiple stakeholders (specifically, the instructors, students and policy makers) for the prevention of plagiarism and the adoption of effective classroom practices, as well as the improvement of the classroom application of the plagiarism deterrent device Turnitin.

Firstly, a detailed honor code (McCabe & Trevino, 1993) and related policies need to be defined and be accessible to all students and instructors for all the departments at universities. This statement needs to be an integral part of all course outlines distributed at the beginning of term. Hayes and Introna (2015) emphasized that the lack of institutional policies regarding plagiarism poses a threat to the academic integrity in higher education. As also pointed out by Ledwith and Risquez (2008) and Balbay and Kilis (2019), it is of utmost importance for the educational institutions to develop, implement and maintain a detailed academic integrity policy, which also involves the disciplinary process, to clearly establish the boundaries of academically dishonest practices for students and to determine the types of punishments in line with the type of plagiarism (See also Brown & Howell, 2001; Gullifer &Tyson, 2014; Wager, 2014). Honor codes could also be used to help students take more responsibility in relation to academic integrity (McCabe & Trevino, 1993), which is also confirmed in another study by Scanlan (2006), indicating a decrease in plagiarism cases than institutions with no such codes. Honesty pledges can be used as another measure to lead students to be more attentive towards the issue of academic integrity. These antiplagiarism policies adopted by universities can be modified or improved through the involvement of "students" (Dozhenko et al., 2016. 852). In line with Mavrinac et al. (2010) we believe that student involvement is likely to be the key factor for success for policy makers as they can assist the disclosure of the motives underlying plagiarism and promote the prevention and reduction of plagiarism. The attitude of faculty members towards academic misconduct, the strict maintenance of university policies and the reporting of plagiarism cases is an important factor in students' attitudes towards plagiarism (Dozhenko et al., 2016). However, faculty members may have a tendency not to report plagiarism incidents or to make minimal efforts to report such cases, as indicated in McCabe and Trevino (1993).

Apart from honor codes and honor pledges, assessment practices may be considered a factor affecting students' plagiarism practices (Patak et al., 2020). Academic integrity should be nurtured through assessment practices of instructors (Patak et al., 2020). High quality assessment schemes could be designed to discourage plagiarism among students (Heron, 2001; Hansen, 2011; Rets & Ilya, 2018), including giving assignments that ask students to activate their higher order thinking skills and creativity. The focus of these assignments should be on the reduction of the students' inclination to plagiarize by engaging them in doing meaningful work, which is likely to give them the idea that doing real work would be easier than plagiarism in any way (Royce, 2003). Portfolios may also be integrated to regular coursework in academic writing classes. (Hansen et al., 2011). Students might be invited to submit all the written drafts together with the final versions of their written works (Hansen et al., 2011). A formative assessment strategy with a focus on the student progress might be adopted in academic writing classes, which might be conducive to the avoidance of student plagiaristic behavior.

Students can also be given online refresher courses where they can be introduced to and re-gain familiarity with academic integrity issues (Jackson, 2006). In line with Galus (2002), emphasis could be put on the development of students' academic writing skills to reduce the number of plagiarism incidents. This could be in the form of an online self-paced training program in academic ethics and plagiarism. Additionally, self-paced information literacy and academic writing modules for students could be introduced, which could be used by students at any time for learning and revision, or by academics in their lectures.

It is advisable for the teachers, instructors and lecturers to be clear about their expectations and requirements for the assignments, to provide a list of specific topics from which students must choose for their essays and research papers. Furthermore, it can be considered useful to require a specific research makeup, and assign the papers in various stages with specific due dates; and to ask students to give oral reports of their papers, which should include responding to questions about the research process, not just the content. It might also be beneficial to necessitate students to write an annotated bibliography as they require an in-depth analysis of each of the sources used. Moreover, it might also be fruitful to require students to write in-class essays about their writing experience as this would help them realize that writing is not only an end-product but also a developmental process and a unique experience of individual authors.

It would also be a good idea to raise the instructors' and students' awareness towards plagiarism: From the instructor's perspective, plagiarism awareness requires understanding both why students cheat and how they cheat. From the student's perspective, plagiarism awareness means students must receive both a clear definition of plagiarism and an unambiguous recitation of the penalties for plagiarizing. Instructors and students might have different viewpoints in their understanding of the concept of plagiarism (Bruton & Childers, 2016). Hence, it might be recommended to discuss what plagiarism is and to reach a consensus on the interpretation of the concept (Balbay & Kilis, 2019; Rets & Illya, 2018) in a shared teaching environment.

Students should also be made aware of the benefits of citing sources. Establishing clear guidelines for the identification and avoidance of plagiarism (Balbay & Kilis, 2019) by providing students with opportunities for citation and referencing practices appear to be crucial steps in maintaining academic integrity (Tran, 2012; Youmans, 2011). Citation instruction may help students gain confidence and improve their citation skills in source-based writing (Fazilatfar et al., 2018). Writing course designers may consider integrating citation instruction into academic writing courses to raise students' awareness towards referencing to avoid plagiarism (Fazilatfar et al., 2018). Instructors are also advised to promote students' academic honesty by promoting their competency in in research skills involving finding, evaluating, organizing, and synthesizing references (Patak et al., 2020), as well as paraphrasing skills (Fenster, 2016). Writing instructors might be recommended to introduce students to anti-plagiarism guidelines to promote academic honesty in academic writing classes (Bennett, 2005).

On the other hand, the findings also pointed out that some improvements should be made to the utilization of Turnitin itself. Participants in the study reported having difficulty using Turnitin. When Turnitin is used for multiple classes, students can get disoriented faced with multiple passwords and class IDs. The integration with other online programs such as Blackboard or Moodle might be a way to overcome this barrier. To help with this and other matters regarding the day-to-day use of Turnitin itself, a series of online materials need to be made available, in interactive form, detailing how students could check their own work through Turnitin before submission to academic staff. This can be integrated with specific (self-paced) 'academic integrity' materials detailed above designed to help students understand the issues surrounding plagiarism. Subject specific requirements for adherence to citation conventions should also be introduced into such support material.

In order to promote the optimum use of Turnitin in academic writing classes, students might be recommended to use Turnitin before they submit their final projects and receive their instructors' feedback based on Turnitin results (Akçapınar, 2015; Amin and Mohammadkariami, 2019). It is also advisable for professors to give their students feedback prior to the latter's submission, and as much as possible provide feedback based on the results of Turnitin, particularly in higher education, to reduce the students' anxiety level (Amin & Mohammadkariami, 2019). In addition, students may be given opportunities to use the PeerMark feature of Turnitin to give online peer feedback (Li & Li, 2017). They may be trained for providing revision-oriented feedback on global areas (e.g., content, organization, and citation) and local areas (e.g., vocabulary, mechanics and format) (Li & Li, 2017).

Regardless of all of the above, it is of utmost importance that (at the beginning of any course where Turnitin is used) students are adequately informed as to how they will be expected to use this text matching software. The purpose and implementation of its use in the course need to be explicitly stated in the syllabus and verbally restated throughout the course. At the same time, students should be provided with ongoing support to get maximum advantage out of the software. Students need to be allowed to resubmit their assignments in cases of texts with a high percentage of match, which will eventually alter and shift student perceptions of the tool from a controlling/policing tool to a learning tool.

FURTHER RESEARCH

The study can be replicated with different cohorts, with different learner and cultural profiles. Comparative studies could also be carried out with different learner profiles having different age and proficiency level. Also, for more global comparisons across learner groups, corpus studies can be conducted with the compilation of corpora of L1 and L2 academic writing samples (Al-Thwaib et al. 2020; Clough & Stevenson, 2009; Gipp et al., 2014; Haneef et al., 2019; Mahmoud & Zrigui, 2018; Taerungruang & Aroonmanakun, 2018). Each sample could be tagged for (a) essay section (b) rhetorical moves, and (b) discoursal elements such as argumentation triggers, and (d) presence of authorial voice. Turnitin could then be utilized to gather text-matching percentages for each distinct extract section/tag identified. With such parallel corpora, student work from diverse academic disciplines can be investigated with the purpose of revealing the common and different features of plagiarism practices and the emergent patterns cross-linguistically comparing L1 and L2 production globally.

REFERENCES

Abasi, A. R., & Akbari, N. (2008). Are we encouraging patchwriting? Reconsidering the role of the pedagogical context in ESL student writers' transgressive intertextuality. *English for Specific Purposes*, 27(3), 267–284. doi:10.1016/j.esp.2008.02.001

Akçapınar, G. (2015). How automated feedback through text mining changes plagiaristic behavior in online assignments. *Computers & Education*, 87, 123–130. doi:10.1016/j.compedu.2015.04.007

Al-Thwaib, E., Hammo, B. H., & Yagi, S. (2020). An academic Arabic corpus for plagiarism detection: Design, construction and experimentation. *International Journal of Educational Technology in Higher Education*, 17(1), 1–26. doi:10.118641239-019-0174-x

Amin, M. Y. M., & Mohammadkarimi, E. (2019). ELT students' attitudes toward the effectiveness the anti-plagiarism software, Turnitin. *Applied Linguisics Research Journal*, 3(5), 63–75.

Angélil-Carter, S. (2000). *Stolen language? Plagiarism in writing*. Pearson Education Limited.

Angelova, M., & Riazantseva, A. (1999). "If you don't tell me, how can I know?" A case study of four international students learning to write the U.S. way. *Written Communication*, 16(4), 491–525. doi:10.1177/0741088399016004004

Arslan, R. Ş., & Üçok-Atasoy, M. (2020). An investigation into EFL teachers' assessment of young learners of English: Does practice match the policy? *International Online Journal of Education & Teaching*, 7(2), 468–484. https://iojet.org/index.php/IOJET/article/view/818

Ashworth, P., Freewood, M., & Macdonald, R. (2003). The student life world and the meanings of plagiarism. *Journal of Phenomenological Psychology*, 34(2), 257–278. doi:10.1163/156916203322847164

Badge, J., & Scott, J. (2009) *Dealing with plagiarism in the digital age*. Retrieved from http://evidencenet.pbworks.com/Dealing-with-plagiarism-in-the-digital-age

Bailey, S. (2015). *Academic writing: A handbook for international students*. Routledge. doi:10.4324/9781315768434

Baker, R., Thornton, B., & Adams, M. (2008). An evaluation of the effectiveness of Turnitin.com as a tool for reducing plagiarism in graduate student term papers. *College Teaching Methods and Styles Journal, 4*(9), 1–4. doi:10.19030/ctms.v4i9.5564

Balbay, S., & Kilis, S. (2019). Perceived effectiveness of Turnitin® in detecting plagiarism in presentation slides. *Contemporary Educational Technology, 10*(1), 25–36. doi:10.30935/cet.512522

Batane, T. (2010). Turning to Turnitin to fight plagiarism among university students. *Journal of Educational Technology & Society, 13*(2), 1–12.

Bennett, R. (2005). Factors associated with student plagiarism in a post-1992 university. *Assessment & Evaluation in Higher Education, 30*(2), 137–162. doi:10.1080/02602930420002642244

Bloch, J. (2001). Plagiarism and the ESL Student: From printed to electronic texts. In D. Belcher & A. Hirvela (Eds.), *Linking literacies: Perspectives on L2 reading-writing connections* (pp. 209–228). The University of Michigan Press.

Born, A. (2003). How to reduce plagiarism. *Journal of Information Systems Education, 14*(3), 223–224.

Breen, L., & Maassen, M. (2005). Reducing the incidence of plagiarism in an undergraduate course: The role of education. *Issues in Educational Research, 15*(1), 1–16.

Bretag, T. (2013). Challenges in addressing plagiarism in education. *PLoS Medicine, 10*(12), e1001574. doi:10.1371/journal.pmed.1001574 PMID:24391477

Brown, V. J., & Howell, M. E. (2001). The efficacy of policy statements on plagiarism: Do they change students' views. *Research in Higher Education, 42*(1), 103–118. doi:10.1023/A:1018720728840

Bruton, S., & Childers, D. (2016). The ethics and politics of policing plagiarism: A qualitative study of faculty views on student plagiarism and Turnitin®. *Assessment & Evaluation in Higher Education, 41*(2), 316–330. doi:10.1080/02602938.2015.1008981

Buranen, L. (1999). But I wasn't cheating: Plagiarism and cross-cultural mythology. In L. Buranen & A. M. Roy (Eds.), *Perspectives on plagiarism and intellectual property in postmodern world* (pp. 63–74). State University of New York Press.

Carrell, S. E., Malmstrom, F., & West, J. E. (2008). Article. *Business Ethics Quarterly*, *10*(1), 33–42. doi:10.2307/3857692

Carroll, J. (2002). *A Handbook for deterring plagiarism in higher education.* Oxford Centre for Staff and Learning Development.

Cheah, S. W., & Bretag, T. (2008). Making technology work for academic integrity in Malaysia. *3rd International Plagiarism Conference Refereed Proceedings*.

Chien, S. C. (2016). Taiwanese college students' perceptions of plagiarism: Cultural and educational considerations. *Ethics & Behavior*, 1–22. doi:10.1080/10508422.2015.1136219

Clough, P., & Stevenson, M. (2009). *Creating a corpus of plagiarised academic texts*. Paper presented at the Corpus Linguistics Conference (CL2009), University of Liverpool.

Compton, J., & Pfau, M. (2008). Inoculating against pro-plagiarism justifications: Rational and affective strategies. *Journal of Applied Communication Research*, *36*(1), 98–119. doi:10.1080/00909880701799329

Currie, P. (1998). Staying out of trouble: Apparent plagiarism and academic survival. *Journal of Second Language Writing*, *2*(2), 1–18. doi:10.1016/S1060-3743(98)90003-0

Dahl, S. (2007). Turnitin(R): The student perspective on using plagiarism detection software. *Active Learning in Higher Education*, *8*(2), 173–191. doi:10.1177/1469787407074110

Davis, M. (2013). The development of source use by international postgraduate students. *Journal of English for Academic Purposes*, *12*(2), 125–135. doi:10.1016/j.jeap.2012.11.008

Davis, M., & Carroll, J. (2009). Formative feedback within plagiarism education: Is there a role for text-matching software? *International Journal for Educational Integrity*, *5*(2), 58–70. doi:10.21913/IJEI.v5i2.614

Deckert, G. D. (1993). Perspectives on plagiarism from ESL students in Hong Kong. *Journal of Second Language Writing*, *2*(2), 131–148. doi:10.1016/1060-3743(93)90014-T

Decoo, W. (2008). Substantial, verbatim, unattributed, misleading: Applying criteria to assess textual plagiarism. In T. S. Roberts (Ed.), *Student plagiarism in an online world: Problems and solutions* (pp. 228–243). Information Science Reference. doi:10.4018/978-1-59904-801-7.ch015

Devlin, M., & Gray, K. (2007). In their own words: A qualitative study of the reasons Australian university students plagiarize. *Higher Education Research & Development, 26*(2), 181–198. doi:10.1080/07294360701310805

Dolzhenko, A. V., Khan, T. M., & Dolzhenko, A. (2016). Strategies and technologies for preventing plagiarism in modern higher education: War against today's plagiarists or nurturing tomorrow's talents. In E. Railean, G. Walker, A. Elçi, & L. Jackson (Eds.), *Handbook of research on applied learning theory and design in modern education* (pp. 840–865). IGI Global. doi:10.4018/978-1-4666-9634-1.ch041

Dryden, L. M. (1999). A distant mirror or through the looking glass? Plagiarism and intellectual property in Japanese education. In L. Bruaunen & A. M. Roy (Eds.), *Perspectives on plagiarism and intellectual property in a postmodern world* (pp. 75–85). State University of New York Press.

Ercegovac, Z., & Richardson, J. V. Jr. (2004). Academic dishonesty: Plagiarism included, in the digital age: A literature review. *College & Research Libraries, 65*(4), 301–318. doi:10.5860/crl.65.4.301

Errey, L. (2002). Plagiarism: Something fishy? Or just a fish out of water? *Teaching Forum, 50*, 17–20.

Espinoza, L.Ü., & Nájera, J.M. (2014). How to correct teaching methods that favour plagiarism: recommendations from teachers and students in a Spanish language distance education university. *Assessment and Evaluation in Higher Education, 40*(8), 1-9. doi:10.1080/02602938.2014.966053

Fazilatfar, A. M., Elhambakhsh, S. E., & Allami, H. (2018). An investigation of the effects of citation instruction to avoid plagiarism in EFL academic writing assignments. *SAGE Open, 8*(2), 1–13. doi:10.1177/2158244018769958

Fenster, J. (2016). Teaching note—Evaluation of an avoiding plagiarism workshop for social work students. *Journal of Social Work Education, 52*(2), 242–248. doi:10.1080/10437797.2016.1151278

Galus, P. (2002). Detecting and preventing plagiarism. *Science Teacher (Normal, Ill.), 69*(8), 35–37.

Gannon-Leary, P., Trayhurn, D., & Home, M. (2009). Good images, effective messages. Working with students and educators on academic practice understanding. *Journal of Further and Higher Education, 33*(4), 435–448. doi:10.1080/03098770903272511

Ghajarzadeh, M., Norouzi-Javidan, A., Hassanpour, K., Aramesh, K., & Emami-Razavi, S. H. (2012). Attitude toward plagiarism among Iranian medical faculty members. *Acta Medica Iranica, 50*(11), 778–781. PMID:23292631

Gibson, N. S., & Chester-Fangman, C. (2011). The librarian's role in combating plagiarism. *RSR. Reference Services Review, 39*(1), 132–150. doi:10.1108/00907321111108169

Gipp, B., Meuschke, N., & Breitinger, C. (2014). Citation-based plagiarism detection: Practicability on a large-scale scientific corpus. *Journal of the Association for Information Science and Technology, 65*(8), 1527–1540. doi:10.1002/asi.23228

Gitanjali, B. (2004). Academic dishonesty in Indian medical colleges. *Journal of Postgraduate Medicine, 50,* 281–284. PMID:15623972

Goddard, R., & Rudzki, R. (2005). Using an electronic text-matching tool (turnitin) to detect plagiarism in an New Zealand university. *Journal of University Teaching & Learning Practice, 2*(3), 58–63.

Goh, E. (2013). Plagiarism behavior among undergraduate students in hospitality and tourism education. *Journal of Teaching in Travel & Tourism, 13*(4), 307–322. doi:10.1080/15313220.2013.839295

Gokmenoğlu, T. (2017). A review of literature: Plagiarism in the papers of Turkish context. *Higher Education Studies, 7*(3), 161–170. doi:10.5539/hes.v7n3p161

Graham-Matheson, L., & Starr, S. (2013). Is it cheating or learning the craft of writing? Using Turnitin to help students avoid plagiarism. *Research in Learning Technology, 21,* 1–13. doi:10.3402/rlt.v21i0.17218

Gullifer, J., & Tyson, G. A. (2010). Exploring university students' perceptions of plagiarism: A focus group study. *Studies in Higher Education, 35*(4), 463–481. doi:10.1080/03075070903096508

Gullifer, J. M., & Tyson, G. A. (2014). Who has read the policy on plagiarism? Unpacking students' understanding of plagiarism. *Studies in Higher Education, 39*(7), 1202–1218. doi:10.1080/03075079.2013.777412

Guraya, S. Y., & Guraya, S. S. (2017). The confounding factors leading to plagiarism in academic writing and some suggested remedies: A systematic review. *Systematic Reviews, 67*(5), 767–773. PMID:28507368

Halgamuge, M. N. (2017). The use and analysis of anti-plagiarism software: Turnitin tool for formative assessment and feedback. *Computer Applications in Engineering Education, 25*(6), 895–909. doi:10.1002/cae.21842

Handa, N., & Power, C. (2005). Land and discover! A case study investigating the cultural context of plagiarism. *Journal of University Teaching & Learning Practice*, *2*(3), 64–86.

Haneef, I., Nawab, R. M. A., Munir, U., & Baiwa, I. S. (2019). Design and development of a large cross-lingual plagiarism corpus for Urdu-English language pair. *Scientific Programming*, *2019*, 1–11. doi:10.1155/2019/2962040

Hansen, B. (2003). Combating plagiarism. *CQ Researcher*, *13*(32), 775–792.

Hayes, N., & Introna, L. D. (2015). Cultural values, plagiarism and fairness: When plagiarism gets in the way of learning. *Ethics & Behavior*, *15*(3), 213–231. doi:10.120715327019eb1503_2

Heckler, N. C., Rice, M., & Bryan, C. H. (2013). Turnitin systems: A deterrent to plagiarism in college classrooms. *Journal of Research on Technology in Education*, *45*(3), 229–248. doi:10.1080/15391523.2013.10782604

Heron, J. L. (2001). Plagiarism, learning dishonesty or just plain cheating: The context and countermeasures in information systems teaching. *Australasian Journal of Educational Technology*, *17*(3), 244–264. doi:10.14742/ajet.1794

Holt, E. A., Fagerheim, B., & Durham, S. (2014). Online plagiarism training falls short in biology classrooms. *CBE Life Sciences Education*, *13*(1), 83–89. doi:10.1187/cbe.13-08-0146 PMID:24591507

Howard, R. M. (1999). *Standing in the shadow of giants: Plagiarists, authors, collaborators*. Ablex.

Hughes, J. M. C., & McCabe, D. L. (2006). Understanding academic misconduct. *Canadian Journal of Higher Education*, *36*(1), 49–63. doi:10.47678/cjhe.v36i1.183525

Hui-Fang, S. (2019). An investigation of plagiarism software use and awareness training on English as a foreign language (EFL) students. *Journal of Computing in Higher Education*, *31*(1), 105–120. doi:10.100712528-018-9193-1

Hyland, F. (2001). Dealing with plagiarism when giving feedback. *ELT Journal*, *55*(4), 375–381. doi:10.1093/elt/55.4.375

Ivanic, R. (2004). Intertextual practices in the construction of multimodal texts in inquiry-based learning. *Uses of intertextuality in classroom and educational research*, 279-314.

Jackson, P. A. (2006). Plagiarism instruction online: Assessing undergraduate students' ability to avoid plagiarism. *College & Research Libraries, 67*(5), 418–428. doi:10.5860/crl.67.5.418

Jereb, E., Perc, M., Lämmlein, B., Jerebic, J., Urh, M., Podbregar, I., & Šprajc, P. (2018). Factors influencing plagiarism in higher education: A comparison of German and Slovene students. *PLoS One, 13*(8), 1–16. doi:10.1371/journal.pone.0202252 PMID:30096189

Jocoy, C. L., & DiBiase, D. (2006). Plagiarism by adult learners online: A case study in detection and remediation. *International Review of Research in Open and Distance Learning, 7*(1), 1–15. doi:10.19173/irrodl.v7i1.242

Johns Hopkins University. (2006). *Deterring and detecting plagiarism with Turnitin. com: A Tip Sheet from Center for Educational Resources*. Retrieved from http://www.cer.jhu.edu/pdf/turnitintips.pdf

Kayaoğlu, M. N., Erbay, S., Flitner, C., & Saltaş, D. (2015). Examining students' perceptions of plagiarism: A cross-cultural study at tertiary level. *Journal of Further and Higher Education*, 1–24. doi:10.1080/0309877X.2015.1014320

Kolich, A. M. (1983). Plagiarism: The worm of reason. *College English, 52*(8), 141–148. doi:10.2307/377221

Köse, Ö., & Arıkan, A. (2011). Reducing plagiarism by using online software: An experimental study. *Contemporary Online Language Education Journal, 1*, 122–129.

Lake, J. (2004). EAP writing: The Chinese challenge; new ideas on plagiarism. *Humanising Language Teaching, 6*(1). Retrieved from http://www.hltmag.co.uk/jan04/mart4.htm

Ledwith, A., & Rísquez, A. (2008). Using anti-plagiarism software to promote academic honesty in the context of peer reviewed assignments. *Studies in Higher Education, 33*(4), 371–384. doi:10.1080/03075070802211562

Lei, J., & Hu, G. (2015). Chinese university EFL teachers' perceptions of plagiarism. *Higher Education, 70*(3), 551–565. doi:10.100710734-014-9855-5

Leki, I., & Carson, J. (1997). Completely different worlds: EAP and the writing experiences of ESL students in university courses. *TESOL Quarterly, 31*(1), 39–69. doi:10.2307/3587974

Li, M., & Li, J. (2017). Online peer review using Turnitin in first-year writing classes. *Composition and Composition, 46*, 21–38. doi:10.1016/j.compcom.2017.09.001

Li, Y. (2013). Text-based plagiarism in scientific publishing: Issues, developments and education. *Science and Engineering Ethics, 19*(3), 1241–1254. doi:10.100711948-012-9367-6 PMID:22535578

LoCastro, V., & Musuko, M. (1997). *Plagiarism and academic writing of NNS learners.* Paper presented at the annual meeting of the Teachers of English to Speakers of Other Languages, Orlando, FL.

Löfström, E. (2011). "Does plagiarism mean anything? LOL." Students' Conceptions of writing and citing. *Journal of Academic Ethics, 9*(4), 257–275. doi:10.100710805-011-9145-0

Löfström, E., & Kupila, P. (2013). The instructional challenges of student plagiarism. *Journal of Academic Ethics, 11*(3), 231–242. doi:10.100710805-013-9181-z

Maddox, T. T. (2008). Plagiarism and the community college. In *Practical issues for academics using the Turnitin plagiarism detection software. International Conference on Computer Systems and Technologies - CompSysTech'08.* Retrieved from http://ecet.ecs.ru.acad.bg/cst08/docs/cp/SIV/IV.1.pdf

Mahmoud, A., & Zrigui, M. (2018). Artificial method for building monolingual plagiarized Arabic corpus. *Computación y Sistemas, 22*(3), 767–776. doi:10.13053/cys-22-3-3019

Marsden, H., Carroll, M., & Neill, J. T. (2005). Who cheats at university? A self-report study of dishonest academic behaviours in a sample of Australian university students. *Australian Journal of Psychology, 57*(1), 1–10. doi:10.1080/00049530412331283426

Martin, D. F. (2005). Plagiarism and technology: A tool for coping with plagiarism. *Journal of Education for Business, 80*(3), 149–152. doi:10.3200/JOEB.80.3.149-152

Mavrinac, M., Brumini, G., Bilić-Zulle, L., & Petrovečki, M. (2010). Construction and validation of attitudes toward plagiarism questionnaire. *Croatian Medical Journal, 51*(3), 195–201. doi:10.3325/cmj.2010.51.195 PMID:20564761

McCabe, D. L., & Trevino, L. K. (1993). Academic dishonesty: Honor codes and other contextual influences. *The Journal of Higher Education, 64*(5), 522538. doi:10.1080/00221546.1993.11778446

McCabe, D. L., Trevino, L. K., & Butterfield, K. D. (2001). Cheating in academic institutions: A decade of research. *Ethics & Behavior, 11*(3), 219–233. doi:10.1207/S15327019EB1103_2

McKeever, L. (2006). Online plagiarism detection services—Saviour or scourge? *Assessment & Evaluation in Higher Education, 31*(2), 155–165. doi:10.1080/02602930500262460

Murphy, R. (1990). Anorexia: The cheating disorder. *College English, 52*(8), 898–903. doi:10.2307/377394

Mustafa, F. (2019). "I think it is not plagiarism": How little do Indonesian undergraduate EFL students understand plagiarism? *Asian EFL Journal, 21*(2), 74–91.

Nova, M., & Utami, W. H. (2018). EFL students' perception of Turnitin for detecting plagiarism on academic writing. *International Journal of Education, 10*(2), 141–148.

O'Donoghue, T. (1996). Malaysian Chinese students' perceptions of what is necessary for their academic success in Australia: A case study at one university. *Journal of Further and Higher Education, 20*(2), 67–80. doi:10.1080/0309877960200206

Park, C. (2003). In other (people's) words: Plagiarism by university students - literature and lessons. *Assessment & Evaluation in Higher Education, 28*(5), 471–488. doi:10.1080/02602930301677

Patak, A. A., Wiraman, H., Abduh, A., Hidayat, R., Iskandar, I., & Dirawan, G. D. (2020). Teaching English as a foreign language in Indonesia: University lecturers' views on plagiarism. *Journal of Academic Ethics* doi:10.100710805-020-09385-y

Paxton, M. (2007). Tensions between textbook pedagogy and the literary practices of the disciplinary community: A study of writing in first year economics. *Journal of English for Academic Purposes, 6*(2), 109–125. doi:10.1016/j.jeap.2007.04.003

Pecorari, D. (2001). Plagiarism and international students: How the English-speaking university responds. In D. Belcher & A. Hirvela (Eds.), *Linking literacies: Perspectives on L2 Reading-Writing Connections* (pp. 229–245). The University of Michigan Press.

Pecorari, D., & Petrić, B. (2014). Plagiarism in second-language writing. *Language Teaching, 47*(3), 269–302. doi:10.1017/S0261444814000056

Pennycook, A. (1996). Borrowing others' words: Text, ownership, memory and plagiarism. *TESOL Quarterly, 30*(2), 201–230. doi:10.2307/3588141

Powell, L. (2012). *Understanding plagiarism: developing a model of plagiarising behavior*. Paper presented at the International Integrity & Plagiarism Conference, Newcastle Upon Tyne, UK. Retrieved from https://pdfs.semanticscholar.org/0903/10b04ade5540c672c5b0db66e868bd805644.pdf

Rakovski, C., & Levy, E. (2007). Academic dishonesty: Perceptions of business students. *College Student Journal*, *41*, 466–481.

Razı, S. (2015a). Cross-checked problems in undergraduate academic writing. K. Dikilitaş, R. Smith, & W. Trotman (Eds.), Teacher-researchers in action (pp. 147-161). Kent, UK: IATEFL.

Razı, S. (2015b). Development of a rubric to assess academic writing incorporating plagiarism detectors. *SAGE Open*, *5*(2), 1–13. doi:10.1177/2158244015590162

Read, B. (2006). Turnitin makes its ivy league debut. *Chronicle of Higher Education*. Retrieved from http://www.chronicle.com/blogs/wiredcampus/turnitin-makes-its-ivy-league-debut/2656

Rets, I., & Ilya, A. (2018). Eliciting ELT students' understanding of plagiarism in academic writing. *Eurasian Journal of Applied Linguistics*, *4*(2), 193–211. doi:10.32601/ejal.464115

Rolfe, V. (2011). Can Turnitin be used to provide instant formative feedback? *British Journal of Educational Technology*, *42*(4), 701–710. doi:10.1111/j.1467-8535.2010.01091.x

Royce, J. (2003). Has turnitin.com got it all wrapped up? (Trust or trussed?). *Teacher Librarian*, *30*(4), 26–30.

Ryan, G., Bonanno, H., Krass, I., Scouller, K., & Smith, L. (2009). Undergraduate and postgraduate pharmacy students' perceptions of plagiarism and academic honesty. *American Journal of Pharmaceutical Education*, *73*(6), 105. doi:10.5688/aj7306105 PMID:19885074

Ryan, S., & Eckersley, C. (2004). *Academic integrity and use of turnitin*. Retrieved from www.newcastle.edu.au/services/academic-integrity

Scaife, B. (2007*). IT Consultancy plagiarism detection software report for JISC Advisory Service*. Retrieved from https://studylib.net/doc/8357192/it-consultancy-plagiarism-detection-software-report-for-jisc

Scanlan, C. L. (2006). Strategies to promote a climate of academic integrity and minimize student cheating and plagiarism. *Journal of Allied Health*, *35*(3), 179–185. PMID:17036675

Scanlon, P. M., & Neumann, D. R. (2002). Internet plagiarism among college students. *Journal of College Student Development*, *43*, 374–385.

Scollon, R. (1994). As a matter of fact: The changing ideology of authorship and responsibility in discourse. *World Englishes*, *13*(1), 33–46. doi:10.1111/j.1467-971X.1994.tb00281.x

Scollon, R. (1995). Plagiarism and ideology: Identity in intercultural discourse. *Language in Society*, *24*(1), 1–28. doi:10.1017/S0047404500018388

Selwyn, N. (2008). 'Not necessarily a bad thing…': A study of online plagiarism amongst undergraduate students. *Assessment & Evaluation in Higher Education*, *33*(5), 465–479. doi:10.1080/02602930701563104

Sentleng, M. P., & King, L. (2012). Plagiarism among undergraduate students in the faculty of applied science at a South African higher education institution. *South African Journal of Libraries and Information Service*, *78*(1), 57–67. doi:10.7553/78-1-47

Sheridan, J., Alany, R., & Brake, D. (2005). Pharmacy students' views and experiences of Turnitin – an online tool for detecting academic dishonesty. *Pharmacy Education*, *5*(374), 241–250. doi:10.1080/15602210500288977

Sherman, J. (1992). Your own thoughts in your own words. *ELT Journal*, *46*(2), 190–198. doi:10.1093/elt/46.2.190

Sohrabi, B., Gholipour, A., & Mohammadesmaeili, N. (2011). Effects of personality and information technology on plagiarism: An Iranian perspective. *Ethics & Behavior*, *21*(5), 367–379. doi:10.1080/10508422.2011.604294

Sowden, C. (2005). Plagiarism and the culture of multilingual students in higher education abroad. *ELT Journal*, *59*(3), 226–233. doi:10.1093/elt/cci042

Standler, R. B. (2012). *Plagiarism in colleges in USA: Legal aspects of plagiarism, academic policy*. Retrieved from http://www.rbs2.com/plag.pdf

Sutherland-Smith, W. (2011). Crime and punishment: An analysis of university plagiarism policies. *Semiotica*, *187*(187), 127–139. doi:10.1515emi.2011.067

Sutherland-Smith, W., & Carr, R. (2005). Turnitin.com: Teachers' perspectives of anti-plagiarism software in raising issues of educational integrity. *Journal of University Teaching & Learning Practice*, *2*(3), 94–101.

Taerungruang, S., & Aroonmanakun, W. (2018). Constructing an academic Thai plagiarism corpus for benchmarking plagiarism detection systems. *GEMA Online® Journal of Language Studies*, *18*(3), 186-202. doi:10.17576/gema-2018-1803-11

Taylor, K. L., Usick, B. L., & Paterson, B. L. (2004). Understanding plagiarism: The intersection of personal, pedagogical, institutional, and social contexts. *Journal on Excellence in College Teaching, 15*(3), 153–174.

Tran, T. T. (2012). The perceptions and attitudes of international students towards plagiarism. *The ACPET Journal for Private Higher Education, 1*(2), 13–21.

Unal, M., Toprak, M., & Baspınar, V. (2012). Bilim etiğine aykırı davranıslar ve yaptırımlar: Sosyal ve beseri bilimler Icin bir çerceve önerisi [Ethical Violations and Sanctions in Scientific Publications: A framework proposal for social sciences and Humanities.]. *Amme Idaresi Dergisi, 45*(3), 1–27.

Wager, E. (2014). Defining and responding to plagiarism. *Learned Publishing, 27*(1), 33–42. doi:10.1087/20140105

Wajda-Johnston, V. A., Handal, P. J., Brawer, P. A., & Fabricatore, A. N. (2001). Academic dishonesty at the graduate level. *Ethics & Behavior, 11*(3), 287–305. doi:10.1207/S15327019EB1103_7

Walker, J. (2010). Measuring *plagiarism:* Researching what students do, not what they say they do. *Studies in Higher Education, 35*(1), 41–59. doi:10.1080/03075070902912994

Williamson, K., & McGregor, J. (2011). Generating knowledge and avoiding plagiarism: Smart information use by high school students. *School Library Research*, 14. Retrieved from http://www.ala.org/aasl/slr/volume14/williamson-mcgregor

Wright, D., Owens, A., & Nigel, D. (2008, June). *Making the case for multiple submissions to Turnitin.* Paper presented at the 3rd International Plagiarism Conference. Retrieved from http://www.plagiarismconference.org/pages/conference2008/conference-proceedings.php

Yamada, K. (2003). What prevents ESL / EFL writers from avoiding plagiarism?: Analyses of 10 North-American college websites. *System, 31*(2), 247–258. doi:10.1016/S0346-251X(03)00023-X

Yazici, A., Yazici, S., & Erdem, M. S. (2011). Faculty and student perceptions on college cheating: Evidence from Turkey. *Educational Studies, 37*(2), 221–231. doi:10.1080/03055698.2010.506321

Youmans, R. J. (2011). Does the adoption of plagiarism-detection software in highereducation reduce plagiarism? *Studies in Higher Education, 36*(7), 749–761. doi:10.1080/03075079.2010.523457

KEY TERMS AND DEFINITIONS

Academic Integrity: Academic practices which involve the submission of original work and the act of giving credit to other people's ideas, which involves the following practices at the tertiary level. The creation and expression of one's own ideas in course work, the acknowledgement of all sources of information, the independent completion of assignments or the acknowledgement of collaboration, the accurate reporting of the results in the course of research conduct and honesty during examination.

Authorship: Usually attributed to persons responsible for the intellectual content of a published work. In the context of articles arising from a research study authorship requires ongoing (rather than occasional) contributions to the study and actual writing/critical review of the paper. It involves, therefore, not only those who do the actual writing but also those who have made substantial scientific contributions to a study.

Plagiarism: Stating, or presenting someone else's work or ideas as one's own, with or without their consent and incorporate it into one's work without acknowledging it fully. Plagiarism cases involve one of the following actions: submitting a paper to be graded or reviewed that one has not written on his/her own, copying answers or text from another classmate and submit it as his/her own, quoting or paraphrasing from another paper without crediting the original author, citing data without giving credit to the original source, proposing another author's idea as if it were one's own, inventing references or using incorrect references, submitting someone else's presentation, work, with only minor alterations.

Plagiarism Detection Software: Online computer programs or web interfaces of such programs developed specifically to identify cases where someone's work is presented totally or partially without giving credit to its owner and without applying proper citation practices.

Source Documentation: The provision of evidence (including the primary and secondary sources) in a research paper.

Textual Borrowing: A natural process underlying academic writing which involves students reading from other sources and integrating facts, research, and scholarship from these sources into their own text. Therefore, textual borrowing should be dealt in such a way that it highlights the improvement of students' critical use of other texts in developing their argument rather than for accusing students of their unorthodox practice, referred to as plagiarism.

Textual Ownership: Stating explicitly which ideas in the text come from the writer and which ideas come from outside sources.

ENDNOTES

[1] In this chapter, the terms pre-test and post–test are being used in solely the temporal sense indicating the time at which each test/survey was administered, before the course and at the end of the course respectively. The terms are not being used in the experimental design sense. This is why although sections were identical, minor lexical additions/wording differences were found in the post-test as well as an additional section on Turnitin related impressions.

[2] There are instances of inaccuracies in the data excepts provided in this chapter due to the participants' use of English as a foreign language. No corrections have been made purposefully to keep the data intact.

APPENDİX A: PRE-TEST QUESTİONNAİRE

Pre-Questionnaire

Please, answer the following questions as *honestly and carefully as* you can. Do NOT write your names. Your answers will be kept confidential. Feel free to use *Turkish* to fill out the questionnaire.

Thank you very much for your cooperation.

A. Defining plagiarism:

1. In your own words, what is **plagiarism**? Try to define it in a **detailed** way. Also write a Turkish equivalent for this term, if you know one.

B. Educational Background regarding writing practices:

Please circle the appropriate answer OR provide the requested information:

Before university:

1. What **type** of **assignments** were you expected do in your previous schooling?

2. At high school, was plagiarism ever **mentioned** to you?
 a) Yes b) No

3. Were you specifically **taught** at high school how to document the sources you mentioned in the report/assignments that you prepared?
 a) Yes b) No

4. Was there a **requirement** to document the sources when you wrote a report/assignment at high school?
 a) Yes b) No
 If yes, HOW were you expected to document your sources?

5. Was plagiarism considered a serious crime at high school?
 a) Yes b) No

6. If your answer to Q. 5 is 'Yes', what was the penalty for plagiarism?

7. How often did any of your teachers in the past schooling ever tell you (i. e., by means of spoken or written comments) that you have plagiarized in your own written work?
 a) never b)1 or 2 times c) more than two times

8. Were **you** ever penalized for copying the words or ideas of other writers without indicating the source before?
a) Yes b) No
Indicate when: ….

At university:

9. At *your university*, was plagiarism ever mentioned or explained to you?
a) Yes b) No

10. Other than for this course, was there a requirement to document the sources when you wrote a report/assignment for any of your classes at *your current university*?
a) Yes b) No

11. In your own opinion, to what extent do you feel that you use the words or ideas of other writers without indicating the source in your assignments? *Please, answer this question without considering whether or not you understood what might be wrong with such a habit.*
a) I usually do it b) I sometimes do it c) I rarely do it d) I never do it

C. Student motives:

8. Why do you think students do plagiarism? Please list as many **reasons** as you can below.
   a)
   b)
   c)
   d)
   e)
   f)
   ……….
   9.

D. Noticing Plagiarism:

Below is a part of a newspaper article a student might use to help him/her in writing a report on the topic **The Loss of Tropical Forests**. Read it carefully so that you can recognize the different ways it is used in the series of student writing samples that follow. After reading each sample, you must decide **if** and to **what extent** the writer committed plagiarism. Simply put a tick in *one* of the following statements for each sample.

To avoid plagiarism in writing what kinds of things MUST be documented?	What things DON'T need to be documented?
- - -	- - -

NOTE: There is <u>at least *one*</u> writing sample to match each of <u>these three possible answers</u>. Be sure to tick an answer for each of the six samples. Do not rush; rather, work carefully.

(This exercise is adapted from Deckert, G. D. (1993).Perspectives on Plagiarism From ESL Students in Hong Kong, <u>Journal of Second Language Writing,</u> 2(2), 131-143).

GLOOM OVER TROPICAL FORESTS*

by Philip Shabecoff
International Herald Tribune, June 9, 1990, p. 3.

Tropical forests, which play a vital role in regulating the global climate, are disappearing much more rapidly than previously estimated, according to an international research group. Each year recently, 40 million to 50 million acres (16 million to 20 million hectares) of tropical forest have been lost as trees are cut for timber and land is cleared for agriculture and development, the World Resources Institute said in its 1990 report. According to this study, the rate of loss in most countries was nearly 50% more in 1987 than in 1980. The report said 1.9 billion acres of tropical forest remained...

1* From "Loss of Tropical Rain Forests Is Found Much Worse Than Was Thought" by Philip Shabecoff, *The New York Times*, June 8, 1990. Reprinted in *International Tribune*, June 9, 1990. Copyright 1990 by New York Times Company. Adapted by permission. (Deckert, 1993)

Sample A

The world is losing its valuable forests at an alarming pace. The Earth's forests which are an important factor in the Earth's climate, were disappearing more quickly in 1987 than previously estimated in 1980. Recently, 40 million to 50 million acres of tropical forest have been lost each year. This is because some forests are cut for timber and some are cleared for other purposes. The group says 1.9 billion acres of tropical forest remain.*

* P. Shabecoff, International Herald Tribune, June 9, 1990, p. 3.
_ The student committed no plagiarism, i. e. no wrong use of the source.
_ The student committed some plagiarism, i. e., some wrong use of the source.
_ The student committed a great amount of plagiarism, i.e., a great amount of wrong use of source.

Sample B

The world is losing its valuable forests at an alarming pace. Tropical forests, which play a vital role in regulating the global climate, are disappearing much more rapidly than previously estimated. An international research group reported that each year recently 40 million to 50 million acres of tropical forest have been lost as forests are cut for timber, and land is cleared for agriculture and development. The rate of loss was more in 1987 than in 1980. The group said 1.9 billion acres of tropical forest remained.*

* P. Shabecoff, International Herald Tribune, June 9, 1990, p. 3.
_ The student committed no plagiarism, i. e. no wrong use of the source.
_ The student committed some plagiarism, i. e., some wrong use of the source.
_ The student committed a great amount of plagiarism, i.e., a great amount of wrong use of source.

Sample C

The world is losing its valuable forests at an alarming pace. According to recent research done by an international research team, the Earth is losing up to 50 million acres of forest each year. According to the investigation, the rate of loss increased by 50% from 1980 to 1987. The 1990 report indicates 1.9 billion acres of forest remain on Earth. A major concern is that this loss may greatly affect patterns of climate.
_ The student committed no plagiarism, i. e. no wrong use of the source.
_ The student committed some plagiarism, i. e., some wrong use of the source.
_ The student committed a great amount of plagiarism, i.e., a great amount of wrong use of source.

Sample D

The world is losing its valuable forests at an alarming pace. Forests, which are an important factor in climatic patterns, are being rapidly cut back for timber, agricultural needs, and land development. Studies over the past decades indicate that the rate of loss increased by 50% between 1980 and 1987. At present there is less than two billion acres of forest remaining, and about 40 to 50 million acres are being lost annually, according to the World Resources Institute.*

* P. Shabecoff, International Herald Tribune, June 9, 1990, p. 3.

_ The student committed no plagiarism, i. e. no wrong use of the source.

_ The student committed some plagiarism, i. e., some wrong use of the source.

_ The student committed a great amount of plagiarism, i.e., a great amount of wrong use of source.

Sample E

The world is losing its valuable forests at an alarming pace. Philip Shabecoff, summarizing a report based upon a recent study done by the World Resources Institute, states, "Each year recently 40 million to 50 million acres ... of tropical forest have been lost as trees are cut for timber and land is cleared for agriculture and development" (International Herald Tribune, 9 June 1990, p. 3). According to the same study, the Earth now has less than two billion acres of forest, and the rate of loss is increasing. The loss of forests can affect global climate.

_ The student committed no plagiarism, i. e. no wrong use of the source.

_ The student committed some plagiarism, i. e., some wrong use of the source.

_ The student committed a great amount of plagiarism, i.e., a great amount of wrong use of source.

Sample F

The world is losing its valuable forests at an alarming pace. A recent article in the International Herald Tribune gives the findings of the World Resources Institute. The findings in this 1990 report are that "at present, each year between 40 million and 50 million acres of forest disappear because people cut them down for wood or remove them to make the land ready for other requirements and only 1.9 acres remain". * Losing so much forest land might affect the climate and cause serious problems.

* P. Shabecoff, International Herald Tribune, June 9, 1990, p. 3.

_ The student committed no plagiarism, i. e. no wrong use of the source.

_ The student committed some plagiarism, i. e., some wrong use of the source.

_ The student committed a great amount of plagiarism, i.e., a great amount of wrong use of source.

Summary Question:

Look at the one or more writing samples you rated as having "**a great amount of plagiarism**". Then circle the letter of the sample which showed the WORST case of plagiarism.
   A B C D E F

E. Perceptions and practices regarding plagiarism:

Look again at the sample you chose as the worst case of plagiarism, that is the writing sample that made the most incorrect use of the newspaper article. To whom is its writer unfair and why is it unfair?

To give your opinion, read each of the following statements and show how much you agree or disagree with each statement by ticking **ONE** of boxes. If you have no opinion about a statement, tick the box "no opinion".

	When one writes this way,	strongly agree	agree	no opinion!	disagree	strongly disagree
1	he/she is unfair to <u>himself/herself</u> because he/she is not being himself/herself. Rather, he/she is pretending to be better than he/she is.					
2	he/she is unfair to the <u>university</u> because it runs counter to the university educational goals which can never be achieved if students just copy information.					
3	he/she is unfair to the <u>writer</u> of the original passage because he/she is taking the credit that the writer deserves for the words and ideas.					
4	When one writes this way, he/she is unfair to <u>class</u> as everybody is processing information in his/her own language whereas by plagiarizing sometimes one may get the same or a better grade.					

5. Do your university instructors have a preference for the sources (internet or library sources) you use?
   Do they indicate their preferences in favor of one or the other?
   If Yes, why do you think they do so?
6. How often do you use <u>library</u> (hardcopy) sources when doing research on an academic topic?
   a) Always b) Often c) Sometimes d) Rarely e) Never
7. How often do you use the <u>internet</u> sources when doing research on an academic topic?

a) Always b) Often c) Sometimes d) Rarely e) Never

8. What do you think of the reliability of the internet sources that you use in your research?

a) Very reliable b) Reliable c) Not much reliable d) Not reliable at all

9. To what extent do you think the internet sources are biased?

1 2 3 4 5

10. How often do you check the reliability of the internet sources that you use?

1 2 3 4 5

11. To what extent do you use the internet websites for academic purposes in Turkish?

1 2 3 4 5

12. To what extent do you use the internet websites for academic purposes in English?

1 2 3 4 5

13. What do you think the role of readily available internet sources have in the rate of plagiarism cases? Please comment.

14. Please recommend things that can be done to prevent student plagiarism by these groups:

By instructors:

By the university/school admin:

By students:

By the community/educational policy makers:

==

15. Please write any additional comments you may want to share:

==

Thank you for your participation!

APPENDIX B: POST-TEST QUESTIONNAIRE

POST-QUESTIONNAIRE

Please, answer the following questions as *honestly and carefully as* you can. Do NOT write your names. Your answers will be kept confidential. Feel free to use *Turkish* to fill out the questionnaire.

Thank you very much for your cooperation.

A. Source documentation practices and the use of the software Turnitin

1. To what extent do you feel you used the words or ideas of other writers without indicating the source in your writing assignments (essays, reflection journals) this semester?
    a) I always did it b) I sometimes did it c) I rarely did it d) I never did it
2. In line with your experience/knowledge you acquired in this course, what kinds of things must be documented?
3. In line with your experience/knowledge you acquired in this course, what kinds of things do not have to be documented?
4. Did you use any sources other than your ideas to while producing to the writing assignments in this course?
    a) Yes b) No
5. If your answer to Question 4 is Yes, did you have any difficulty documenting your sources in your written work this semester?
    a) Yes b) No
6. If your answer to Question 4 is Yes, how often did you have any difficulty documenting your sources?
    a) Always b) Often c) Sometimes d) Rarely
4. What types of difficulties did you have documenting sources? Please explain.
5. To what extent do you think the software Turnitin has been beneficial for you? Please circle your choice.
    a) Very beneficial b) Beneficial c) Not much beneficial d) Not beneficial at all
6. In what specific way(s) do you think you have benefited from the software Turnitin?
7. To what extent do you think the software Turnitin is helpful to avoid plagiarism?
    a) Very beneficial b) Beneficial c) Not much beneficial d) Not beneficial at all
8. Did you check the rate of plagiarism in your work after you submitted it to the Turnitin?
    a) Yes b) No
10. Has the program ever detected high rates of plagiarism in your work?
    a) Yes b) No
11. If your answer to Question 10 is Yes, what did you do about it?
12. In what ways do you think the software Turnitin is not effective?
    a.
    b.
    c.

d.
e.

13. How often did you use internet sources when preparing your written assignments for this class?

a) Always b) Often c) Sometimes d) Rarely e) Never

14. How often did you use library (hardcopy) sources when preparing your written assignments for this class?

a) Always b) Often c) Sometimes d) Rarely e) Never

15. What do you think of the reliability of the internet sources that you used in your assignments in this class?

a) Very reliable b) Reliable c) Not much reliable d) Not reliable at all

16. To what extent did you check the reliability of the internet sources that you used in your written assignments for this class?

a) Always b) Often c) Sometimes d) Rarely e) Never

B. Noticing Plagiarism

Below is a part of a Politics textbook. Read it carefully so that you can recognize the different ways it is used in the series of student writing samples that follow. After reading each sample, you must decide **if** and to **what extent** the writer committed plagiarism. Simply put a tick in *one* of the following statements for each sample.

NOTE: There is at least *one* writing sample to match each of these three possible answers. Be sure to tick an answer for each of the six samples. Do not rush; rather, work carefully.

ORIGINAL TEXT:

Gorbachev declared that the countries of the world shared mutual interests and faced mutual threats that went beyond class conflict. This was a revolutionary perspective for a Soviet leader, because a Marxist-Leninist class conflict was the ultimate driving force behind history (Papp, 1994: 290).

(Adapted from Cormack, J. and Slaght, J. (2005). *Extended writing skills and research skills coursebook*. Reading, UK: Garnet Publishing Ltd.)

Sample A

But by this time tings were changing in Russia. The new leader, Gorbachev, argued that all countries in the world had interests in common, which were not connected with class. This was very different from the traditional Soviet view (Papp, 1994: 290).

_ The student committed no plagiarism, i. e. no wrong use of the source.

_ The student committed some plagiarism, i. e., some wrong use of the source.

_ The student committed a great amount of plagiarism, i.e., a great amount of wrong use of source.

Sample B

But by this time things were changing in Russia. Gorbachev declared that the countries of the world shared mutual interests and faced mutual threats that went beyond class conflict. This was a revolutionary perspective for a Soviet leader, because a Marxist-Leninist class conflict was the ultimate driving force behind history. The West reacted to this new way of talking…

_ The student committed no plagiarism, i. e. no wrong use of the source.

_ The student committed some plagiarism, i. e., some wrong use of the source.

_ The student committed a great amount of plagiarism, i.e., a great amount of wrong use of source.

Sample C

But by now things were changing in Russia. Established Soviet dogma was being abandoned by the new leader, whose views concerning the common interests of different countries in the world, both East and West, clearly represented a revolutionary perspective for a leader of the USSR. The West reacted to such changes by…

_ The student committed no plagiarism, i. e. no wrong use of the source.

_ The student committed some plagiarism, i. e., some wrong use of the source.

_ The student committed a great amount of plagiarism, i.e., a great amount of wrong use of source.

Sample D

But by now things were changing in Russia. The new leader was expressing views about the need for international action that were so different from established Soviet ideology that they represented a "revolutionary perspective for a Soviet leader" (Papp, 1994: 290). The West reacted to the new Soviet mood by…

_ The student committed no plagiarism, i. e. no wrong use of the source.

_ The student committed some plagiarism, i. e., some wrong use of the source.

_ The student committed a great amount of plagiarism, i.e., a great amount of wrong use of source.

Sample E

But by now things were changing in Russia. The new leader was expressing views that were very different from traditional Soviet ideology, in that they represented a revolutionary perspective for a leader of the USSR in which the class struggle was the driving force. The West reacted to such changes ...
  _ The student committed no plagiarism, i. e. no wrong use of the source.
  _ The student committed some plagiarism, i. e., some wrong use of the source.
  _ The student committed a great amount of plagiarism, i.e., a great amount of wrong use of source.

Sample F

But by now things were changing in Russia. The new leader was expressing views which were very different from traditional Soviet ideology. As one theorist puts it:

Gorbachev declared that the countries of the world shared mutual interests and faced mutual threats that went beyond class conflict. This was a revolutionary perspective for a Soviet leader, because a Marxist- Leninist class conflict was the ultimate driving force behind history (Papp, 1994: 290).

  _ The student committed no plagiarism, i. e. no wrong use of the source.
  _ The student committed some plagiarism, i. e., some wrong use of the source.
  _ The student committed a great amount of plagiarism, i.e., a great amount of wrong use of source.

C. Perceptions regarding plagiarism:

Look at the one or more writing samples you rated as having "**a great amount of plagiarism**" above. Then circle the letter of the sample which showed the <u>WORST</u> case of plagiarism.
  A B C D E F
Think about to whom its writer is unfair to and why is it unfair? Next, to give your opinion, read each of the following statements and show how much you agree or disagree with each statement by ticking **ONE** of boxes. If you have no opinion about a statement, tick the box "no opinion".

14. Please recommend things that can be done to <u>prevent student plagiarism</u> by these groups:

	When one writes this way,	strongly agree	agree	no opinion!	disagree	strongly disagree
1	he/she is unfair to himself/herself because he/she is not being himself/herself. Rather, he/she is pretending to be better than he/she is.					
2	he/she is unfair to the university because it runs counter to the university educational goals which can never be achieved if students just copy information.					
3	he/she is unfair to the writer of the original passage because he/she is taking the credit that the writer deserves for the words and ideas.					
4	When one writes this way, he/she is unfair to class as everybody is processing information in his/her own language whereas by plagiarizing sometimes one may get the same or a better grade.					

By instructors
By the university/school admin:
By students:
By the community/educational policy makers:
===

15. Please write any additional comments you may want to share:

===

Thank you for your participation!

Compilation of References

Abasi, A. R., & Akbari, N. (2008). Are we encouraging patchwriting? Reconsidering the role of the pedagogical context in ESL student writers' transgressive intertextuality. *English for Specific Purposes*, *27*(3), 267–284. doi:10.1016/j.esp.2008.02.001

Adamson, B. (2002). Barbarian as a foreign language: English in China's schools. *World Englishes*, *21*(2), 231–243. doi:10.1111/1467-971X.00244

Afonso, A. S., & Gilbert, J. K. (2013). The role of 'popular' books in informal chemical education. *International Journal of Science Education. Part B*, *3*(1), 77–99.

Airey, J. (2011). The disciplinary literacy discussion matrix: A heuristic tool for initiating collaboration in higher education. *Across the Disciplines*, *8*(3).

Akçapınar, G. (2015). How automated feedback through text mining changes plagiaristic behavior in online assignments. *Computers & Education*, *87*, 123–130. doi:10.1016/j.compedu.2015.04.007

Akçayır, M., & Akçayır, G. (2017). Advantages and challenges associated with augmented reality for education: A systematic review of the literature. *Educational Research Review*, *20*, 1–11. doi:10.1016/j.edurev.2016.11.002

Al Kayed, M., & Al-Ghoweri, H. (2019). A socio-pragmatic study of speech act of in Jordanian arabic. *European Journal of Scientific Research*, *153*(1), 105–117.

Alacapinar, F. (2008). Effectiveness of project-based learning. *Eurasian Journal of Educational Research*, *32*, 17–35.

Al-Jamal, D. A. (2017). Students' Fossilized Writing Errors: EFL Postgraduates at Jordanian Universities as a Model. *Journal of Al-Quds Open University for Research and Studies*, *19*(6), 1-17.

Allami, H., & Smavarchi, L. (2012). Giving condolence by Persian EFL learners: A contrastive sociopragmatic study. *International Journal of English Linguistics*, *2*(1), 71–78.

Alsagoff, L. (2010). English in Singapore: Culture, capital and identity in linguistic variation. *World Englishes*, *29*(3), 336–348. doi:10.1111/j.1467-971X.2010.01658.x

Compilation of References

Al-Thwaib, E., Hammo, B. H., & Yagi, S. (2020). An academic Arabic corpus for plagiarism detection: Design, construction and experimentation. *International Journal of Educational Technology in Higher Education*, *17*(1), 1–26. doi:10.118641239-019-0174-x

Amin, M. Y. M., & Mohammadkarimi, E. (2019). ELT students' attitudes toward the effectiveness the anti-plagiarism software, Turnitin. *Applied Linguisics Research Journal*, *3*(5), 63–75.

Amin, N. (2001). Nativism, the native speaker construct, and minority immigrant women teachers of English as a second language. *The CATESOL Journal*, *13*(1), 89–107.

Anderson, J., & Rainie, L. (2017). The Future of Truth and Misinformation Online. Report. *Internet & Technology*. https://www.pewinternet.org/2017/10/19/the-future-of-truth-and-misinformation-online/

Anderson, B. (1983). *Imagined communities: Reflections on the origin and spread of nationalism*. Verso.

Anderson, B. (1991). *Imagined communities: Reflections on the origins and spread of nationalism* (Rev.ed.). Verso. (Original work published 1983)

Anderson, R. D. (2002). Reforming science teaching: What research says about inquiry. *Journal of Science Teacher Education*, *13*(1), 1–12. doi:10.1023/A:1015171124982

Angélil-Carter, S. (2000). *Stolen language? Plagiarism in writing*. Pearson Education Limited.

Angelova, M., & Riazantseva, A. (1999). "If you don't tell me, how can I know?" A case study of four international students learning to write the U.S. way. *Written Communication*, *16*(4), 491–525. doi:10.1177/0741088399016004004

Annamalai, E. (2003). Medium of power: The question of English in education in India. In J. W. Tollefson & A. B. M. Tsui (Eds.), *Medium of instruction policies: Whose agenda? Which agenda?* (pp. 177–193). Lawrence Erlbaum.

Arnot, M. (2014). *School approaches to the education of EAL students: Language development, social integration and achievement*. The Bell Foundation. https://www.educ.cam.ac.uk/research/projects/ealead/Fullreport.pdf

Arslan, R. Ş., & Üçok-Atasoy, M. (2020). An investigation into EFL teachers' assessment of young learners of English: Does practice match the policy? *International Online Journal of Education & Teaching*, *7*(2), 468–484. https://iojet.org/index.php/IOJET/article/view/818

ASER 2018. (2019). *Annual status of education report (rural) 2018*. http://img.asercentre.org/docs/ASER%202018/Release%20Material/aserreport2018.pdf

Ashworth, P., Freewood, M., & Macdonald, R. (2003). The student life world and the meanings of plagiarism. *Journal of Phenomenological Psychology*, *34*(2), 257–278. doi:10.1163/156916203322847164

Asylum in the UK. (n.d.). *The UN Refugee Agency.* Retrieved June 28, 2020 from https://www.unhcr.org/asylum-in-the-uk.html

Badge, J., & Scott, J. (2009) *Dealing with plagiarism in the digital age.* Retrieved from http://evidencenet.pbworks.com/Dealing-with-plagiarism-in-the-digital-age

Bailey, S. (2015). *Academic writing: A handbook for international students.* Routledge. doi:10.4324/9781315768434

Baird, R., Baker, W., & Kitazawa, M. (2014). The complexity of ELF. *Journal of English as a Lingua Franca, 3*(1), 171–196. doi:10.1515/jelf-2014-0007

Baker, R., Thornton, B., & Adams, M. (2008). An evaluation of the effectiveness of Turnitin.com as a tool for reducing plagiarism in graduate student term papers. *College Teaching Methods and Styles Journal, 4*(9), 1–4. doi:10.19030/ctms.v4i9.5564

Baker, W. (2009). The Cultures of English as a Lingua Franca. *TESOL Quarterly, 43*(4), 567–592. doi:10.1002/j.1545-7249.2009.tb00187.x

Baker, W. (2012). From Cultural Awareness to Intercultural Awareness: Culture in ELT. *ELT Journal, 66*(1), 62–70. doi:10.1093/elt/ccr017

Balbay, S., & Kilis, S. (2019). Perceived effectiveness of Turnitin® in detecting plagiarism in presentation slides. *Contemporary Educational Technology, 10*(1), 25–36. doi:10.30935/cet.512522

Ball, J. (2017). *Post–Truth: How Bullshit Conquered the World.* Biteback Publishing Ltd. Print

Bandura, A. (1997). *Self-efficacy: The exercise of control.* Freeman.

Barkhuizen, G., & de Klerk, V. (2006). Imagined identities: Pre-immigrants' narratives on language and identity. *The International Journal of Bilingualism, 10*(3), 277–299. doi:10.1177/13670069060100030201

Batane, T. (2010). Turning to Turnitin to fight plagiarism among university students. *Journal of Educational Technology & Society, 13*(2), 1–12.

Bayyurt, Y. (2006). Non-native English Language Teachers' Perspective on Culture in English as a Foreign Language Classrooms. *Teacher Development, 10*(2), 233–247. doi:10.1080/13664530600773366

Beare, K. (2019, November 18). How many people learn English? *ThoughtCo.* https://www.thoughtco.com/how-many-people-learn-english-globally-1210367

Beekes, R. (2010). *Etymological Dictionary of Greek.* Brill.

Beglar, D. (2017). *Teaching speaking: The key is scaffolding.* Paper presented at the 2017 International JALT Conference, Tsukuba.

Bennett, R. (2005). Factors associated with student plagiarism in a post-1992 university. *Assessment & Evaluation in Higher Education, 30*(2), 137–162. doi:10.1080/0260293042000264244

Blizzard, B., & Batalova, J. (2019). *Refugees and Asylees in the United States.* Migration Policy Institute. https://www.migrationpolicy.org/article/refugees-and-asylees-united-states

Bloch, J. (2001). Plagiarism and the ESL Student: From printed to electronic texts. In D. Belcher & A. Hirvela (Eds.), *Linking literacies: Perspectives on L2 reading-writing connections* (pp. 209–228). The University of Michigan Press.

Block, F. (2003). Karl Polanyi and the writing of the great transformation. *Theory and Society, 32*, 1–32.

Boix Mansilla, V., Miller, W. C., & Gardner, H. (2000). On disciplinary lenses and interdisciplinary work. In S. Wineburg & P. Grossman (Eds.), *Interdisciplinary curriculum: Challenges of implementation* (pp. 17–38). Teachers College Press.

Bolton, K., & Graddol, D. (2012). English in China today: The current popularity of English in China is unprecedented, and has been fuelled by the recent political and social development of Chinese society. *English Today, 28*(3), 3–9. doi:10.1017/S0266078412000223

Borg, S. (2013). *Teacher research in language teaching: A critical analysis.* Cambridge University Press.

Born, A. (2003). How to reduce plagiarism. *Journal of Information Systems Education, 14*(3), 223–224.

Boudon, R. (1995). *Le juste et le vrai: études sur l'objectivité des valeurs et de la connaissance.* Fayard.

Bourdieu, P. (1977). *Outline of a theory of practice.* Cambridge University Press.

Bourdieu, P. (1991). *Language and symbolic power.* Harvard University Press.

Bourne, J. (2007). Focus on literacy: ELT and educational attainment in England. In J. Cummins & C. Davison (Eds.), *International handbook of English language teaching* (pp. 199–210). Springer Verlag. doi:10.1007/978-0-387-46301-8_15

Braine, G. (1989). Writing in science and technology: An analysis of assignments from ten undergraduate courses. *English for Specific Purposes, 8*(1), 3–15. doi:10.1016/0889-4906(89)90003-3

Braine, G. (2010). *Non-native-speaker English teachers: Research, pedagogy, and professional growth.* Routledge. doi:10.4324/9780203856710

Braine, G. (2013). *Non-native educators in English language teaching.* Routledge. doi:10.4324/9781315045368

Brandt, C. (2006). *Success on your certificate course in English language teaching.* Sage.

Braun, S. (2007). Integrating corpus work into secondary education: From data-driven learning to needs-driven corpora. *ReCALL, 19*(3), 307–328. doi:10.1017/S0958344007000535

Breen, L., & Maassen, M. (2005). Reducing the incidence of plagiarism in an undergraduate course: The role of education. *Issues in Educational Research*, *15*(1), 1–16.

Breidbach, S., & Viebrock, B. (2012). CLIL in Germany: Results from recent research in a contested field of education. *International CLIL Research Journal*, *1*(4), 21–35.

Bretag, T. (2013). Challenges in addressing plagiarism in education. *PLoS Medicine*, *10*(12), e1001574. doi:10.1371/journal.pmed.1001574 PMID:24391477

Brickhouse, N. W., Dagher, Z. R., Shipman, H. L., & Letts, W. J. (2002). Evidence and warrants for belief in a college astronomy course. *Science and Education*, *11*(6), 573–588. doi:10.1023/A:1019693819079

British Council | China. (2019). Retrieved January 19, 2019, from https://www.britishcouncil.cn/en

Brown, V. J., & Howell, M. E. (2001). The efficacy of policy statements on plagiarism: Do they change students' views. *Research in Higher Education*, *42*(1), 103–118. doi:10.1023/A:1018720728840

Bruton, S., & Childers, D. (2016). The ethics and politics of policing plagiarism: A qualitative study of faculty views on student plagiarism and Turnitin®. *Assessment & Evaluation in Higher Education*, *41*(2), 316–330. doi:10.1080/02602938.2015.1008981

Bryant, C. W. (2010). How did language evolve? https://science.howstuffworks.com/life/evolution/language-evolve.htm

Bull, H. (1982). Civilian Power Europe: A Contradiction in Terms. *JCMS*, *21*(2), 149–170. doi:10.1111/j.1468-5965.1982.tb00866.x

Buranen, L. (1999). But I wasn't cheating: Plagiarism and cross-cultural mythology. In L. Buranen & A. M. Roy (Eds.), *Perspectives on plagiarism and intellectual property in postmodern world* (pp. 63–74). State University of New York Press.

Burbules, N. C. (2006). Rethinking the virtual. In J. Weiss, J. Nolan, J. Hunsinger, & P. Trifonas (Eds.), *The international handbook of virtual learning environments* (pp. 37–58). Springer. doi:10.1007/978-1-4020-3803-7_1

Burdea, G. C., & Coiffet, P. (2003). *Virtual reality technology*. John Wiley & Sons. doi:10.1162/105474603322955950

Burnaby, B. (1998). ESL policy in Canada and the United States: Basis for comparison. In T. Ricento (Ed.), *Language and politics in the United States and Canada: Myths and realities* (pp. 243–267). Routledge.

Butler, C. D. (n.d.). North And South, The (Global). *International Encyclopedia of the Social Sciences*. Retrieved July 15, 2019 from Encyclopedia.com: https://www.encyclopedia.com/social-sciences/applied-and-social-sciences-magazines/north-and-south-global

Byers-Heinlein, K., & Lew-Williams, C. (2013). Bilingualism in the early years: What the science says. *LEARNing Landscapes*, *7*(1), 95–112. https://www.ncbi.nlm.nih.gov/pmc/articles/PMC6168212/. doi:10.36510/learnland.v7i1.632 PMID:30288204

Byram, M. (1997). *Teaching and assessing intercultural communicative competence*. Multilingual Matters.

Cardinal, L., & Lěger, R. (2018). The politics of multilingualism in Canada: A neo-institutional approach. In P. A. Kraus & F. Grin (Eds.), *The politics of multilingualism: Europeanisation, globalization and linguistic governance* (pp. 19–37). John Benjamins. doi:10.1075/wlp.6.02car

Carmigniani, J., & Furht, B. (2011). Augmented reality: an overview. In B. Furht (Ed.), *Handbook of augmented reality* (pp. 3–46). Springer. doi:10.1007/978-1-4614-0064-6_1

Carrell, S. E., Malmstrom, F., & West, J. E. (2008). Article. *Business Ethics Quarterly*, *10*(1), 33–42. doi:10.2307/3857692

Carroll, J. (2002). *A Handbook for deterring plagiarism in higher education*. Oxford Centre for Staff and Learning Development.

Caruana, V. (2010). Global citizenship for all: Putting the 'Higher" back into UK higher education? In F. Maringe & N. Foskett (Eds.), *Globalization and internationalization in higher education: Theoretical, strategic and management perspective*. Continuum. doi:10.5040/9781350091122.ch-0004

Castek, J., & Beach, R. (2013). Using apps to support disciplinary literacy and science learning. *Journal of Adolescent & Adult Literacy*, *56*(7), 554–564. doi:10.1002/JAAL.180

Castells, M. (2009). *The Rise of the Network Society*. Blackwell. doi:10.1002/9781444319514

Center for Advanced Research on Language Acquisition. (2019). *What is a speech act?* Retrieved from carla.umn.edu/speechacts/definition.html

Central Intelligence Agency. (2020). *The World Factbook: People and Society*. Retrieved from https://www.cia.gov/library/publications/resources/the-world-factbook/geos/xx.html

Chang, Y. J. (2014). Learning English Today: What can World Englishes Teach College Students in Taiwan? *English Today, 30*(1), 21-27.

Chao, T. C. (2016). A preliminary study of Taiwanese NNETS' self-assessment of intercultural communicative competence in English language teaching. *Taiwan Journal of TESOL.*, *13*(1), 71–103.

Cheah, S. W., & Bretag, T. (2008). Making technology work for academic integrity in Malaysia. *3rd International Plagiarism Conference Refereed Proceedings*.

Cheers 快樂工作人雜誌 (2017). 2017最佳大學指南 [Best Universities 2017]. Retrieved January 31, 2018 https://topic.cheers.com.tw/issue/2017/college/article/2-2.aspx

Chen, A. H. (2013). An Evaluation on Primary English Education in Taiwan: From the Perspective of Language Policy. *English Language Teaching*, *6*(10), 158–165. doi:10.5539/elt.v6n10p158

Cheng, K.-H., & Tsai, C.-C. (2013). Affordances of augmented reality in science learning: Suggestions for future research. *Journal of Science Education and Technology*, *22*(4), 449–462. doi:10.100710956-012-9405-9

Cheuk, T. (2016). Discourse practices in the new standards: The role of argumentation in common core-era next Generation Science Standards Classrooms for English Language Learners. *The Electronic Journal of Science Education*, *20*(3), 92–111.

Chien, S. C. (2016). Taiwanese college students' perceptions of plagiarism: Cultural and educational considerations. *Ethics & Behavior*, 1–22. doi:10.1080/10508422.2015.1136219

Chomsky, N. (1965). *Aspects of the theory of syntax*. MIT Press.

Chomsky, N. A. (1965). *Aspects of the Theory of Syntax*. MIT.

Clark, E., & Paran, A. (2007). The employability of non-native-speaker teachers of EFL: A UK survey. *System*, *35*(4), 407–430. doi:10.1016/j.system.2007.05.002

Clemente, A., & Higgins, M. J. (2008). *Performing English with a postcolonial accent: Ethnographic narratives from Mexico*. Tufnell Press.

Clough, P., & Stevenson, M. (2009). *Creating a corpus of plagiarised academic texts*. Paper presented at the Corpus Linguistics Conference (CL2009), University of Liverpool.

Compton, J., & Pfau, M. (2008). Inoculating against pro-plagiarism justifications: Rational and affective strategies. *Journal of Applied Communication Research*, *36*(1), 98–119. doi:10.1080/00909880701799329

Cook, G. (1998). The uses of reality: A reply to Ronald Cater. *ELT Journal*, *52*(1), 57–64. doi:10.1093/elt/52.1.57

Cook, V. (1999). Going beyond the native speaker in language teaching. *TESOL Quarterly*, *33*(2), 185–209. doi:10.2307/3587717

Corder, S. P. (1967). The significance of learner's errors. *International Review of Applied Linguistics in Language Teaching*, *5*(4), 161–170.

Coskun, A. (2011). Future English Teachers' Attitudes towards EIL Pronunciation. *Journal of English as an International Language*, *6*(2), 46–67.

Court of Justice of the European Union. (n.d.). *The Institution: Language arrangements*. Retrieved from https://curia.europa.eu/jcms/jcms/Jo2_10739/en/

Coyle, D. (2012). *CLIL: Content and Language Integrated Learning*. Cambridge University Press.

Compilation of References

Coyle, D. (2013). Listening to learners: An investigation into successful learning across CLIL contexts. *International Journal of Bilingual Education and Bilingualism*, *16*(3), 244–266. doi:10.1080/13670050.2013.777384

Crystal, D. (1990). Liturgical language in a sociolinguistic perspective. In D. Jasper & R. C. D. Jasper (Eds.), *Language and the worship of the church* (pp. 120–146). Macmillan. doi:10.1007/978-1-349-20477-9_7

Crystal, D. (2003). *English as a global language* (2nd ed.). Cambridge University Press. doi:10.1017/CBO9780511486999

Cummins, J. (1996). *Negotiating identities: Education for empowerment in a diverse society*. California Association for Bilingual Education.

Cummins, J. (2000). *Language, Power and Pedagogy. Bilingual Children in the Crossfire*. Multilingual Matters Ltd.

Currie, P. (1998). Staying out of trouble: Apparent plagiarism and academic survival. *Journal of Second Language Writing*, *2*(2), 1–18. doi:10.1016/S1060-3743(98)90003-0

Dahl, S. (2007). Turnitin(R): The student perspective on using plagiarism detection software. *Active Learning in Higher Education*, *8*(2), 173–191. doi:10.1177/1469787407074110

David, M. K. (2018, January). *Performing Speech Acts- focussing on local cultural norms in the Englishes we use*. Plenary Paper presented at the International Conference on Teaching and Assessing English Language and Literature, Chennai, India.

David, M. K. (2018, July). *Social media- a treasure house for pedagogical resources: Focusing on responses to the speech act of congratulations and condolences*. Plenary Paper presented at the International Conference on English Language Teaching (CONELT), Kuningan, Indonesia.

David, M. K. (2005). Cultural capsules and reading texts: Triggers to cross-cultural language awareness. *TEFLIN Journal*, *16*(2), 209–222.

David, M. K. (2011). Extracting discourse norms from novels. *Pratibimba Journals of IMIS*, *11*, 24–32.

Davies, A. (1991). *The native speaker in applied linguistics*. Edinburgh University Press.

Davies, A. (2003). *The native speaker: Myth and reality*. Multilingual Matters. doi:10.21832/9781853596247

Davies, W. D., & Dubinsky, S. (2018). *Language conflict and language rights: Ethnolinguistic perspectives on human conflict*. Cambridge UP. doi:10.1017/9781139135382

Davis, M. (2013). The development of source use by international postgraduate students. *Journal of English for Academic Purposes*, *12*(2), 125–135. doi:10.1016/j.jeap.2012.11.008

Davis, M., & Carroll, J. (2009). Formative feedback within plagiarism education: Is there a role for text-matching software? *International Journal for Educational Integrity*, *5*(2), 58–70. doi:10.21913/IJEI.v5i2.614

Davison, C. (2005). *Information technology and innovation in language education* (Vol. 1). Hong Kong University Press.

de Bot, K. (2004). *The psycholinguistics of multilingualism*. Benjamins.

de Jong, N. (2017). Fluency in second language assessment. In D. Tsagari & J. Banerjee (Eds.), *Handbook of second language assessment* (pp. 203–218). Mouton de Gruyter.

Deci, E. L., & Ryan, R. M. (2000). The what and why of goal pursuits: Human needs and the self-determination of behavior. *Psychological Inquiry*, *11*(4), 227–268. doi:10.1207/S15327965PLI1104_01

Deckert, G. D. (1993). Perspectives on plagiarism from ESL students in Hong Kong. *Journal of Second Language Writing*, *2*(2), 131–148. doi:10.1016/1060-3743(93)90014-T

Decoo, W. (2008). Substantial, verbatim, unattributed, misleading: Applying criteria to assess textual plagiarism. In T. S. Roberts (Ed.), *Student plagiarism in an online world: Problems and solutions* (pp. 228–243). Information Science Reference. doi:10.4018/978-1-59904-801-7.ch015

Dede, C. (2009). Immersive interfaces for engagement and learning. *Science*, *323*(5910), 66–69. doi:10.1126cience.1167311 PMID:19119219

DeKeyser, R. (2007). *Practice in a second language: Perspectives from applied linguistics and cognitive psychology*. Cambridge University Press. doi:10.1017/CBO9780511667275

Deniz, E. B., Özkan, Y., & Bayyirt, Y. (2016). English as a Lingua Franca: Reflections on ELF-Related Issues by Pre-Service Language Teachers in Turkey. *The Reading Matrix: An International Online Journal*, *16*(2), 144–161.

Devlin, M., & Gray, K. (2007). In their own words: A qualitative study of the reasons Australian university students plagiarize. *Higher Education Research & Development*, *26*(2), 181–198. doi:10.1080/07294360701310805

Dijk Van, T. (1998). *Ideology: A Multidisciplinary Approach*. Sage.

Dimitriadou, C., Palaiologou, N., & Nari, E. (2014). E-Learning Training Courses on Multricultural Education: An Example from Greece. In V. Zuzeviciute, E. Butrime, D. Adžgauskiene, V. Fomin, & K. Papadakis (Eds.), *E-Learning as a Socio-Cultural System: A Multidimensional Analysis* (pp. 322–345). IGI Global. doi:10.4018/978-1-4666-6154-7.ch006

Dolzhenko, A. V., Khan, T. M., & Dolzhenko, A. (2016). Strategies and technologies for preventing plagiarism in modern higher education: War against today's plagiarists or nurturing tomorrow's talents. In E. Railean, G. Walker, A. Elçi, & L. Jackson (Eds.), *Handbook of research on applied learning theory and design in modern education* (pp. 840–865). IGI Global. doi:10.4018/978-1-4666-9634-1.ch041

Compilation of References

Dörnyei, A. (2003). Attitudes, orientations, and motivations in language learning: Advances in theory, research, and applications. *Language Learning*, *53*(S1), 3–32. doi:10.1111/1467-9922.53222

Dryden, L. M. (1999). A distant mirror or through the looking glass? Plagiarism and intellectual property in Japanese education. In L. Bruaunen & A. M. Roy (Eds.), *Perspectives on plagiarism and intellectual property in a postmodern world* (pp. 75–85). State University of New York Press.

Dyrberg, N. R., Treusch, A. H., & Wiegand, C. (2017). Virtual laboratories in science education: Students' motivation and experiences in two tertiary biology courses. *Journal of Biological Education*, *51*(4), 358–374. doi:10.1080/00219266.2016.1257498

Dzialtuvaite, J. (2006). The role of religion in language choice and identity among Lithuanian immigrants in Scotland. In *Explorations in the Sociology of Language and Religion* (pp. 79–85). John Benjamins. doi:10.1075/dapsac.20.08dzi

Eckstein, B. (1976). Overcoming non-cognitive problems in interdisciplinary engineering work. *European Journal of Engineering Education*, *1*(3), 217–221. doi:10.1080/03043797608903428

Eisen, A., Hall, A., Soon Lee, T., & Zupko, J. (2009). Teaching water: Connecting across disciplines and into daily life to address complex societal issues. *College Teaching*, *57*(2), 99–104. doi:10.3200/CTCH.57.2.99-104

Eisenchlas, S. A., Schalley, A. C., & Guillemin, D. (2013). The importance of literacy in the home language: The view from Australia. *SAGE Open*, *3*(October – December), 1–14. doi:10.1177/2158244013507270

Ellis, R. (1994). *The Study of Second Language Acquisition*. Oxford University Press.

Ellis, R., & Shintani, N. (2013). *Exploring language pedagogy through second language acquisition research*. Routledge. doi:10.4324/9780203796580

Elwood, K. (2004). *"Congratulations": A cross cultural analysis of responses to another's happy news*. Retrieved from: http://dspace. Wil. waseda.ac.jp/dspace/handle/2065/6097

English is GREAT. (2019). Retrieved January 19, 2019, from https://www.britishcouncil.cn/en/EnglishGreat

Ercegovac, Z., & Richardson, J. V. Jr. (2004). Academic dishonesty: Plagiarism included, in the digital age: A literature review. *College & Research Libraries*, *65*(4), 301–318. doi:10.5860/crl.65.4.301

Errey, L. (2002). Plagiarism: Something fishy? Or just a fish out of water? *Teaching Forum*, *50*, 17–20.

Espinoza, L.Ü., & Nájera, J.M. (2014). How to correct teaching methods that favour plagiarism: recommendations from teachers and students in a Spanish language distance education university. *Assessment and Evaluation in Higher Education*, *40*(8), 1-9. doi:10.1080/02602938.2014.966053

Compilation of References

Eur-lex. (1958, April 15). *EEC Council: Regulation No 1 determining the languages to be used by the European Economic Community.* Brussels: The Council. Retrieved from https://eur-lex.europa.eu/LexUriServ/LexUriServ.do?uri=CELEX:31958R0001:EN:HTML

Eur-lex. (1976, February 9). *Resolution of The Council and of The Ministers of Education, Meeting Within the Council: comprising an action programme in the field of education.* Retrieved from https://eur-lex.europa.eu/legal-content/EN/TXT/PDF/?uri=CELEX:41976X0219&from=EN

Eur-lex. (2018, May 22). *Proposal for a Council Recommendation on a comprehensive approach to the teaching and learning of languages.* Retrieved from https://eur-lex.europa.eu/resource.html?uri=cellar:1cc186a3-5dc7-11e8-ab9c-01aa75ed71a1.0001.02/DOC_1&format=PDF

Eur-lex. (n.d.a). *Culture Programmes.* Retrieved from https://eur-lex.europa.eu/summary/chapter/culture/1002.html?root=1002&obsolete=true

Eur-lex. (n.d.b). *International cultural relations — an EU strategy.* Retrieved from https://eur-lex.europa.eu/legal-content/EN/TXT/HTML/?uri=LEGISSUM:4298957&from=EN

European Commission. (2012, November 20). *Commission Staff Working Document: Language competences for employability, mobility and growth.* Retrieved from https://eur-lex.europa.eu/legal-content/EN/TXT/PDF/?uri=CELEX:52012SC0372&from=en

European Commission. (2013, September 26). *Frequently asked Questions on Languages in Europe.* Retrieved from https://europa.eu/rapid/press-release_MEMO-13-825_en.htm

European Commission. (2016, December). *The ABC of EU Law.* Retrieved from https://op.europa.eu/webpub/com/abc-of-eu-law/en/

European Commission. (2019, May 29). *Multilingual communication, a vehicle to bring international organisations closer to the citizens.* Retrieved from https://ec.europa.eu/info/news/multilingual-communication-vehicle-bring-international-organisations-closer-citizens-2019-may-29_en

European Commission. (2020, December 11). *Commission welcomes political agreement on Erasmus+ programme.* Retrieved from: https://ec.europa.eu/commission/presscorner/detail/en/IP_20_2317

European Commission. (n.d.a). *About Multilingualism Policy.* Retrieved from https://ec.europa.eu/education/policies/multilingualism/about-multilingualism-policy_en

European Commission. (n.d.b). *Erasmus+; Key figures.* Retrieved from https://ec.europa.eu/programmes/erasmus-plus/about/key-figures_en

European Council. (2017, December 14). *European Council Meeting Conclusions.* Retrieved from https://www.consilium.europa.eu/media/32204/14-final-conclusions-rev1-en.pdf

European Parliament. (2000). *Lisbon European Council 23 and 24 March 2000 Presidency Conclusions.* Retrieved from: https://www.europarl.europa.eu/summits/lis1_en.htm

Eurostat. (2019, April). *Foreign Language Skills Statistics*. Retrieved from https://ec.europa.eu/eurostat/statistics-explained/index.php/Foreign_language_skills_statistics#Number_of_foreign_languages_known

Fasold, R. (1984). *The Sociolinguistics of Society*. Blackwell.

Fazilatfar, A. M., Elhambakhsh, S. E., & Allami, H. (2018). An investigation of the effects of citation instruction to avoid plagiarism in EFL academic writing assignments. *SAGE Open*, *8*(2), 1–13. doi:10.1177/2158244018769958

Fenster, J. (2016). Teaching note—Evaluation of an avoiding plagiarism workshop for social work students. *Journal of Social Work Education*, *52*(2), 242–248. doi:10.1080/10437797.2016.1151278

Ferguson, C. (1992). Foreword to the first edition. In B. B. Kachru (Ed.), The other tongue: English across cultures (2nd ed., pp. xiii–xvii). Chicago, IL: University of Illinois Press.

Ferguson, C. (1982). Religious factors in language spread. In R. L. Cooper (Ed.), *Language spread* (pp. 95–106). Indiana University Press.

Fillmore, Ch. (1976). Frame semantics and the nature of language. *Annals of the New York Academy of Sciences*, *280*(1 Origins and E), 20–32. doi:10.1111/j.1749-6632.1976.tb25467.x

Fischer, A. R., Tobi, H., & Ronteltap, A. (2011). When natural met social: A review of collaboration between the natural and social sciences. *Interdisciplinary Science Reviews*, *36*(4), 341–358. doi:10.1179/030801811X13160755918688

Fishman, J. A. (1966). *Language loyalty in the United States. The maintenance and perpetuation of non-English mother tongues by American ethnic and religious groups*. Mouton.

Fishman, J. A. (1971). *Sociolinguistics: a Brief Introduction*. Mouton.

FrankeM.HeriardP. (2018, September). *Language Policy*. Retrieved from https://www.europarl.europa.eu/ftu/pdf/en/FTU_3.6.6.pdf

Frankfurt, H. G. (2005). *On Bullshit*. Princeton UP.

Freeden, M. (2003). *Ideology: A Very Short Introduction*. Oxford: UP.

Fromkin, V., Rodman, R., & Hyams, N. (2014). *An introduction to language* (10th ed.). Cengage Learning.

Fukuyama, F. (1992). *The End of History and the Last Man*. Free Press.

Galloway, N. (2013). Global Englishes and English Language Teaching (ELT)-Bridging the Gap between Theory and Practice in a Japanese Context. *System*, *41*(3), 786–803. doi:10.1016/j.system.2013.07.019

Galloway, N., & Rose, H. (2014). Using Listening Journals to Raise Awareness of Global Englishes in ELT. *ELT Journal*, *68*(4), 386–396. doi:10.1093/elt/ccu021

Galloway, N., & Rose, H. (2015). *Introducing Global Englishes*. Routledge. doi:10.4324/9781315734347

Galus, P. (2002). Detecting and preventing plagiarism. *Science Teacher (Normal, Ill.)*, *69*(8), 35–37.

Gannon-Leary, P., Trayhurn, D., & Home, M. (2009). Good images, effective messages. Working with students and educators on academic practice understanding. *Journal of Further and Higher Education*, *33*(4), 435–448. doi:10.1080/03098770903272511

Gao, Y., & Chen, L. (2013, October). China's English fervor under scrutiny. *People's Daily Online*. http://en.people.cn/203691/8426108.html

Gardner, H. (2008). *Five Minds for the Future*. Harvard Business School Publishing. doi:10.1086/591814

Garner, R., Zhao, Y., & Gillingham, M. (Eds.). (2002). *Hanging out: Community-based after school programs for children*. Greenwood.

Gass, S., & Selinker, L. (2008). The role of the native language: An historical overview. In *Second Language Acquisition: An Introductory Course*. Routledge.

Geeraerts, D. (1997). *Diachronic Prototype Semantics*. Clarendon Press.

Ghajarzadeh, M., Norouzi-Javidan, A., Hassanpour, K., Aramesh, K., & Emami-Razavi, S. H. (2012). Attitude toward plagiarism among Iranian medical faculty members. *Acta Medica Iranica*, *50*(11), 778–781. PMID:23292631

Gibson, N. S., & Chester-Fangman, C. (2011). The librarian's role in combating plagiarism. *RSR. Reference Services Review*, *39*(1), 132–150. doi:10.1108/00907321111108169

Giere, R. (1991). *Understanding Scientific Reasoning* (3rd ed.). Holt, Rinehart & Winston.

Gil, J. (2016). English language education policies in the People's Republic of China. In R. Kirkpatrick (Ed.), *English language education policy in Asia* (pp. 49–90). Springer. doi:10.1007/978-3-319-22464-0_3

Ginsburgh, V., & Moreno-Ternero, J. D. (2020, May). *Brexit and Multilingualism in the European Union*. ECARES Working Paper 16.

Gipp, B., Meuschke, N., & Breitinger, C. (2014). Citation-based plagiarism detection: Practicability on a large-scale scientific corpus. *Journal of the Association for Information Science and Technology*, *65*(8), 1527–1540. doi:10.1002/asi.23228

Gitanjali, B. (2004). Academic dishonesty in Indian medical colleges. *Journal of Postgraduate Medicine*, *50*, 281–284. PMID:15623972

Glaveanu, V. P. (2017). Psychology in the Post-Truth Era. Editorial. *Europe's Journal of Psychology*, *13*(3), 375–377. doi:10.5964/ejop.v13i3.1509 PMID:28904590

Gobbo, F. (2018). How to measure linguistic justice? Theoretical considerations and the South Tyrol case study of the Calvet Language Baromer. In P. A. Kraus & F. Grin (Eds.), *The politics of multilingualism: Europeanisation, globalization and linguistic governance* (pp. 145–165). John Benjamins. doi:10.1075/wlp.6.07gob

Goddard, R., & Rudzki, R. (2005). Using an electronic text-matching tool (turnitin) to detect plagiarism in an New Zealand university. *Journal of University Teaching & Learning Practice*, *2*(3), 58–63.

Goh, E. (2013). Plagiarism behavior among undergraduate students in hospitality and tourism education. *Journal of Teaching in Travel & Tourism*, *13*(4), 307–322. doi:10.1080/15313220.2013.839295

Gokmenoğlu, T. (2017). A review of literature: Plagiarism in the papers of Turkish context. *Higher Education Studies*, *7*(3), 161–170. doi:10.5539/hes.v7n3p161

Govardhan, A. K., Nayar, B., & Sheorey, R. (1999). Do U.S. MATESOL programs prepare students to teach abroad? *TESOL Quarterly*, *33*(1), 114–125. doi:10.2307/3588194

Graddol, D. (2006). *English next*. The British Council.

Graham-Matheson, L., & Starr, S. (2013). Is it cheating or learning the craft of writing? Using Turnitin to help students avoid plagiarism. *Research in Learning Technology*, *21*, 1–13. doi:10.3402/rlt.v21i0.17218

Granger, S. (2002). A bird's-eye view of learner corpus research. In S. Granger, J. Hung, & S. Petch-Tyson (Eds.), *Computer Learner Corpora, Second Language Acquisition and Foreign Language Teaching* (pp. 3–36). John Benjamins. doi:10.1075/lllt.6.04gra

Granger, S. (2003). The International Corpus of Learner English: A new resource for foreign language learning and teaching acquisition research. *TESOL Quarterly*, *37*(3), 538–546. doi:10.2307/3588404

Granger, S. (2009). The contribution of learner corpora to second language acquisition and foreign language teaching: A critical evaluation. In A. Karin (Ed.), *Corpora and Language Teaching* (pp. 13–32). John Benjamins. doi:10.1075cl.33.04gra

Gras-Velázquez, A. (2019). *Project-based learning in second language acquisition: Building communities of practice in higher education*. Routledge. doi:10.4324/9780429457432

Gullifer, J. M., & Tyson, G. A. (2014). Who has read the policy on plagiarism? Unpacking students' understanding of plagiarism. *Studies in Higher Education*, *39*(7), 1202–1218. doi:10.1080/03075079.2013.777412

Gullifer, J., & Tyson, G. A. (2010). Exploring university students' perceptions of plagiarism: A focus group study. *Studies in Higher Education*, *35*(4), 463–481. doi:10.1080/03075070903096508

Gupta, D. (2005). ELT in India: A brief historical and current overview. *Asian EFL Journal*, *7*(1), 197–207.

Guraya, S. Y., & Guraya, S. S. (2017). The confounding factors leading to plagiarism in academic writing and some suggested remedies: A systematic review. *Systematic Reviews*, *67*(5), 767–773. PMID:28507368

Halgamuge, M. N. (2017). The use and analysis of anti-plagiarism software: Turnitin tool for formative assessment and feedback. *Computer Applications in Engineering Education*, *25*(6), 895–909. doi:10.1002/cae.21842

Hall, S. (1992). The west and the rest: Discourse and power. In S. Hall & B. Gieben (Eds.), Formation of modernity (pp. 275–320). Cambridge: Polity in Association with Open University.

Hall, S. (2013). The work of representation. In S. H. Stuart, E. Jessica, & Nixon (Eds.), Representation (2nd ed., pp. 1–59). London: Sage.

Halliday, M. A. K., & Martin, J. R. (1993). *Writing science: Literacy and discursive power*. The Falmer Press.

Hall, J. K. (2002). *Teaching and researching language and culture*. Pearson Education.

Hamdi, S. (2005). *An analysis of written grammatical errors of Tunisian learners of English in EFL context*. ISEAH Institute of Kef.

Hamdi, S. (2016). An analysis of lexical errors in the English compositions of EFL Tunisian learners. *International Journal of Humanities and Cultural Studies*, *2*(4), 643–652.

Handa, N., & Power, C. (2005). Land and discover! A case study investigating the cultural context of plagiarism. *Journal of University Teaching & Learning Practice*, *2*(3), 64–86.

Hand, B. M., Alvermann, D. E., Gee, J. P., Guzzetti, B. J., Norris, S. P., Phillips, L. M., Prain, V., & Yore, L. D. (2003). Message from the "Island Group": What is literacy in science literacy? *Journal of Research in Science Teaching*, *40*(7), 607–615. doi:10.1002/tea.10101

Hand, B. M., Wallace, C., & Yang, E. M. (2006). Using a Science Writing Heuristic to enhance learning outcomes from laboratory activities in seventh-grade science: Quantitative and qualitative aspects. *International Journal of Science Education*, *26*(2), 131–149. doi:10.1080/0950069032000070252

Haneef, I., Nawab, R. M. A., Munir, U., & Baiwa, I. S. (2019). Design and development of a large cross-lingual plagiarism corpus for Urdu-English language pair. *Scientific Programming*, *2019*, 1–11. doi:10.1155/2019/2962040

Hansen, B. (2003). Combating plagiarism. *CQ Researcher*, *13*(32), 775–792.

Han, Z. (2004). Fossilization: Five central issues. *Journal of Applied Linguistics*, *14*(2), 212–242. doi:10.1111/j.1473-4192.2004.00060.x

Harrison, G. P., Macpherson, D. E., & Williams, D. A. (2007). Promoting Interdisciplinarity in Engineering Teaching. *European Journal of Engineering Education*, *32*(3), 285–293. doi:10.1080/03043790701276775

Compilation of References

Harris, R., Leung, C., & Rampton, B. (2001). Globalisation, diaspora and language education in England. In D. Block & D. Cameron (Eds.), *Globalization and language teaching* (pp. 29–46). Routeledge.

Hartman, E., Kiely, R., Bottcher, C., & Friedrichs, J. (2018). *Community-based global learning: The theory and practice of ethical engagement at home and abroad.* Sterling, VA: *Stylus*.

Hatipoğlu, Ç. (2016). The impact of the university entrance exam on EFL education in Turkey: Pre-service English language teachers' perspective. *Procedia: Social and Behavioral Sciences*, *232*, 136–144. doi:10.1016/j.sbspro.2016.10.038

Hayes, N., & Introna, L. D. (2015). Cultural values, plagiarism and fairness: When plagiarism gets in the way of learning. *Ethics & Behavior*, *15*(3), 213–231. doi:10.120715327019eb1503_2

Heckler, N. C., Rice, M., & Bryan, C. H. (2013). Turnitin systems: A deterrent to plagiarism in college classrooms. *Journal of Research on Technology in Education*, *45*(3), 229–248. doi:10.1080/15391523.2013.10782604

Henderson, M. H. (2019). Grammar in the Spanish/English bilingual classroom: Three methods for teaching academic language. In M. D. Devereaux & C. C. Palmer (Eds.), *Teaching language variation in the classroom: Strategies and models from teachers and linguists* (pp. 101–108). Routledge. doi:10.4324/9780429486678-18

Heron, J. L. (2001). Plagiarism, learning dishonesty or just plain cheating: The context and countermeasures in information systems teaching. *Australasian Journal of Educational Technology*, *17*(3), 244–264. doi:10.14742/ajet.1794

Hino, N. (2018). *EIL education for the Expanding Circle: A Japanese model.* Routledge.

Holliday, A. (2005). *The struggle to teach English as an international language.* Oxford University Press.

Holmes, J. (2007). Designing agents to support learning by explaining. *Computers & Education*, *48*(4), 523–547. doi:10.1016/j.compedu.2005.02.007

Holt, E. A., Fagerheim, B., & Durham, S. (2014). Online plagiarism training falls short in biology classrooms. *CBE Life Sciences Education*, *13*(1), 83–89. doi:10.1187/cbe.13-08-0146 PMID:24591507

Howard, R. M. (1999). *Standing in the shadow of giants: Plagiarists, authors, collaborators.* Ablex.

Huang, H. M., Rauch, U., & Liaw, S. S. (2010). Investigating learners' attitudes toward virtual reality learning environments: Based on a constructivist approach. *Computers & Education*, *55*(3), 1171–1182. doi:10.1016/j.compedu.2010.05.014

Hu, G. (2005). English language education in China: Policies, progress, and problems. *Language Policy*, *4*(1), 5–24. doi:10.100710993-004-6561-7

Hughes, J. M. C., & McCabe, D. L. (2006). Understanding academic misconduct. *Canadian Journal of Higher Education*, *36*(1), 49–63. doi:10.47678/cjhe.v36i1.183525

Hui-Fang, S. (2019). An investigation of plagiarism software use and awareness training on English as a foreign language (EFL) students. *Journal of Computing in Higher Education*, *31*(1), 105–120. doi:10.100712528-018-9193-1

Hyland, F. (2001). Dealing with plagiarism when giving feedback. *ELT Journal*, *55*(4), 375–381. doi:10.1093/elt/55.4.375

Ibrahim, A. (1999). Becoming Black: Rap and hip-hop, race, gender, identity, and the politics of ESL learning. *TESOL Quarterly*, *33*(3), 349–369. doi:10.2307/3587669

Interpreting and Translating for Europe. (n.d.). Retrieved from http://cdt.europa.eu/sites/default/files/documentation/pdf/qd0117611en.pdf

İrican, E. S. (2017). A comparative study on basic education curricula of Finland and Turkey in foreign language teaching. *International Journal of Curriculum and Instruction*, *9*(2), 137–156.

Ivanic, R. (2004). Intertextual practices in the construction of multimodal texts in inquiry-based learning. *Uses of intertextuality in classroom and educational research*, 279-314.

Izumi, S., Ikeda, M., & Watanabe, Y. (2012). CLIL: Content and language integrated learning: New challenges in foreign language education at Sophia University: Vol. 2. *Practices and Applications*. Sophia University Press.

Jackson, L., Meyer, W., & Parkinson, J. (2006). A study of the writing tasks and reading assigned to undergraduate science students at a South African University. *English for Specific Purposes*, *25*(3), 260–281. doi:10.1016/j.esp.2005.04.003

Jackson, P. A. (2006). Plagiarism instruction online: Assessing undergraduate students' ability to avoid plagiarism. *College & Research Libraries*, *67*(5), 418–428. doi:10.5860/crl.67.5.418

Jaspal & Coyle. (2010). Arabic is the language of the Muslims --- that's how it was supposed to be? Exploring language and religious identity through reflective accounts from young British-born South Asians. *Mental Health, Religion and Culture*, *13*(1), 17-36.

Jenkins, J. (2003). *World Englishes: A resource book for students*. Routledge.

Jenkins, J. (2006). Current perspectives on teaching World Englishes and English as a lingua franca. *TESOL Quarterly*, *40*(1), 157–181. doi:10.2307/40264515

Jereb, E., Perc, M., Lämmlein, B., Jerebic, J., Urh, M., Podbregar, I., & Šprajc, P. (2018). Factors influencing plagiarism in higher education: A comparison of German and Slovene students. *PLoS One*, *13*(8), 1–16. doi:10.1371/journal.pone.0202252 PMID:30096189

Jha, S. K. (2014). An ethnographic insight into the causal factors of degrading English education in Ethiopia, Libya, and India. *International Journal of Language and Linguistics*, *2*(2), 44–55.

Jocoy, C. L., & DiBiase, D. (2006). Plagiarism by adult learners online: A case study in detection and remediation. *International Review of Research in Open and Distance Learning, 7*(1), 1–15. doi:10.19173/irrodl.v7i1.242

Johns Hopkins University. (2006). *Deterring and detecting plagiarism with Turnitin.com: A Tip Sheet from Center for Educational Resources*. Retrieved from http://www.cer.jhu.edu/pdf/turnitintips.pdf

Joseph, J. E. (2006). The shifting role of languages in Lebanese Christian and Muslim identities. In *Explorations in the Sociology of Language and Religion* (pp. 165–179). John Benjamins. doi:10.1075/dapsac.20.14jos

Kachru, B. (1992). *The other tongue: English across cultures*. University of Illinois Press.

Kachru, B. B. (2013). History of World Englishes. In C. A. Chapelle (Ed.), *The encyclopedia of Applied Linguistics*. Blackwell Publishing Ltd.

Kachru, Y., & Nelson, C. L. (2006). *World Englishes in Asian contexts*. Hong Kong UP.

Kachru, Y., & Smith, L. E. (2008). *Cultures, contexts and world Englishes*. Routledge. doi:10.4324/9780203891346

Kanda, E. P. T. (2007). *KEPT*. Kanda University of International Studies.

Kaplan, R. B., & Baldauf, R. B. (1997). *Language planning from practice to theory*. Multilingual Matters.

Kayaoğlu, M. N., Erbay, S., Flitner, C., & Saltaş, D. (2015). Examining students' perceptions of plagiarism: A cross-cultural study at tertiary level. *Journal of Further and Higher Education*, 1–24. doi:10.1080/0309877X.2015.1014320

Ke, I. C. (2012). English as a lingua franca (ELF) in intercultural communication: Findings from ELF online projects and implication for ELTC in Taiwan. *Taiwan Journal of TESOL, 9*(2), 63–93.

Kelly, G. J., & Takao, A. (2002). Epistemic levels in argument: An analysis of university oceanography students' use of evidence in writing. *Science Education, 86*(3), 314–342. doi:10.1002ce.10024

Kemp, C. Defining Multilingualism. In L. Aronin & B. Hufeisen (Eds.), *The Exploration of Multilingualism* (pp. 11–26). John Benjamins Publishing Company.

Kırkgöz, Y. (2005). English language teaching in Turkey: Challenges for the 21st century. In G. Braine (Ed.), *Teaching English to the world: History, curriculum, and practice* (pp. 159–175). Lawrence Erlbaum Associates.

Kırkgöz, Y. (2007). English Language Teaching in Turkey: Policy Changes and their implementations. *RELC Journal, 38*(2), 216–228. doi:10.1177/0033688207079696

Kırkgöz, Y. (2017). English education policy in Turkey. In R. Kirkpatrick (Ed.), *English language education policy in the Middle East and North Africa* (pp. 235–256). Springer. doi:10.1007/978-3-319-46778-8_14

Kirkpatrick, A. (2007). *World English Implications for International Communication and English Language Teaching*. Cambridge University Press.

Klein, J. T. (1990). *Interdisciplinarity: History, Theory, and Practice*. Wayne State University Press.

Kolich, A. M. (1983). Plagiarism: The worm of reason. *College English*, *52*(8), 141–148. doi:10.2307/377221

Kormos, J. (2006). *Speech production and second language acquisition*. Lawrence Erlbaum Associates.

Köse, Ö., & Arıkan, A. (2011). Reducing plagiarism by using online software: An experimental study. *Contemporary Online Language Education Journal*, *1*, 122–129.

Krajcik, J. S., & Sutherland, L. M. (2010). Supporting students in developing literacy in science. *Science*, *328*(5977), 456–459. doi:10.1126cience.1182593 PMID:20413490

Kramsch, C. (1997). The privilege of the nonnative speaker. *Modern Language Association*, *112*(3), 359–369. doi:10.1632/S0030812900060673

Krashen, S. D., & Terrell, T. D. (1983). *The natural approach: Language acquisition in the classroom*. The Alemany Press.

Kubota, R., & Lin, A. (2009). *Race, culture, and identities in second language education: Exploring critically engaged practice* (R. Kubota & A. Lin, Eds.). Routledge. doi:10.4324/9780203876657

LaDousa, C. (2014). *Hind is our ground, English is our sky: Education, language, and social class in contemporary India*. Berghahn Books.

Lake, J. (2004). EAP writing: The Chinese challenge; new ideas on plagiarism. *Humanising Language Teaching*, *6*(1). Retrieved from http://www.hltmag.co.uk/jan04/mart4.htm

Lakoff, G. (1987). *Women, Fire and Dangerous Things: What Categories Reveal About the Mind*. University Press. doi:10.7208/chicago/9780226471013.001.0001

Lakoff, G., & Johnson, M. (1980). *Metaphors We Live By*. University Press.

Lasonen, J. (2011). Multiculturalism in the Nordic countries. In C. A. Grant & A. Portera (Eds.), *Intercultural and multicultural education: Enhancing global interconnectedness* (pp. 261–278). Routledge.

Lawless, K. A., Brown, S. W., Rhoads, C., Lynn, L., Newton, S. D., Brodowiksa, K., Oren, J., Riel, J., Song, S., & Wang, M. (2018). Promoting students' science literacy skills through a simulation of international negotiations: The GlobalEd 2 Project. *Computers in Human Behavior*, *78*, 389–396. doi:10.1016/j.chb.2017.08.027

Lawrance, G., & Cohen, E. (2018). Examing International Telecollaboration in Language Teacher Education. In D. Tafazoli, M. Gómez Parra, & A. Cristina (Eds.), *Cross-Cultural Perspectives on Technology-Enhanced Language Learning* (pp. 264–282). IGI Global. doi:10.4018/978-1-5225-5463-9.ch018

Ledwith, A., & Rísquez, A. (2008). Using anti-plagiarism software to promote academic honesty in the context of peer reviewed assignments. *Studies in Higher Education, 33*(4), 371–384. doi:10.1080/03075070802211562

Lee, P. (2016, March 10). English most common home language in Singapore, bilingualism also up: Government survey. *The Straits Times.* https://www.straitstimes.com/singapore/english-most-common-home-language-in-singapore-bilingualism-also-up-government-survey

Leech, G. (1998). Learner corpora: What they are and what can be done with them. In S. Granger (Ed.), Learner English on computer. London: Addison Wesley Longman.

Lee, E. (2008). The other(ing) costs of ESL: A Canadian case study. *Journal of Asian Pacific Communication, 18*(1), 91–108.

Lee, O., Buxton, C. A., Lewis, S., & LeRoy, K. (2006). Science inquiry and student diversity: Enhanced abilities and continuing difficulties after an instructional intervention. *Journal of Research in Science Teaching, 43*(7), 607–636. doi:10.1002/tea.20141

Lee, O., Llosa, L., Grapin, S., Haas, A., & Goggins, M. (2019). Science and language integration with English learners: A conceptual framework guiding instructional materials development. *Science Education, 103*(2), 317–337. doi:10.1002ce.21498

Lee, O., Quinn, H., & Valdés, G. (2013). Science and language for English language learners in relation to Next Generation Science Standards and with implications for Common Core State Standards for English language arts and mathematics. *Educational Researcher, 42*(4), 223–233. doi:10.3102/0013189X13480524

Lei, J., & Hu, G. (2015). Chinese university EFL teachers' perceptions of plagiarism. *Higher Education, 70*(3), 551–565. doi:10.100710734-014-9855-5

Leki, I., & Carson, J. (1997). Completely different worlds: EAP and the writing experiences of ESL students in university courses. *TESOL Quarterly, 31*(1), 39–69. doi:10.2307/3587974

Lemke, J. L. (1990). *Talking science: Language, Learning and Values.* Ablex.

Lengeling, M., & Pablo, I. M. (2012). A critical discourse analysis of advertisements: Inconsistencies of our EFL profession. In R. Roux, A. M. Vazquez, & N. P. T. Guzman (Eds.), *Research in English language teaching: Mexican perspectives* (pp. 91–105). Palibrio.

Lim, L. (2001). Ethnic group varieties of Singapore English: Melody or harmony? In Evolving Identities. The English language in Singapore and Malaysia (pp. 53-68). Singapore: Times Academic Press.

Li, M. C., & Tsai, C. C. (2013). Game-based learning in science education: A review of relevant research. *Journal of Science Education and Technology, 22*(6), 877–898. doi:10.100710956-013-9436-x

Li, M., & Li, J. (2017). Online peer review using Turnitin in first-year writing classes. *Composition and Composition, 46*, 21–38. doi:10.1016/j.compcom.2017.09.001

Lim, C. P., Nonis, D., & Hedberg, J. (2006). Gaming in a 3D multiuser virtual environment: Engaging students in science lessons. *British Journal of Educational Technology, 37*(2), 211–231. doi:10.1111/j.1467-8535.2006.00531.x

Lim, S. (1995). A review of reading and writing research in Singapore: Implications for language education. In M. Tickoo (Ed.), *Reading and writing: Theory into practice* (pp. 492–513). SEAMEO Regional Language Centre.

Lin, S. Y., Wu, M. T., Cho, Y. I., & Chen, H. H. (2015). The effectiveness of a popular science promotion program on nanotechnology for elementary school students in I-Lan City. *Research in Science & Technological Education, 33*(1), 22–37. doi:10.1080/02635143.2014.971733

Liu, G. Z., Chiu, W. Y., Lin, C. C., & Barrett, N. E. (2014). English for Scientific Purposes (EScP): Technology, trends, and future challenges for science education. *Journal of Science Education and Technology, 23*(6), 827–839. doi:10.100710956-014-9515-7

Liu, P. H., & Cheng, Y. C. (2017). Attitudes toward English as an International Language: A Comparative Study of College Teachers and Students in Taiwan. *English as an International Language Journal, 12*(1), 66–85.

Liu, W. (2016). The changing pedagogical discourses in China: The case of the foreign language curriculum change and its controversies. *English Teaching, 15*(1), 74–90. doi:10.1108/ETPC-05-2015-0042

Li, Y. (2013). Text-based plagiarism in scientific publishing: Issues, developments and education. *Science and Engineering Ethics, 19*(3), 1241–1254. doi:10.100711948-012-9367-6 PMID:22535578

LoCastro, V., & Musuko, M. (1997). *Plagiarism and academic writing of NNS learners.* Paper presented at the annual meeting of the Teachers of English to Speakers of Other Languages, Orlando, FL.

Löfström, E. (2011). "Does plagiarism mean anything? LOL." Students' Conceptions of writing and citing. *Journal of Academic Ethics, 9*(4), 257–275. doi:10.100710805-011-9145-0

Löfström, E., & Kupila, P. (2013). The instructional challenges of student plagiarism. *Journal of Academic Ethics, 11*(3), 231–242. doi:10.100710805-013-9181-z

Low, E.-L., & Hashim, A. (Eds.). (2012). *English in Southeast Asia. Features, policy and language in use.* John Benjamins Publishing Company.

Compilation of References

Lyons, U. (1992). Secretary Bennett versus equal educational opportunity. In J. Crawford (Ed.), *Language loyalties: A source book on the official English controversy* (pp. 363–366). University of Chicago Press.

Maddox, T. T. (2008). Plagiarism and the community college. In *Practical issues for academics using the Turnitin plagiarism detection software. International Conference on Computer Systems and Technologies - CompSysTech'08*. Retrieved from http://ecet.ecs.ru.acad.bg/cst08/docs/cp/SIV/IV.1.pdf

Mahapatra, S., & Mishra, S. (2019). Articulating identities – the role of English language education in Indian universities. *Teaching in Higher Education, 24*(3), 346–360. doi:10.1080/13562517.2018.1547277

Mahboob, A., & Golden, R. (2013). Looking for native speakers of English: Discrimination in English language teaching job advertisements. *Voices in Asia Journal, 1*(1), 72–81.

Mahboob, A., Newman, K., Uhrig, K., & Hartford, B. (2004). Children of a lesser English: Status of nonnative English speakers as college-level English as a second language teachers in the United States. In L. D. Kamhi-Stein (Ed.), *Learning and teaching from experience: Perspectives on nonnative English-speaking professionals* (pp. 100–120). University of Michigan Press.

Mahmoud, A., & Zrigui, M. (2018). Artificial method for building monolingual plagiarized Arabic corpus. *Computación y Sistemas, 22*(3), 767–776. doi:10.13053/cys-22-3-3019

Makransky, G., Terkildsen, T. S., & Mayer, R. E. (2017). Adding immersive virtual reality to a science lab simulation causes more presence but less learning. *Learning and Instruction*, 1–12.

Maniam, K. S. (2003). *Between Lives*. Penguin Books Ltd.

Manners, I. (2008, February 1). *The normative ethics of the European Union*. doi:10.1111/j.1468-2346.2008.00688.x

Manners, I., & Diez, T. (2007). Reflecting on Normative Power Europe. In F. Berenskoetter & M. J. Williams (Eds.), *Power in World Politics* (pp. 173–188). Routledge.

Marsden, H., Carroll, M., & Neill, J. T. (2005). Who cheats at university? A self-report study of dishonest academic behaviours in a sample of Australian university students. *Australian Journal of Psychology, 57*(1), 1–10. doi:10.1080/00049530412331283426

Martin Levi, J. (2015). Ideology. *Sociológia, 77*, 9–31.

Martin, D. F. (2005). Plagiarism and technology: A tool for coping with plagiarism. *Journal of Education for Business, 80*(3), 149–152. doi:10.3200/JOEB.80.3.149-152

Martinez, G., Naranjo, F. L., Pérez, A. L., Suero, M. I., & Pardo, P. J. (2011). Comparative study of the effectiveness of some learning environments: Hyper-realistic virtual simulations, traditional schematic simulations and traditional laboratory. *Physical Review Special Topics. Physics Education Research, 7*(2), 020111-1, 020111–020112. doi:10.1103/PhysRevSTPER.7.020111

Martinez, M. D., Ranjeet, B., & Marx, H. A. (2009). Creating study abroad opportunities for first-generation college students. In R. Lewin (Ed.), *The handbook of practice and research in study abroad: Higher education and the quest for global citizenship* (pp. 527–542). Routledge.

Matsuda, A. (2003). Incorporating World Englishes in Teaching English as an International Language. *TESOL Quarterly, 37*(4), 719–729. doi:10.2307/3588220

Matsumoto, N. (2008). Bridges between Cognitive Linguistics and second language pedagogy: The case of corpora and their potential. *SKY Journal of Linguistics, 21*, 125–153.

Mavrinac, M., Brumini, G., Bilić-Zulle, L., & Petrovečki, M. (2010). Construction and validation of attitudes toward plagiarism questionnaire. *Croatian Medical Journal, 51*(3), 195–201. doi:10.3325/cmj.2010.51.195 PMID:20564761

McCabe, D. L., & Trevino, L. K. (1993). Academic dishonesty: Honor codes and other contextual influences. *The Journal of Higher Education, 64*(5), 522538. doi:10.1080/00221546.1993.11778446

McCabe, D. L., Trevino, L. K., & Butterfield, K. D. (2001). Cheating in academic institutions: A decade of research. *Ethics & Behavior, 11*(3), 219–233. doi:10.1207/S15327019EB1103_2

McEnery, A. M., Xiao, R., & Tono, Y. (2005). *Corpus-based language studies*. Routledge.

McEnery, T., & Wilson, A. (1996). *Corpus linguistics*. Edinburgh University Press.

McKay, S. L., & Freedman, S. W. (1990). Language minority education in Great Britain: A challenge to current U.S. Policy. *TESOL Quarterly, 24*(3), 385–405. doi:10.2307/3587226

McKeever, L. (2006). Online plagiarism detection services—Saviour or scourge? *Assessment & Evaluation in Higher Education, 31*(2), 155–165. doi:10.1080/02602930500262460

McLaughlin, B. (1987). *Theories of Second Language Learning*. Arnold Publishers.

McNeill, K. L. (2008). Teachers' use of curriculum to support students' in writing scientific arguments to explain phenomena. *Science Education, 93*(2), 233–268. doi:10.1002ce.20294

Medgyes, P. (1992). Native or non-native: Who's worth more? *ELT Journal, 46*(4), 340–349. doi:10.1093/elt/46.4.340

Medgyes, P. (2001). When the teacher is a non-native speaker. In M. Celce-Murcia (Ed.), *Teaching English as a second or foreign language* (pp. 429–442). Heinle & Heinle.

Mee, C. Y. (2002). English language teaching in Singapore. *Asia Pacific Journal of Education, 22*(2), 65–80. doi:10.1080/0218879020220207

Mercer, N., Dawes, L., Wegerif, R., & Sams, C. (2004). Reasoning as a scientist: Ways of helping children to use language to learn science. *British Educational Research Journal, 30*(3), 359–377. doi:10.1080/01411920410001689689

Metz, M. (2019). Principles to navigate the challenges of teaching English language variation: A guide for nonlinguists. In M. D. Devereaux & C. C. Palmer (Eds.), *Teaching language variety in the classroom: Strategies and models from teachers and linguists* (pp. 69–75). Routledge. doi:10.4324/9780429486678-14

Migration Advisory Committee. (2018). *Impact of international students in the UK*. https://assets.publishing.service.gov.uk/government/uploads/system/uploads/attachment_data/file/739089/Impact_intl_students_report_published_v1.1.pdf

Min, C. Y. (2018, February 5). Singapore still 2nd freest economy in the world but gap with top-ranked Hong Kong widens. *The Straitstimes*. https://www.straitstimes.com/business/economy/singapore-still-2nd-freest-economy-in-the-world-but-gap-with-top-ranked-hong-kong-0

Ministry of Education, Culture, Science, Sports, and Technology – MEXT. (2017). *Report on the survey of English language skills of English teachers in Japan*. Retrieved from: http://www.mext.go.jp/component/a_menu/education/detail/__icsFiles/afieldfile/2017/04/07/1384236_01_1.pdf

Ministry of Education. (1991). *English language syllabus*. Curriculum Planning Division, Ministry of Education.

Ministry of Education. (2011). *English curriculum standard*. Beijing Normal University Press.

Mitchell, R., & Myles, F. (2004). *Second language learning theories*. Edward Arnold.

Mohan, B. A. (1986). *Language and content*. Addison-Wesley.

Monfared, A., & Safarzadeh, M. M. (2014). Pronunciation issues and varieties of English from an EIL perspective: A survey of outer and expanding circle learners' beliefs. *International Journal of Applied Linguistics and English Literature*, *3*(6), 212–223.

Moore, D., & Gajo, L. (2009). French Voices on Plurilingualism and Pluriculturalism: Theory, Significance and Perspectives. *International Journal of Multilingualism and Multiculturalism*, *6*(2), 137–153. doi:10.1080/14790710902846707

Morrison, W. M. (2019). *China's economic rise: History, trends, challenges, and implications for the United States*. Congressional Research Service.

Murphey, T., & Arao, H. (2001). Reported belief changes through near-peer role modeling. *TESL-EJ*, *5*(3).

Murphy, J. (2014). Intelligible, Comprehensible, non-native models in ESL/EFL Pronunciation Teaching. *System*, *42*, 258–269. doi:10.1016/j.system.2013.12.007

Murphy, R. (1990). Anorexia: The cheating disorder. *College English*, *52*(8), 898–903. doi:10.2307/377394

Mustafa, F. (2019). "I think it is not plagiarism": How little do Indonesian undergraduate EFL students understand plagiarism? *Asian EFL Journal*, *21*(2), 74–91.

National Academy for Educational Research. (2015). 十二年國民基本教育語文領域(英語、第二外語)課程綱要研修說明公聽會版本(國民中小學及普通型高中) [The Curricula for English Guidelines of 12 year Education: The Language Arts Learning Area]. Taipei: National Academy for Educational Research. Retrieved June 11, 2017 from http://www.naer.edu.tw/files/15-1000-10472,c639-1.php?Lang=zh-tw

National Academy for Educational Research. (2016). 中華民國教育年報105年版 [The Republic of China Education Yearbook 2016]. Taipei: National Academy for Educational Research. Retrieved November 1, 2017 from https://www.naer.edu.tw/files/15-1000-13943,c1310-1.php?Lang=zh-tw

National Academy for Educational Research. (2017). 十二年國民基本教育課程綱要國民中小學暨普通型高級中等學校語文領域-英語文課程手冊初稿更新第五版 [The Curricula for English Guidelines of 12 year Curriculum: The Language Arts Learning Area (The fifth version)]. Taipei: National Academy for Educational Research. Retrieved November 1, 2017 from https://www.naer.edu.tw/files/11-1000-1590-1.php?Lang=zh-tw

National Center for Education Statistics. (2018). *English language learners in public schools*. https://nces.ed.gov/programs/coe/indicator_cgf.asp

National Centre for Education Development Research. (2008), *National report on mid-term assessment of education for all in China*. National Centre for Education Development Research, Chinese National Commission for Unesco. http://planipolis.iiep.unesco.org/upload/China/China_EFA_MDA.pdf

National Research Council (NRC). (1996). *National science education standards*. National Academic Press.

National Research Council. (2012). *A framework for K-12 science education: Practices, crosscutting concepts, and core ideas*. National Academies Press.

Nation, I. S. P. (2013). *What should every EFL teacher know?* Compass.

Nation, I. S. P. (2014). Developing fluency. In T. Muller, J. Adamson, P. S. Brown, & S. Herder (Eds.), *Exploring EFL fluency in Asia* (pp. 11–25). Palgrave Macmillan.

Nation, I. S. P. (2015). *Learning vocabulary in another language* (2nd ed.). Cambridge University Press.

Nation, I. S. P., & Newton, J. (2009). *Teaching ESL/EFL listening and speaking*. Routledge.

Nemser, W. (1971). Approximative systems of foreign language learner. *International Journal of Applied Linguistics*, *9*, 115–124.

Next Generation Science Standards Lead States. (2013). *Next Generation Science Standards: For states, by states*. The National Academies Press.

Ngo, M. (2014). Canadian youth volunteering abroad: Rethinking issues of power and privilege. *Current Issues in Comparative Education*, *16*(1), 49–61.

Compilation of References

Nickerson, C. (2013). English for specific purposes and English as a lingua franca. In B. Paltridge & S. Starfield (Eds.), *The handbook of English for specific purposes* (pp. 446–460). Wiley-Blackwell.

Nishino, T., & Watanabe, M. (2008). Communication-oriented policies versus classroom realities in Japan. *TESOL Quarterly*, *42*(1), 133–138. doi:10.1002/j.1545-7249.2008.tb00214.x

Norriss, S. P., & Phillips, L. M. (2003). How literacy in its fundamental sense is central to scientific literacy. *Science Education*, *87*(2), 224–240. doi:10.1002ce.10066

Norton, B. (1997). Language, identity and ownership of English. *TESOL Quarterly*, *31*(3), 409–429. doi:10.2307/3587831

Norton, B. (2001). Non-participation, imagined communities, and the language classroom. In M. Breen (Ed.), *Learner contributions to language learning: New directions in research* (pp. 159–171). Pearson Education Limited.

Norton, B., & Toohey, K. (2001). Identity, language learning, and social change. *Language Teaching*, *44*(4), 412–446.

Nova, M., & Utami, W. H. (2018). EFL students' perception of Turnitin for detecting plagiarism on academic writing. *International Journal of Education*, *10*(2), 141–148.

Nunan, D. (2003). The Importance of English as a Global Language on Educational Policies and Practices in the Asia-Pacific Region. *TESOL Quarterly*, *37*(4), 589–613. doi:10.2307/3588214

Nye, S. J. (2008, March). Public Diplomacy and Soft Power. *AAPSS*, 94-109. Retrieved from https://journals.sagepub.com/doi/pdf/10.1177/0002716207311699

Nye, S. J. (1990, Autumn). Soft Power. *Foreign Policy*, (80), 153–171. https://www.jstor.org/stable/1148580. doi:10.2307/1148580

Nye, S. J. (2004). *Soft Power The Means to Success in World Politics*. Public Affairs.

Nye, S. J. (2009). Get Smart Combining Hard and Soft Power. *Foreign Affairs*, *88*(4), 160–164. https://www.jstor.org/stable/20699631?seq=4#metadata_info_tab_contents

O'Donoghue, T. (1996). Malaysian Chinese students' perceptions of what is necessary for their academic success in Australia: A case study at one university. *Journal of Further and Higher Education*, *20*(2), 67–80. doi:10.1080/0309877960200206

Odeh, L. E. (2010). A comparative analysis of Global North and Global South economies. *Journal of Sustainable Development in Africa*, *12*(3), 338–348.

Omoniyi, T. (Ed.). (2010). *The Sociology of Language and Religion: Change, Conflict and Accommodation*. Palgrave Macmillan. doi:10.1057/9780230304710

Omoniyi, T., & Fishman, J. A. (Eds.). (2006). *Explorations in the sociology of language and religion*. John Benjamins. doi:10.1075/dapsac.20

Onoda, S. (2015). Effects of issue logs on L2 oral fluency development. *Proceedings of the 4th Annual International Conference on Language, Literature, & Linguistics* (pp. 156-163). Singapore: Global Science and Technology Forum. 10.5176/2251-3566_L315.29

Onoda, S. (2000). Effectiveness of adopting productive activities in Media English learning with a primary focus on the use of group projects. *Journal of Current English Studies, 39*, 87–102.

Onoda, S. (2012). Effects of repetition of selected news stories on speaking fluency in Media English learning. *Media English and Communication, 1*, 89–105.

Onoda, S. (2014). An exploration of effective teaching approaches for enhancing the oral fluency of EFL students. In T. Muller, J. Adamson, P. S. Brown, & S. Herder (Eds.), *Exploring EFL fluency in Asia* (pp. 120–142). Palgrave Macmillan.

Onoda, S. (2019a). Effects of CLIL-based approaches on pre-service teachers' learning in teacher education programs. In R. Raul & A. Lopes (Eds.), *Current issues in language teaching* (pp. 111–122). Editorial Académica Española.

Onoda, S. (2019b). Enhancing L2 interactional skills through interactive pair presentations with small-group discussion. *JALT CUE Journal, 37*(1), 25–37.

Onoda, S., & Miyashita, O. (2018). Improving learners' interactional skills through innovative undergraduate English teacher education programs. *Juntendo Journal of Global Studies, 3*, 45–60.

Onoda, S., Miyashita, O., & Yoshino, Y. (2017). Innovating in undergraduate English teacher education programs. *Juntendo Journal of Global Studies, 2*, 58–65.

Ortega, L. (2010). *The Bilingual Turn in SLA*. Plenary delivered at the Annual Conference of the American Association for Applied Linguistics, Atlanta, GA.

Osborne, J. (2001). Integrating corpora into a language-learning syllabus. In B. Lewandowska Tomaszczyk (Ed.), *PALC 2001: Practical applications in language corpora* (pp. 479–492). Peter Lang.

Osborne, J. (2002). Science without literacy: A ship without a sail? *Cambridge Journal of Education, 32*(2), 203–218. doi:10.1080/03057640220147559

Owens, J. (1995a). Minority languages and urban norms: A case study. *Linguistics, 33*(2), 305–358. doi:10.1515/ling.1995.33.2.305

Owens, J. (1995b). Language in the graphic mode: Arabic among the Kanuri of Nigeria. *Language Sciences, 17*(2), 181–199. doi:10.1016/0388-0001(95)91152-F

Owens, J. (2001). Arabic Sociolinguistics. *Arabica, 48*(4), 419–469. doi:10.1163/157005801323163816

Özen, E. N. (2013). *Turkey National needs assessment of state school English language teaching*. https://www.britishcouncil.org.tr/sites/default/files/turkey_national_needs_assessment_of_state_school_english_language_teaching.pdf

Özmen, K., Çakır, A., & Cephe, P. (2018). Conceptuation of English Culture and Accent: Idealized English among Teachers in the Expanding Circle. *Asian EFL Journal*, *20*(3), 8–30.

Paikeday, T. M. (1985). *The native speaker is dead!* Paikeday Publishing Co.

Pan, Z., Cheok, A. D., Yang, H., Zhu, J., & Shi, J. (2006). Virtual reality and mixed reality for virtual learning environments. *Computers & Graphics*, *30*(1), 20–28. doi:10.1016/j.cag.2005.10.004

Pargament, K. I., & Mahoney, A. (2005). Sacred Matters: Sanctification as a Vital Topic for the Psychology of Religion. *The International Journal of Religion*, *15*(3), 179–198. doi:10.120715327582ijpr1503_1

Park, C. (2003). In other (people's) words: Plagiarism by university students - literature and lessons. *Assessment & Evaluation in Higher Education*, *28*(5), 471–488. doi:10.1080/02602930301677

Parkinson, J. (2000). Acquiring scientific literacy through content and genre: A theme-based language course for science students. *English for Specific Purposes*, *19*(4), 369–387. doi:10.1016/S0889-4906(99)00012-5

Park, J. S., & Wee, L. (2009). The Three Circles redux: A market–theoretic perspective on World Englishes. *Applied Linguistics*, *30*(3), 389–406. doi:10.1093/applin/amp008

Patak, A. A., Wiraman, H., Abduh, A., Hidayat, R., Iskandar, I., & Dirawan, G. D. (2020). Teaching English as a foreign language in Indonesia: University lecturers' views on plagiarism. *Journal of Academic Ethics* doi:10.100710805-020-09385-y

Patterson, E. W. (2001). Structuring the composition process in scientific writing. *International Journal of Science Education*, *23*(1), 1–16. doi:10.1080/09500690117425

Pavlenko, A., & Norton, B. (2007). Imagined communities, identity, and English language learning. In J. Cummins & C. Davison (Eds.), *International handbook of English language Teaching* (pp. 669–680). Springer. doi:10.1007/978-0-387-46301-8_43

Paxton, M. (2007). Tensions between textbook pedagogy and the literary practices of the disciplinary community: A study of writing in first year economics. *Journal of English for Academic Purposes*, *6*(2), 109–125. doi:10.1016/j.jeap.2007.04.003

Pearson, D., Moje, E. B., & Greenleaf, C. (2010). Literacy and science: Each in the service of the other. *Science*, *328*(5977), 459–463. doi:10.1126cience.1182595 PMID:20413491

Pecorari, D. (2001). Plagiarism and international students: How the English-speaking university responds. In D. Belcher & A. Hirvela (Eds.), *Linking literacies: Perspectives on L2 Reading-Writing Connections* (pp. 229–245). The University of Michigan Press.

Pecorari, D., & Petrić, B. (2014). Plagiarism in second-language writing. *Language Teaching*, *47*(3), 269–302. doi:10.1017/S0261444814000056

Pelger, S., & Nilsson, P. (2016). Popular science writing to support students' learning of science and scientific literacy. *Research in Science Education*, *46*(3), 439–456. doi:10.100711165-015-9465-y

Pennycook, A. (1996). Borrowing others' words: Text, ownership, memory and plagiarism. *TESOL Quarterly, 30*(2), 201–230. doi:10.2307/3588141

Pennycook, A. (2007). *Global English and transcultural flows*. Routledge.

Pennycook, A. (2017). *The cultural politics of English as an international language. TESOL Matters*. Routledge. doi:10.4324/9781315225593

Pérez Paredes, P., Sánchez Tornel, M., & Alcaraz Calero, J. M. (2011). *The role of corpus linguistics in developing innovation in data-driven language learning*. Academic Press.

Phillipson, R. (1992). *Linguistic imperialism*. Oxford University Press.

Phillipson, R. (Ed.). (1991). *Foreign/second language pedagogy research*. Multilingual Matters.

Pintrich, P. R., & Zusho, A. (2002). The development of academic self-regulation: The role of cognitive and motivational factors. In A. Wigfield & J. S. Eccles (Eds.), *Development of achievement motivation* (pp. 249–284). Academic Press. doi:10.1016/B978-012750053-9/50012-7

Pishghadam, R., & Morady, M. M. (2013). Investigating condolence responses in English and Persian. *International Journal of Research Studies in Language Learning, 2*(1), 39–47.

Powell, L. (2012). *Understanding plagiarism: developing a model of plagiarising behavior*. Paper presented at the International Integrity & Plagiarism Conference, Newcastle Upon Tyne, UK. Retrieved from https://pdfs.semanticscholar.org/0903/10b04ade5540c672c5b0db66e868bd805644.pdf

Power. (2019). In *Oxford Dictionaries*. Retrieved from https://en.oxforddictionaries.com/definition/power

Prapinwong, M. (2018). Blended learning course design and implementation to foster the intercultural awareness of preservice teachers in an EFL context. *Asian EFL Journal, 20*(12.2), 131-152.

Pryke, W. Y. (n.d.). Singapore's journey: Bilingualism and role of English language in our development. *British Council*. https://www.britishcouncil.cl/sites/default/files/escrito-way-yin-pryke.pdf

Radford, J. (2019). *Key findings about U.S. immigrants*. Pew Research Center. https://www.pewresearch.org/fact-tank/2019/06/17/key-findings-about-u-s-immigrants/

Rahal, A. (2016). *Phonetic Fossilization in the Speech of Advanced Tunisian English Students: The English Department of Kairouan as a case study* (Unpublished MA thesis). Faculty of Letters and Humanities of Kairouan.

Rakovski, C., & Levy, E. (2007). Academic dishonesty: Perceptions of business students. *College Student Journal, 41*, 466–481.

Compilation of References

Ramanathan, V. (2007). A critical discussion of the English-Vernacular divide in India. In J. Cummins & C. Davison (Eds.), *International handbook of English language teaching* (pp. 51–61). Springer. doi:10.1007/978-0-387-46301-8_5

Rampton, M. B. H. (1990). Displacing the native speaker: Expertise, affiliation and inheritance. *The Language Ethnicity and Race Reader*, *44*(2), 97–101.

Rao, A. G. (2013). The English-only myth: Multilingual education in India. *Language Problems and Language Planning*, *37*(3), 271–279. doi:10.1075/lplp.37.3.04rao

Razı, S. (2015a). Cross-checked problems in undergraduate academic writing. K. Dikilitaş, R. Smith, & W. Trotman (Eds.), Teacher-researchers in action (pp. 147-161). Kent, UK: IATEFL.

Razı, S. (2015b). Development of a rubric to assess academic writing incorporating plagiarism detectors. *SAGE Open*, *5*(2), 1–13. doi:10.1177/2158244015590162

Read, B. (2006). Turnitin makes its ivy league debut. *Chronicle of Higher Education.* Retrieved from http://www.chronicle.com/blogs/wiredcampus/turnitin-makes-its-ivy-league-debut/2656

Registrar General & Census Commissioner. (2011). *Census of India 2011: Report on post enumeration survey.* https://www.censusindia.gov.in/2011Census/pes/Pesreport.pdf

Rets, I., & Ilya, A. (2018). Eliciting ELT students' understanding of plagiarism in academic writing. *Eurasian Journal of Applied Linguistics*, *4*(2), 193–211. doi:10.32601/ejal.464115

Ricento, T. K. (1997). Language policy and education in the United States. In R. Wodak & D. Corson (Eds.), *Encyclopedia of language and education: Language policy and political issues in education* (pp. 137–148). Springer. doi:10.1007/978-94-011-4538-1_13

Richards, J. C. (2002). Theories of teaching in language learning. In J. C. Richards & W. A. Renandya (Eds.), *Methodology in language teaching: An anthology of current practice* (pp. 19–26). Cambridge University Press. doi:10.1017/CBO9780511667190.004

Rivers, D. J. (2018). Speakerhood as segregation: The construction and consequence of divisive discourse in TESOL. In B. Yazan & N. Rudolph (Eds.), *Criticality, teacher identity, and (in)equity in English language teaching. Educational linguistics* (pp. 179–197). Springer International Publishing. doi:10.1007/978-3-319-72920-6_10

Robins, R. H., & Crystal, D. (2020). Language. In *Encyclopædia Britannica.* Encyclopædia Britannica, Inc. https://www.britannica.com/topic/language

Rohlfs, G. (1984). Quer durch Afrika. Wissenschaftliche: Buchgesellschaft, Darmstadt. (Original publication 1874)

Rolfe, V. (2011). Can Turnitin be used to provide instant formative feedback? *British Journal of Educational Technology*, *42*(4), 701–710. doi:10.1111/j.1467-8535.2010.01091.x

Romaine, S. (1989). *Bilingualism*. Blackwell.

Rosch, E. (1973). Natural categories. *Cognitive Psychology*, *4*(3), 328–350. doi:10.1016/0010-0285(73)90017-0

Rosch, E. (1977). Human categorization. In E. N. Warren (Ed.), *Advances in cross-cultural psychology* (p. 49). Academic Press.

Rosch, E. (1978). Principles of categorization. In E. Rosch & B. B. Lloyd (Eds.), *Cognition and Categorization*. Erlbaum.

Rosch, E., & Mervis, C. B. (1975). Family resemblance: Studies in the internal structure of categories. *Cognitive Psychology*, *7*(4), 573–605. doi:10.1016/0010-0285(75)90024-9

Rosowsky, A. (2006). The role of liturgical literacy in UK Muslim communities. In *Explorations in the Sociology of Language and Religion* (pp. 309–324). John Benjamins. doi:10.1075/dapsac.20.24ros

Rosowsky, A. (2008). *Heavenly Readings: Liturgical Literacy in a Multilingual Context*. Multilingual Matters.

Rosowsky, A. (2012). Performance and Flow: The Religious Classical in Translocal and Transnational Linguistic Repertoires. *Journal of Sociolinguistics*, *16*(5), 5. doi:10.1111/j.1467-9841.2012.00542.x

Rosowsky, A. (2018). Globalisation, the practice of devotional songs and poems and the linguistic repertoires of young British Muslims. *Culture and Religion*, *19*(1), 90–112. doi:10.1080/14755610.2017.1416645

Royal Geographical Society. (n.d.). *A 60 second guice to the Global North/South divide*. Retrieved July 15, 2019. https://www.rgs.org/CMSPages/GetFile.aspx?nodeguid=9c1ce781-9117-4741-af0a-a6a8b75f32b4&lang=en-GB

Royce, J. (2003). Has turnitin.com got it all wrapped up? (Trust or trussed?). *Teacher Librarian*, *30*(4), 26–30.

Ruecker, T., & Ives, L. (2015). White native English speakers needed: The rhetorical construction of privilege in online teacher recruitment spaces. *TESOL Quarterly*, *49*(4), 733–756. doi:10.1002/tesq.195

Ryan, S., & Eckersley, C. (2004). *Academic integrity and use of turnitin*. Retrieved from www.newcastle.edu.au/services/academic-integrity

Ryan, G., Bonanno, H., Krass, I., Scouller, K., & Smith, L. (2009). Undergraduate and postgraduate pharmacy students' perceptions of plagiarism and academic honesty. *American Journal of Pharmaceutical Education*, *73*(6), 105. doi:10.5688/aj7306105 PMID:19885074

Sadler, T. D. (2009). Situated learning in science education: Socio-scientific issues as contexts for practice. *Studies in Science Education*, *45*(1), 1–42. doi:10.1080/03057260802681839

Samarin, W. J. (1976a). The Language of Religion. In Language in Religious Practice (pp. 3-13). Newbury House.

Samarin, W. J. (1976b). *Language in religious practice*. Newbury House.

Saquing, J. (2018). Intercultural communicative competence of Bachelor of Science in Secondary Education (BSED) major in English students: A basic for a proposed integration of internationalization in the BSED major in English curriculum. *Asian EFL Journal, 20*(2), 8–29.

Sato, K. (2012). *Changing a teaching culture: From individual practice to curriculum development*. Paper presented at the 2012 International JALT conference, Nagoya.

Saussure De, F. (1921). *Cours de Linguistique Générale*. Payot.

Scaife, B. (2007). *IT Consultancy plagiarism detection software report for JISC Advisory Service*. Retrieved from https://studylib.net/doc/8357192/it-consultancy-plagiarism-detection-software-report-for-jisc

Scanlan, C. L. (2006). Strategies to promote a climate of academic integrity and minimize student cheating and plagiarism. *Journal of Allied Health, 35*(3), 179–185. PMID:17036675

Scanlon, P. M., & Neumann, D. R. (2002). Internet plagiarism among college students. *Journal of College Student Development, 43*, 374–385.

Schifflin, D. (1996). Narrative as Self-Portrait: Sociolinguistic Constructions of Identity. *Language in Society, 25*(2), 167–203. doi:10.1017/S0047404500020601

Schutter, H. (2018). Linguistic justice and English as a lingua franca. In P. A. Kraus & F. Grin (Eds.), *The politics of multilingualism: Europeanisation, globalisation, and linguistic governance* (pp. 167–199). John Benjamins. doi:10.1075/wlp.6.08des

Scollon, R. (1994). As a matter of fact: The changing ideology of authorship and responsibility in discourse. *World Englishes, 13*(1), 33–46. doi:10.1111/j.1467-971X.1994.tb00281.x

Scollon, R. (1995). Plagiarism and ideology: Identity in intercultural discourse. *Language in Society, 24*(1), 1–28. doi:10.1017/S0047404500018388

Segalowitz, N. (2010). *The cognitive bases of second language fluency*. Routledge. doi:10.4324/9780203851357

Seidlhofer, B. (2005). English as a lingua franca. *ELT Journal, 59*(4), 339–341. doi:10.1093/elt/cci064

Selinker, L. (1972). Interlanguage. *International Journal of Applied Linguistics, 10*, 203–230.

Selvi, A. F. (2010). All teachers are equal, but some teachers are more equal than others: Trend analysis of job advertisements in English language teaching. *WATESOL NNEST Caucus Annual Review, 1*, 156–181.

Selwyn, N. (2008). 'Not necessarily a bad thing… ': A study of online plagiarism amongst undergraduate students. *Assessment & Evaluation in Higher Education, 33*(5), 465–479. doi:10.1080/02602930701563104

Sentleng, M. P., & King, L. (2012). Plagiarism among undergraduate students in the faculty of applied science at a South African higher education institution. *South African Journal of Libraries and Information Service, 78*(1), 57–67. doi:10.7553/78-1-47

SGO (Steering Group Office for Survey of Language Situation in China). (2006). *Zhongguo Yuyan Wenzi Shiyong Qingkuang Diaocha Ziliao* [Findings and Documents of Survey of Language Situation in China]. Language Press.

Sharifian. (2013). Globalization and Developing Metacultural Competence in Learning English at an International Language. *Multilingual Education, 3*(7), 1-11.

Sharma, R. L. (2018). Communication in the Era of Post-truth. In *Communication, Entrepreneurship and Finance: Renegotiating Diverse Perspectives. Co-edited by Manpreet Arora and Roshan Sharma*. Anamika Publishers & Distributors (P) Ltd.

Sharma, S. K. (1980). Practical and Theoretical Consideration involved in Error Analysis. *Indian Journal of Applied Linguistics, VI*, 74–83.

Sheridan, J., Alany, R., & Brake, D. (2005). Pharmacy students' views and experiences of Turnitin –an online tool for detecting academic dishonesty. *Pharmacy Education, 5*(374), 241–250. doi:10.1080/15602210500288977

Sherman, J. (1992). Your own thoughts in your own words. *ELT Journal, 46*(2), 190–198. doi:10.1093/elt/46.2.190

Shi, J. L. (2017). English language education in China: Progress, problems, and reflections. *Journal of Literature and Art Studies, 7*(7), 935–938.

Shi, Y., & Ariza, E. (2018). A study on the Natural Approach (NA) and teaching proficiency through reading and storytelling (TPRS). In *Proceedings of the 6th international conference on social science, education and humanities research (SSEHR 2017)*. Atlantis Press. 10.2991sehr-17.2018.92

Shuck, G. (2006). Racializing the nonnative English speaker. *Journal of Language, Identity, and Education, 5*(4), 259–276. doi:10.120715327701jlie0504_1

Siemund, P., Schulz, M. E., & Schweinberger, M. (2014). Studying the linguistic ecology of Singapore: A comparison of college and university students. *World Englishes, 33*(3), 340–362. doi:10.1111/weng.12094

Sifakis, N. C. (2007). 'The education of the teachers of English as a lingua franca: A transformative perspective. *International Journal of Applied Linguistics, 17*(3), 355–375. doi:10.1111/j.1473-4192.2007.00174.x

Sifakis, N. C., & Sougari, A. M. (2005). Pronunciation Issues and EIL Pedagogy in the Periphery: A Survey of Greek State School Teachers' Beliefs. *TESOL Quarterly, 39*(3), 467–485. doi:10.2307/3588490

Simon, B. (2004). *Identity in Modern Society: A Social Psychological Perspective*. Blackwell. doi:10.1002/9780470773437

Sinclair, J. (1996). The search for units of meaning. *Textus, 9*, 75–106.

Skutnabb-kangas, T., & Phillipson, R. (1994). Linguistic human rights: Past and present. In Linguistic human rights: Overcoming linguistic discrimination (pp. 71–110). Berlin: Mouton de Gruyter.

Sljusareva, N.A. (1980). The heart of F. De Saussure's theory of language. *STUF - Language Typology and Universals, 33*(1-6), 541-545.

Smith, R. (2016). ELT and the British Council, 1935-2014: Research notes. *Warwick ELT Archive*. https://warwick.ac.uk/fac/soc/al/research/collections/elt_archive/research_projects/britishcouncil/

Smith, K. E. (2005). Beyond the Civilian Power debate. *Politique Europeenne, 1*(17), 63–82. doi:10.3917/poeu.017.0063

Smith, L. E. (Ed.). (1983). *Readings in English as an International Language*. Pergamon Press.

Snow, M. A., Kamhi-Stein, L. D., & Brinton, D. M. (2006). Teacher Training for English as a Lingua Franca. *Annual Review of Applied Linguistics, 26*, 261–281. doi:10.1017/S0267190506000134

Soederberg, S. (2006). *Global governance in question: Empire, class and the new common sense in managing North-South relations*. Pluto Press.

Sohrabi, B., Gholipour, A., & Mohammadesmaeili, N. (2011). Effects of personality and information technology on plagiarism: An Iranian perspective. *Ethics & Behavior, 21*(5), 367–379. doi:10.1080/10508422.2011.604294

Soler, V. (2011). Comparative and contrastive observations on scientific titles written in English and Spanish. *English for Specific Purposes, 30*(2), 124–137. doi:10.1016/j.esp.2010.09.002

Solga, H. (2016). The social investment state and the myth of meritocracy. In A. Gallas, H. Herr, F. Hoffer, & C. Scherrer (Eds.), *Combating inequality: The Global North and South* (pp. 199–211). Routledge.

Solono, T. (2014). *Spanish Interference in EFL Writing Skills: A Case of Ecuadorian Senior High Schools* (Vol. 7). English Language Teaching Journal.

Somekh, B. (2007). *Pedagogy and learning with ICT: Researching the art of innovation*. Routledge. doi:10.4324/9780203947005

Sowden, C. (2005). Plagiarism and the culture of multilingual students in higher education abroad. *ELT Journal, 59*(3), 226–233. doi:10.1093/elt/cci042

Speaking English does not mean forgetting our traditions, says Raja Permaisuri Agung. (2019, Oct. 14). *The Star Online*. Retrieved from https://www.malaymail.com/news/malaysia/2019/10/14/speaking-english-does-not-mean-forgetting-our-traditions-says-raja-permaisu/1800182?fbclid=IwAR3hBpBUkPcpYIkZ9Em23MrYGzzms3AXVUZA4O4hRIxT3YOQCL5yO7jvZmc

Spelt, E. J. H., Biemans, H. J. A., Tobi, H., Luning, P. A., & Mulder, M. (2009). Teaching and learning in interdisciplinary higher education: A systematic review. *Educational Psychology Review*, 21(4), 365–378. doi:10.100710648-009-9113-z

Spelt, E. J. H., Luning, P. A., Van Boekel, M. A. J. S., & Mulder, M. (2015). Constructively aligned teaching and learning in higher education in engineering: What do students perceive as contributing to the learning of interdisciplinary thinking? *European Journal of Engineering Education*, 40(5), 459–475. doi:10.1080/03043797.2014.987647

Spolsky, B. (2004). *Language policy*. Cambridge University Press.

Sridhar, K., & Sridhar, S. (1986). Bridging the paradigm gap: Second language acquisition theory and indigenized varieties of English. *World Englishes*, 5(1), 3–14. doi:10.1111/j.1467-971X.1986.tb00636.x

Standler, R. B. (2012). *Plagiarism in colleges in USA: Legal aspects of plagiarism, academic policy*. Retrieved from http://www.rbs2.com/plag.pdf

Stanley, T. (2014). Antiracism without guarantees: A Framework for rethinking racisms in schools. *Critical Literacy: Theories and Practices*, 8(1), 4–19.

Statista. (2019). *The most spoken languages worldwide (native speakers in millions)*. Retrieved from https://www.statista.com/statistics/266808/the-most-spoken-languages-worldwide/

Stein, P. (2008). *Multimodal Pedagogies in Diverse Classrooms: Representation, rights and resources*. Routledge.

Stewart, W. (1968). A sociolinguistic typology for describing national multilingualism. In J. A. Fishman (Ed.), *Readings in the sociology of language* (pp. 531–545). Mouton. doi:10.1515/9783110805376.531

Sutherland-Smith, W. (2011). Crime and punishment: An analysis of university plagiarism policies. *Semiotica*, 187(187), 127–139. doi:10.1515emi.2011.067

Sutherland-Smith, W., & Carr, R. (2005). Turnitin.com: Teachers' perspectives of anti-plagiarism software in raising issues of educational integrity. *Journal of University Teaching & Learning Practice*, 2(3), 94–101.

Swift, J. (1892). *Gulliver's Travels*. Retrieved from globalgreyebooks.com

Taerungruang, S., & Aroonmanakun, W. (2018). Constructing an academic Thai plagiarism corpus for benchmarking plagiarism detection systems. *GEMA Online® Journal of Language Studies*, 18(3), 186-202. doi:10.17576/gema-2018-1803-11

Taher, A. (2011). *Error analysis: a study of Swedish junior high school students' texts and grammar knowledge* (Unpublished thesis). Uppsala Universitet.

Tan, A. (2003). *The Opposite of Fate: a Book of Musing*. G. P. Putnam's Sons.

Tan, P. K. W. (2012). English in Singapore. *International Journal of Language. Translation and Intercultural Communication, 1*(1), 123–138. doi:10.12681/ijltic.14

Taylor, K. L., Usick, B. L., & Paterson, B. L. (2004). Understanding plagiarism: The intersection of personal, pedagogical, institutional, and social contexts. *Journal on Excellence in College Teaching, 15*(3), 153–174.

TESOL. (2006). *Position statement against discrimination of nonnative speakers of English in the field of TESOL*. Retrieved from https://www.tesol.org/docs/pdf/12305.pdf?sfvrsn=2&sfvrsn=2

The Digital Language Diversity Programme. (n.d.). Retrieved from http://www.dldp.eu/en/content/project

The Republic of Turkey Ministry of Foreign Affairs. (n.d.). *The United Nations Organization and Turkey*. Retrieved from http://www.mfa.gov.tr/the-united-nations-organization-and-turkey.en.mfa

The Star. (2008a, Oct. 25). Blast heist. *The Star*.

The Star. (2008b, Oct. 25). Ways to ensure safety of kids. *The Star*.

The Treaty of Rome. (1957, March 25). Retrieved from. https://ec.europa.eu/archives/emu_history/documents/treaties/rometreaty2.pdf

The UN Migration Agency. (2018). *World migration report 2018*. https://www.iom.int/sites/default/files/country/docs/china/r5_world_migration_report_2018_en.pdf

Thirusanku, J. & Yunus. (2014). Status of English in Malaysia. *Asian Social Science, 10*(14), 254–260.

Thormann, W. E. (1969). The Audio-Lingual Method in the past: "Anti-grammar" in Seventeenth-century France. *Modern Language Journal, 53*(5), 327–329.

Tomlinson, B. (2013). Introduction: Principles and procedure of material development. In B. Tomlinson (Ed.), *Materials development in language teaching* (2nd ed., pp. 25–47). Cambridge University Press.

Tomlinson, B., & Masuhara, H. (2018). *The complete guide to the theory and practice of materials development for language learning*. Wiley Blackwell.

Tomul, E., & Savasci, H. (2012). Socioeconomic determinants of academic achievement. *Educational Assessment, Evaluation and Accountability, 24*(3), 175–187. doi:10.100711092-012-9149-3

Torricelli, P. (2006). Il segno metaforico. Tra motivazione e relatività linguistica. In R. Bombi & G. Cifoletti (Eds.), Studi linguistici in onore di Roberto Gusmani, (vol. 3, pp. 1715-1729). Alessandria: Edizioni dell'Orso.

Torricelli, P. (2019). *Ammetto di non conoscere l'Africa*. Retrieved from http://www.focusonafrica.info/ammetto-di-non-conoscere-lafrica/

Tran, T. T. (2012). The perceptions and attitudes of international students towards plagiarism. *The ACPET Journal for Private Higher Education*, *1*(2), 13–21.

Treaty of Lisbon Amending the Treaty on European Union and the Treaty Establishing the European Community. (2007, December 17). Retrieved from http://publications.europa.eu/resource/cellar/688a7a98-3110-4ffe-a6b3-8972d8445325.0007.01/DOC_19

Treaty on European Union. (1992). Retrieved from https://europa.eu/european-union/sites/europaeu/files/docs/body/treaty_on_european_union_en.pdf

Tse, K. P. (1987). *Language Planning and English as a Foreign Language in Middle School Education in the Republic of China*. Crane Publishing Co.

Tsou, W. (2015). From Globalization to Glocalization: Rethinking English Language Teaching in Response to the ELF Phenomenon. *English as a Global Language Education (EaGLE). Journal*, *1*(1), 47–63.

Tsou, W., & Chen, F. (2014). EFL and ELF College Students' Perceptions toward Englishes. *Journal of English as a Lingua Franca*, *3*(2), 363–386. doi:10.1515/jelf-2014-0021

Tsui, A. B. M., & Tollefson, J. W. (2007). Language policy and the construction of national cultural identity. In A. B. M. Tsui & J. W. Tollefson (Eds.), *Language policy, culture, and identity in Asian contexts* (pp. 1–21). Lawrence Erlbaum Associates.

Unal, M., Toprak, M., & Baspınar, V. (2012). Bilim etiğine aykırı davranıslar ve yaptırımlar: Sosyal ve beseri bilimler Icin bir çerceve önerisi [Ethical Violations and Sanctions in Scientific Publications: A framework proposal for social sciences and Humanities.]. *Amme Idaresi Dergisi*, *45*(3), 1–27.

United Nations. (n.d.). *Official Languages*. Retrieved from https://www.un.org/en/sections/about-un/official-languages/index.html

Vaish, V. (2008). *Biliteracy and globalization: English language education in India*. Multilingual Matters. doi:10.21832/9781847690340

van Dijk, T. A. (2015). Critical discourse analysis. In D. Tannen, H. Hamilton, & D. Schiffrin (Eds.), Handbook of discourse analysis (2nd ed., pp. 466–485). Chichester: Wiley Blackwell. doi:10.1002/9781118584194.ch22

van Dijk, T. A. (1993). Principles of critical discourse analysis. *Discourse & Society*, *4*(2), 249–283. doi:10.1177/0957926593004002006

Van Merriënboer, J. J. G. (1997). *Training complex cognitive skills: A four-component instructional design model for technical training*. Educational Technology.

Vandewalle, L. (2014). *In-depth Analysis; The increasing role of the EU's culture, education and science diplomacy in Asia*. Retrieved from https://www.europarl.europa.eu/RegData/etudes/IDAN/2015/549050/EXPO_IDA(2015)549050_EN.pdf

Vargas-Silva, C., & Rienzo, C. (2019). *Migrants in the UK: An overview*. The Migration Observatory. https://migrationobservatory.ox.ac.uk/resources/briefings/migrants-in-the-uk-an-overview/

Vázquez, C. P., Molina, M. P., & López, D. J. A. (2014). Perceptions of teachers and students of the promotion of interaction through task-based activities in CLIL. *Porta Linguarum: Revista Internacional de Didáctica de las Lenguas Extranjeras, 23*, 75–91.

Vettorel, P., & Corrizzato, S. (2016). Fostering Awareness of the Pedagogical Implications of World Englishes and ELF in Teacher Education in Italy. *Studies in Second Language Learning and Teaching, 6*(3), 487–511. doi:10.14746sllt.2016.6.3.6

Vijayalakshmi, M., & Babu, M. S. (2014). A brief history of English language teaching in India. *International Journal of Scientific and Research Publications, 4*(5), 1-4.

Vurdien, R., & Puranen, P. (2018). Intercultural Learning Via Videoconferencing: Students' Attitudes and Experiences. In D. Tafazoli, M. Gómez Parra, & A. Cristina (Eds.), *Cross-Cultural Perspectives on Technology-Enhanced Language Learning* (pp. 264–282). IGI Global., doi:10.4018/978-1-5225-5463-9.ch015

Wager, E. (2014). Defining and responding to plagiarism. *Learned Publishing, 27*(1), 33–42. doi:10.1087/20140105

Wajda-Johnston, V. A., Handal, P. J., Brawer, P. A., & Fabricatore, A. N. (2001). Academic dishonesty at the graduate level. *Ethics & Behavior, 11*(3), 287–305. doi:10.1207/S15327019EB1103_7

Wajnryb, R. (2008). *You know what I mean?: Words, contexts and communication*. Cambridge University Press. doi:10.1017/CBO9780511487064

Walker, J. (2010). Measuring *plagiarism:* Researching what students do, not what they say they do. *Studies in Higher Education, 35*(1), 41–59. doi:10.1080/03075070902912994

Wang, X., & Gao, Y. (2013, October). Beijing expected to see exam reforms in 2014. *People's Daily Online*. http://english.people.com.cn/203691/8432022.html#

Wang, A.-L. (2013). Engaging students in language learning via successful cross-cultural video-conferencing. In M. Hamada (Ed.), *E-learning: New technology, application and future trends* (pp. 241–256). Nova Publishers.

Wang, L., & Lin, T. (2013). The representation of professionalism in native English-speaking teachers recruitment policies: A comparative study of Hong Kong, Japan, Korea and Taiwan. *English Teaching, 12*(3), 5–22.

Wang, Q. (2007). The national curriculum changes and their effects on English language teaching in the People's Republic of China. In J. Cummins & C. Davison (Eds.), *International handbook of English language teaching* (pp. 87–105). Springer. doi:10.1007/978-0-387-46301-8_8

Wendt, J. L., & Rockinson-Szapkiw, A. (2014). The effect of online collaboration on middle school student science misconceptions as an aspect of science literacy. *Journal of Research in Science Teaching*, *51*(9), 1103–1118. doi:10.1002/tea.21169

Wentrup, R., Nakamura, H. R., & Ström, P. (2017). Online services: An equalising force between the Global North and the Global South? In N. Beerepoot, B. Lambergts, & J. Kleibert (Eds.), *Globalisation and service-driven economic growth: Perspectives from the Global North and South* (pp. 55–71). Routledge.

Widdowson, H. G. (1978). *Teaching language as communication*. Oxford University Press.

Williamson, K., & McGregor, J. (2011). Generating knowledge and avoiding plagiarism: Smart information use by high school students. *School Library Research*, *14*. Retrieved from http://www.ala.org/aasl/slr/volume14/williamson-mcgregor

Witherell, S., & Department of State. (2016). *Open doors 2016 executive summary*. https://www.iie.org/en/Why-IIE/Announcements/2016-11-14-Open-Doors-Executive-Summary

Wolfram, W. (2019). Language awareness in education: A linguist's response to teachers. In M. D. Devereaux & C. C. Palmer (Eds.), *Teaching language variation in the classroom: Strategies and models from teachers and linguists* (pp. 61–66). Routledge. doi:10.4324/9780429486678-12

Wollensak, A. (2002). Curricular modules: 3D and immersive visualization tools for learning. *Computers & Graphics*, *26*(4), 599–602. doi:10.1016/S0097-8493(02)00110-3

Wright, D., Owens, A., & Nigel, D. (2008, June). *Making the case for multiple submissions to Turnitin*. Paper presented at the 3rd International Plagiarism Conference. Retrieved from http://www.plagiarismconference.org/pages/conference2008/conference-proceedings.php

Wu, W.-H., Wu, Y.-C. J., Chen, C.-Y., Kao, H.-Y., Lin, C.-H., & Huang, S.-H. (2012). Review of trends from mobile learning studies: A meta-analysis. *Computers & Education*, *59*(2), 817–827. doi:10.1016/j.compedu.2012.03.016

Yahya, L. (1980). *Fossilized Errors Among Second-cycle Students at the Faculté des Lettres et Sciences Humaines* (MA thesis). University of Tunis.

Yakout, K., & Amel, M. H. (2019). The EFL Learners' Fossilization of the /θ/ and /ð/ Sounds. Case Study: First Year EFL Students at Tahri Mohamed University, Bechar, Algeria. *International Journal of Linguistics. Literature and Translation*, *2*(4), 219–228.

Yamada, K. (2003). What prevents ESL / EFL writers from avoiding plagiarism?: Analyses of 10 North-American college websites. *System*, *31*(2), 247–258. doi:10.1016/S0346-251X(03)00023-X

Yamazaki, A. (2006). Eigokakyosyokukatei no genjo to kadai [Current situation and problems of university English teacher education programs]. *Musashi University of Technology. Faculty of Environment and Technology Journal, 7,* 103–112.

Yan, C. (2015). 'We can't change much unless the exam change': Teachers' dilemmas in the curriculum reform in China. *Improving Schools, 18*(1), 5–19. doi:10.1177/1365480214553744

Yang, J. H., & Wong, W. (2009, November). *Linguistic standards and realities of English use for international business interaction.* Paper presented at the 2009 Applied Linguistics and Sociolinguistics: The Form and the Content, Taipei, Taiwan.

Yang, J. H. (2013). Taiwanese Perceptions of Indian English: A Perceptual Change in the Learning of English Variation. *English Teaching & Learning, 37*(4), 91–146. doi:10.6330/ETL.2013.37.4.03

Yang, P. (2018). Developing TESOL Teacher Intercultural Identity: An Intercultural Communication Competence Approach. *TESOL Journal, 9*(3), 525–541. doi:10.1002/tesj.356

Yashima, T. (2002). Willingness to communicate in a second language: The Japanese EFL context. *Modern Language Journal, 86*(1), 54–66. doi:10.1111/1540-4781.00136

Yazici, A., Yazici, S., & Erdem, M. S. (2011). Faculty and student perceptions on college cheating: Evidence from Turkey. *Educational Studies, 37*(2), 221–231. doi:10.1080/03055698.2010.506321

Yore, L. D., & Treagust, D. F. (2006). Current realities and future possibilities: Language and science literacy—empowering research and informing instruction. *International Journal of Science Education, 28*(2-3), 291–3142. doi:10.1080/09500690500336973

Yore, L., Bisanz, G. L., & Hand, B. M. (2003). Examining the literacy component of science literacy: 25 years of language arts and science research. *International Journal of Science Education, 25*(6), 689–725. doi:10.1080/09500690305018

Youmans, R. J. (2011). Does the adoption of plagiarism-detection software in highereducation reduce plagiarism? *Studies in Higher Education, 36*(7), 749–761. doi:10.1080/03075079.2010.523457

Zacharias, N.T. (2014). Integrating EIL Pedagogy in a Pre-service Teacher Education Program. *TEFLIN Journal: A Publication on the Teaching and Learning of English, 25*(2), 217-232.

Zalta, E. N. (Ed.). (2010). *Stanford Encyclopedia of Philosophy.* Stanford University.

Zhang, L. J. (2006). The ecology of communicative language teaching: Reflecting on the Singapore experience. In *Proceeding of the annual CELEA international conference: Innovating English teaching: Communicative Language Teaching (CLT) and other approaches.* China English Language Education Association (CELEA) and Guangdong University of Foreign Studies, Guangzhou, China.

Zhang, L. J., Aryadoust, V., & Zhang, D. (2016). Taking stock of the effects of strategies-based instruction on writing in Chinese and English in Singapore primary classrooms. In R. E. Silver & W. D. Bokhorst-Heng (Eds.), *Quadrilingual education in Singapore: Pedagogical innovation in language education* (pp. 103–126). Springer. doi:10.1007/978-981-287-967-7_7

Zimmerman, B. J. (2000). Attaining self-regulation: A social cognitive perspective. In M. Boekaerts, P. R. Pintrich, & M. Zeidner (Eds.), *Handbook of self-regulation: Theory, research, and applications* (pp. 13–39). Academic Press. doi:10.1016/B978-012109890-2/50031-7

About the Contributors

Veysel Altunel is a Ph.D. student in English Language Teaching at Hacettepe University.

Manpreet Arora is an Assistant Professor of Management in the Central University of Himachal Pradesh, Dharamshala (HP). With around sixteen years of teaching experience she has varied interest areas. A Gold medalist at undergraduate and postgraduate levels, she obtained her PhD in International Trade from Himachal Pradesh University, Shimla. Her areas of research interest include Accounting and Finance, Entrepreneurial Leadership, and Communication Skills. She has been guiding research at the doctoral level and has worked in the area of Microfinance. She has keen interest in delivering invited talks on Finance, Business Communication, Interpersonal skills, Entrepreneurship and Skill Development. She is a motivational speaker and conducts workshops on communication and motivation. She has published more than 35 papers/chapters in various journals of national and international repute. She is an active social worker also and is working towards the protecting the rights of women. She also works for community in various village development programs.

Aliyyah Nuha Faiqah binti Azman Firdaus is a recipient of the Japanese Government (Monbukagakusho: MEXT) Postgraduate Scholarship 2020. She is currently pursuing her PhD studies at the Graduate School of Humanities and Social Sciences, Hiroshima University, Japan in applied linguistics and environmental discourse. She has been involved in capacity building projects in Malaysia, Cambodia and Laos. She has also conducted some research in discourses of expert views on obesity in Malaysia and Sweden, environmental and professional communication and higher educational leadership policies in ASEAN. Currently, she is an active executive committee member of the Malaysian Association of Applied Linguistics (MAAL) and previously served as MAAL's Assistant Secretary from 2016-2018.

About the Contributors

Ethan Fu-Yen Chiu is an assistant professor of Applied English at National Chin-Yi University of Technology. Dr. Chiu double majored in English Language and Literature and Japanese Language and Culture. He obtained his master's degree in Teaching English to Speakers of Other Languages (TESOL) and finished his Ph.D. in TESOL. He is also a licensed secondary school English and Japanese language teacher. His research interests include Global Englishes, intercultural education, teacher education, and corpus assisted language teaching.

Neriman Hocaoğlu Bahadır is an Assistant Professor of International Relations in Kırklareli University. She received her doctorate in EU Politics and International Relations from Marmara University. Her research interests include the EU, identity, language policy, migration policy and Turkey – EU relations.

Awad Ibrahim is a professor curriculum theory and social foundations at the Faculty of Education of the University of Ottawa. He has more than 100 publications including numerous books, book chapters, and journal articles.

Hale Işık-Güler works as an Associate Professor of Linguistics at the Department of Foreign Language Education, Middle East Technical University, Ankara where she mainly teaches courses on Pragmatics, Discourse/Conversation Analysis, Corpus Linguistics and the analysis of Spoken Interaction at the graduate level, and Linguistics and Research methods courses as well as practicum at the undergraduate level. She holds a PhD in Foreign Language Education and has worked more specifically within the fields of Pragmatics, Discourse Analysis and Corpus Linguistics. Her academic interests mainly lie within the domains of cross-cultural (im)politeness research, spoken corpora, conversation analysis, discourse and gender, intercultural communication, applied linguistics, and the teaching of English and Turkish as a foreign language, and English taught programs and internationalization.

Işıl Günseli Kaçar is an English instructor at the Department of Foreign Language Education at Middle East Technical University (METU) in Turkey. She is interested in pre-service language teacher education, pre-service teacher identity, English as a Lingua Franca, flipped instruction, mentoring, the integration of technologies into English language teaching, telecollaboration, and teaching writing. She worked as a tutor at the academic writing center at METU previously. She is currently coordinating a number of national and international research projects on pre-service teacher education and e-mentoring.

Maya Khemlani David is a Master Trainer for the CLMV Programme parked with the Asia-Europe Institute, University of Malaya. She has written, edited and published widely in the field of sociolinguistics and is also a Certified Executive Coach and Counsellor. Her passion for research and publication consumes her and she currently conducts workshops on research methodology, qualitative research, critical thinking, academic writing and supervisory skills.

Kazuhiko Nakae is Professor of Linguistics and Semitic Linguistics, mainly working on Arabic language. The research interest is Language Contact and Linguistic Typology.

Sakae Onoda is a Professor of English Education in the Faculty of International Liberal Arts, Juntendo University, Japan. He has over 20 years' experience of English teacher training as well as extensive experience of teaching English in high schools. His research interests include English teacher education, materials development, and the development of listening, speaking, and writing fluency, the improvement of interactional skills, and facilitating self-regulated language learning in all four skills as well as vocabulary in learners of English as a Second or Foreign Language. His Ed.D. dissertation was entitled "Self-regulation: Its relation to motivation and proficiency." He also conducted research in speaking fluency development under the supervision of Professor Paul Nation at Victoria University, New Zealand during a one-year sabbatical conferred on me by Kanda University of International Studies in 2010. He is an Oxford Teachers' Academy certified trainer and frequently conduct seminars with secondary school and university teachers of English. He frequently presents at international conferences, including "New Trends in Language Teaching" (Spain) and the Japan Association of Language Teaching (JALT). He has also published a range of research articles in internationally-refereed journals, including "Examining relationships between self-efficacy, effort regulation strategy use, and English vocabulary skills" in Studies in Self-Access Learning, and in internationally-refereed edited volumes, including "An exploration of effective teaching approaches for enhancing the oral fluency of EFL students" in Exploring EFL Fluency in Asia (Palgrave Macmillan), and "Effects of expanded 10-minute writing on L2 speaking and writing fluency development" in New Trends in Foreign Language Teaching: Methods, Evaluation, Innovation (Cambridge Scholars Publishing).

Lanqing Qin is a Ph.D. student at the Faculty of Education of the University of Ottawa.

Aicha Rahal is a Tunisian researcher in English linguistics. She was a former online teacher assistant with the US Department of State and the University of Oregon. She is the co-editor of the upcoming book 'World Englishes and Language Assessment'.

Roshan Lal Sharma is a Professor of English in the Department of English & European Languages, Central University of Himachal Pradesh, Dharamshala. He has been a Senior Fulbright Fellow at the University of Wisconsin-Madison (USA) during 2007-08. He has authored Shorter Fiction of Raja Rao (2009), Walt Whitman (2000), co-authored Som P. Ranchan: Dialogue Epic in Indian English Poetry (2012); co-edited, Communication in Contemporary Scenario: Its Multiple Dimensions (2017), Mapping Diaspora Identities (2017), and Communication, Entrepreneurship and Finance: Renegotiating Diverse Perspectives (2018).He has more than fifty published papers and book chapters to his credit. His areas of interest include Indian Writing in English, Literary and Cultural Theory, Mystical Poetry of Diverse Literary Traditions, Communication Studies, and New Media Ecology.

Patrizia Torricelli is a Full Professor of Linguistics, University of Messina, Italy.

Xiaoli Yu is a lecturer at the Department of Foreign Language Education at Middle East Technical University.

Azlin Zaiti Zainal is Senior Lecturer at the Department of English, Faculty of Languages and Linguistics, University of Malaya. Her research interests include teacher education, technology in language education, second language writing, oral communication, and discourse studies.

Index

A

academic integrity 243, 245-251, 254-258, 261, 263-264, 274-279, 282, 289, 292
academic integrity awareness 243
academic writing course 243, 260
Arabic 54-56, 58-69, 73, 83, 119, 280, 287
authorship 244, 252-254, 290, 292

B

Bourdieu 83, 89, 102, 109

C

China 11-12, 30, 88-89, 95-98, 106, 109, 132-134, 145-149, 151-158, 231, 240-241
CLIL 159, 161-163, 167, 169-170, 172, 179-181, 183
collaborative learning 174, 211
communication 4, 9-10, 17, 22, 35-37, 40, 42-44, 46, 48-53, 55, 59, 62, 65-66, 68, 74, 82-87, 91, 95, 120-122, 124-125, 128, 132-135, 138, 142, 144, 146, 148-151, 156, 158, 164, 170, 176, 182, 188, 197, 200, 202, 205, 207-208, 211, 217, 219-220, 222-223, 225-226, 232-234, 237, 239, 242, 245, 265, 280, 282
Condolences 73, 77-81, 84, 86
Congratulations 73, 80, 82, 84, 86
Contrastive Analysis Theory 185-186, 193, 196
Corpus Linguistics 191-192, 195-196, 282
critical thinking skills 159-164, 166-170, 172-174, 179, 198, 256
Cross-Sectional Approach 196
cultural norms 71, 73-75, 77, 80-84

D

developed countries 1, 12-14, 18
developing countries 1, 13-15, 18, 21, 26
dialect 1, 4-7, 27
diglossia 54, 59-60, 67
discourse analysis 71, 88-89, 94-95, 110, 112

E

educational policy 131-132, 158, 274-275, 300, 305
EFL 26, 73, 83, 86, 109-110, 133, 137, 153, 158, 160, 162-163, 165, 173, 178, 181-183, 190-191, 193-194, 196, 240-241, 243-245, 247-248, 250-255, 257, 259-260, 262-264, 268, 270, 275-276, 280, 283, 285-286, 288, 291
EFL preservice teachers 243, 255, 259, 262-264, 268, 270, 275-276
ELF 158, 185, 193, 221-226, 235-237, 239, 241
ELT 86, 88-96, 99, 104, 108-109, 111, 134, 138-139, 141, 147-148, 152-153, 156-158, 192, 194, 220, 222, 224-225, 236, 238-239, 241, 260, 280, 285, 289-290
English education 131-132, 142, 144, 148-150, 153, 171, 220-221, 225, 239
English learning 94, 131, 143-144, 148,

160, 163, 175, 179, 181-182, 220-221
English varieties 9, 27, 219-221, 223-225, 229, 234-236, 238
Error Analysis Theory 185-187, 193, 196
ESL 26, 75, 84, 110, 137, 139-140, 152, 158, 162, 178, 181, 240, 243-244, 248, 250-253, 280-282, 286, 291, 296
ethics 45-46, 48, 50, 129, 246, 248, 261, 264, 277, 281-282, 285, 287-288, 290-291
Ethnocentric 27
European Union 113, 115, 117-119, 121, 123, 127-130, 145
Expanding Circle 10, 19, 73, 84, 131, 133-134, 145, 147, 149-151, 158, 223, 230, 236-237, 240-241

F

fake news 47-48, 50-51

G

Global English 9-10, 27, 97, 100, 102, 111
Global North 1, 11-13, 22, 24-27
Global South 1, 11-13, 22, 24-25, 27
greetings 71, 80, 86
group projects 159, 162, 168-175, 177, 179, 181

I

ideology 10, 27-28, 30-31, 34, 36-37, 39, 91-92, 108, 114, 117, 137-138, 290, 303-304
imagination 28-29, 31-36, 39, 42, 44, 57-61, 63, 67, 210
inequality 1-4, 6-8, 11-12, 16, 18, 20, 23, 25, 27, 49, 95, 144, 148, 150-151
Inner Circle 9, 19, 131, 133-135, 140, 143, 150-151, 158, 223-225, 234, 236, 238
integration 113-114, 124, 130, 143, 152, 162, 200, 203, 215, 241, 245, 254, 270, 278
intercultural communication 71, 86, 156, 222, 232, 237, 239, 242
intercultural communicative competence 221, 238, 241

intercultural education 1, 16-18, 22, 27, 225
interdisciplinary 56, 197-200, 202-205, 207-208, 211-213, 217, 231
Interlanguage Theory 185-187, 193, 196
intrinsic motivation 165-168, 170, 172-174

L

L2 interactional skills 159, 166, 168, 172, 174, 182
L2 learning 159, 163, 165-170, 185, 187, 191
language 1-10, 16, 18-20, 22-27, 29, 32-39, 41-75, 80-87, 89-96, 98-105, 107-111, 113-114, 118-144, 146, 148-173, 175, 178-213, 215-218, 220-222, 224-226, 230, 232-234, 236-245, 247, 249, 252, 260, 265, 275-276, 280, 282-283, 285-286, 288, 290, 293, 296
language learning 19, 25-26, 69, 72, 83-85, 138, 140, 142-143, 156, 159-163, 169, 171, 181-182, 187-188, 191, 194-195, 202-204, 240-242, 247, 252
language policy 8, 56, 70, 113-114, 118-122, 124, 126, 128, 130, 138, 141, 146, 148-149, 153, 155-156, 158, 239
learner language 184-185, 187, 192-193, 196
linguistic strategies 28, 33, 46
liturgical language 54-55, 57-68
longitudinal study 72, 190, 196

M

majority 1, 4, 14-16, 18, 149, 185, 219, 224, 231, 233, 246-248, 256, 264, 268-270
meaning value 28, 32, 35
minority 1, 6-9, 14-16, 18, 69, 109, 113-114, 123, 137, 139, 149, 154, 264
misuse of language 43, 52
multicultural education 1, 16-17, 24, 27
multilingualism 6, 8-9, 17, 23-25, 66, 70, 113, 121-124, 128, 130, 142, 180, 191, 195

N

native speaker 16, 82, 88-96, 99-100, 103-105, 107-109, 111-112, 138, 189, 220, 224, 234
Nativised Discourse Norms 86
nativised speech acts 71, 82

O

online 12-13, 21, 25-26, 48, 50-52, 85, 88-89, 94-95, 111, 152, 157, 160, 177, 206, 208, 217, 225-226, 239, 246, 249-250, 255-258, 263, 267, 269-271, 273-274, 276-280, 282, 285-286, 288, 290, 292
oral fluency 159, 166-168, 170, 172-174, 182
Outer Circle 9, 19, 131, 133-134, 140, 144, 146-151, 158, 223, 230, 236

P

pedagogy 16, 84, 91, 132, 138, 143, 152, 181, 187, 191-193, 195, 217, 224-226, 237, 241-242, 288
plagiarism 243-259, 261-266, 268-292, 294-304
plagiarism detection software 257, 282, 287, 289, 292
post-truth 43, 45-53
power 6-7, 10, 13, 21, 23-24, 45, 49, 52, 58-60, 67, 75, 84, 91, 95, 99, 101, 103, 107-110, 113-119, 125-127, 129-130, 147, 151, 214, 248, 256, 266, 285

R

religious identity 54-55, 57-59, 64-65, 67-68
representation 8, 32, 85, 88, 90, 92-93, 96, 98, 105, 107, 110, 112, 135, 232

S

scientific literacy 197, 199-203, 206-208, 212, 216-217
second language acquisition 72, 90, 160, 175, 178, 181, 184-186, 189, 193-194, 196
self-discovery 243
self-efficacy 159, 163, 166, 168-170, 172-174, 179-180
self-regulated learning 168, 170
SLA 175, 184-186, 191-193, 195, 202
social imagination 28-29, 31-33, 36
Social interaction 87
social media 43, 46-47, 49-51, 71, 77, 80, 167
soft power 113-118, 126, 129-130
source documentation 245, 247-248, 252, 254, 261-262, 264, 266-269, 275, 292, 301
speech act 73-75, 77-84, 86-87

T

teacher training programs 219, 231
technology 12, 25-26, 47, 51-52, 100, 102, 140, 143, 148-149, 151, 161, 181-183, 197-199, 203, 205-213, 215, 217, 219, 228, 233, 244-246, 249, 255, 260, 280-282, 284-285, 287, 289-290
text-matching software 243-244, 246, 255, 270, 282
textual borrowing 244, 292
textual ownership 244, 252, 292
Three Circle Model 131, 133, 135, 140
tool 4, 7, 36, 46, 50, 91, 113-114, 118, 125-126, 130, 134, 141, 144, 151, 187, 192-193, 205, 207, 211-212, 222-223, 226, 232, 234, 237, 256-258, 261, 270, 279, 281, 284, 287, 290
Turnitin 243-246, 255-258, 262, 268-276, 278-282, 284-291, 293, 301

W

we 1-2, 4-5, 7, 10, 12-15, 19, 22, 29, 31, 33-34, 36-40, 44-47, 49-52, 57, 59, 63-64, 71-74, 76-77, 80, 83-84, 89-90, 92-99, 102-105, 107-108, 112, 133, 146, 157-158, 177, 186-187, 199-200, 203, 206-207, 209, 211, 221-222, 224,

226, 232, 235-236, 263-264, 270, 272, 277, 280
Whiteness 89, 92, 105, 108

World Englishes 9-10, 24, 27, 110, 133, 138, 151, 153, 155-156, 158, 185, 194, 196, 221, 230, 235, 238-241, 290

Purchase Print, E-Book, or Print + E-Book

IGI Global's reference books can now be purchased from three unique pricing formats:
Print Only, E-Book Only, or Print + E-Book.
Shipping fees may apply.

www.igi-global.com

Recommended Reference Books

ISBN: 978-1-5225-1955-3
© 2017; 397 pp.
List Price: $205

ISBN: 978-1-5225-8217-5
© 2019; 102 pp.
List Price: $135

ISBN: 978-1-5225-8163-5
© 2019; 393 pp.
List Price: $185

ISBN: 978-1-5225-6061-6
© 2019; 396 pp.
List Price: $265

ISBN: 978-1-5225-7195-7
© 2019; 310 pp.
List Price: $195

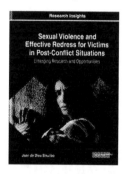

ISBN: 978-1-5225-8194-9
© 2019; 328 pp.
List Price: $145

Looking for free content, product updates, news, and special offers?
Join IGI Global's mailing list today and start enjoying exclusive perks sent only to IGI Global members.
Add your name to the list at **www.igi-global.com/newsletters**.

Publisher of Peer-Reviewed, Timely, and Innovative Academic Research

IGI Global
DISSEMINATOR OF KNOWLEDGE

www.igi-global.com   Sign up at www.igi-global.com/newsletters   facebook.com/igiglobal   twitter.com/igiglobal

Ensure Quality Research is Introduced to the Academic Community

Become an IGI Global Reviewer for Authored Book Projects

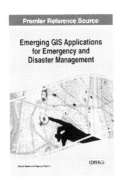   

The overall success of an authored book project is dependent on quality and timely reviews.

In this competitive age of scholarly publishing, constructive and timely feedback significantly expedites the turnaround time of manuscripts from submission to acceptance, allowing the publication and discovery of forward-thinking research at a much more expeditious rate. Several IGI Global authored book projects are currently seeking highly-qualified experts in the field to fill vacancies on their respective editorial review boards:

Applications and Inquiries may be sent to:
development@igi-global.com

Applicants must have a doctorate (or an equivalent degree) as well as publishing and reviewing experience. Reviewers are asked to complete the open-ended evaluation questions with as much detail as possible in a timely, collegial, and constructive manner. All reviewers' tenures run for one-year terms on the editorial review boards and are expected to complete at least three reviews per term. Upon successful completion of this term, reviewers can be considered for an additional term.

If you have a colleague that may be interested in this opportunity, we encourage you to share this information with them.

IGI Global Proudly Partners With eContent Pro International

Receive a 25% Discount on all Editorial Services

Editorial Services

IGI Global expects all final manuscripts submitted for publication to be in their final form. This means they must be reviewed, revised, and professionally copy edited prior to their final submission. Not only does this support with accelerating the publication process, but it also ensures that the highest quality scholarly work can be disseminated.

English Language Copy Editing

Let eContent Pro International's expert copy editors perform edits on your manuscript to resolve spelling, punctuaion, grammar, syntax, flow, formatting issues and more.

Scientific and Scholarly Editing

Allow colleagues in your research area to examine the content of your manuscript and provide you with valuable feedback and suggestions before submission.

Figure, Table, Chart & Equation Conversions

Do you have poor quality figures? Do you need visual elements in your manuscript created or converted? A design expert can help!

Translation

Need your documjent translated into English? eContent Pro International's expert translators are fluent in English and more than 40 different languages.

Hear What Your Colleagues are Saying About Editorial Services Supported by IGI Global

"The service was very fast, very thorough, and very helpful in ensuring our chapter meets the criteria and requirements of the book's editors. I was quite impressed and happy with your service."

– Prof. Tom Brinthaupt,
Middle Tennessee State University, USA

"I found the work actually spectacular. The editing, formatting, and other checks were very thorough. The turnaround time was great as well. I will definitely use eContent Pro in the future."

– Nickanor Amwata, Lecturer,
University of Kurdistan Hawler, Iraq

"I was impressed that it was done timely, and wherever the content was not clear for the reader, the paper was improved with better readability for the audience."

– Prof. James Chilembwe,
Mzuzu University, Malawi

Email: customerservice@econtentpro.com   www.igi-global.com/editorial-service-partners

Celebrating Over 30 Years of Scholarly Knowledge Creation & Dissemination

www.igi-global.com

InfoSci®-Books

A Database of Over 5,300+ Reference Books Containing Over 100,000+ Chapters Focusing on Emerging Research

GAIN ACCESS TO **THOUSANDS** OF REFERENCE BOOKS AT **A FRACTION** OF THEIR INDIVIDUAL LIST **PRICE**.

InfoSci®-Books Database

The **InfoSci®-Books** database is a collection of over 5,300+ IGI Global single and multi-volume reference books, handbooks of research, and encyclopedias, encompassing groundbreaking research from prominent experts worldwide that span over 350+ topics in 11 core subject areas including business, computer science, education, science and engineering, social sciences and more.

Open Access Fee Waiver (Offset Model) Initiative

For any library that invests in IGI Global's InfoSci-Journals and/or InfoSci-Books databases, IGI Global will match the library's investment with a fund of equal value to go toward **subsidizing the OA article processing charges (APCs) for their students, faculty, and staff** at that institution when their work is submitted and accepted under OA into an IGI Global journal.*

INFOSCI® PLATFORM FEATURES

- No DRM
- No Set-Up or Maintenance Fees
- A Guarantee of No More Than a 5% Annual Increase
- Full-Text HTML and PDF Viewing Options
- Downloadable MARC Records
- Unlimited Simultaneous Access
- COUNTER 5 Compliant Reports
- Formatted Citations With Ability to Export to RefWorks and EasyBib
- No Embargo of Content (Research is Available Months in Advance of the Print Release)

*The fund will be offered on an annual basis and expire at the end of the subscription period. The fund would renew as the subscription is renewed for each year thereafter. The open access fees will be waived after the student, faculty, or staff's paper has been vetted and accepted into an IGI Global journal and the fund can only be used toward publishing OA in an IGI Global journal. Libraries in developing countries will have the match on their investment doubled.

To Learn More or To Purchase This Database:
www.igi-global.com/infosci-books
eresources@igi-global.com • Toll Free: 1-866-342-6657 ext. 100 • Phone: 717-533-8845 x100

www.igi-global.com

Publisher of Peer-Reviewed, Timely, and Innovative Academic Research Since 1988

IGI Global's Transformative Open Access (OA) Model:
How to Turn Your University Library's Database Acquisitions Into a Source of OA Funding

In response to the OA movement and well in advance of Plan S, IGI Global, early last year, unveiled their OA Fee Waiver (Read & Publish) Initiative.

Under this initiative, librarians who invest in IGI Global's InfoSci-Books (5,300+ reference books) and/or InfoSci-Journals (185+ scholarly journals) databases will be able to subsidize their patron's OA article processing charges (APC) when their work is submitted and accepted (after the peer review process) into an IGI Global journal. *See website for details.

How Does it Work?

1. When a library subscribes or perpetually purchases IGI Global's InfoSci-Databases and/or their discipline/subject-focused subsets, IGI Global will match the library's investment with a fund of equal value to go toward subsidizing the OA article processing charges (APCs) for their patrons.
   Researchers: **Be sure to recommend the InfoSci-Books and InfoSci-Journals to take advantage of this initiative.**

2. When a student, faculty, or staff member submits a paper and it is accepted (following the peer review) into one of IGI Global's 185+ scholarly journals, the author will have the option to have their paper published under a traditional publishing model or as OA.

3. When the author chooses to have their paper published under OA, IGI Global will notify them of the OA Fee Waiver (Read & Publish) Initiative. If the author decides they would like to take advantage of this initiative, IGI Global will deduct the US$ 2,000 APC from the created fund.

4. This fund will be offered on an annual basis and will renew as the subscription is renewed for each year thereafter. IGI Global will manage the fund and award the APC waivers unless the librarian has a preference as to how the funds should be managed.

Hear From the Experts on This Initiative:

"I'm very happy to have been able to make one of my recent research contributions, "Visualizing the Social Media Conversations of a National Information Technology Professional Association" featured in the *International Journal of Human Capital and Information Technology Professionals*, freely available along with having access to the valuable resources found within IGI Global's InfoSci-Journals database."

– **Prof. Stuart Palmer**,
Deakin University, Australia

For More Information, Visit: www.igi-global.com/publish/contributor-resources/open-access/read-publish-model
or contact IGI Global's Database Team at eresources@igi-global.com.

IGI Global offers book authorship and editorship opportunities across 11 subject areas, including business, computer science, education, science and engineering, social sciences, and more!

Benefits of Publishing with IGI Global:

- Free, one-on-one editorial and promotional support.
- Expedited publishing timelines that can take your book from start to finish in less than one (1) year.
- Choose from a variety of formats including: Edited and Authored References, Handbooks of Research, Encyclopedias, and Research Insights.
- Utilize IGI Global's eEditorial Discovery® submission system in support of conducting the submission and blind review process.
- IGI Global maintains a strict adherence to ethical practices due in part to our full membership with the Committee on Publication Ethics (COPE).
- Indexing potential in prestigious indices such as Scopus®, Web of Science™, PsycINFO®, and ERIC – Education Resources Information Center.
- Ability to connect your ORCID iD to your IGI Global publications.
- Earn royalties on your publication as well as receive complimentary copies and exclusive discounts.

Get Started Today by Contacting the Acquisitions Department at:
acquisition@igi-global.com

www.igi-global.com/infosci-ondemand

InfoSci®-OnDemand

Continuously updated with new material on a weekly basis, InfoSci®-OnDemand offers the ability to search through thousands of quality full-text research papers. Users can narrow each search by identifying key topic areas of interest, then display a complete listing of relevant papers, and purchase materials specific to their research needs.

Comprehensive Service
- Over 125,000+ journal articles, book chapters, and case studies.
- All content is downloadable in PDF and HTML format and can be stored locally for future use.

No Subscription Fees
- One time fee of $37.50 per PDF download.

Instant Access
- Receive a download link immediately after order completion!

"It really provides an excellent entry into the research literature of the field. It presents a manageable number of highly relevant sources on topics of interest to a wide range of researchers. The sources are scholarly, but also accessible to 'practitioners'."

- Lisa Stimatz, MLS, University of North Carolina at Chapel Hill, USA

"It is an excellent and well designed database which will facilitate research, publication, and teaching. It is a very useful tool to have."

- George Ditsa, PhD, University of Wollongong, Australia

"I have accessed the database and find it to be a valuable tool to the IT/IS community. I found valuable articles meeting my search criteria 95% of the time."

- Prof. Lynda Louis, Xavier University of Louisiana, USA

Recommended for use by researchers who wish to immediately download PDFs of individual chapters or articles.

www.igi-global.com/e-resources/infosci-ondemand

IGI Global
DISSEMINATOR OF KNOWLEDGE
www.igi-global.com

Printed in the United States
By Bookmasters